Foreword by Mike Adams

I can't think of a better way to start than to tell the story of my first day in the Moors.

I received a phone call from an old friend I had not heard from for a long while. He talked enthusiastical [illegible] and what sounded like a raving lunatic who was spearheading the campaign. He suggested we meet u[illegible] Although I was highly sceptical my interest was pricked. I made some positive noises and agreed to meet. What followed was simply [illegible] moor for well over an hour by people who seemed to fall a bit short of 'knowing exactly where they were', with much debate and frantic checking of mobile phones. To say I had lowered my expectation was an understatement. Then without warning we dropped down and a crag-line loomed into view; my hopes lifted instantly. I was relieved when we came to some decent looking boulders, then confused when we walked straight past them with only a few mumblings of done problems. I was led into the trees and shown unclimbed projects and strange sandstone blocs, in particular an overhanging blank arête that just looked outstanding and impossible in equal measure. I had a fantastic day's climbing and found myself warming to the mad man who had led us here. The place was Kay Nest, the project arête became Mixed Emotions 8b+ and the 'mad man' was none other than Lee Robinson.

The story above in a lot of ways effectively sums up bouldering in the North York Moors; you will find you have to put in a bit of effort. Venues are quite often a hike away and are often not that concentrated. They can be difficult to locate and you'll probably have to do some cleaning. This effort however will be rewarded with some nice moves on great boulder problems with fantastic views, providing a good day out. The areas covered are never likely to become too popular, as they are so far away from the main areas of British climbing, giving an almost unique sense of solitude. The small local climbing scene is as quirky as it is friendly. The locals are always willing to help, sharing advice and information and they are keen for people to come and climb in their area. All they ask is that you respect the 'spirit of the Moors'. I have felt privileged to be involved with the development of these areas and very much enjoyed my time climbing and exploring the boulders. I have many fond memories that will stay with me forever from my days out on the Moors.

Happy exploring!

Mike Adams

Sunset over Farndale

Contents

The Elephant Boulder High Crag

They are many more blocks and edges to be enjoyed on the moors.

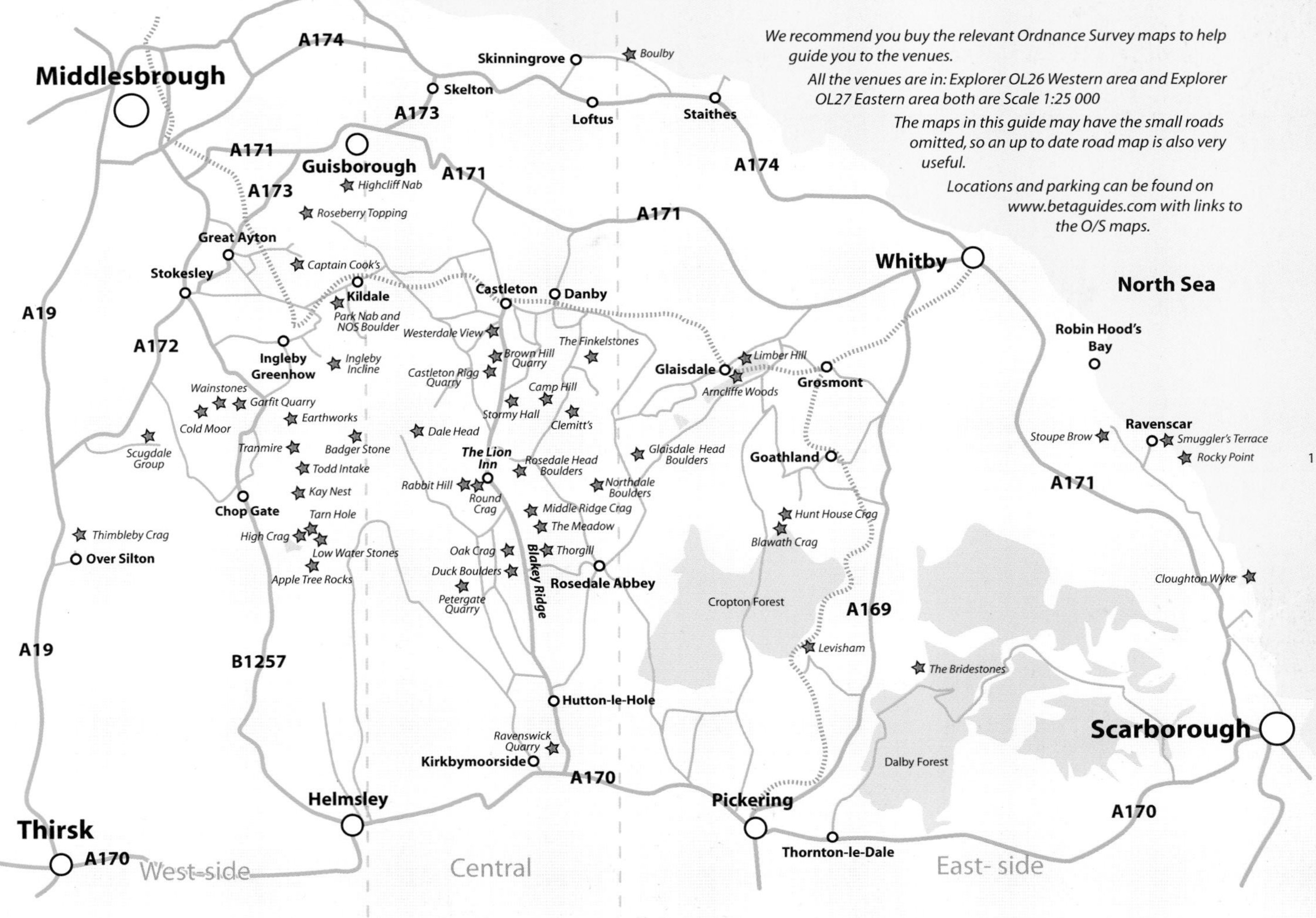

We recommend you buy the relevant Ordnance Survey maps to help guide you to the venues.
All the venues are in: Explorer OL26 Western area and Explorer OL27 Eastern area both are Scale 1:25 000
The maps in this guide may have the small roads omitted, so an up to date road map is also very useful.
Locations and parking can be found on www.betaguides.com with links to the O/S maps.
Middlesbrough
A174
Skinningrove
Boulby
Skelton
A173
Loftus
Staithes
A171
Guisborough
A171
A174
A173
Highcliff Nab
Roseberry Topping
A171
Great Ayton
Whitby
Captain Cook's
Stokesley
Castleton
Danby
North Sea
Kildale
A19
Park Nab and NOS Boulder
Westerdale View
A172
The Finkelstones
Robin Hood's Bay
Brown Hill Quarry
Limber Hill
Ingleby Greenhow
Ingleby Incline
Castleton Rigg Quarry
Glaisdale
Grosmont
Arncliffe Woods
Wainstones
Camp Hill
Garfit Quarry
Cold Moor
Earthworks
Stormy Hall
Clemitt's
Ravenscar
Dale Head
Stoupe Brow
Smuggler's Terrace
Scugdale Group
Tranmire
Badger Stone
Glaisdale Head Boulders
Goathland
Rocky Point
The Lion Inn
Rosedale Head Boulders
Todd Intake
Northdale Boulders
A171
Rabbit Hill
Kay Nest
Round Crag
Chop Gate
Middle Ridge Crag
Hunt House Crag
Tarn Hole
The Meadow
Thimbleby Crag
High Crag
Blawath Crag
Oak Crag
Thorgill
Over Silton
Low Water Stones
Blakey Ridge
Duck Boulders
Rosedale Abbey
Cloughton Wyke
Apple Tree Rocks
Petergate Quarry
Cropton Forest
A169
A19
B1257
Levisham
The Bridestones
Hutton-le-Hole
Scarborough
Ravenswick Quarry
Kirkbymoorside
A170
Dalby Forest
Helmsley
Pickering
A170
Thirsk
A170
Thornton-le-Dale
West-side
Central
East- side

Disclaimer

Be aware that bouldering is a form of unroped climbing and as such is an inherently dangerous activity which requires care and attention at all times. Participation in climbing and spotting carries the risk of serious injury and even death. Users of this book should be aware of the potential risks involved and responsible for their own actions. The decision to climb is your own responsibility. Be wise and look after each other. The authors and publishers of this guide therefore accept no liability for any accident, injury and damage incurred whilst using this book, either to climbers themselves, third parties or property. Please also note that use of the information within this guide does not give you the right of access to climb on these rocks.

Access

Please check the BMC website for access information: www.thebmc.co.uk
Also check www.naturalengland.org.uk for details of open access land in the North York Moors.

Behaviour

Be polite and respect local residents and landowners at all times.
During the shooting season there are often shooting parties on the moor, so keep out of their way. If asked to leave, then do so. Remember, if it wasn't for the management of the heather moorland for the purposes of game-keeping and sheep farming, it would look vastly different. Please do not block any farm gates and park considerably, as any issues with parking could affect future access. Avoid short-cuts across private land and stick to the approaches described. Close any gates after you and avoid climbing over fences and walls. Most of the venues in this guide either do not allow dogs or have restrictions during shooting season. Please read the information sections to each venue to let you know about any issues. This information is not conclusive. Please make every effort to be aware of shooting season times and permitted rights of way and access.

Ethics

Please respect the rock and areas you climb in and abide by the countryside code. Follow these simple rules:

- Do not drop litter anywhere. Take it home with you.
- Do not chip or damage any rock. The use of crampons and dry-tooling are strictly forbidden.
- Do not use resin or drill fixed-bolts anywhere.
- Do not use wire or hard nylon brushes . Keep brushing to a minimum.
- Please use as little chalk as possible and avoid tick marking. Lightly brush away any chalk after you've finished.
- Please do not remove any vegetation.
- Use a bouldering mat wherever possible, to decrease the impact on vegetation.
- Do not climb on wet sandstone.

A soft brush is perfect for preserving the life of the rock

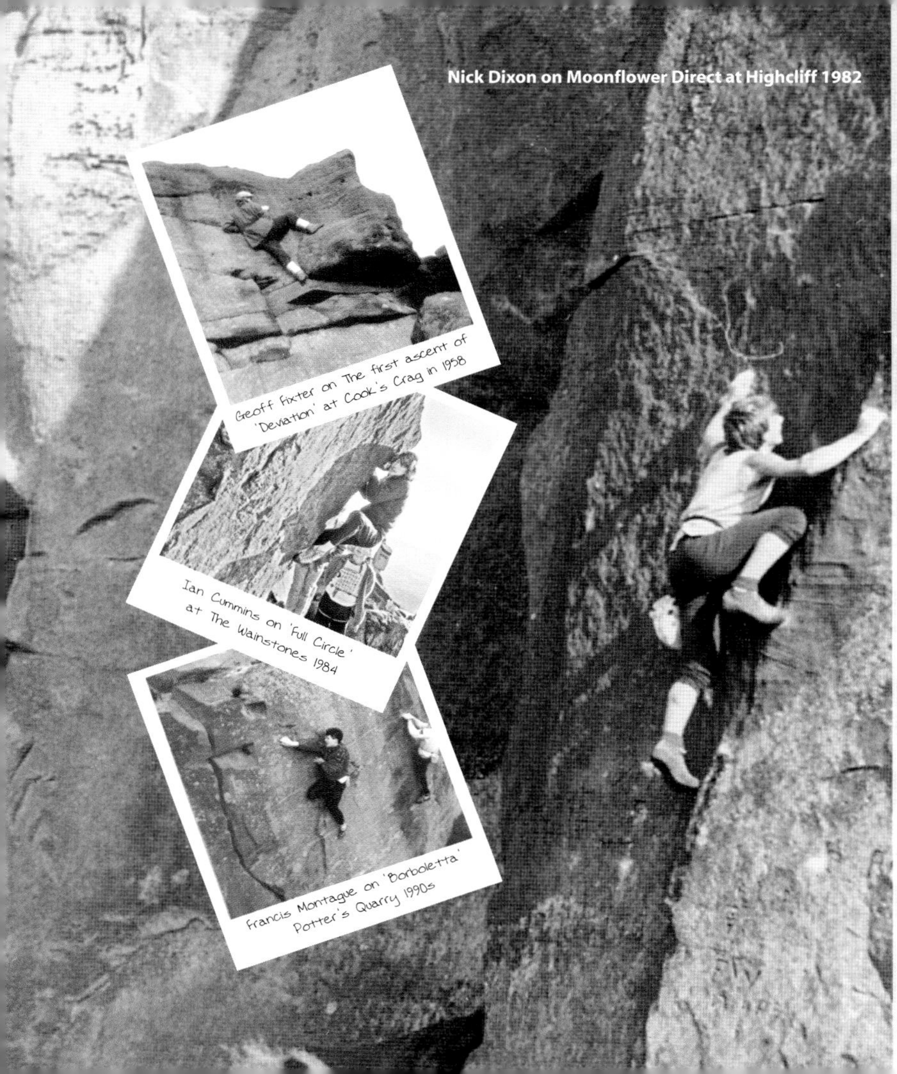

Nick Dixon on Moonflower Direct at Highcliff 1982

Geoff Fixter on The first ascent of 'Deviation' at Cook's Crag in 1958

Ian Cummins on 'Full Circle' at The Wainstones 1984

Francis Montague on 'Borboletta' Potter's Quarry 1990s

Bouldering in the Moors *A Brief History by Steven Phelps*

Although climbing on The North York Moors may have been going on for centuries, it wasn't until organised climbing began at the end of the nineteenth century that climbs were recorded, though information for this period is lacking.

What we do have seems to start with early pioneers such as E.E. Roberts, E.Creighton and Arthur Barker in the early part of the 20th century on the popular outcrops of The Wainstones and Scugdale. Both are areas that are still the most popular of the moors today, indicating the quality of these early problems and venues, still being enjoyed by generations of climbers. The Wainstones was probably the first venue to be explored for bouldering by those early climbers, with the features on the boulders offering obvious challenges in addition to the routes up on the main edge.

Development continued throughout the middle part of the 20th century involving people such as Eric Marr and Geoff Fixter adding new routes to already popular crags and first ascents at new venues such as Cook's Crag. Moors regular Tony Marr was also starting his developments about this time and observed some of the bouldering up on the Wainstones one day in 1959, "We were treated to some impressive climbing that day by two local climbers, Eric (Spider) Penman and John Cheesmond. The pair moved from boulder to boulder, choosing only the hardest problems, encouraging each other to "go for it". In fact, I can clearly remember two of the many problems they climbed that day....located on what is now called the A Boulder: Pebble Climb and The Crack". Bouldering was already an activity in its own right on the moors.

This was also around the time that the Cleveland Mountaineering Club started recording their exploits, opening up further venues, doing maintenance for access and providing a focal point for local enthusiasts: a valuable commodity.

In the 1970s and 80s standards started to reach a new level of difficulty and problems perceived as unclimbable or too dangerous were finally breached by the likes of Dave Paul, Nick Dixon, Alan Taylor and Paul Ingham. Many of the well-regarded highball problems of today were ascended in a much bolder fashion back then as it was before the advent of the bouldering mat. Boundaries were being pushed and at Scugdale tales of Taylor's false claims were quashed in front of doubting and dazzled audiences as he flawlessly demonstrated where the future realms of difficulty lay.

Things continued apace throughout this period with stories being told of climbers even using car seats for softer landings beneath the extremely bold unprotected slabs of Highcliff Nab to breach the tantalising highball variations of Moonflower, definitely a sign of things to come. The 1980s saw the publication of the first dedicated climbing guide for the moors, along with the discovery of fresh venues well-suited to bouldering such as The Bridestones, with its grassy landings and enigmatic blocks with relatively short elevation. The 1990s experienced a flurry of new additions at already developed venues by the likes of Martin Parker, Francis Montague, Karin Magog and Steve Crowe, including another venue ideally suited to bouldering at Earthworks Rocks. All of this culminated in what would become 'Climbing in North East England' published in 2003. At this point bouldering mats began to be seen across the country, undoubtedly a welcome addition to any climber's kit, replacing their beer towel or piece of carpet. The North York Moors themselves seem to have been historically late to adjust to bouldering and have only recently adopted a foreign grading system, much better suited to bouldering than traditional British grading. After the impetus created by the last guidebook to the moors the amount of activity gradually decreased, though recently there has been a renewed interest in development, especially on the bouldering scene. New venues have been identified which were previously unknown even to local climbers and further problems have been added to the boulders at already popular crags. As a result this first dedicated bouldering guide to the North York Moors has been created to highlight the wealth of bouldering across the moors and surrounding area.

Ravenswick Limestone at night

Geology *Written by Dave Warburton, local climber and geologist*

The Cleveland Hills, Howardian Hills and North Yorkshire Moors are sculpted from Jurassic-age strata which formed around 200 million years ago. The fertile Moorland valleys such as Rosedale and the base of the Cleveland Hills, which are in stark contrast to the acidic moorland, see the oldest outcropping strata: the black-coloured shales of the Lower Jurassic. The shale is often inter-bedded with harder limestone (best seen on wave-cut platforms on the coast) and was formed when the area was an extensive, generally muddy sea. The Lower Jurassic Shales are host to some of the most famous commodities of the area, including the Cleveland Ironstone, Whitby Jet and Alum, which have been extensively worked both inland and on the coast; for Iron-ore, jewellery and cloth dye respectively. Similarly, commonly found fossils such as ammonites and belemnites are found alongside more exotic plesiosaurs and even a lone pterosaur in these Lower Jurassic horizons.

The muddy seas existed for millions of years, allowing a great thickness to develop. But eventually the sea levels fell in relation to the land and this marked the beginning of the Middle Jurassic. This allowed the development of freshwater deltas sourcing sediment from eroding land to the north. Thus providing the major sandstone formations of the area which were formed from the deposition of sand and mud by river channels in a large scale delta system. Fossils of vegetation, usually logs and leaves and the more rarely found, but far more impressive dinosaur footprints showed that reptiles roamed these fern and horsetail rich river deltas.

At several times during the Middle Jurassic the river delta was submerged by shallow seas ending sandstone deposition. However, it wasn't long before the deltas re-established, with each episode providing a slightly different character of sandstone. The sandstones of the Middle Jurassic are major feature forming units holding out against erosion; a perfect example being the sandstone-capped Roseberry Topping.

By the Upper Jurassic however the area was once again totally submerged by the sea. This sea was shallow, tropical and provided the area with coral reefs giving rise to clays, calcareous sandstones but most importantly Limestones which are found in the south of the region.

Since the Upper Jurassic, around 145 million years ago, the sediments were buried to great depth by the formation of younger strata. This allowed rock forming to occur. During the Tertiary volcanism at Mull in Scotland resulted in the formation of an igneous intrusion, the Cleveland Dyke, which cross-cuts Jurassic and older rocks.

Tectonic uplift resulted in the general southward dip of the strata and created numerous smaller-scale dome structures (Robin Hoods Bay being a perfect example). Subsequent erosion removed the younger strata and brought the Jurassic-aged rocks towards the surface. The current geography of the area is due to the interaction of ice and water with the bedrock during the last Ice age 20-120,000 years ago. Glaciers cut broad valleys such as Eskdale, while melt waters cut and over deepened the north-south trending valleys such as Farndale, Bilsdale and most famously Newtondale. The crags and boulders that adorn the Moors and coast have been further weathered to leave the outcrops and boulders we find today.

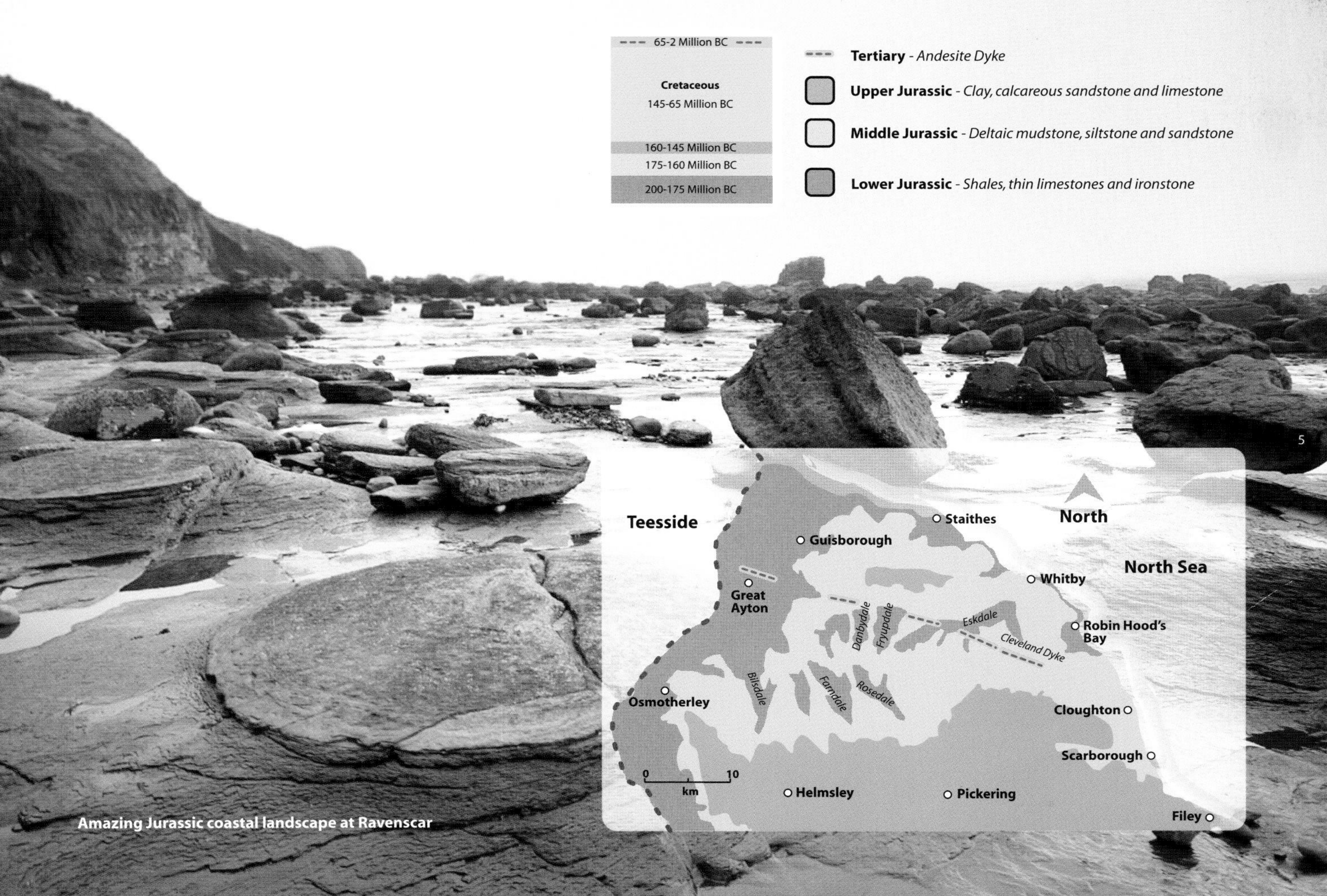
65-2 Million BC
Cretaceous
145-65 Million BC
160-145 Million BC
175-160 Million BC
200-175 Million BC
Tertiary - *Andesite Dyke*
Upper Jurassic - *Clay, calcareous sandstone and limestone*
Middle Jurassic - *Deltaic mudstone, siltstone and sandstone*
Lower Jurassic - *Shales, thin limestones and ironstone*
Teesside
Staithes
North
Guisborough
Whitby
North Sea
Great Ayton
Danbydale
Fryupdale
Eskdale
Cleveland Dyke
Robin Hood's Bay
Bilsdale
Farndale
Rosedale
Osmotherley
Cloughton
Scarborough
0
10
km
Helmsley
Pickering
Filey

Amazing Jurassic coastal landscape at Ravenscar

The Human Effect *Written by Dave Warburton*

The Moors contain an amazing wealth of archaeological remains of all periods, dating from the end of the last Ice Age - the flint tools and camps of the first hunters - through to the concrete and steel bunkers of the Cold War.

When you look at the North York Moors, what do you see? Although the moors seem wild and natural, their appearance is entirely the result of human activity. The evidence of this can be found all around us, if you learn how to read the signs. Each generation has left its own mark, manipulating and managing the land to meet their own needs. With just a little knowledge, it is possible to look at the countryside and settlements here and imagine what was happening hundreds or thousands of years ago. Some aspects of this story may surprise you, opening up a vision of the past which will change your perception of the present.

Ever since Mesolithic settlers arrived, crossing from mainland Europe 10,000 years ago, the area has been altered to suit the needs of the population. Indeed, evidence of settlements and flint tools allow us an insight into their moors, which were quite different, mainly due to a thick covering of deciduous woodland.

By 5,000 years ago the widespread woodland on the upland plateau was being cleared away for settlement and farming. Evidence of these early Neolithic farmers can be seen throughout the moors, particularly so in the south where concentrations of small stoney mounds (clearance cairns; cairnfields) and boundary banks can be found. There are also well-preserved settlement sites comprising enclosures and traces of huts, together with burial mounds. It is around this time that some of the most famous relics of the moors date. The moors around Stoupe Brow is also home to many examples of 'rock art' carvings, which are believed to date from the Late Neolithic to the Bronze Age. The purposes of the carvings are not conclusively known; whether astronomical markers, grave markers, territorial boundary markers, way markers or some the work of shepherds on the hills?

From the Late Bronze Age and through the Iron Age, more imposing monuments were constructed. Huge dykes, comprising rows of banks and ditches, built with nothing more than primitive tools and the sweat of human hands, divided up the landscape into different territories. A chance discovery by the National Park has led to a major archaeological investigation in partnership with English Heritage: the new research and fieldwork near Roulston Scar have revealed that the whole plateau was occupied by a hillfort, believed to date back to around 400BC. Covering an area of 60 acres and defended by a perimeter 1.3 miles long, this is the largest Iron Age fort of its kind in the north of England and within the 20 largest of the country as a whole.

By the Bronze Age, 4,000 years ago, much of the forest had been cut down and settlements existed upon the high moors plateau. Again, numerous artifacts offer an insight into a way of life associated with the limited period of upland farming, before it was abandoned leaving soils deficient in nutrients. This nutrient-poor land was colonised by heathland, the start of the rolling heather moorland of today.

Young Ralph Cross The emblem of the National Park

After the Romans withdrew in the early 5th century, the area was settled by Germanic and subsequently Norse incomers from the late 8th to 11th century. Both are notable for worshipping numerous gods, including Odin, known as Woden by the Anglo-Saxons. Odin's importance led to the naming of 'Odins Hill' what is now Roseberry Topping, one of the most recognisable features of the Moors. The peak is still iconic to this day, though now sculptured by the hand of man.

Although Christianity was introduced during the Roman Empire, the pagan incursion mentioned above caused it's virtual demise. Christianity was re-introduced to the region by missionaries from Ireland and Rome in the 7th century AD. By 657AD a monastery was established in Whitby and its ruins remain today, as one of the most photographed images of the area. Conflict between the two branches of 'Celtic' and 'Roman' christinaity resulted in the important Synod of Whitby in 664AD, attended by King Oswiu, where it was decided that the church in Northumbria would use the Roman method to calculate the date of Easter.
Times soon changed however, with Viking raiding parties laying waste to religious buildings and later settling in the region. Many of the current place names are derived from Danish dialect; Danby being a classic example.

The development of Christian monastic life in the medieval period did much to shape the Moors as seen today. Rievaulx and Byland Abbeys and Mount Grace Priory posessed sheep farms on their lands and developed the land to acommodate grazing. A series of Monks 'Trods' were built to provide path systems between markets. Arncliff Woods path is a fine example. These paths were often well constructed with large flag-stones and they appear to have joined the fishing coastline with the interior of the moors.

Some of the most obvious landscape alterations occurred in the 17th to 19th centuries, with the development of the Alum, Iron-ore and Jet industries. Although these industries, Jet in particular, had been extracting for many centuries it was only in the 17th to 19th centuries that the scale grew due to external demands. The Jet industry was soon booming for usage in jewellery after its use as mourning jewellery by Queen Victoria, while large scale alum quarries such as at Stoupe Brow, Carlton Bank and Boulby grew with the demands of the time for cloth-dye. The nature of the mining leaves its mark even today with shale heaps and slopes devoid of vegetation. Likewise, the Rosedale iron-workings which decorate the tranquil valley are also an example of this sudden growth. Within 70 years (1856 to 1926) the village swelled in population attracting miners from all over the country. A railway was built to Teesside and a series of kilns and furnaces were fashioned upon the Moors. Market changes and scientific advancement put an end to these extractive industries and once again the Moors returned to an agricultural economy.

A very different landscape The Rosedale Mining Works

Ecology *Written by Mike Gray, local climber and ecologist*

The defining features of the North York Moors are the open moorlands plunging into crag-rimmed grassy dales, yet the tumbling coastline to the east and proud limestone cliffs to the west are as much a part of the landscape. The variation in the Moors' geology, topography and climate over its relatively compact area gives rise to a diversity of habitats and species, many of which are recognised as internationally important. The crags and boulders where we climb allow us to visit some of the most valued and sensitive of these features: bogs and heaths of the moorland plateaux through which we curse and stumble; ancient woodlands in gills and valleys, rich in bryophytes, invertebrates and ferns, including the extremely rare Killarney Fern; streams and seeping flushes supporting rare flowers and mammals; or the rocks themselves and their delicate mosaics of lichens.

The heather moorland that dominates the Moors is the largest continuous expanse of moorland in England and is carefully managed for sheep grazing and grouse shooting, but with an increasing awareness of its sensitive ecology. The winter burning of the heather and the resulting patchwork quilt of heather, as well as the noisy weeks following the 'Glorious Twelfth' and scattered bee hives, are clear reminders of the economic importance of the moorland landscape. The warmer months following the quiet, often snow-clad winter, bring spectacular sights and sounds: breeding birds of prey and waders arrive in spring with their twilight calls and reeling flights; the rare Pearl-bordered Fritillary or Duke of Burgundy butterflies emerge in early summer; and the stunning late-summer carpet of purple heather brims with invertebrate life.

The natural world of the Moors is both vibrant and peaceful, and you'll be surrounded by unique sights and sounds whenever and wherever you climb. Tread carefully and enjoy.

Trumpet Lichen at Low Water Stones

Ferns at Thimbleby

Beetle at Kay Nest

Arncliffe Flora

Glaisdale Shooting Butts

Ingleby Grouse Couple

Rosedale Ewe and her lamb

Please be very careful when driving around the Moors

Campsites

There are an abundance of camping sites near the national park, most of which are open throughout the year. Here is a list of those that are suitable in regards to facilities or location for the venues documented in this guide.

Park Farm Campsite and Camping Barn, Kildale (01642 722847)

Jet Miners Inn, Great Broughton (01642 712642)

Cote Ghyll Campsite, Osmotherly (01609 883425)

Rigg Farm Caravan and Camping Park, Stainsacre, Whitby (01947 880430)

Pexton Moor Farm, Dalby Forest (01751 460294)

Rosedale Abbey Caravan and Camping Park, Rosedale Abbey (01751 417272)

Outdoor Shops

All of the closest outdoor stores lie outside the moors area. Whitby, Scarborough, Pickering and Helmsley have outdoor shops which sell general outdoor equipment. The nearest that sell climbing and bouldering gear are in Middlesbrough which has amongst others a Nevisport and further west is a large Go Outdoors store just off the A19 near Stockton, which sells everything you need.

Pubs

There are hundreds of pubs in and around the moors with each village usually having at least one. Here is a list of some that are close by a few of the bouldering venues.

The Arncliffe Arms, Glaisdale

The Lion Inn, Blakey Ridge

The White Horse Inn, Rosedale Abbey

The Eskdale Inn, Castleton

The Buck Inn, Chop Gate

Cafes and tea rooms

These can be found in most villages and towns throughout the area but there are several good ones conveniently located near the venues at Castleton, Danby, Lealholm, Rosedale Abbey, Hutton-le-Hole, Swainby, Goathland, Ravenscar (near the parking for Smuggler's Terrace) and Lord Stones Cafe high on Carlton Bank. Most are open year-round but some have restricted opening times over the winter.

Transport

The National Park has a good railway link system from the main line at Middlesbrough through the Esk Valley and finishing at Whitby. Several of the stations provide a useful way of getting to the venues, such as the stops at Battersby, Kildale, Castleton, Lealholm and Grosmont. Alternatively the Pickering to Grosmont North York Moors steam railway can take you to the heart of the moors.
There are also buses running from 24th March to the 27th October that go through the moors from Hull, Malton, Teeside, Thirsk and Northallerton. A full bus timetable can be found at **www.northyorkmoors.org.uk/visiting/public-transport**

Heritage and tourist sites

Whitby Town - An historic fishing town with modern facilities including seafront arcades, galleries, shopping and simply the best fish and chips in the country. Attractions include the Captain Cook Memorial Museum, Whitby Museum in Pannett Park, the famous 199 steps up to the church of St. Mary, the historic medieval ruins of St. Hilda's Abbey which dominate the town high up on the east cliff, plus the Dracula Experience. There are also regular festivals throughout the year including the Whitby Folk Week, Whitby 60s Festival and the famous Goth Weekend.

North York Moors Heritage Steam Railway - The popular rail line running between Pickering and Whitby is an excellent way of getting to some of the bouldering venues and to see some of the most beautiful moorland scenery on offer.

Dalby Forest - A fantastic day out for all can be had in the forest with activities such as walking and cycle trails for all levels of skill, tree-top adventures at 'Go Ape', paintballing, archery and even Segway rides through the forest. There's also a large visitor centre.

Rievaulx Abbey - The ruins of this medieval Cistercian monastic complex are the most atmospheric and complete of England's Abbey ruins. They are set in a spectacularly picturesque valley to the north-west of Helmsley.

Helmsley Town and Castle - A market town and gateway to the moors with shops, holiday cottages, an arts centre and the ruins of a medieval castle in a fantastic location.

Mount Grace Priory - The best preserved Carthusian monastery in England and the last monastery to be founded in Yorkshire. The monks' cells, each of which are small houses, are very well-preserved and accessible to the public. One has replica furniture and a herb garden. There's also a 13th century manor house on the site. The priory is located below a wooded hillside just off the A19.

Guisborough Priory - An ancient priory in some fantastic grounds in the historic market town.

Whorlton Castle - Situated just outside the village of Swainby is an 11th century earthwork motte and bailey castle, an excellent place to visit and explore for free.

Tom Leonard Mining Museum - Is located in the coastal village of Skinningrove and provides an insight into some of the important local industrial history and geology of the area, some of which has shaped the bouldering venues themselves.

Ryedale Folk Museum - An excellent place to visit with a wealth of re-constructed original and replica ancient buildings showing life from the Iron Age to the 1950s on a six acre site in the very picturesque village of Hutton-le-Hole.

Scaling Dam - A large reservoir located just off the A171 and a venue for sailing, canoeing and fishing. Also an excellent setting for walking.

Goathland - Otherwise known as Aidensfield in ITV's Heartbeat is a popular tourist spot and a nice place for a stroll, if in the area.

Other attractions that lie outside or close by are: Flamingo Land theme park , zoo and holiday park near Malton; Castle Howard, the large stately home and gardens also near Malton (the location for the 'Brideshead Revisited' series and film); The Howardian Hills south of the moors, which are far less travelled than they deserve and offer excellent walking.

Tourist Information

Whitby Tourist Information Centre, Langborne Road, Whitby (01723 383636)
The Moors National Park Centre, Lodge Lane, Danby (01439 772737)
Sutton Bank National Park Centre (01845 597246)

Grades

This guide has adopted the Font grading system, utilising the colour coding of problems throughout the range of grades, yet still respecting UK traditional grades as most of the historical climbing/bouldering in the North Yorkshire Moors was climbed without the use of pads. As with Fontainebleau grades, the problem is the same grade whether you use a pad or not and however high you climb.

The range of grade colour codes are:

- **Orange = 1 to 4+**
- **Blue = 5 to 5+**
- **Red = 6a to 6c+**
- **Black = 7a to 8b+**
- **White = Unclimbed lines, some of which are not so hard.**

Be aware! Some of the problems are a conversion of older British traditional grades, given in a time when British 6a-6b was considered the limit that a climber would grade, so people were reluctant to grade higher even if it had taken quite a while to climb a project. So don't feel too bad if an 'old school' 5+ batters your ego a bit, it's more of a testament to how good the climbers were back in the day.

Note regarding sit-starts: '**SS**' in bold capitals after the problem name indicates a sitting start to a problem, though occasionally an additional sit-start to a problem will be mentioned at the end of the description, generally where the historical original start did not include one. Some sit-starts have deliberately been left out of the description as they are not consistent with the flow of the climbing above. Omission of the sit-start does not necessarily mean it has not been climbed.

Thanks

Countless people have done so much for climbing in the Moors and many have helped me produce this guide, without whom it would not exist. Here are the names of but a few. Sorry if I have missed anyone out.
Lisa Robinson, Steven Phelps, James Rennardson, Mike Adams, Mike Gray, James Kitson, Tony Marr, Eric Marr, Steve Ramsden, Dave Warburton, Franco Cookson, Steve Crowe, Karin Magog, Jason and Scott Wood, Martin Parker, Francis Montague, Paul Ingham, Steve and Tom McClure, Nick Dixon, Sam Marks, Matthew Ferrier, Tom Barr, Jake Hampshire, Nigel Poustie, Tom Crane, Mark Wilson, Chris Carr, Neil Furniss, Clare Jennings, Aido Holt, Tony Simpson, Andy Jennings, John Cheesmond, Eric "Spider" Penman, Terry Sullivan, Joe Tasker, Johnny Adams, Colin Read, Les Brown, Pete Holden, Alan Dewison, Ron Lake, Ken Jackson, Rick Graham, Chris Shorter, Alan Hinks, Alan Taylor, Richard Waterton, Niall Grimes, Rob Lonsdale, Martin Whitton, Liam and Brandon Copley, Dan Crawford and many more who know who they are.

I am looking forward to seeing the next generation of Moors climbers. I hope they will continue adding to what is recorded in this guide, pushing the barriers even further..........

Contact: *lee@betaguides.com*

Use the grade converter below if you already use the British Technical or American Vermin grading system

Font	UK	V Grade
1	D	
2	S	
3	4a	VB
	4b	V0
	4c	
4		
4+	5a	V1
	5b	
5		
5+	5c	V2
6a		V3
6a+	6a	V4
6b		
6c		V5
6c+	6b	
7a		V6
7a+		V7
7b	6c	V8
		V9
7c		V10
	7a	
8a		V11
		V12
8b	7b	V13
8b+		V14
8c		V15

Introduction

I have thought long and hard about how to introduce this guide. How do you describe a climbing area in a few words? For me the answer was carved into a mighty boulder at Kay Nest in Tripsdale. The words were written in Latin by John Hart, a man of Bilsdale in 1849. The words read:

"All things are full of the creator"

This sums up the North York Moors for me, millions of years for nature and humans to create a landscape, the end result being a beautiful yet diverse place, with a set of venues that have very different outlooks and feel. It can take a while to understand how to navigate around the Moors and know when each venue is at its best, but after a bit of effort its charms and tranquillity are the perfect place to lose yourself in a problem or two, whatever grade you climb.

The North York Moors lends itself to bouldering well, with blocks and micro edges in abundance, plenty of climbs for the beginner and choice test-pieces at the harder end of the spectrum.

Significantly it was the first place I ever climbed as a youth, on a school trip from Hull, venturing into Dalby Forest to The Bridestones. This experience opened my mind to the possibilities that rock climbing could offer both personally and socially, filling a void that city living can cause. It brought fulfillment in my life, experiencing both landscape and gymnastic movement within a sport that is very accessible and keeps you fit. It also takes you to some of the most stunning places in the UK and Ireland - what a way to meet new friends.

I can recommend bouldering to anyone. It's a very social way to enjoy climbing for the first time - all you need is a pad, shoes and somewhere to go and the North York Moors is the perfect place to start.

All I hope from this guide is that it will inspire climbers new and old to explore these places and enjoy them when they are at their best.

Please also take the time to look at the culture and food the area has to offer. It's warm-hearted, full of history, charm and culinary delights.

Lee Robinson

Pattie and Chips, then a stroll around Whitby.

My top four culinary experiences to hunt out whilst in the area:

Western Area – Helmsley – Thomas the Baker – Buy a large scone (Fat Scamp) and a coffee, sit in the square, chill out and watch the world go by.
Other great local delicatessens sell a wide range of quality freshly baked sweet and savory delights.

Central Area – Middleton Service Station/Londis Supermarket - just north of Pickering – First choice is a Glaves pork pie (the best in the world), second is a curry pasty. The pies sell out fast! 5 star dining outdoors.
Pickering also has a good selection of pie shops, cafes and pubs, Hutton-le-Hole and Castleton also have good pubs and tea shops with some fine grub.

Eastern Area – Glaisdale - Arncliffe Arms – Chicken Parmo (chicken beaten flat, covered in breadcrumbs and smothered with a béchamel sauce and cheese) Teeside's kebab equivalent. So bad but so tasty.

Coastal Area – Robin Hoods Bay - Maryondale Fisheries – Fish and chips by the sea. Perfection.
Whitby also has some fine fish and chip establishments. Best of all is the famed 'The Magpie Café' but be prepared to queue as it is very popular.

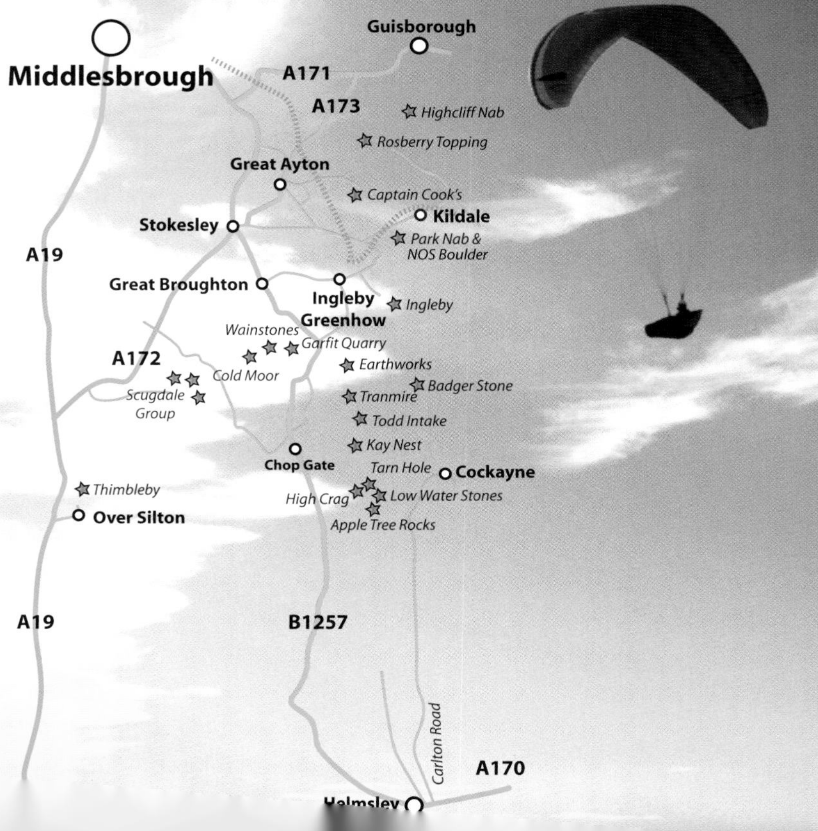

Western Edges

The most popular area of the North York Moors due to its easy access for the local population of Teesside, accessibility from the gritstone edges of Yorkshire to the west and The Peak District further south. There is a rich history connected with this western area, where several ground-breaking ascents have been made over the years. Recent development have uncovered several new venues, some giving a bouldering aspect to existing traditional crags. There are well known areas, such as Scugdale, The Wainstones, Captain Cook's and Ingleby Boulders, along with other lesser known, though worthy venues.
Even though this western area is more popular compared to further east, some venues still have an isolated feel and the potential for further exploration.

Venues are usually ordered south to north, although some will be grouped according to access and locality.

Paragliding over Potter's Quarry

Low Water Stones

A remote cluster on East Bilsdale Moor, with a roof section to the left and some thin slabby walls to the right.

Approach: Park at the lay-by near The Grange on the B1257 between Helmsley and Chop Gate (grid reference (SE 572961). Walk south and take the farm track to the left and the next track left to High Cowhelm farm. At the T-junction, turn right, pass the farm and also Low Cowhelm Farm. At the next farm (Apple Tree Hurst) a leftwards path by the first barn leads through fields and up onto the moor. On reaching the top the path becomes boggy and follows the edge of the moor northwards. After a few hundred metres the boulders can be seen up on the right. Cross the heather to reach them. An alternate flatter (though longer) approach is via parking in Bransdale on Pockley Moor and following a moorland track northwards until the rocks can be approached from above.

OS Map: SE 592970
Walk: 45 minutes
Faces west

The Low Water Stones

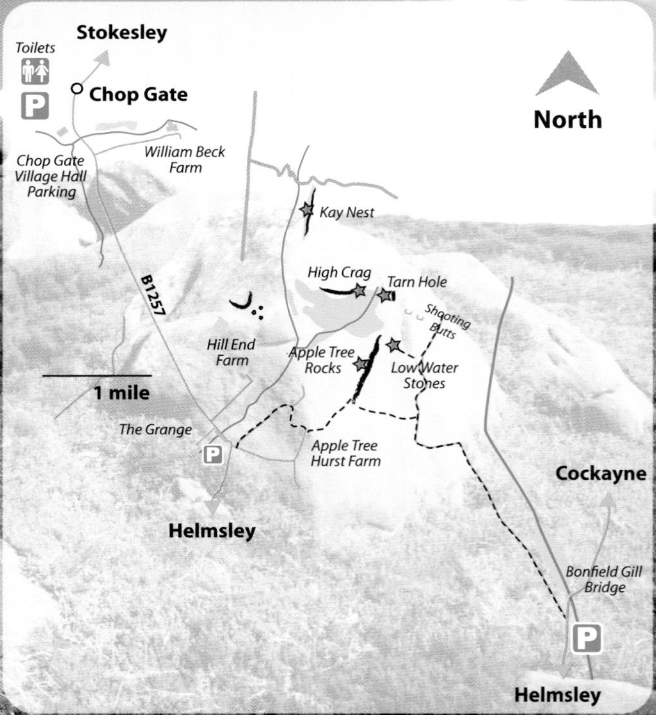

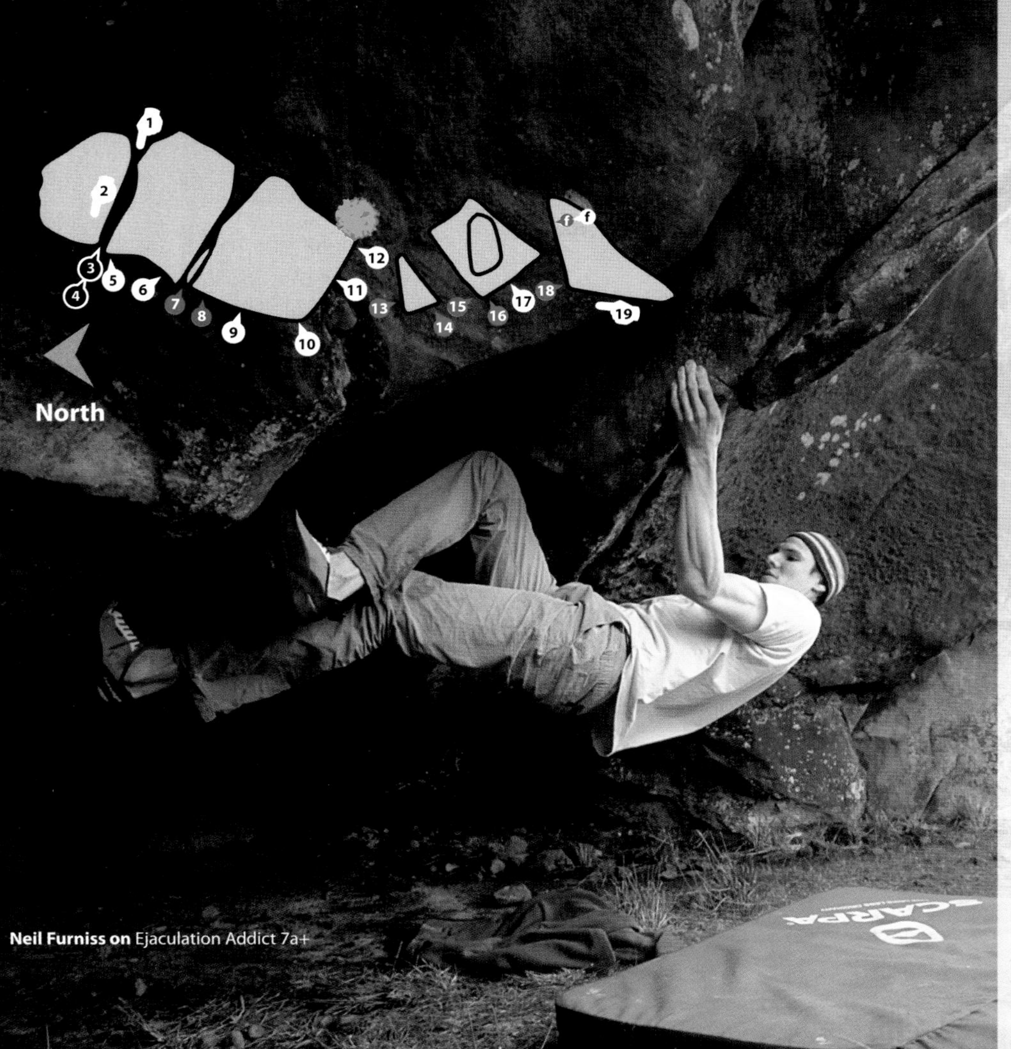

Neil Furniss on Ejaculation Addict 7a+

The Low Water Stones have some rare features for moors sandstone and some hard project possibilities.

1. Project Start way back at the start of the crack.
2. Project The crimpy rails, using the left block only.
3. Corpus Hypercubus 7a SS Start with a left hand sidepull and the right on a shallow pocket. Place your feet on the lower ledge, pull up hard or knee-bar to gain the painful jam in the crack with the right hand. Then use the rounded hold low down on the left wall. Sort your feet out to gain the top.
4. Ejaculation Addict 7a+ SS Start as above, then spin your feet on the left wall and work your way up the prow undercutting. Once you reach the crack over the prow top-out left.
5. Project As above, without using the left block.
6. Project The right arête without any other blocks.
7. Lobster Telephone 6a SS Climb the crack avoiding the block underneath.
8. The Persistance of Memory 6a Use the left undercut and the right mono to get the feet up and gain the arête. Follow this to the top. No other blocks allowed.
9. Project The centre of the slab.
10. Project The rounded arête is best climbed via some levitation techniques!
11. Project The central groove.
12. Project The right arête with the tricky start.
13. Surrealist 5+ Use a giant bear hug, then latch the top.
14. Galatea of the Spheres 5+ SS Climb the rounded arête on its left side.
15. Honey is Sweeter than Blood 6a No French starts! Get established on the right arête plus a sloping crimp for the left hand, then pop for the top.
16. Chupa Chups 5+ SS A stiff pull to gain the arête, with a slopey mantel finish.
17. Project No arêtes allowed. A desparate pull off the ground. Might be easier for the shorter in stature!
18. Salvador 7a From the scooped pocket make some awkward moves leftwards on slopers to gain the rounded flutings on the left side of the block, then top-out.
19. Project The extension of Salvador from sitting. Start on the good lip. Getting round the corner is going to be tricky.

High Crag Boulders These isolated boulders are scattered over a small area below High Crag Right Hand Buttress, which is about two hundred metres east of the main buttresses of High Crag itself. There are a good range of problems on clean solid sandstone including some excellent arêtes and some steep overhangs, with the boulders staying clean throughout the year, due to their open aspect. Keep dogs on a lead.

Approach: Parking can be found on the B1257 Helmsley to Great Broughton road towards Chop Gate. Park at the village hall at the southern edge of the village and on the west side of the road straight after the village sign. Cross over the small bridge, cross the road and follow the public right of way over the stile and across the fields to William Beck Farm, or take the farm track a little further down the road. Go through the farm after which the track becomes a bridleway and takes you onto the moor top via three gates. Where the footpath meets the bridleway turn south for 100m, then take the path to the east, down into Tripsdale on a zig-zag track. Cross the river and follow the track up onto Hagg House Moor. You can either go south along the top of Kay Nest and then break off across the moor through the heather or follow the main track east onto the moor. As the track begins to level out towards the grouse butts, there's another track going right (if you've reached the shooting houses, you've gone too far). Take this across the moor until you reach a dry stone wall field boundary. The boulders are to the south. An alternative approach from a large lay-by about 2.5 miles south of Chop Gate is possible although fraught with difficulties, including a river, a bog and undefined paths. Although a shorter route, this way is not recommended.

OS Map: SE 589978
Walk: 1 hour 20 minutes
Faces south

Dry Stone Wall
Moor Top
Stokesley
Toilets
Chop Gate
Chop Gate Village Hall Parking
William Beck Farm
Kay Nest
High Crag
B1257
Hill End Farm
1 mile
High Crag Approach
The Grange
Helmsley
North
High Crag Boulders

Lee Robinson on Numb 6c

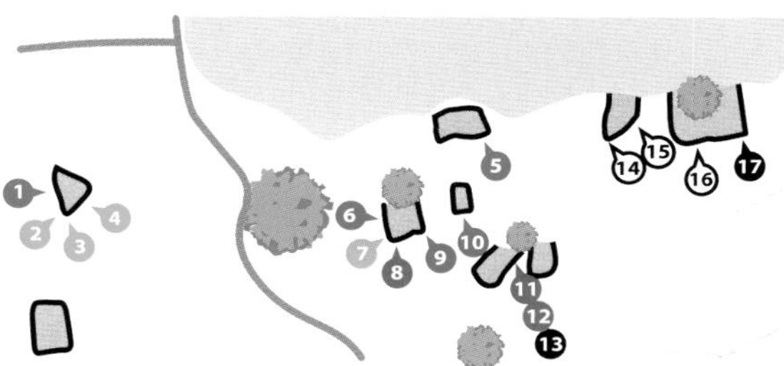

The first arête block.

1. Isolation 5+ Start just left of the arête and without using it gain the top.
2. Repression 4 Climb the arête on its left.
3. Born Again 4 Climb the arête on its right. The sit-start has not been done.
4. Social Connections 4+ Gain the undercut and climb direct.

Below the arête is a lichen-covered slab that needs a clean!

The next block over the fence can be green, as the tree keeps it in the shade.

5. In The Shade 6a SS Start on a crimp ledge with feet under the block, climb up and right to find the good hold at the top.

Just down the slope from this block are:

6. Misdeed 5 SS Climb the sidewall starting below the flake.
7. Perfectly Weathered 4 SS Climb the left arête on its left side
8. Delusions of Reality 6c SS Start on the left side of the front face, make a big move right to gain the sloping lip, then left on pockets. Pull over the bulge and finish up the slab.
9. Confusion 5 Start on the right side of the block, gain the slab, then finish right of the crackline.

Next is a nice little slab.

10. Follow 5+ Mount the slab, then climb up using the left arête.

The sideways prow block.

11. Numb 6c+ SS Start low from an undercut for the left hand and a spike for your right. Work your way left on slopers, then climb round the nose of the prow and grovel over with the help from a blunt arête.
12. Hollow 6c+ SS With the left hand on the undercut pocket and right on the spike at the base of the crack, pull up and slap up left to get the sloping shelf. Finish direct.
13. Shades of Green 7a SS Start in the same place but this time have your right on the undercut pocket and left on the flake at the base of the crack. This time follow the crackline up right.

The craggy alcove.

14. Project The left side of the split block.
15. Project The centre of the split block.
16. Smooth sloper pocket project
17. Skyfall 7a+ Climb the left-hand side of the arête above the less than ideal landing, making a long move to gain the pocket (more positive than it looks) then gain the top.

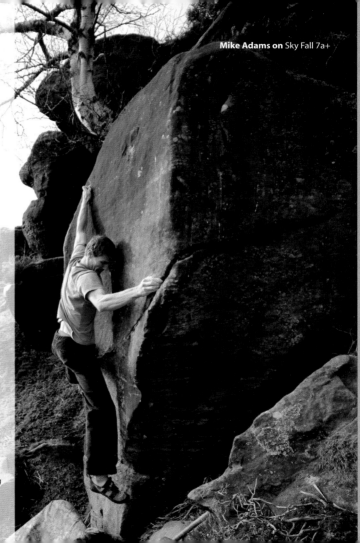

Mike Adams on Sky Fall 7a+

James Rennardson on The Thief of Always 7b+

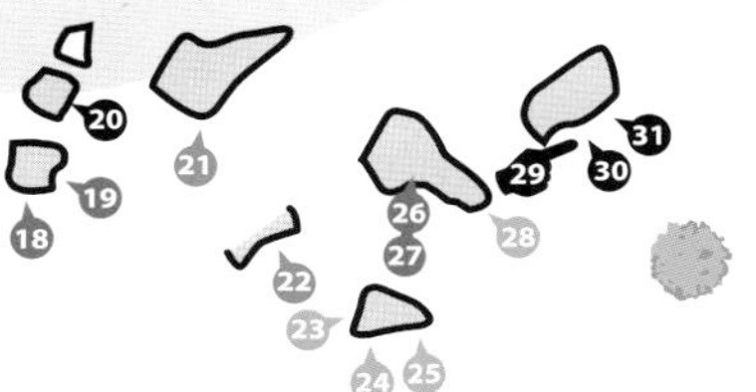

The small, dark, weathered block has two interesting problems.

18. Ape 6c SS Hug the hanging block then gain the ledge and mantel.
19. Dance Monkey Dance 6a SS Pull up from the right-hand pocket to gain the ledge, rock into the groove and top-out.

Just up the hill to the left.

20. Ripples of Desire 7b SS Climb up the face of the block in the mini gully. With both hands on the low break and feet on the block only, pull up and make difficult moves to gain and get established on the crimp line and climb an easier finish via the blob.

To the right of the last problem is a highball arête located on the Right-Hand Buttress.

21.Cool as Ice 5+ (E1 5b) The tall arête is climbed on its left side to a serious mantel finish.

The short curved block below.

22. Solitude 5+ SS Climb the right side of the curved wall directly below the crack.

The next slab block down the hill.

23. Remote 4 Climb the arête on its left side.
24. Lonely 3 Climb the front slab.
25. Mirage 3 The right arête on the front face.

The next block along has a small roof.

26. Man of Steel 6a SS Starting under the block, climb rightwards to gain the front face and a nipple feature.
27. Swearing Down 6b SS Start as Man of Steel, then move left under the bulge to tricky moves to gain the arête and top.
28. Delicacy 3 Gain the slab and finish up the crack, delicate.

Next is a fine block with a rising lip and some perfect slopers.

29. The Thief of Always 7b+ SS Traverse the lip rightwards around the nose and follow the arête to gain the top, before rocking out to finish.
30. Autolycus 7a+ SS With the right hand in the pockets and left on the low left lip of the boulder, mantel the lip of the boulder directly using the lefthand crack.
31. Prometheus 7a+ SS Using the flakes to slap up to the lip, trend right to reach the right-hand crackline and finish up this.

Lee Robinson on Prometheus 7a+

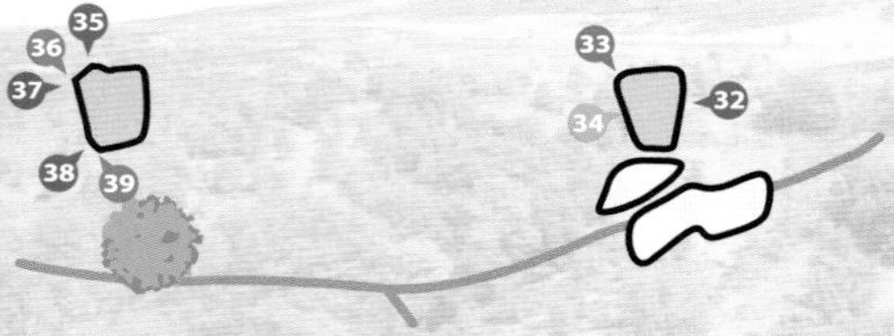

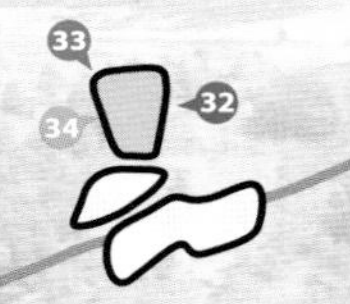

At the bottom of the hill are two good blocks.

32. Hagg 6a Climb the centre of the block using the undercut rail and a small right crimp.
33. Short Arse 5+ SS The sloping corner is trickier than it looks.
34. Ripple 4 SS Climb the centre face on the diagonal features.

The Elephant Block

Can you see it? This block holds three classics up the trunk and head.

35. Never Forget 6a Climb the leaning left side of the arête.
36. Truncation 5+ Start at the base of the trunk-like feature and climb the right side of the arête.
37. Elephantitus 6c+ Start as for the last problem. Once off the floor move up and right to a sidepull and a side-sloper, before making a dynamic bid rightwards to finish.
38. Nelly 6c From a reachy start, climb using the arête only and finishing mantelling on its left side.
39. Rear-ended 5 Start on the right side of the far arête at the flake. Pull up to reach an obvious hold then move round for the same finish as Nelly.

Steve Dennison on Hagg 6a

Steve Dennison on Elephantitus 6c+

Kay Nest, located in the hidden valley of Tripsdale is a wonderous collection of boulders unlike anywhere else. There's a diverse range of climbing in and around a wooded hillside below a large broken crag. The rock is excellent quality throughout and the boulders themselves do not give up their secrets easily. The problems cover all grades from 1 all the way up to the dizzy heights of 8b+, with enough to keep the avid boulderer busy for a full day. In high summer bracken can usually be avoided and there are plenty of shaded areas. In winter it can stay surprisingly dry, as much of it is out in the open.

Approach: Park at Chop Gate village hall, to the south of the village on the B1257 Helmsley to Stokesley road. Cross over the small bridge, then cross the road and follow the public right of way either crossing the stile and cutting across the fields or straight down the farm track to William Beck Farm, a little further down the road. Continue through the farm and up the hill, where the track becomes a footpath and takes you onto the moor top via three gates. Where the footpath meets the bridleway turn south for 100m, then take the track to the east, which takes a zig-zag route down into Tripsdale. The Eagle Stone is located 150m to the right at the first tight left turn. For the main area follow the track down to the river and at the first tight left turn going uphill, take a faint path south through some reeds, keeping left of the dry stone wall. The first blocks reached are the Capsized and Hull blocks, with The Ship just below. The other blocks are to the south on roughly the same contour line.

OS Map: SE 582986
Walk: 45 to 55 minutes.
Faces west

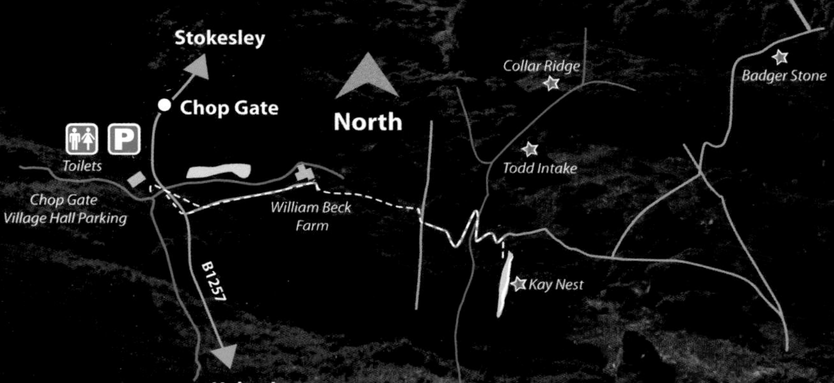

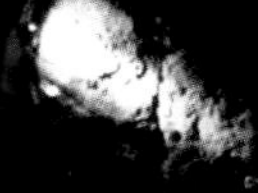

Moonlight bouldering on The Ship Stone

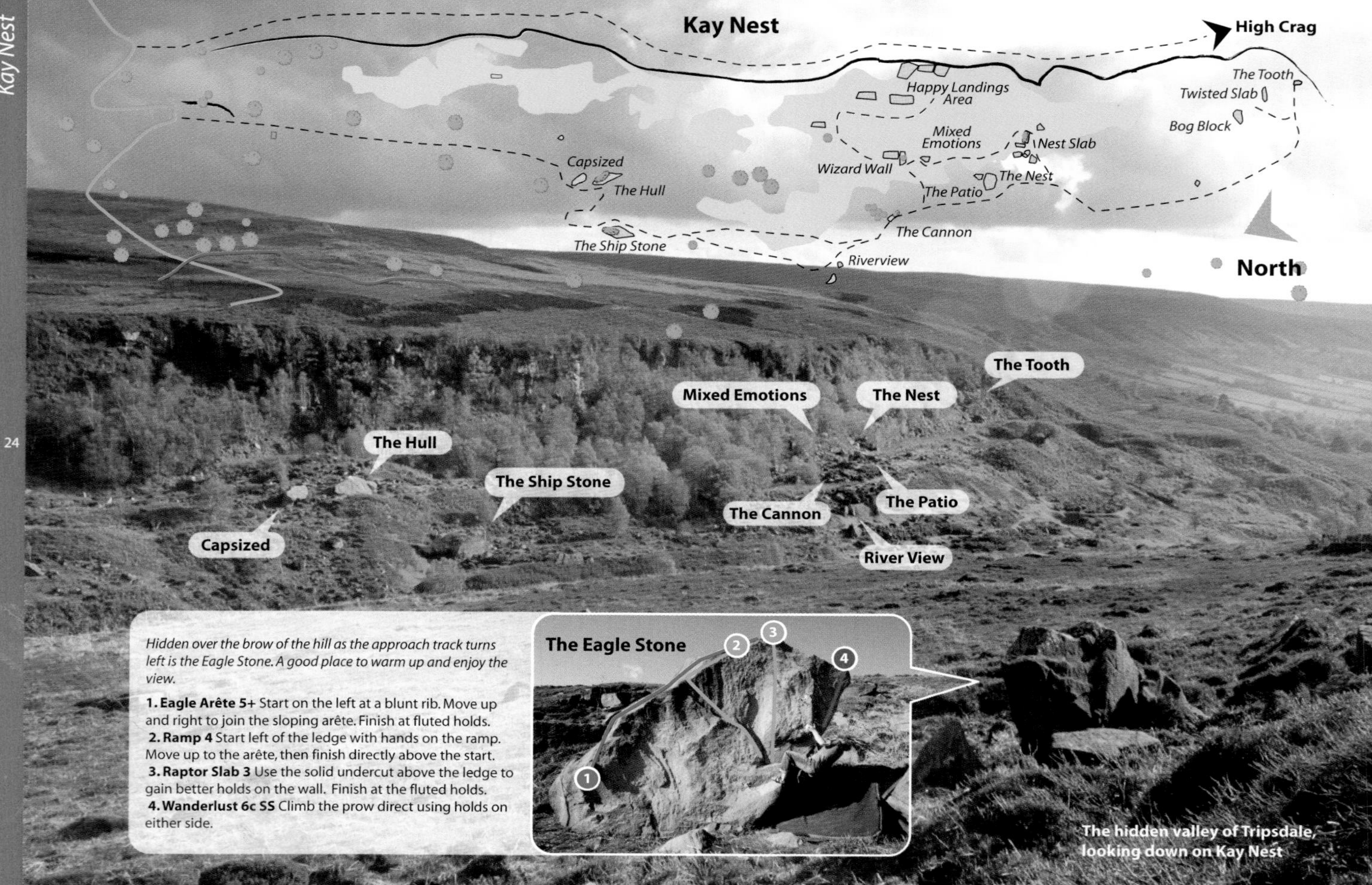

Hidden over the brow of the hill as the approach track turns left is the Eagle Stone. A good place to warm up and enjoy the view.

1. Eagle Arête 5+ Start on the left at a blunt rib. Move up and right to join the sloping arête. Finish at fluted holds.

2. Ramp 4 Start left of the ledge with hands on the ramp. Move up to the arête, then finish directly above the start.

3. Raptor Slab 3 Use the solid undercut above the ledge to gain better holds on the wall. Finish at the fluted holds.

4. Wanderlust 6c SS Climb the prow direct using holds on either side.

The hidden valley of Tripsdale, looking down on Kay Nest

Capsized

A scooped leaning block with some hard little test-pieces.

1. 5+ The arête, hard top-out.
2. The Quaker 6c SS From the left-hand pinch and right-hand thread pull to a trangular pinch, then swing leftwards to the top.
3. Man Overboard 7a SS on the left side of the pit on pockets, gain the lip of the bulge to a tricky mantel finish on slopey edges.
4. Capsize 7a SS Just left of the pit is a slight arête. Start beneath this on pockets and pull up to gain the lip of the bulge and a gaston, mantel to finish.
5. Dick Ritchie 7a+ SS From the lowest break make a stiff pull to the slot above, then over the top to the left-hand sloper/poor crimp, rock over onto the face using the right-hand sidepulls.

James Rennardson on Dick Ritchie 7a+

The Hull

Fine slab climbing with good height at the apex.

1. 3 The shortest line on the block.
2. 4 The undercut flake, then direct.
3. 4+ The delightful curving flake.
4. 6a Mount the block with some difficulty, carefully reach the curved scoop then gain the top using nice moves to finish.
5. 5 Use the ribs and features just left of the scoop.
6. 6a Delicate climbing up the scoop.
7. 5 The features right of the scoop.
8. Alabama Worley 6a+ Traverse from the right-hand side and finish on the left arete and top-out. A sloping magical mystery tour.

Jim Conbery on Problem 3

The Ship Stone - East Face

This impressive block looks like a giant battleship. The full circuit provides a good workout on its own.

1. 5 Start just left of a small ledge at a thin slot and make a direct one move wonder.
2. 5 Start beneath a hairline crack and climb to a large slot using crimps.
3. 4 The corner scoop on good holds.
4. 6a Start 1m left, climb up to a sloper then reach up and right for a good hold to finish.
5. 5 Start 2m left and climb up to the curving rail, then finish direct or follow left.
6. 6b+ Start in front of a small boulder and climb past slots direct to a sidepull, where a very long reach may gain the top.
7. 5 Start 3m right of the arête and climb past slots moving left near the top.
8. 5+ The line just right of the arête, past a large slot and finishing on flakes. No use of arête.

Carved into the the Ship Stone is a Latin inscription reputedly the work of a schoolmaster named John Hart.

DEI PLENA SUNT OMNIA. JOANNES CERVUS, BILSVALLENSIS ANNO MDCCCXLIX

Which translates: All things are full of the Creator. John Hart, a man of Bilsdale, 1849.

Mike Gray on Problem 8

The Ship Stone - West Face

The west side is a bit steeper and most problems are harder than they look.

9. 4+ Gain the ledge and climb the face.
10. 6a Climb up on flakes and sidepulls to reach pockets in the arête. Finish past a ledge.
11. 5+ Start with a good hold at head height, then gain a rising left to right traverse leading to the arête to finish as for the last problem.
12. 6b Same start as the last problem, but take a direct line with a difficult mantel finish slightly left.
13. 5+ Start just left and climb direct to flakes at the top, with a tricky mantel.
14. 6a+ Make difficult moves up to a thin flake, then a reachy finish.
15. 6a Straight up using another line of flakes.
16. 6a SS Start at a layaway and make thin moves following the weakness, then finishing just to the right.

The short wall on the left has possibilities but needs a clean and a haircut!

Steven Phelps on Problem 14

Just south of The Ship and down the hill are a couple of good blocks.

River View

1. Riverview 6a A bold pop up to a good pocket. The sit will be tricky.

2. For me to know and you to find out 6a SS Climb the right-hand arête of the block.

A fine low arête just below Riverview.

3. No Bouldering Here 6a SS Climb the arête, finishing at the apex.

The next block up the hill and a bit south is a very rare almost rounded prow feature.

The Cannon

4. The Cannon 8a+ SS From under the turret of rock, not on the boulder pull and and slap your way to the front face and a stiff lock to the top via a mono. Hard!

Venture into the woods next and you will find old mossy slabs, blank walls and something a bit special and impossible-looking.

5. Mixed Emotions 8b+ SS The sharp angled arête without any real holds has been climbed! Rock onto the slab as the climbing eases. A classic test-piece. **(See front cover photograph)**.

Mike Adams on The Cannon 8a+

Lee Robinson on Riverview 6a

James Rennardson on No Bouldering Here 6a

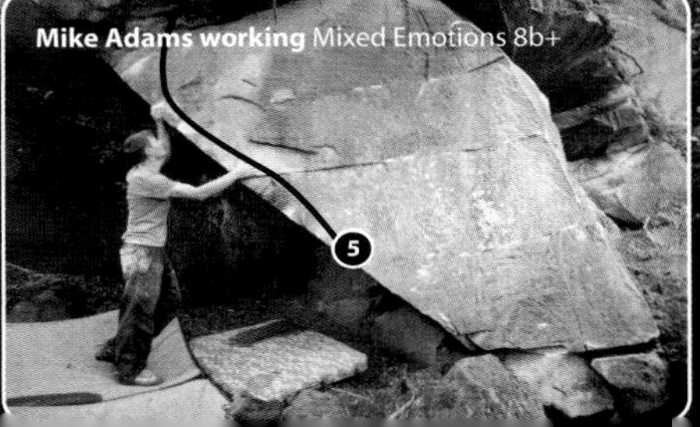

Mike Adams working Mixed Emotions 8b+

The next blocks are south again, just outside the woods.

The Patio Area

The blocks around the large flat block.

1. Elliott Blitzer 5 Climb the left arête.
2. Clifford Worley 6a The wall right of the arête, not using the arête.
3. Nicky Dimes 6a The central line on smears and not much else.
4. Wurlitzer 5+ Climb the right arête.
5. Little Gem SS 6b On the back of the block, gain the sidepull, then the top.
6.The Patio 6c SS Tricky moves to gain the face and top.
7. BBQ 5 Climb the hanging right end of the block.
8. Ribs 6b SS Climb just left of the rib.
9. Full Rack 6a+ SS Climb Just right of the rib.

The Nest

A dense mass of blocks with a rounded egg-shaped blob on top.

10. Floyd 6a The wall heading left on small holds.
11. Elvis 5 The middle arête/groove on good holds and long reaches.
12. Alabama Whitman 4+ Climb the micro VS crack. Over far too soon!
13. Drexl 6a The right-hand arête with a long move at the top.
14. True Romance 6c SS The arête and mono. Make a stiff pull for the twin monos and then the funky arête hold.
15. Project Not to be dismissed and very bold. Not yet climbed.
16. Project From a low sit on its south side climb directly over the bulge on rails and bizarre features. Bad landing!

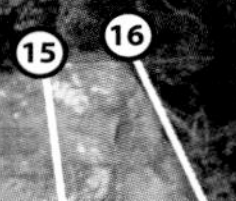

The Nest

10 11 12 13 14 15 16

Go into the woods here to get to
Vermillion and Nest Slab
Beware of holes in the rocky ground!

James Rennardson on Clarence Worley 7a

Mike Adams on Vermillion 7c

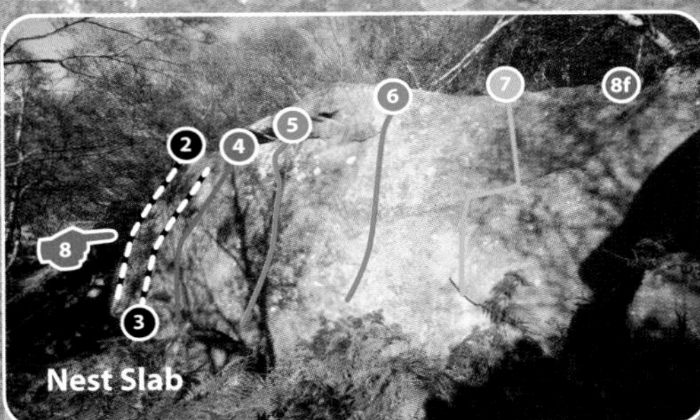

Vermillion Block

Just before you get to the Nest Slab, to the left is a block with a fine lip traverse.

1. Vermillion 7c From crouching, traverse the lip from the far right using the undercut, then rock-over to top-out using the left corner.

Nest Slab

2. Clarence Worley 7a SS Start with your right hand on the ironstone hold and use a left heel-hook to gain the arête, then carefully work your way up. **6a** from standing.
3. Will Scarlet 7b SS Start with a right-hand layaway and make your way up the slab on small holds without the arête.
4. Police Captain Quiggle 6a+ SS Start at a small ledge. Climb direct using obvious edges.
5. The King 5+ Climb the slanting rail without use of the large ledge. Finish direct over the small roof.
6. Big Don 5 Mantel the smaller left side of the ledge.
7. Little Don 4 Mantel the broader right side of the ledge.
8. I like you Clarence, always have and always will. 6a+ Traverse the wall from the standing start to 'Clarence Worley' and finish up the far right ramp line.

Steve Webster on Fifty Six 6c

Happy Landings Area

Further up through the woods are some very serious crag-based highball projects, a hanging arête block and a vague featured slab. Just north and below this are two leaning blocks.

1. Fifty Six 6c SS Start on a flat hold (shorties may only get one hand on this). Climb the wall via a finger hold and layaways.

2. Fear and Loathing 7b SS Using small edges pull up and dyno to the flat slopey hold. Hold the swing, then finish boldly up the wall. **6c+** from standing.

3. Rocky 6b+ From crouch gain the ledge, then use a sidepull to top-out. Possible sit-start.

Mike Adams on Fear and Loathing 7b

Two worthy problems at the far south end of the crag.

Twisted Slab

The long slab up the hill looks easier than it is:

4. Twisted Arête 6a Start at the right end of the block working up the rising arête.

The Tooth

The large tooth-shaped face up the hill. Take care, the landing is quite serious!

5. The Dentist 7a Climb the face finishing up the left arête.

Lee Robinson on The Dentist 7a

34 21 32 8 4

Tranmire Rocks are situated in the valley of Bilsdale. They stretch for about a mile across the edge of Broad Ings Moor and can always be combined with a visit to Earthworks Rocks, which is not too far north. The rock is good quality and the many boulders and edges offer much variety throughout the grades, from the short difficult problems of Tranmire North to the highball challenges of Far Tranmire. Some areas can suffer from bracken during the summer months, but much of it can usually be avoided. Only the climbing on the boulders and some smaller select parts of the edge are included in this guide, although a mat can be used for much of the main crag. For more information on the routes here see **www.climbonline.co.uk**

Approach: From the B1257 Helmsley to Stokesley road, take the turn to the east signposted 'St Hilda's Church', just north of the village of Chop Gate. Continue uphill through Seave Green village and follow the track through Bilsdale Hall farmyard after which you'll see St Hilda's church up on the right. Do not park anywhere near Bilsdale Hall Farm; instead park at the side of the road near the church. Please park sensibly as there have been access issues in the past. Walk back through the farm and go through the gate bearing the 'No Parking' sign. Follow a bridleway through the woods and uphill passing through two more gates to reach a red-tiled barn and gate in the dry-stone wall beyond. For Tranmire Crag boulders turn right before the gate past the barn and follow the stone wall to the crag. For the rest go through the gate past the barn. For the northern area walk up for 50 metres, take a path going north above the quarry and drop down onto the boulders. To get to Streamside Buttress take an immediate right after the gate. For the South Rocks and Far Tranmire Rocks, after 50 metres turn right on a faint path that crosses two small flagstone bridges towards the plantation. The South Rocks are by the wood next to the track. The Far Tranmire Rocks are reached by following this track south alongside the trees until you see them on the right.

OS Map:
Tranmire North NZ 572011
Crag Boulders NZ 573007
South Rocks NZ 575004
Far Tranmire SE 576999
Walk: 20 to 30 minutes
Faces west

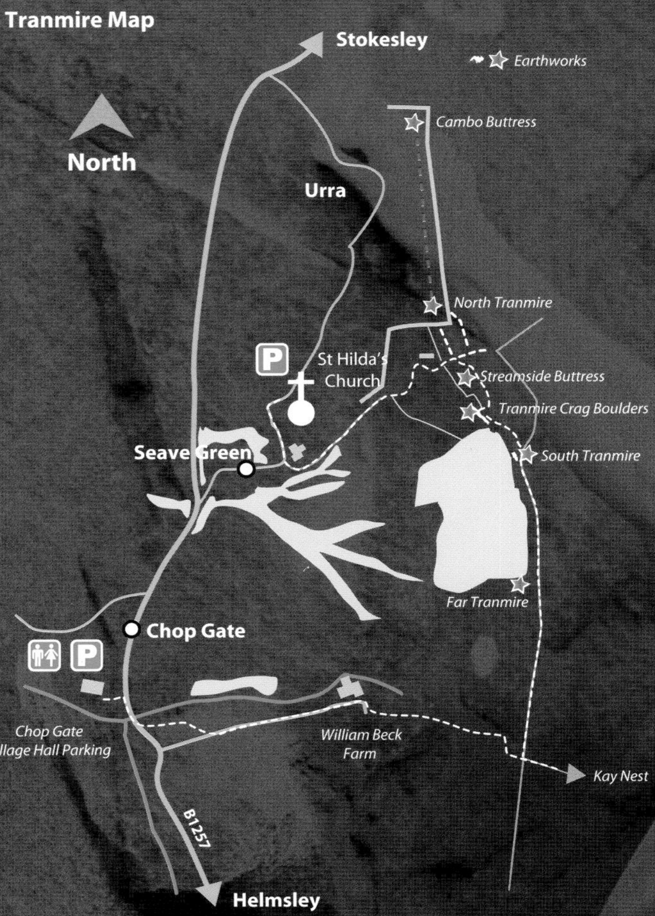

Scott Gibson on 42 7a

This section describes the Tranmire bouldering areas from north to south. starting with:

North Tranmire

1. Game Theory 4+ SS The arête and shelf on the left of the wall.
2. 42 7a+ SS From an undercut on the right wall and a sloping crimp on the left, work up the sustained arête. A real test of efficient climbing.
2a. 84.21 7b+ Climb the the arête of 42 but be very strict, not using holds on the face left of the arête. Use the arête holds only and those on the right face. Twice as hard and half as good.
3. Core 6a SS Using the pocket and the arête, gain the top. Will be difficult without the arête.

Directly below is a rising arête.

4. Repdigit 5 SS Traverse the rising arête from left to right to a mantel top-out.

The next block directly opposite and downhill has a hanging lip and an arête.

5. Thermodynamics 6b+ SS Start under the block using the sidepull rail and a hand on the sloper at the lip, then climb onto the slab using slopers and crimps. To increase the grade, start further back under the block.
6. The Differential 7b SS Starting at the base, climb the overhanging arête.

The next broken block downhill.

7. Combinatorics SS 6a Starting low on the lip, move up and left, then rock around left topping out on the apex.
8. Stressed Ribbon 6b SS A jamming start gets you out of the bivi hole. This starts where a small boulder blocks an even longer extension of this problem.
9. Pythagoreanism 6a+ SS Use the right arête starting on a low left hold, before gaining the good sloping shelf and topping out left of the apex.
9a. Variational Principle 7b+ Climb the wall left of the arête of Pythagoreanism. Start with the left hand on the bottom of the high layaway and the right hand just below. Pull on, match, then gain the left arête lip and mantel the middle of this to finish, still not using the right arête.
10. Point of Inertia 7c SS Start under the the left arête. Pull on using terrible slopers and make a difficult slap up and right, then match. Top-out using everything. It can be finished by mantelling out direct after matching, which is slightly harder but does not increase the grade.

Just over the wall in the quarry on a large slabby block are:

1. Easy Slab 1 The easy-angled slab just left of the arête.
2. Interloper 1+ Start round the corner and follow the slanting fault to finish up the top corner.
3. Holy Holy 1+ The wall on the right. past the holes.

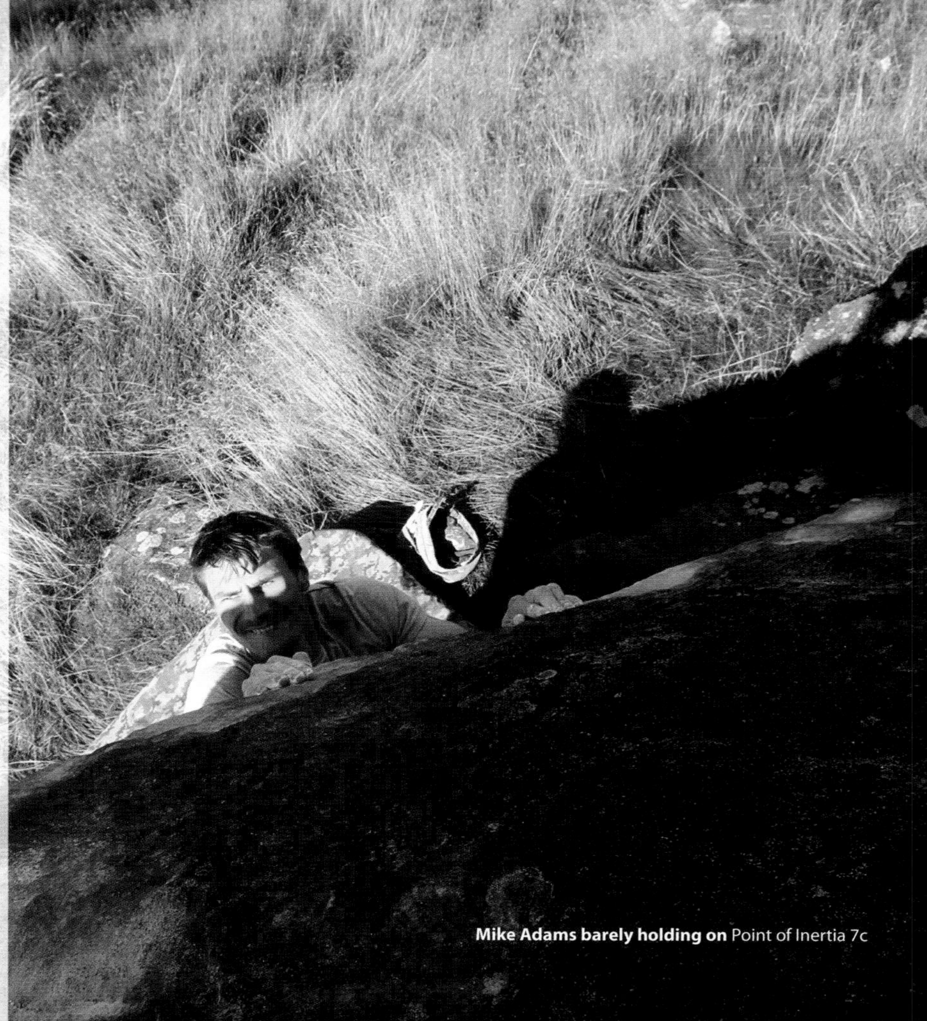

Mike Adams barely holding on Point of Inertia 7c

James Rennardson on The Differential 7b

Streamside Buttress

This is the first buttress you get to when you reach the top of the moor.

1. Cassini 6a Use low steps and crimps to gain the wall, then go for a direct finish using the arête.
2. Banana 3 The obvious curving feature.
3. Gravity Groove 2 Layback up the heathery groove.
4. Slab and Mantel 2 The thin crack in the slab.
5. The Ripper 5 The excellent steep corner.
6. Shallow Corner 3+ The pleasant feature at the right side.
7. Obscure Arête 5+ The small arête on the next section climbed mainly on its right.
8. Open Groove 5+ Follow layaways to the top.
9. Child In Time 6a Climb the wall and bulge without use of the ledge on the right.
10. Slab Mantelshelf 1+ Mantel onto the ledge 3m up, then finish direct.
11. Slab Groove 1+ Up the slab and finish up the groove.
12. Slab Face 1 Up the face just left of the edge.
13. Slab Edge 1+ Follow the right edge of the wall on good holds.

25m to the right is another buttress.

Twin Buttress

14. Twin Traverse 3+ SS A low-level traverse using the obvious break on the left buttress.
15. Linda 2 Start at the left end of the undercut base wall. Climb to the flat ledge, then finish direct.
16. Spikey 3+ Start 2m right. Climb the centre of the undercut-based wall to finish by a small spike.
17. Long Player 1 Start right of the undercut and climb the slab at the right side.

Over the wall are the next problems.

18. Vee 3+ Climb the crack in the left side of the wall.
19. The Thug 5 Climb the crack and short wall right of Vee.

About 20m right is an obvious pinnacle in front of the main crag.

Tranmire Pinnacle

20. RD's 1 The left side of the pinnacle.
21. Centre Line 5 The centre of the front face direct.
22. Gee Bee 1+ Follow the right side using the arête and small crack.

Tranmire Crag Boulders

North
Hanging Slab
Bitter Block
The Chocolate Bar
Fossil Block
Hidden Arête Block
and Short Prow
Two Prows
First and Last
The Bivi Block
Hanging Slab
The Chocolate Bar
Fossil Block
Bitter Block
First and Last
Two Prows
The Bivi Block

Twin Prows

First and Last

First and Last

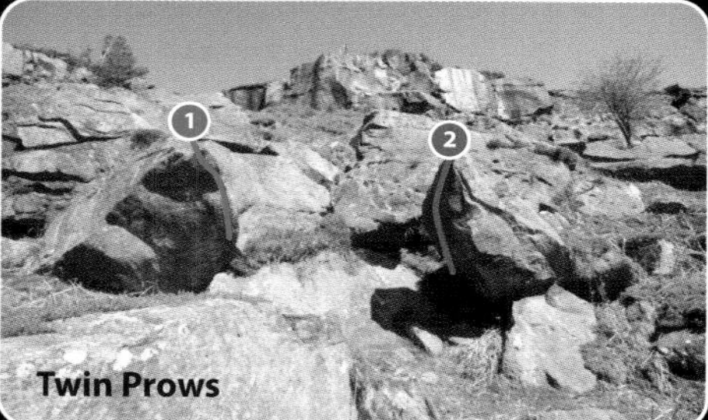

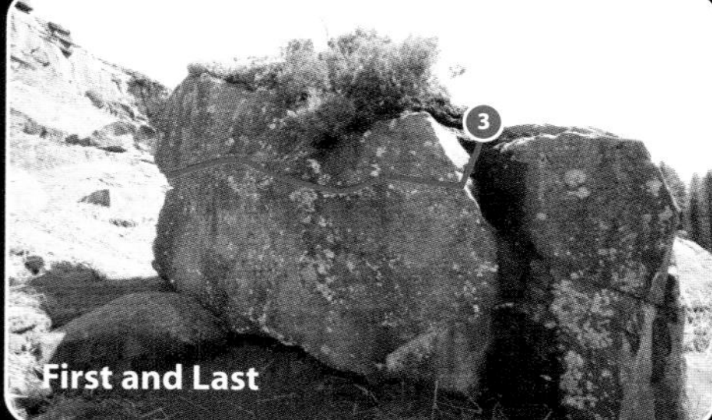

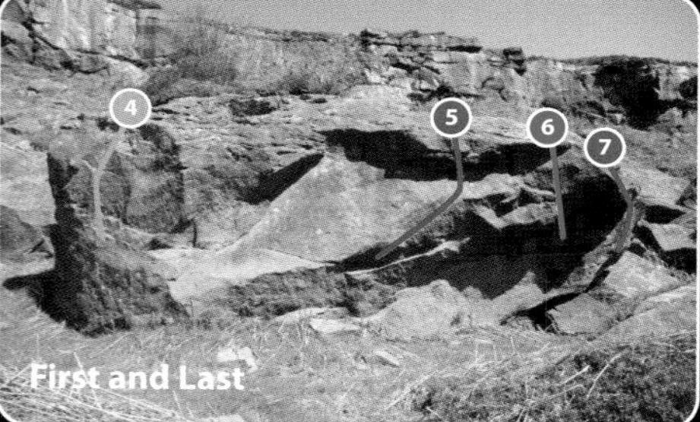

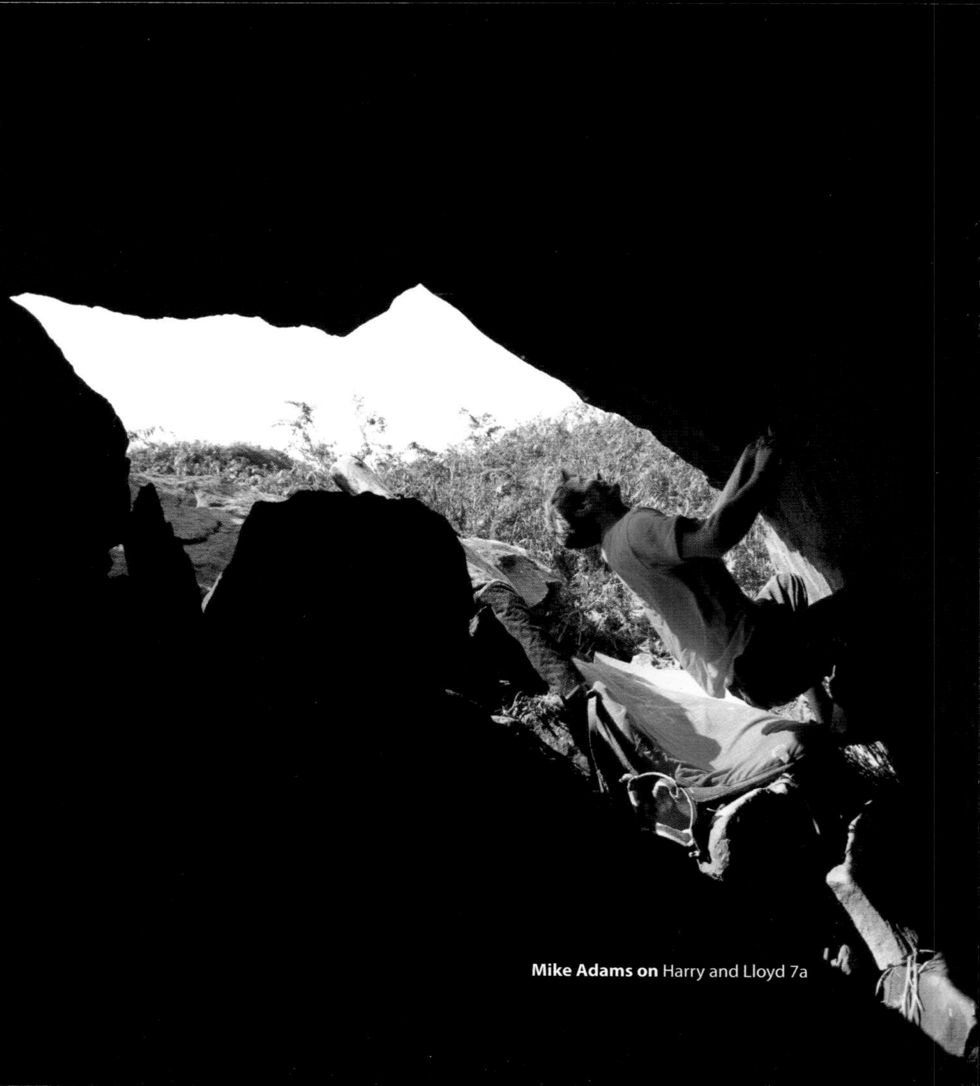

Mike Adams on Harry and Lloyd 7a

Main Crag Boulders

Twin Prows

Two good problems on the way in, harder than they look.

1. Left Prow 5 Use the lower block for feet and the right arête to gain a sloper. Mantel to finish.
2. The Pinch 6b SS Climb the prow utilising the left ledge.

First and Last Block

A good starting block, quality sandstone with some good problems.

3. Butch and Sundance 6c SS Traverse the block from left to right, passing some great slopers.
4. Tom Selleck 4 SS The first problem on the left end.
5. Hot Yogurt 6c SS The sloping ledge starting on a left sidepull heading rightwards.
6. Canal Street 5+ SS From a small ledge pop to the top.
7. Carb Goggles 6a SS From the small ledge pull for the top, and mantel.

Bivi Block

Looks so promising, yet has some poor rock in places. Still holds some good problems however.

8. Peaches and Herb 3 The first left groove on the slabby side of the block.
9. Shake Your Groove Thing 5+ Climb the sweet groove just right of Peaches and Herb.
10. The Other Place 1 Smooth slab climbing.
11. Harry and Lloyd 7a SS Starting under the bivi cave use a small left undercut and a right sloping crimp. Pull hard to gain the lip and rock over, no dabs allowed.
12. True Bromance 6b SS Traverse the lip rightwards to finish up the crack.
13. Grey Queen 7a+ SS Climb the left side of the arête, staying left and going directly for the top. Take care as the rock is a little friable.
14. The Brownie King 7b SS Start below the right arête of the face and climb direct, taking care as the rock is a little friable.
15. Hugs 5 SS Start at the right side. Use the arête and holds out right making long moves to the jugs above and an awkward finish.

The Fridge

16. Domestic Bliss 5+ SS Use sidepulls to gain success.

The block featured in the photograph is up the hill on the ***Chocolate Box****.*

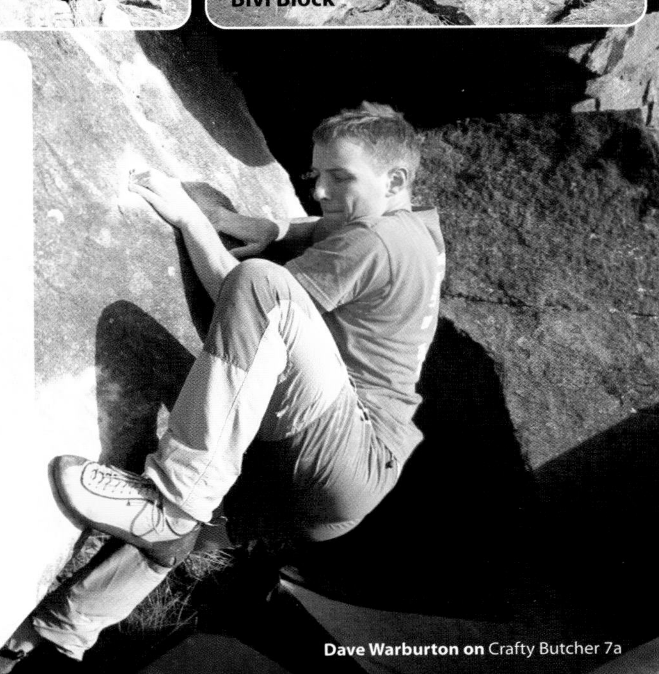

Dave Warburton on Crafty Butcher 7a

Steven Phelps on Chocolate Log 5+

The next block is up the hill below the crag.

Hanging Slab

1. 5+ The left side of the slab, passing a large flake low down.
2. 5 The centre of the slab, passing a good hold on the upper slab.
3. 3 The right side of the slab using positive holds.

The Chocolate Bar

The long block has some good short challenges.

4. Cocktail 5+ Climb, starting on the left arête.
5. Jack Twist 6b Start with hands on the nose of the right arête and gain the top. Use of the left arête is allowed at this grade. A sit-start will add an extra challenge.
6. Crafty Butcher 7a Hang the lip and rock-up left to a crease feature. The direct mantel is still unclimbed.

The hanging block to the right has a worthy mantel..

7. Brad Majors 6a+ Jump or just reach (depending on how tall you are) and flop over the ledge direct. Topping out right is just wrong, don't even think about it!

Just south of this is:

Fossil Block

8. Project Thin holds to dyno to the top.
9. Chocolate Log 5+ Climb through the fossilised tree feature.

Hidden Arête Block

10. The Scorpion and the Frog 5 SS Gain the top via some composed layaways.

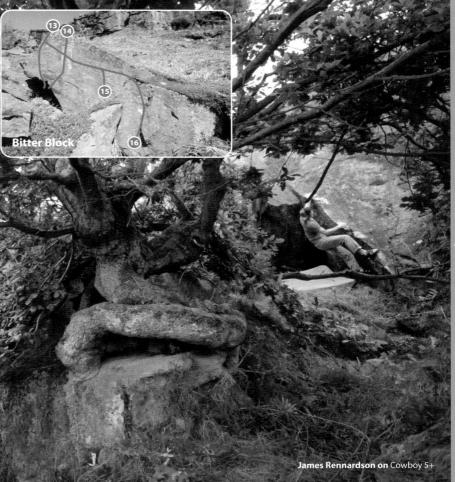

More problems hidden away behind the curly oak tree.

Short Prow

11. Han and Chewie 6a SS Hug the arêtes before moving left to top-out.

Hidden Arête Block

12. Cowboy 5+ SS From the good hold, climb the arête until you are forced to mantel.

Bitter Block

13. Best Bitter 6a+ SS Start under the overhang with hands on holds just above. Pull up and traverse left on crimps to the arête and continue up.

14. Lager Than Life 6a SS Start as for the last problem. This time pull round onto the slab to gain a good pocket higher up. Finish direct.

15. Bitter Taste 6b Start at the right side. Pull onto the wall using a thin side crimp, then traverse left to the pocket and finish as the last problem.

16. Badger Breath 6b+ Starting lower down and right, climb across the block avoiding the top, finishing as for Bitter Taste.

James Rennardson on Cowboy 5+

South Tranmire

South Tranmire

The Hourglass

The leaning block has some tricky little problems.

1. Tower of the Winds 6a The left face of the leaning block has a tricky top-out.
2. The Flow 6b The right face direct.
3. In Time 6b+ SS Climb the left-hand hanging arête until the overhang forces you to rock onto the slab.

Just right is a bulging roof block that needs some gardening.

4. Half-life 6a SS A good problem just left of the vegetated roof.

Mumbo Block

A fine block with a mixed contrast of problems.

5. Project SS The left wall of the Mumbo block.
6. Liquid Clocks 7a SS Use the big starting pocket and make a long move to climb the hanging arête. Standing start goes at **6a.**
7. Mumbo 1 Climb the left side of the small wall.
8. Jumbo 1 The right side of the small wall.

The Nose

The large-roofed nose block.

9. Project From stand under the right side of the nose, climb the 'chicken heads' to gain a frustrating mantel. Be very careful as the 'chicken heads' may break.
10. Iron Pendulum 6b SS Start quite far back on the right side of the nose in a recess. Climb out of this, using a good ledge for feet and mantel over via the right hand-hold and sloping lip.

Nothing has been recorded on the little buttress to the right below The Nose. 'Platform Wall' looks good, with some tricky mantel finishes.

Next is an excellent low sloping traverse block.

11. Jigawatts 7a SS Start at the right end of the block and make the sloping journey leftwards to a mantel top-out. Just right of this is a high arête on the crag edge.
12.1981 4+ SS Start on the huge thread pocket and climb the arête to a long move for the top.

More problems on the next walls - with dodgy landings!

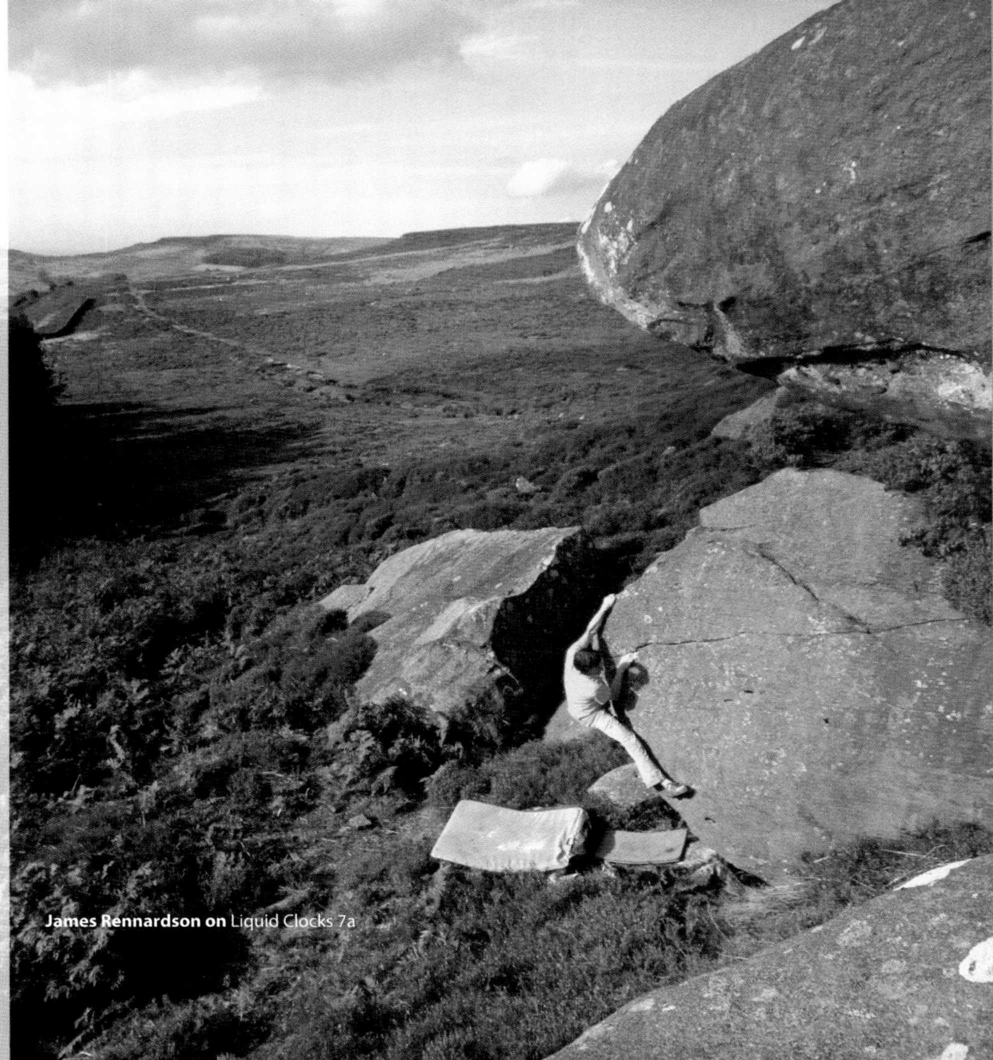

James Rennardson on Liquid Clocks 7a

Far Tranmire

The Clock Tower

Mike Adams on Flux 7c

Main Edge

There are some fine highballs to be had on this crag.

1. Intake Arête 2 Start with a high left foot and long reach to gain the ledge. Move right into a niche to finish.

2. Intake Wall 1+ Take a central line up the wall to the right.

3. Hanging Crack 6a+ Just opposite Intake Wall is a hanging crackline, follow this direct.

4. Cyclops 6c The highball blunt arête using a sidecrimp out on the left wall.

5. The Last Heroes 5+ Gain the ledge via a deep pocket. Finish using holds above the left side of the ledge.

6. Project Take a direct line up the blank wall via the thin ledge.

7. Neolithic Flake 2 Follow the flake system near the corner to an awkward exit.

8. Rocket Launcher 5+ The overhanging blocks just left of Slape Slab on their right edge.

9. Slape Slab 1 Climb the right-most slab then move off right to finish.

The Clock Tower

A large slab block with a normally damp east face and a drier west face.

10. Family Ties 7b SS Start at the base of the arête in the entrance to the cave. Pull up and rock onto the slab with difficulty, before making a balancey slap to better holds. Trend left with the arête to finish.

11. Doc Brown 6c+ Start just to the right and climb the slab via a dynamic move up to the good edges.

12. Bird Watching 6b Climb to the flake using crimps and undercuts to a bold top-out up the arête.

13. Delorean DMC-12 5c+ SS The arête on its right-hand side. A highball expedition up the arête from the ground.

14. Nobody calls me 'Chicken' 6b Climb the slab just right of the very thin crack.

The Capacitor Blocks

Two blocks behind the Clock Tower.

15. Banana Skin 3 SS Climb the left arête.

16. Flux 7c SS Start in the corridor on the left side of the low shelf. Climb out to the lip then rock up the middle of the slab above using the line of layaways in the slight rising groove-line. At this grade do not use the crack or the block right of the crack to start and stay right of the arête and the big hold close to it at the top.

17. Buford "Mad Dog" Tannen 1 The left side of the eroded face.

18. Biff Tannen Jr 3 The centre of the eroded face.

19. Tannen the Barbarian 3 The right end of the eroded face.

20. Marty McFly 5 Use the curved flake to pull over onto the slab. Aim for the hole to finish.

21. Back in Time 6b Start from crouch low on the rising lip utilizing eroded holds, head right and gain a good curved flake then carry on right and top out when you reach the nose.

22. Plutonium 6b SS With one hand on the low arête and the other high, climb to the nose and top-out.

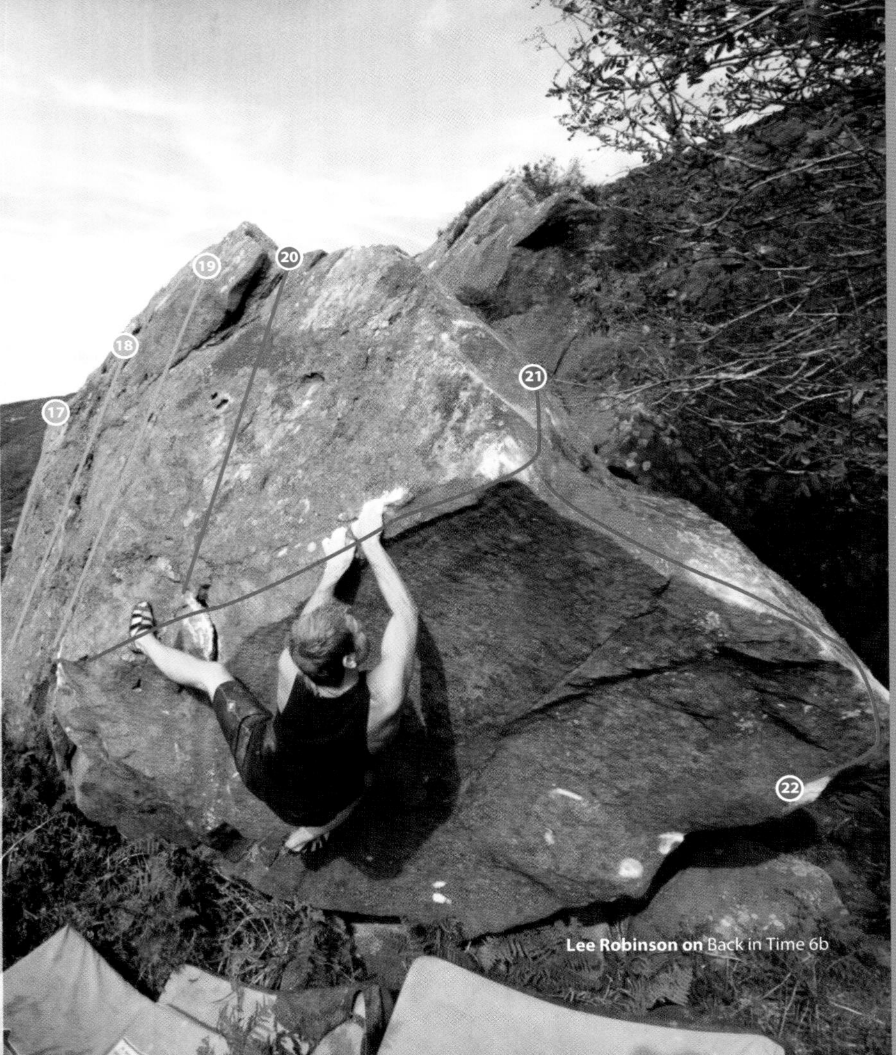

Lee Robinson on Back in Time 6b

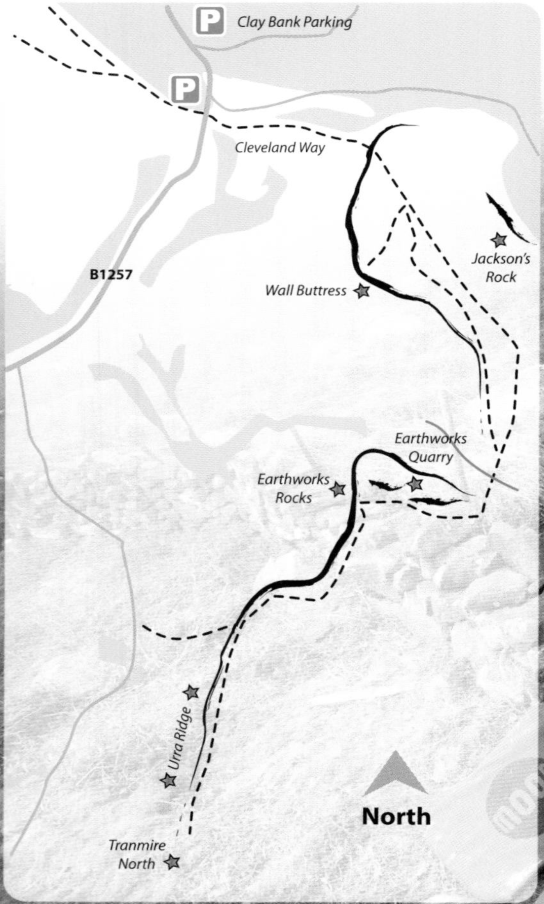

The Earthwork Edges

are a collection of scattered edges and blocks, some of which are clean and weathered, others are less so. The best venue is at **Earthworks Rocks**, but if you're a wandering explorer who doesn't mind the odd one move wonder or micro crag, it might be worth a look along the ridge.

Approach: On the B1257 between Chop Gate and Great Broughton park either at the large Clay Bank viewpoint car park or preferably any of the lay-bys further up the hill nearer the Cleveland Way Path, where it crosses the B1257. Take the Cleveland Way east up the hill passing two small gates. Once you go through the second gate at the top of the hill take a smaller path that heads rightwards. This takes you along the edge of the moor where Earthworks will clearly be visible across a large gully. Cross the stream in the gully and once the path levels out on the other side the top of the main buttress will clearly be visible 30m on your right.

See map on page 52 for Clay Bank parking.

Good moves on Wall Buttress

Steve Crowe on Red and White 6a+

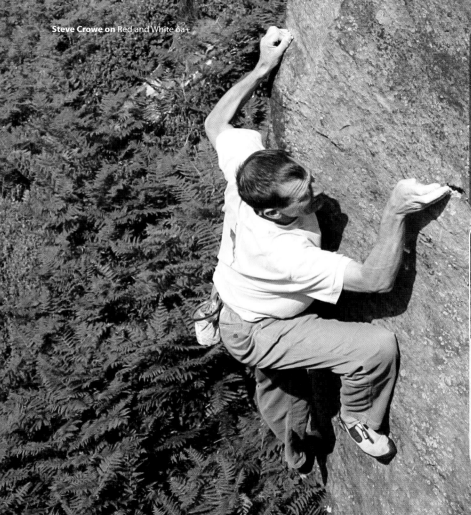

Earthworks Rocks

A small remote outcrop located on the edge of Urra Moor with fine views into Bilsdale and beyond. It's a very pleasant place to spend several hours and has some strange formations and features with some good highball problems on excellent weathered sandstone in the low to mid grades. The highlights are on Arch Buttress, though there are other nice slabs and arêtes at this location.

OS Map: NZ 577021
Walk: 30 minutes
Faces north and west

The bouldering is described left to right. The path leads to the Main Wall at the right end of the cluster. Head east to get to the first problems described.

The Red Corners

The eastern edge of the rocks.

1. Red Arête 4 The far arête direct.
2. Red and White 6a+ The impressive central arête with a hard move to reach the top.
3. Slab of Redness 4 The next arête on the slabby side.
4. Red Wall 4 Climb the short arête.

* *Some problems have not been recorded here, just the obvious lines.*

Arch Buttress

The next large block with some good test- pieces.

1. Arch Rivals 4 Start just right of the block then follow the blunt arête.
2. Hole Shot 6b+ SS Start on flakes above the lip just left of Under the Arch. Reach a hold on the blunt arête then throw out left to a hole. From here top-out direct.
3. Under the Arch 6a Make thin moves up the slab to finish over the roof direct.
4. The Arch 5+ Climb the scoop then move leftwards across the slab to a powerful finish over the roof.
5. Archway 4 Start as for the last problem, but this time finish rightwards.

Steve Ramsden on Hole Shot 6b+

Main Buttress

1. No Work 3 Climb the pocketed wall.
2. Hard Work 3+ Start at the foot of the buttress and climb up a short diagonal crack to the large ledge, then finish direct over the blunt nose.
3. Easy Work 1+ Climb the steep wall to the ledge, then finish up the deep crack.
4. Worked Out 2+ The green wall on the right at the back of the Lower Slab.
5. Work Work Work 4+ Climb up the smooth wall by the arête, left of the large letterbox.
6. Three Ps 6c Tackle the slab direct once the large letterbox is gained.
7. Nice Work 4 Climb up the smooth wall just right of the large letterbox.
8. Entropy 2+ Climb the outside edge of the slab.

Lower Slab

9. Lower Slab Left-Hand 5 Start 1m in from the left edge. Using a left-hand sidepull and a right-hand iron nodule pull onto the slab and follow to finish.
10. Lower Slab Direct 3+ The centre of the slab using a good right-hand hold to start.
11. Inside Right 1 Start 1m in from the right edge and climb direct.
12. Outside Right 1+ Start as for the last problem but move to the right edge, then follow this to the top.

Urra Ridge

Just south of Earthworks Rocks is a strewn-out ridge of scattered edges and small blocks.

A windy winter ascent of Inside Right 1

Wainstones and Cold Moor Map

Great Broughton

Maynard's Plant Centre

B1257

Parking

Broughton Plantation

Faster but steeper approach, can be muddy

Flattest approach

Clay Bank Parking

Cleveland Way

Ingleby

Cleveland Way

Wainstones

End Buttress

Garfit Quarry

Cold Moor

Central Area

Plantation Area

Wall Buttress

North

B1257

Carlton

Chop Gate

Cloud inversion leaving Cold Moor

Steve Ramsden on The Prow 7a

35

15

49

16

2

The Wainstones consist of an outcrop and boulders perched high on the Cleveland Hills at the western end of Hasty Bank, with excellent views in all directions. The history of man's influence stretches back to the Neolithic or Bronze Age period when rock carvings were made for possible way-marking, territorial or ritual purposes.

More recently the boulders themselves will have held obvious challenges to the early climbers between leads on the main edge. This is likely to have been the start of bouldering as we know it on the North York Moors. The Wainstones possess many different problems extending across the grades, from easy-angled slabs to desperate arêtes with most of the boulders being a short distance from one another. The rock itself is solid weather-worn sandstone of excellent quality with the odd ironstone intrusion, which adds interest and variation to the problems. The only part of the actual edge included here is Broughton Buttress, which with its unprotected aspect and flat grassy landings lends itself to bouldering. More details of the routes can be found at: **www.climbonline.co.uk.**

Approach: Use the same parking as Earthworks, which is the car park or lay-bys on top of Clay Bank, just before Great Broughton, on the B1257 Helmsley to Stokesley road. Take the Cleveland Way up the steps and where the path splits either follow the Cleveland Way through the gate onto the moor and up onto Hasty Bank to approach from the top or take the track which borders the forest to approach from the bottom. Both ways take about the same time, though the lower way avoids the long steep hill near the start. There is also a shorter but steeper walk-in reached by taking the turn off the bend at Maynard's Plant Centre, just south of Great Broughton. From here head south down Bank Lane towards the wooded bank. Where the track bends to the right you'll see the path to the Broughton Plantation on the corner. Park at a small lay-by round the bend and take the path up through the woods. This route can get muddy and use of an OS map is recommended.

OS Map: NZ 558035
Walk: 30 minutes
Open aspect

View of the Wainstones from Cold Moor

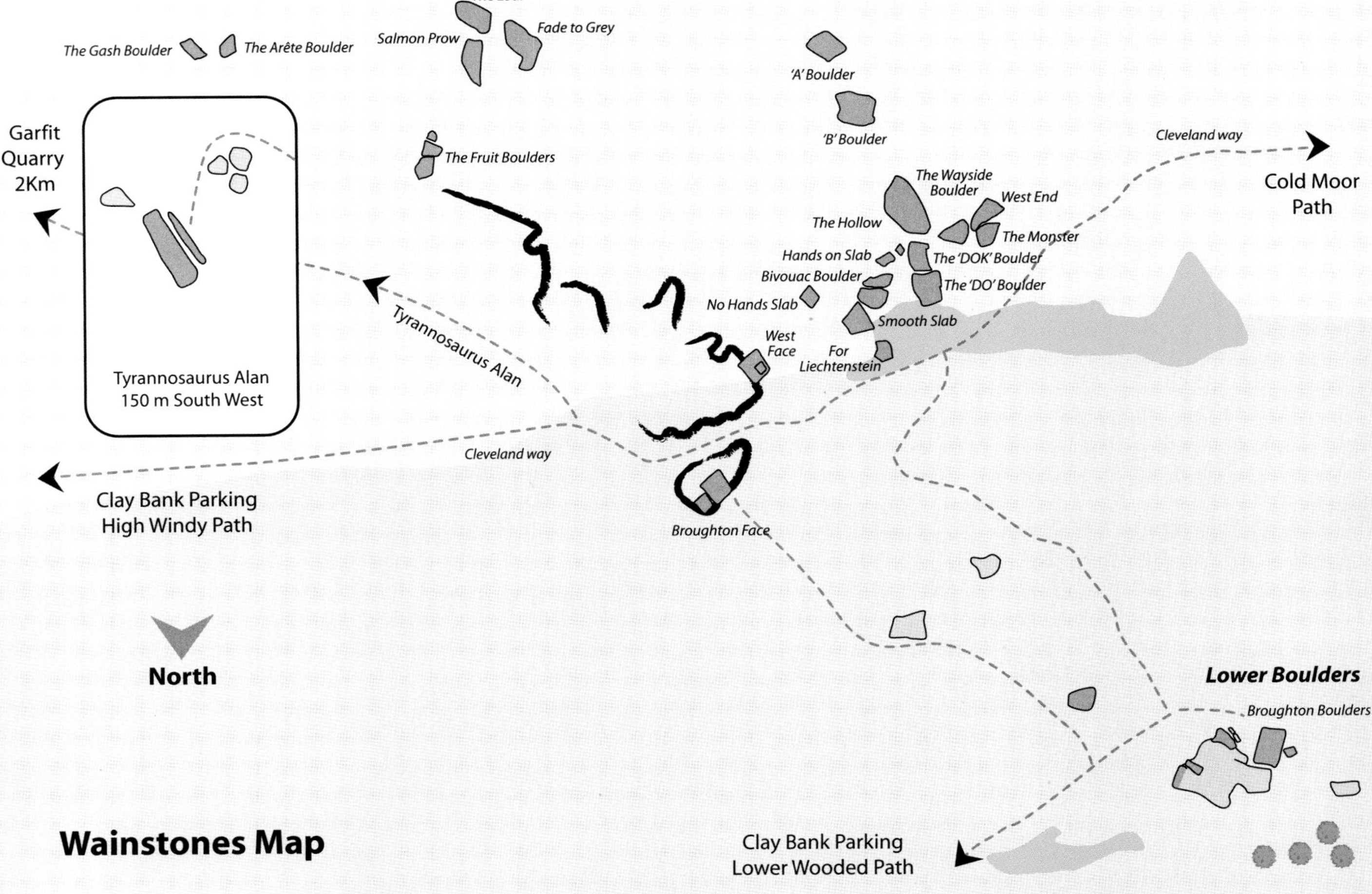
The Loaf
Fade to Grey
Salmon Prow
The Gash Boulder
The Arête Boulder
'A' Boulder
'B' Boulder
Garfit Quarry 2Km
The Fruit Boulders
Cleveland way
Cold Moor Path
The Wayside Boulder
West End
The Hollow
The Monster
Hands on Slab
The 'DOK' Boulder
Bivouac Boulder
The 'DO' Boulder
No Hands Slab
Smooth Slab
Tyrannosaurus Alan
West Face
For Liechtenstein
Tyrannosaurus Alan 150 m South West
Cleveland way
Clay Bank Parking High Windy Path
Broughton Face
North
Lower Boulders
Broughton Boulders
Wainstones Map
Clay Bank Parking Lower Wooded Path

Mike Adams on Cruel Intentions 7c

Broughton Boulders

The first cluster of blocks at the lower path.

1. The Filler SS 6a The short block on the left of the steep prow has an interesting top-out.
2. The Prow 7a SS Start at the left-hand bottom of the hanging prow and top-out just before the apex. Can be extended by topping out right then direct **2a. 7a+.**
3. Cruel Intentions 7c SS The Prow's right arête, strictly on its left side, with no pockets. **3a Enigma Variation 6c SS** From the same start work your way across the prow without the top and with the pockets. Can be finished direct.
4. Slabbiness 6a+SS The pleasant slab from sit, without the small cracked blocks for feet.
5. Strongbow 7b+ SS The aptly-named cave roof.
6. Strongbow Crack 5+ SS Start in the cave as far back as you can, follow the crack right out and over the top.
7. Off-beat 5+ SS The left arête of the block.
8. The Palmist 6a SS From the small overhanging right corner, traverse leftwards to the middle of the slab, then straight up. Finishing direct is also good.
9. Button Nose 6a SS From the far back of the short prow climb the right-hand edge and top out in the centre of the prow. No cheating!
10. Long Slab 2+ A fine slab problem on good holds.
11. The Loner 5+ The arête on its right side. Delicate.
12. The Trick 6a Climb the face on the left side of the arête.
13. You've Pulled 7a SS From a low start make a hard pull on a crimp and the arête to gain better holds.

Lee Robinson on You've Pulled 7a

Franco Cookson on Psycho Syndicate 7a+

Just up the hill from the lower boulders are a few testing high-balls.

Broughton Face

1. Broughton Ridge 2 Starting left, gain the ridge/arête and finish direct.
1a. Broughton Ridge Direct 4+ The smooth arête/ridge on its left side.
2. Benchmark Crack 3+ Follow the obvious corner crack with interest.
3. Benchmark Wall 6a+ The line just right of the crack, up a shallow groove finishing direct.
4. Psycho Syndicate 7a+ A direct line up the peg-scarred wall. One of the region's most testing problems.
5. Tiny's Arete Direct 5 Start on the left side of the arête then follow direct.
6. Tiny's Dilemma 4+ Climb up the face right of the arête avoiding use of the crack and corner on the right.

Broughton Face

The next problems are just west of the Broughton Face next to the path on the Cleveland Way, below the needle.

The first described face the path and can be green; but dry out very quickly when the sun comes round in an afternoon.

The remainder are on the opposite side and catch the sun for most of the day.

Simon Walker on DO Wainstones 1984

Tony Marr on DO 6b+

Steve Ramsden on For Liechtenstein 7a

Needle Boulders

1. West Face Direct 7a A classic high-ball up the centre of the impressive needle-face goove. Take some spotters.

2. The Shield 5 SS Hands on both arêtes, finish direct.

3. For Liechtenstein 7a SS From a left-hand crimp and a right-hand pinch, swing up right for the top!

4. The Path 6a Start on top of the thin block and hand-traverse the lip leftwards round the corner and up the steep path-side, then round to touch the block on the east side then reverse....

Smooth Slab

5. The Frog 6b SS Climb the left side of the arête. Tricky to start and can be green.

6. Left Arête 5+ Getting established onto the arête can be awkward.

7. Rock On 6a Start just right of the curving overlap. Rock-on to a small edge then reach up for the arête. A finish straight up without using any of the chipped holds is **6b**.

8. Smooth Centre 5+ The centre of the slab using chipped holds. Without them is **6a+**.

9. Right Arête 4+ The left side of the right arête is good. The right side can be climbed at the same grade.

'DO' Boulder

10. Dead Point 6c SS Tackle the left side of the arête from a right crimp and the arête for hands, plus a small foothold. Good luck.

11. 'DO' 6b+ Climb the centre of the block on large lay-aways, then find the good top hold. From standing **5**.

12. Project SS The right arête, Has been done from standing **6a**

13. Full Circle 5+ A full traverse of the whole block can be awkward.

'DOK' Boulder (North Side)

14. Rocky 6a SS Start on the overhanging edge and rock up onto the face to finish.

15. Nibble 3 Straight up the centre of the block.

16. Fruit Machine 6b+ SS A tricky start hugging the obvious arête feature.

The Wayside Boulder (North Side)

17. The Wayside 2 Climb the oft green pebbly slab.

18. It Only Gets Better 6c SS Start low on the right side of the pebbly arête and work your way right to some good sloping ledges. It's still not over, top out avoiding the block on the right.

Just to the right is another block.

19. The Monster 6a SS From the large slot gain the top.

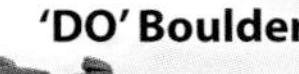

1
3
4
10
11
12
13
'DOK' Boulder
14
15
16
The Wayside Boulder
17
18
19
Next problems this way
Needle Boulders

The Wayside Boulder (South Side)

1. Airbag 6a+ Tackle the left side of the south facing arête with a bad landing.

2. The Road to Jericho 6a+ SS Climb into the Good Samaritan from the left.

3. Good Samaritan 2+ Climb the wall direct.

Just one more line to the west.

4. West End 5 SS A short but sweet climb on good rock at the end of the cluster.

Dave Warburton on Airbag 6a+

Steve Ramsden on The Crack Left-Hand 6c **(block on next page)**

Walk through a gully over small blocks to find:

The Hollow

1. The Finger 7c Gain the top via the hideous mono! Possible sit-start!?

2. The Hollow 6c+ SS Follow the hanging groove to gain the top.

The 'DOK' Boulder (South Side)

3. 'DOK' 6a+ Step off the block and hand-traverse across the ledges on the leaning wall to holds on the top, then move along towards the corner and top-out. Has been started from sitting and mantelled out direct at **6b+**.

4. South Wall 4 Start from the small layaway flake below the right of the ledge then climb direct. **3+** if you start by hanging the ledge first.

5. 'KOD' 6c SS The right arête starting in the corner where the blocks touch. Use a good left hold and a thin sloping crimp round the arête for the right, pull hard to gain a jam with the right. (the only use of the block to the right). Mantel to finish.

The smaller block to the right.

6. Abutment 1+ The short blunt arête.

Hands on Slab

7. Lifeline 6a+ SS Powerful moves gain the slab from under the lip.

8. Hands On 3 Step off the boulder and climb straight up the slab.

Further uphill are:

Bivouac Boulder

1. West Face 6b The thin hanging slab facing away from the crag.

The next problems have many variations, most of which are very entertaining. Some involve long-forgotten techniques. Take a few pads.

2. The Crack Left-Hand 6c SS From the small block under the block climb out via the crack, then gain the right arête and follow to the top. The problem can also can be laybacked from stand facing right at **6a+**.

3. *Tackling the crack direct via jams and skin grinding thrutching. Was originally graded English **6a.** Have a go. Mental!*

4. Layback Crack Right-Hand 7a+ SS Same start from the block under the crack. Gain the right side of the crack then rock onto the slab, with difficulty. **4** from standing.

5. Old Wall 7a+ SS A painful sitter on crimps and sharp pockets. The standing start is much more pleasant **3+**.

No Hands Slab

6. Left Edge 1 Use small edges to step onto the higher boulder.

7. Right Edge 1 Up scratches to step onto the higher boulder.

The large block south-east.

'B' Boulder

1. Stock Slab 1+ Up the easy slab on the left.

2. Cross The Line 2 Traverse beneath the roof in either direction.

3. Redhead's Roof 6b+ Start beneath the roof and climb directly over it using an obvious crimp. If it feels too easy for the grade you're too far left.

4. On The Edge 4 Make long reaches over the bulge to finish up the arête.

5. The Shelf 6b+ SS The leaning wall climbed via the sloping ledge is tough. From standing is **5+.** The left exit from the shelf is **4+**

James Rennardson on Redhead's Roof 6b+

Just across from the B Boulder is:

'A' Boulder

1. Button It 6b+ The right side of the arête eliminating the crack to the right. Pop up to the top of the crack using just the sharp pebbles on its left side.
2. The Crack 5 This excellent crack feature is a Wainstones classic. **6a+** from sitting.
3. Super Crackless 6b Avoiding both cracks climb direct.
4. Steel Fingers 6a SS Follow the slanting crackline rightwards to a nice finish. Still good from standing at **5+**.
5. Temper Arête 6b SS Climb the right side of the arête. From standing is **4+**.
6. Cracking Up 6a SS Climb the crack without the arête, then mantel on the slab.
7. Tapered Slab 1 Gain the slab in a slight depression, then finish leftwards. Can be done without hands.
8. Mother Slab 1+ Climb the right edge via a shallow depression.
9. Sloper Motion 6a SS Trickier than it looks. Top-out at the apex on its left side.
10. Normal Route 4 Start by climbing the diagonal feature to finish up the slab. Can be climbed with no hands for quite a test-piece.
11. 'A' Route 5 Start just right, climb up to the small rounded spike and finish on flutings. To eliminate the spike and climb with just the crimps makes a good **6a+**.
12. Pebble Climb 6b Climb the slabby arête via a pebble, finishing on flutings. Classic.

Nick Dixon on Pebble Climb 1978

Claire Jennings on Pebble Climb 6b

'A' Boulder - North Face

1
2
3
4
5

West Face

6
7
8

South Face

9

East Face

10
11
12

Lisa Robinson on Southern Slab Right-hand 1

A little south of the 'A' Boulder.

Southern Boulders

1. Southern Slab 1 Climb the centre of the slab on excellent rock. Left and right variations climb at about the same grade.

2. Southern Nose 4 The bulging nose just to the right.

3. South-east Face Left 4 SS Take the left side of the leaning wall on good holds. From standing is **3**.

4. South-east Face Right 5 SS Climb the right side of the leaning wall. From standing is **3+**.

5. Softie 4 Climb the slab up the gully on some nice features.

6. Siamese Twin 3+ The blunt arête to the right is good for its size. Can be done with no hands at **6b**.

7. Conjoined 4+ Climb the wall to the right, tackle the left or right finish, it's your choice. Both are good.

A traverse of the main boulder can be made keeping hands below the top on the slab sides at **4+**.

Just up the hill and south are:

1. Fade to Grey 7a SS Traverse the block from right to left. Top-out up the thin feature.

The Loaf

2. The Loaf Direct 6b SS The left-most line on the block over the bulge. From standing is **5**.

3. Breadline 5 Start beneath the bulge, but move right onto the slab to finish.

4. Beneath the Breadline 6c SS Start on poor slopers to rock-over onto the slab using crimps. From standing is **6a+**.

5. Way Below the Breadline 7c SS Start at Beneath the Breadline and traverse the lip all the way across to top-out past Loaf Traverse.

6. Central Route 6a+ SS From more poor slopers rock over the bulge onto the slab. From standing is **6a.**

7. Daily Bread 6b+ SS Right hand in iron nodule pocket and left hand in mono then up to crimps. Finish up the slab. From standing is **6a+**.

8. Loaf Traverse 4 Start on the right corner and foot traverse along a thin horizontal crackline to finish at the far right of the slab.

Claire Jennings on Beneath the Breadline 6c

Just up the hill from The Loaf is a rounded prow.

1. Salmon Prow 6c+SS The small prow is quite a grovel over over the nose.

Further up the hill are three blocks with a cracking traverse.

2. Fruit of the Gods 6c SS Start with feet on the small block and make your way right across the lip and crack of the two blocks. This leads to better holds to finish.

Neil Furniss on Salmon Prow 6c+

James Rennardson on Fruit of the Gods 6c

Follow the top edge of the crag south and you will find:

The Arête Block

1. Slanting Crack 3+ Climb the thin crack up the groove.
2. Arête Left-side 4+ Climb the arête on its left. **3+** on its right side.

The Gash Block

3. North Wall 6b Climb direct from crimps with no use of the arêtes or bridging.
4. Smooth 5 The arête on its left side on nodules.
5. Moon 3 The left end of the block, feels quite bold at the top.
6. The Gash 2+ Start at the left and gain the slab to the break, then follow right, topping out on the nose
7. The Gash Direct 6a SS From the large break, gain the flake then mount the slab and finish direct. **5+** from standing.
8. The End 5+ SS The arête starting in the large break. **5** from standing.

The last blocks further south on the top of the moor have a must-see block with teeth and one eye.

Tyrannosaurus Alan

9. Alan's Breakfast 6a+ SS Climb direct through Alan's mouth. Trickier than it looks as the reach is longer than you think.
10. Tyrannosaurus Alan 6c+ SS An ultra-direct variation climbing over the nose, mantelling direct to finish. Easier topping out left or right.
11. Alan's Friend 6c SS Another direct variation, bear-hugging up the front face of the short leaning block, to mantel direct. Easier topping out left or right.

Rob Lonsdale on Tyrannosaurus Alan 6c+

Garfit Quarry is an excellent little venue with solid rock in a fantastic location, tucked away round the back of Hasty Bank. The problems all follow strong lines making many eliminates possible. It's a good place to stop off on the way back from the Wainstones or Cold Moor.

Approach: From the Wainstones parking at Clay Bank, follow the Cleveland Way path via the steps, to the gate accessing the moor and near the bench. Go through the gate and head left on a small path that goes across the moor and gradually uphill to a more well-defined path. As it starts levelling out above the farm the quarry is relatively close by on the right. **See map on page 52.**

OS Map: NZ 567032
Walk: 10 minutes
Faces south

Garfit Quarry Main Wall

Guardian of the Quarry

Garfit Quarry

1. Garfit Arête 2 The left arête mainly on its right side.

2. Garfit of Passion 6c SS Start 1m right of the arête at some crimps using the JM carving. Make a difficult move to a sidepull, then a dynamic finish via the break. Can be done using the crack out left, reducing the grade. From standing is **6b+**.

3. JM SS 6c Start as for the last problem; but break out rightwards once the sidepull is reached. The finish is the same as problem 4.

4. 6a Start using a sidepull on the vertical scar for the left hand and the horizontal crack of Garfoid for the right. Move up to the good hold on the base of the green groove. Finish direct.

5. Garfoid 5+ Start at the obvious slanting ramp and use crimps to gain the horizontal crack. Follow this leftwards and finish as the last problem.

6. Garfoid Direct 5 Make the first move of the original to the break, then finish direct on good holds. Be careful of loose stone.

7. Garfit Crack 6a The excellent slanting crackline has tricky moves.

8. 1962 7b The line on the right wall, using an old peg hole and thin crimps.

Just to the right is a smaller section.

9. 6a SS Start at the obvious pocket, make a hard move to gain more pockets, then finish left or dyno rightwards. **5+** from standing.

10. 5 The arête on its left side. Very satisfying.

11. 4+ The green slab is climbed direct on crimps just left of a hairline crack.

To the right is more rock. An obvious corner crack has been done before, as have several other lines. Have a go.

Mike Adams on 1962 7b

Cold Moor, previously called Mount Vittoria is a collection of boulders and buttresses across the edge of the moor and visible from the much more popular Wainstones. It holds a good variety of problems and high challenges, mostly with good landings which blur the line between bouldering and routes at times. The rock is good moorland sandstone throughout and very solid in character, much like the Wainstones. Some of the buttresses haven't seen much attention in a while and are suffering from lack of traffic, with lichen, overgrown heather and bracken problematic in high summer, although much of the bracken can be avoided by using the faint path that runs along the top of the rocks.

Approach: From the Wainstones follow the main path that goes west across Garfit Gap. Go through a gate, take a left turn and follow a path up the hillside towards the first buttress, which is Cold Moor End Buttress. Other faint paths running along the top and bottom lead to the rest of the crag. Cold Moor can also be approached from Bank Lane in a slightly shorter time but the walk up is much steeper. **See map on page 52**.

OS Map: NZ 5540334
Approach: 30 minutes
Faces east

Wall Buttress
Plantation Area
Central Area
Cold Moor
North
End Buttress
The Nose
Pathside Block
Wainstones

Approaching Cold Moor in perfect conditions

On the right fork in the path is a block with a couple of interesting problems.

Pathside Block

1. The Edge 6b SS Start underneath the arête. Move up via the mono pocket onto the arête and finish with a dynamic slap for better holds near the top, to finish direct. Use of the blocks below allowed for feet. Trickier than you think.

2. Absolute Zero 6c SS Start with the mono pocket for the left hand. Make a stiff pull using holds on the face and finish direct.

Just before the first buttress is a sloping prow.

The Nose

3. Cold Turkey 6c SS Start with a crimp on the lip for the left hand and a hold beneath the roof for the right. Make difficult and powerful moves leftwards up the sidewall.

4. The Placebo Grenade 7a+ SS Climb from the right-hand side of the prow/roof and heel-hook your way leftwards along the lip to a good crimp. Use this to gain the pocket and then the top.

Martin Parker on The Placebo Grenade 7a+

4

The Nose

Pathside Block

The Nose

300m north is the next and most popular buttress.

Cold Moor Buttress

1. Twinkle Toes 2+ The stepped slab on the left.
2. Cold Cut 3 Up the shallow groove/crack.
3. Cold Fusion 5 Start at the right of the bulge and move up leftwards until it's possible to join Cold Cut.
4. True Fusion 5+ Start as for the last problem, but climb the blunt arête.
5. Oblique Crack 1 The obvious slanting hand-crack on the main buttress is followed until a step right can be made to a heathery finish.
6. Cold Sweat 6a+ (E1 6a) Over to the right start beneath the hanging block and use the flake for the initial step only, then pull onto the slab and climb to the block via a scoop to finish direct.
7. Chilled Out 6a+ (E2 6a) An eliminate between Cold Sweat and Beak Ridge, following the thin slab and finishing direct over the small roof.
8. Beak Ridge 3+ (HS 4b) The classic of Cold Moor. Follow the ridge/arête starting on the right. Can also be done from sitting, starting from down on the left side.
9. Cool Dude 6a SS Start about 2m to the right of the last problem and climb the wall direct. The original from standing is **5**.
10. Cold Shoulder 1+ Up the corner crack.
11. Cool Juggler 5 The difficult leaning wall to the right.

Lee Robinson on Cool Dude 6a

Steven Phelps on Cold Sweat 6a+

Cold Moor Buttress

Central Area

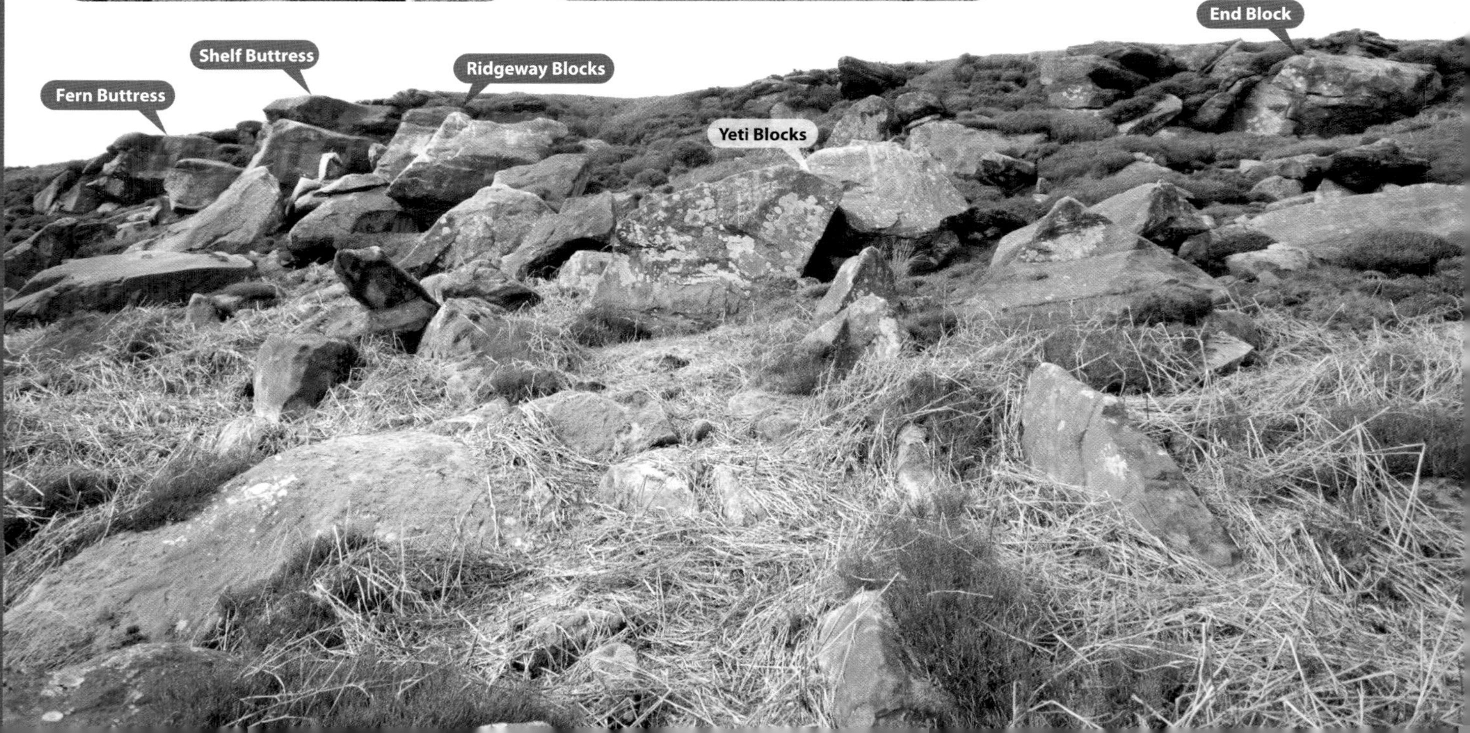

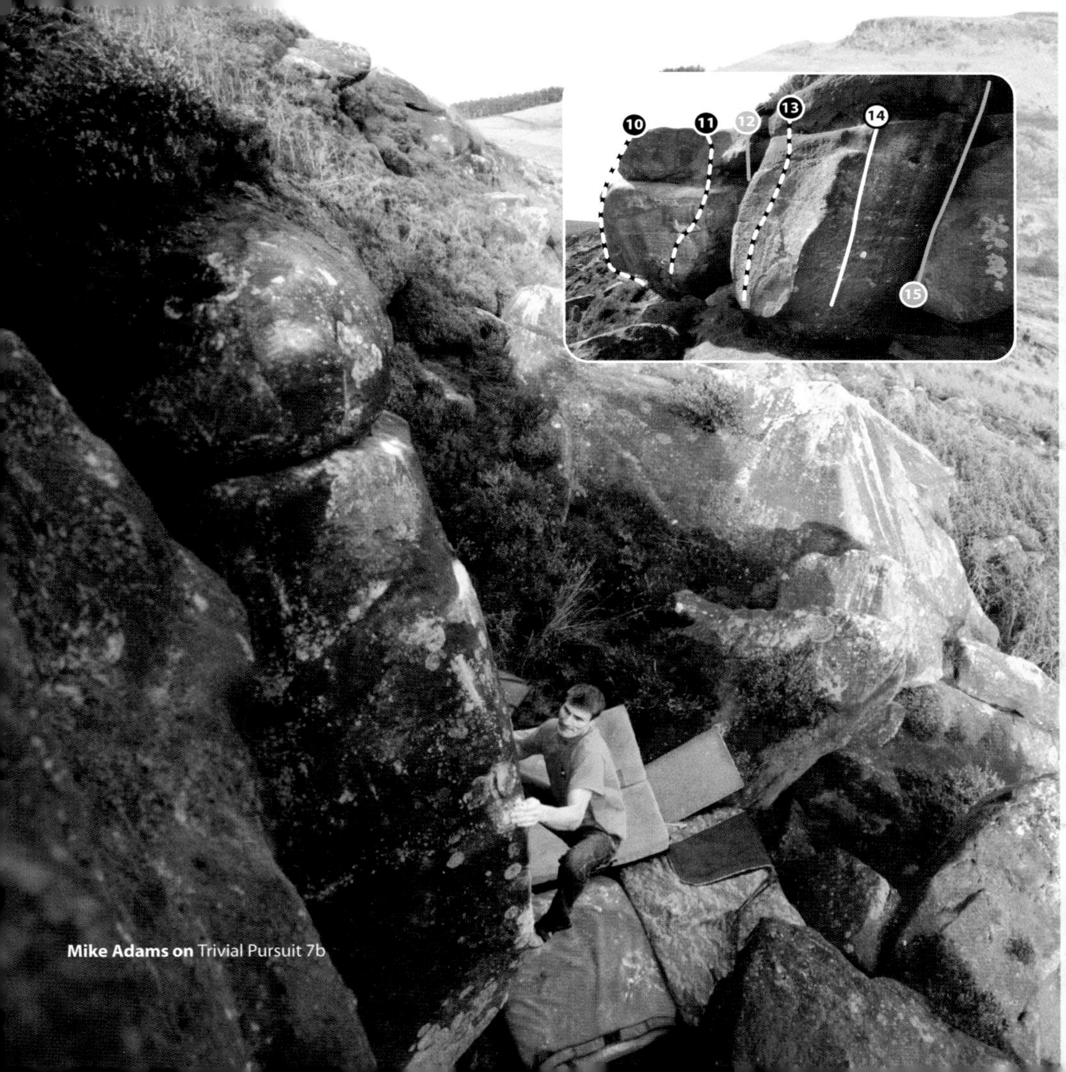

Fern Buttress

1. Fern Crack 2 The short crack.
2. Hungover 1 Follow the chimney, stepping right then left to escape over the down-pointing block.
3. Fern Groove 5 The fine leaning corner. Start by climbing the wall just right for a few moves until it is possible to pull into the crack to finish.
4. Fern Gully 1 The dirty stepped gully.
5. Fern Gully Variation 4 Start up the gully but move leftwards using the crack under the capstone.

Little Shelf Buttress

6. Over The Hill SS 5+ The undercut arête has short but good moves. The original problem without the sit-start is **4**.
7. Little Shelf 3+ Gain a standing position on the small shelf, then finish left up the arête.

Shelf Buttress

8. White Slab 1+ Start at the foot of the gully then step onto the light-coloured front face and finish up this.
9. Left Chasing Desire 7c SS Start on holds under White Slab then traverse right towards the arête and follow to finish.
10. Chasing Desire 7c SS Use very small holds under the small roof to gain the arête then finish up this. From standing is **7a.**
11. Oblivion 7c+ SS Use the obvious lower hold on the face to dyno for the hold beneath the shelf, compose yourself and finish over the often-damp shelf to the top.
12. Frank's Chimney 1+ Follow the filthy chimney.
13. Trivial Pursuit SS 7b The front face with a difficult start and a finish moving left. The original from standing is **5.**
14. Project The arête on its right using small crimps.
15. Leaning Corner 1+ The dirty little corner is possible.

Mike Adams on Trivial Pursuit 7b

Shelf Buttress Boulders and the Ridgeway

Steven Phelps on Lay Z Day 4+

James Rennardson on Cold Cut 6b

Lee Robinson on Problem 9

Shelf Buttress Boulders

1. Frank's Slab 1 The short enjoyable slab, keeping as central as possible.
2. Lay Z Day 4+ Start by pulling over the overlap, then follow the steepening slab keeping right of the arête to an extremely bold (for its size) finish. Starting from sit extends the climbing but does not change the grade.

The next problems start beneath Lay Z Day on a flat-topped boulder.

The Ridgeway

3. Cold Cut 6b SS The first boulder can be traversed from right to left with a difficult rockover finish.
4. The Ridgeway 1 Mantel the first boulder and walk up to the second. The second boulder is climbed by its left wall exiting around an obvious capstone. After this climb from the gap in the ridge next to the left wall to finish.

The next group of problems all make use of the final boulder on The Ridgeway.

The Ridgeway Variations

5. Variation 3+ The last of the three boulders can be climbed by crossing the slab on the lip of the overhang gaining the ridge/arête and following to the top.
6. 7b+ SS Starting under the roof, pull onto the slab via a painful mono! Finish direct.
7. 7b SS Start as the last problem then move right finishing up the arête. **6a** from standing.
8.7b SS Start right of the overhang on an undercut, climb left on sloping crimps then over the nose of the arête to finish up the slab with use of the arête/ridge. **6a** from standing.
9. 7a SS Start as the last problem, gain a good sloper then step up to gain a sloping layaway and pull over onto the slab to finish. **6a** from standing.
10. 1+ Pull onto the slab on the right, which is slightly higher up at an obvious good hold.

Yeti Blocks

11. Under Pressure 5 Traverse the block rightwards using holds on the face to finish at the far end.
12. Hoppings 3 The centre of the short slab.
13. Ice Ice Baby 4 SS Start the arête then pull round to the slab via a sidepull, finish direct.
14. Vanilla Ice 4 SS The short arête direct.
15. Yeti 6c+ SS Starting on two undercut holds surmount the slab using the left arête and right hand hold on the slab, finish delicately. A contrasting problem of two halves.
16. 6b SS Traverse the block on slopers to the far arête and rock onto the slab.
17. Sasquatch 3+ SS The right arête.

Further uphill at a bulging boulder just on the edge of the moor is the last problem of the area.

End Block

18. Uptime 2 Start at the obvious sloping shelf, then use a flake crack to pull over the bulge.

Mike Adams on Problem 2

Midget Gem Block

1. 7a SS Gain the pockets, rocking onto the slab to finish.
2. 7b SS Using a thin crack finish up the groove.
3. Midget Gem 5 Climb up the shallow overhanging groove on the east face of the boulder.
4. 7a SS Climb the bulge just right of Miget Gem.
5. Project SS The overhanging crack.

Three Tier Buttress

6. Three Tier Climb 3 Move up the stepped buttress direct to finish at the right arête.

Little Buttress

7. Small Time 1+ Climb up the arête. Can also be extended following a rising ledge rightwards.
8. Child's Play 4 Climb direct up the undercut flake.
9. Kiddie Time 5 The side wall on pockets to the right.

Delta Slab

10. Delta Force 4 The centre of the slab to an awkward finish.
11. Delta Slab 2 Start at the right hand corner, gain a diagonal crack and follow it leftwards to finish up a thin crack.
12. Delta Slab Arête 3 Start as the last problem and follow the arête direct.

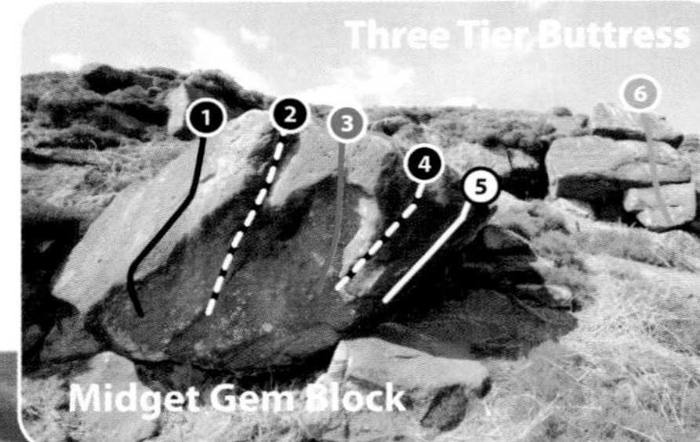

Steven Phelps on Nebula (Severe)

Capstone Buttress

1. Insatiable Desire 6a+ This takes the central rib passing the wedged block in the break.

2. Capstone Corner 1+ The leaning corner.

Neb Buttress

3. Out of Reach 6a Start just left of the chimney in the shallow alcove. Move up the alcove and escape slightly left to a ledge. Precarious moves lead to the top.

4. Nebula (Severe) The brilliant chimney is a struggle.

5. Buttress Route 4+ Start just right of Nebula and gain the ledge above the nose. Finish up the blunt arête.

6. Neb Direct 6a+ Straight up the overhanging nose by way of a shallow flake/groove. Finish direct.

7. Harum Scarum 6a Climb the undercut wall direct past a thin diagonal crack near the top.

8. Tough Enough 5 The awkward wall to the dirty shelf, finishing left or right.

Plantation Buttress

Dead Tree Buttress

Undercut Buttress

Bilsdale Buttress

James Rennardson on Letterbox Wall 6b+

The next buttresses are:

Plantation Buttress

1. Project Arête/wall
2. Endgame 4 Climb the bulge just right of the central corner via the curving ledge.
3. Fraggle Rock 1+ The next bulge to the right.

The next buttress looks as if it gets little to no traffic, it's very green and includes heathery finishes.

Dead Tree Buttress

4. Bravo 3 The bulging slab at the left side of the buttress has a difficult exit.
5. Stumpy 3 Gain the groove in the corner, direct or from the left.
6. Dead Tree Wall 4 An eliminate between Stumpy and Dead Tree Crack.
7. Dead Tree Crack 2 Cross the wall, move right to gain the vertical crack, then finish.
8. Dead Tree Groove 1+ The groove/crack in the centre.
9. Dead Loss 3+ The shallow flaked groove, crossing the bulge.
10. Dead End 1 Up the dirty ledges leading to a slanting groove.

20m right is the next buttress with some high problems.

Undercut Buttress

11. All In One 3+ A shallow flake edge leads up to a rounded break. Finish using pockets above.
12. Classic Rock 4 Climb the steep slab rightwards to finish up the arête. Can be started direct up the arête at **5**.

The next 2 problems can be finished by traversing leftwards once the break is reached.

13. No Limits Direct Start 6b (E1 6a) Start from the obvious boulder on the left and climb straight up to the break by use of small holds and a thin flake. Finish as for the original No Limits.
14. No Limits 5+ (HVS 5c) Start in the centre of the undercut wall on the left end of the flake block, pull up to gain the break and follow this leftwards to finish just right of the arête.
15. No Limits Direct Finish 6a+ (E1 6a) Start as No Limits to the break, then move slightly left finishing direct on small holds.
16. Sickle Direct 4+ (VS 5a) Make a pull over the undercut to the sickle-shaped ledge, then finish direct.
17. Sickle 2 From a sloping ledge move left to the curving ledge, step left then back right to finish.

The next problem is down to the right and is included for historical reasons only.
Easy Slab - Gardener's World 1 *Up the dirty slab trending right.*

20m to the right is the next buttress.

Bilsdale Buttress

18. Facade 3+ The centre of the slab on the left. Step right near the top or to increase the difficulty go direct to exit.
19. Letterbox Wall 6b+ SS Move up the narrow wall making use of the slot to finish over the final block. The original from standing is **5**.
20. Party Piece 5 Gain a curving ledge direct without use of the sidepull, then move up and left to escape.
21. Vice Versa 1 Start up the corner to gain the overgrown break. Follow this to finish as the last problem.

Wall Buttress

The buttress at the far left of the edge hasn't seen much traffic over the years and is very green and overgrown.

1. **Opening Gambit 3+** Start left of the stone wall and climb the face behind the tree.
2. **Wall and Crack 2** Mantel the heathery ledge above the stone wall and finish up the crack.
3. **Crack 4** The overhanging crack on the right is more testing.
4. **Desiree 3+** From the right gain the nose and move up the slab above.
5. **Optical Trap 6a** Start on the left arête to gain the sidewall of the buttress, then hug each arête to gain the top.

Lee Robinson on Optical Trap 6a

Thimbleby Crag is hidden in the forest above Over Silton village. The highlight of the venue is the Great Wall which reaches a height of seven metres and holds some excellent and sustained highball problems, amongst others. Further problems are situated on separate blocks, though these have mostly inferior rock. It's advisable to check the top of the Great Wall before an ascent and if possible abseil down to clean the holds. There are trees at the top to abseil off or set up slings if needed for safe exits.

Approach: Either park in Over Silton village or follow the track north out of the village parking at a small sandstone quarry on the left. Follow the main forestry track that goes north-east for about a mile to a crossroads at the top. From here take the main track straight down Thimbleby Bank, which is the third on the left. As the track bears right there is a small path on the left which leads to a large rock and popular viewpoint. Take a right turn onto the overgrown path and follow to where the crag will be visible down on your left.

OS Map: SE 460949
Walk: 20 minutes
Faces north-west and gets the evening sun. Best in cool dry conditions as the rock gets sweaty in summer.

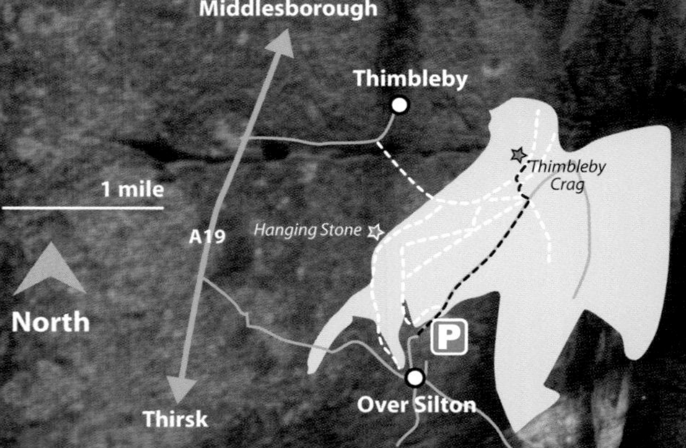

Steven Phelps on White Star Line 6a+

The Great Wall

1. Meteor Shower 6c Start on the left with a sidepull and a thin break. Climb up with good moves between nice holds and the crux sequence to reach a multitude of pockets. Finish direct, eliminating the low jug and mid height slot to the right.
2. Shotgun 6a Mantel the ledge to gain the large slot. From here move up leftwards to join the last route and finish up this.
3. Project Climb Shotgun until you can find a way across the wall rightwards.
4. White Star Line 6a+ Climb to the shelf then move right to a good hold. From here move past a crimp to the next shelf and a rest. Then use a small crimp reach for a good right-hand hold and follow with the hole out left. Finish direct.
5. Project Tackle the blunt rib direct passing a shelf.
6. Big Bang 5+ The right arête of the main wall using the pockets.
7. Project Climb up Big Bang before a traverse left can be made to the rib.

A short wall opposite.

8. Curious Rover 4+ Climb the weakness to an awkward finish.
9. Rocket 6a Climb through the overlap to the pocket to gain the top.
10. Venus in Transit 5 The far right arête with a foot in the crack to a long reach finish.

Mike Adams on Prowess 6b

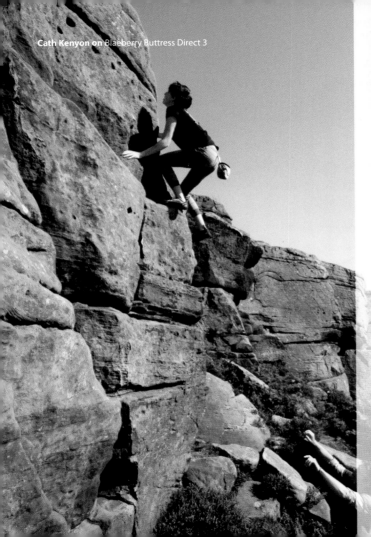

Cath Kenyon on Blaeberry Buttress Direct 3

Scugdale crags are probaby the most visited of all the moorland venues, as they are accessible for locals and a short uphill approach is all that is needed to reach them. The crags sit prominently on the hillside above the parking and stretch out for several miles all the way to the farthest area which is White Stone. The main area of Scot Crags is the most popular, being directly above the parking. It hosts fine boulder problems and routes, most with friendly landings. Then it's onto the less-trodden areas of Barker's Crags further south, Stoney Wicks which holds mostly short easy problems and finally at the far end of the valley is White Stone which doesn't see much traffic but does hold some good problems and is dominated by the West Wall.

Approach: Take the turning off the A172 for the village of Swainby. The river runs between the two parallel High Streets, you'll need the river on your left to keep going south, so cross over the bridge at the church if you are on the other side. Continue driving south and take the left turn onto Scugdale Road, just outside the village. This road is very narrow for several miles, so take extra care as it gets extremely tight in places. Pass through Heathwaite, pass the 'dead-end' sign and eventually you'll see Raikes Farm on the left. The parking is located after Raikes Farm, directly below Scot Crags with enough space for up to five cars in the lay-by and several spaces either side of the road. Please park responsibly as the road is often used by tractors.

Scot Crags

The most popular of the venues has something for everyone, from short easy-going slabs through to high overhanging arêtes. The sandstone is well-weathered and solid, apart from the odd easy line which gets far too much attention and bears broken holds due to the amount of traffic; but most of the problems are fine and a good day will be had by anyone visiting.

Approach: Cross a stile just above the main parking then pass over a small stream. Follow the diverted path, keeping right of the wall and passing over several more stiles, after which the path will bring you out in front of Beginner's Slab.

OS Map: NZ 516004
Walk: 5 minutes
Faces south

* *Countless variations and other problems are at Scugdale, though the best on the most solid rock have been included here.*

The first buttress at the far left end of the crag.

Rake's Buttress

1. Off Spring 6a SS Make a long move up to a flake from good holds, using the main roof block for feet. No using the sidewall.
2. Auntie's 5 Start at the left side of Rake's Buttress and climb the left edge of the wall without bridging onto the boulder on the left.
3. Rake's Progress 1 Start at Auntie's, move right following the ledge to the right edge, then finish up the flutes on the arête.
4. Uncle's 4 Start 2m right, climb a short crack then the upper wall past three pockets.
5. Mother's Little Helper 2 Start as for Uncle's, then follow the ramp to exit up the arête right of the three pockets.
6. Straight and Narrow 1 From the base of the buttress, climb up and right to finish up the flutes.
7. Moderator 1 Start beneath the roof and climb the left wall to gain the ledge. Exit up the fluted wall.
8. Direct Version 5 Climb the centre of the roof without using any other block.
9. Easy Stages 1 Climb the overhang on the right then finish left up the main fluted wall.

10m to the right.

Oriel Wall

10. Left Side 2 Climb the wall left of the protruding nose.
11. The Mounting Block 2 Climb the concave wall right of the nose.
12. Nutcrackers Wall 5+ SS Start left of The Nutcrackers at a small overhang, use slopers to move straight up via a break. Finish direct.
13. The Nutcrackers 1 Climb the awkward crack.
14. Spiral Stairs 1+ Climb the right side of the undercut arête using a pocket.

Just right of this is:

The Parson's Nose Buttress

15. Parson's Chimney 1 The short cleft at the left side of the wall opposite the last problem.
16. Hand Jive 5+ Climb the wall right of the last problem, using small holds with a difficult finish. No use of the embedded block or left edge.
17. Jiver's Wall 4+ The wall just right of centre via small holds.
18. Bop Route 2+ The arête starting on the right side, using a crack and finishing at a small corner.
19. Bopped 5 Climb straight over the overlap and finish direct.
20. Zoot Route 1+ Take the leaning wall on good holds.
21. The Nose 5+ Climb the overhang on its right.

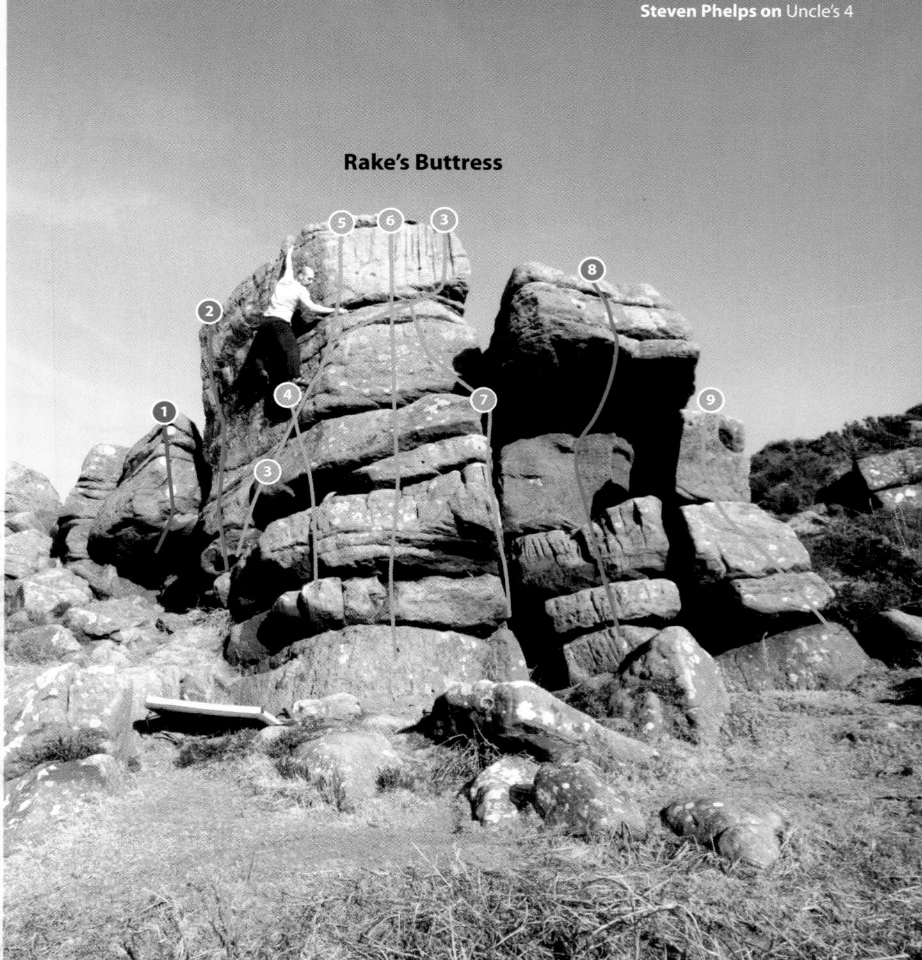

Steven Phelps on Uncle's 4

The Parson's Nose Buttress
Oriel Wall
10
11
12
13
14
15
16
17
18
19
20
21

Neb Buttress

Scot Buttress

1 2 3 4 5 6 7 8 9 10 11 12 13 14 15

20m right is:

Neb Buttress

1. The Neb Buttress 1 The slabby buttress to the left of The Neb, starting at the lowest point.
2. The Neb 5+ This is in the alcove on the left side of the buttress. Climb up left of the undercut nose to the break, step right then straight over the top.

Scot Buttress.

3. Vallum 2 Climb the left edge of the wall and finish up a short crack.
4. Hadrian's Wall 3 Start up a short diagonal crack and finish up the centre of the wall.
5. Corner Direct Left 2 Start at the arête and climb the left side.
6. Corner Direct Right 3 Start at the right side and climb into the niche 'Nook'. Finish up the right edge of the arête.
7. Nook and Cranny 2 Climb the left side of the arête into the 'Nook', traverse right to the flake 'Cranny' and finish with this.
8. Direct Start 3 Start below the final flake crack or 'Cranny', pull over the bulge using a flake and finish as problem 7.
9. Highland Fling 5 (E1 5b) Climb straight up the rounded arête between the last route and Bawbee Crack to finish up a shallow vertical fault, no use of the 'Cranny'.
10. Bawbee Crack 1+ Step off the block to climb the awkward crack.
11. Blaeberry Buttress Slab 4 An eliminate between the two cracks.
12. Blaeberry Crack 1 The slanting crack is followed to a junction with the last route. Finish up this.
13. Blaeberry Buttress Direct 3 Climb the wall right of Blaeberry Crack via a short vertical crack.
14. Blaeberry Buttress 1 Start just right of the arête, step up and traverse up leftwards using a sloping shelf for the hands and finish at the top of Blaeberry Crack.
15. Blaeberry Buttress Variation 1+ Climb the right arête to the top then traverse left into Blaeberry Crack.

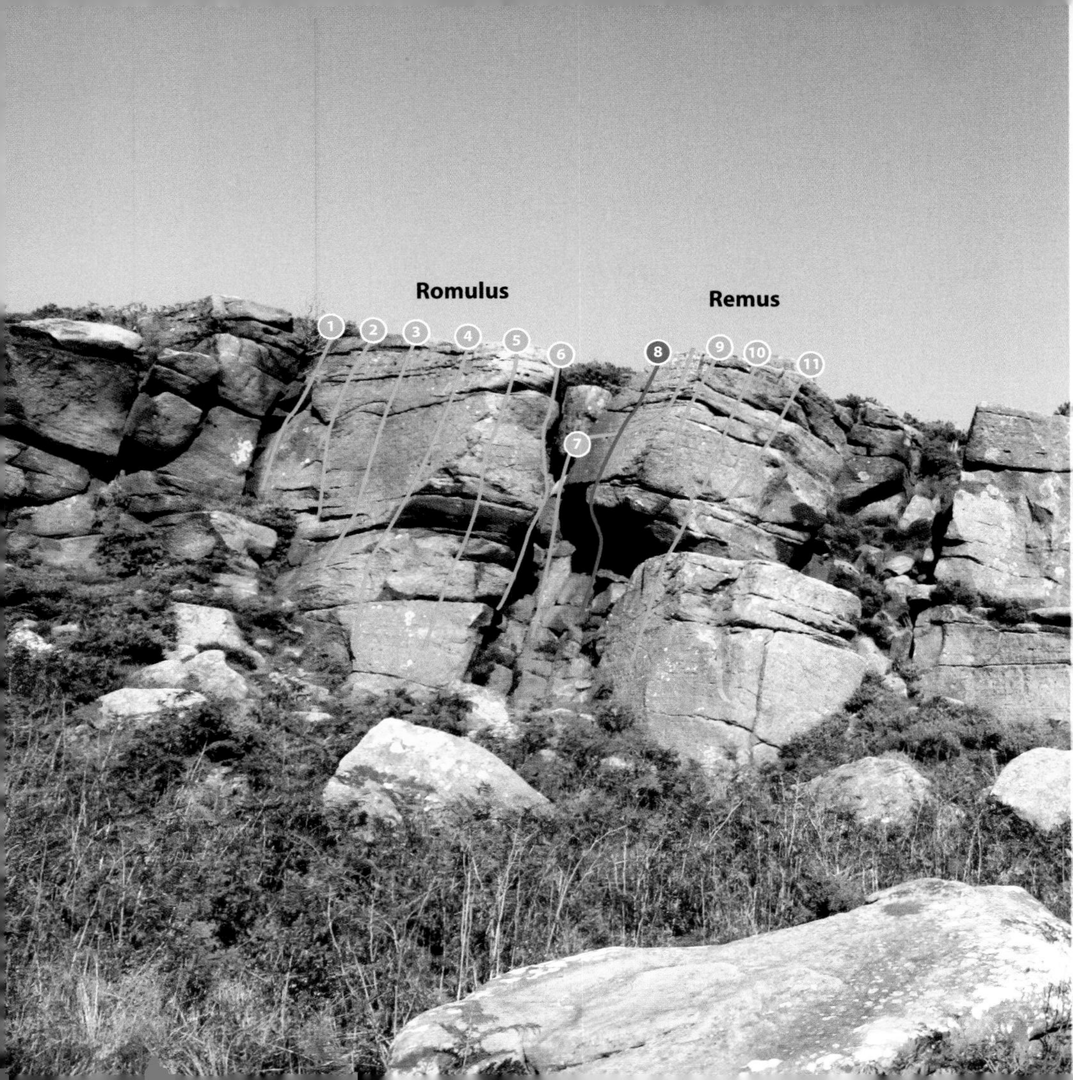

Romulus

Remus

*The small overhanging broken buttress to the left holds three problems. The left arête and wall on its left are **3** and the thin hanging crack right of these is **3+**.*

Romulus and Remus

1. Wolf Wall Corner 1 Climb the corner with the heathery shelf beneath it.
2. Wolf Wall 2 Climb a thin crack and the wall 1m right of the corner.
3. Wolf Whistle 3 Ascend the wall using small holds in the centre.
4. Woodpecker Wall 2 Move up the wall using well defined pockets on the upper slab.
5. Romulus 3 Climb the blunt arête left of the chimney.
6. Tiber Chimney 1 Ascend the wide chimney.
7. Decline and Fall 3+ (HS 4b) Climb up the chimney for 4m, then using both walls traverse right above the roof to finish up the right side of the slab.
8. Tiber Wall 6a (E1 5c) Start at the base of the chimney then surmount the overhanging wall at its centre. Continue direct, no bridging.
9. Remus Left Hand VS 4c Sloping holds lead to a large ledge then follow the left arête using a hidden pocket.
10. Remus VS 4c Start the same as the last problem, then go straight up the centre of the buttress with a long reach to finish .
11. Remus Right Hand VS 5a Starting in a shallow groove, climb to the ledge and finish up the right arête.

4m to the right is:

The Prow Area

1. Halyards 1 Straight up the left arête on the raised platform.
2. Little By Little 1+ The groove just to the right.
3. Eliminate Wall 5+ Climb the wall between Little By Little and Main Mast Crack on a steepening flake, layback and reach up to the flake avoiding the right arête. Another reach should lead to the top.
4. Main Mast Crack 2 The splendid corner crack.
5. Stewker 6a (E1 5c) Start in the centre and climb direct up the wall using a sidepull to reach the obvious pocket. Continue up the wall via small holds. An excellent and bold problem.
6. Prowess 6c (E3 6b) The wall right of Stewker using the right edge. Even bolder.
7. The Prow 5 (E1 5a) Straight up the edge of the arête. The essential problem.
8. Galley Chimney 1 The wide chimney.
9. The Heads 2+ The right arête of Galley Chimney. Start either side of the arête to finish up the left side on flakes.
10. The Bulkhead 3+ The fine overhanging crack. For a variation finish, climb the crack to half-height then reach for the slanting flake on the right and finish round the corner in a niche.
11. The Keel 5 Start at a short crack to the right, climb this and gain a slanting flake on the upper wall. Follow the flake to finish.

***Plimsoll Line 4+** A low level traverse in either direction from Little By Little to the variation finish of The Bulkhead.*

5m right is:

Adam

12. Jill's Delight 1 Climb the wall left of the arête.
13. Right Hand Side 1 Climb the right side of the arête.

Eve

The first problem is not in the photo and is around the back.

14. Evens 4+ Start in the gully opposite Adam, then step into the obvious pocket, gain the shallow scoop above and finish.
15. Curving Arete 4+ Follow the blunt arête right of Evens.
16. Jack's Delight 4 Start at the toe of the buttress, then pull up leftwards and up the delicate wall.
17. Eve (Left Hand) 4+ (HVS 5a) Climb up the left side of the high sharp arête, with a bad landing.
18. Eve (Right Hand) 5 (E2 5b) Climb up the disconcerting right side of the sharp arête.
19. Hob Nobs 6b+ (E3 6a) Start 1m right of the arête and climb the delicate wall direct.
20. Serpent 6b+ (E3 6a) This climbs the slanting crack and follows it until it's possible to step left, using small pockets up to the top.

Megabite 6a *A traverse starting at the gully of Evens, crossing Jack's Delight and turning the awkward corner (feet in a horizontal break at 2m), then traversing a delicate wall to finish in the corner-right of Serpent.*

Directly below the main edges is a low prow.

Shark's Head Block

21. Shark's Head Left 5 SS Climb the left-hand side of the head from the low jug, using a pocket out left and avoiding the lodged block.
22. Napoleon Dynamite 7a SS Traverse right to left below the lip using a shallow dish and topping out past a vertical crack.

Mike Kenyon on Stewker 6a

Just along from Serpent.

Green Walls

1. Green Wall 1 Climb up the wall just right of the holly tree.

2. Archer's Arête 3 The arête to the right, keeping hands and feet on the right side.

3. Archer's Crack 1+ Start in the corner just right of Green Wall and bridge the corner until holds can be used on the slab out right.

4. Clarence 1+ Start 2m right, then step onto the slab and climb trending rightwards past a break.

5. Clarence Direct 5 Start under the overlap below and right and climb up the wall without using the block on the right.

6. Clarence Arête 4 The undercut arête just to the right.

The Pulpit

7. The Pulpit 5 Climb the wide crack on the left then traverse out right to a difficult finish direct up the nose. Can be climbed with a direct start at a similar grade.

8. Lazing on a Sunny Afternoon 5+ Start up the crack as for The Pulpit, then move right and pull straight over the roof on small holds.

9. Choir 1+ The blunt arête right of the main overhang. Up the slope to a wide gully.

10. Lost Arête 4 Without using the boulders in the gully, climb the left-hand arête starting in a shallow groove.

11. Anvil Chorus 5 Climb the right side of the arête.

12. Forgotten Wall 4 The centre of the wall.

13. Forgotten Arête 4 The right-hand arête.

14. Lost Chimney 1 The chimney in the corner.

15. Wall and Crack 2 Climb the short wall just right of the chimney and finish up a steep crack.

16. Tried in Vein 6a+ SS Start at the right arête. Once positioned move across the slab and straight up the left arête all without using the faint flake on the slab.

Low Level Traverse 3 *Traverse from Lost Arête to Lost Chimney, with hands in the first break.*

Fràncis Montague on The Pulpit 5 **In the 1990s**

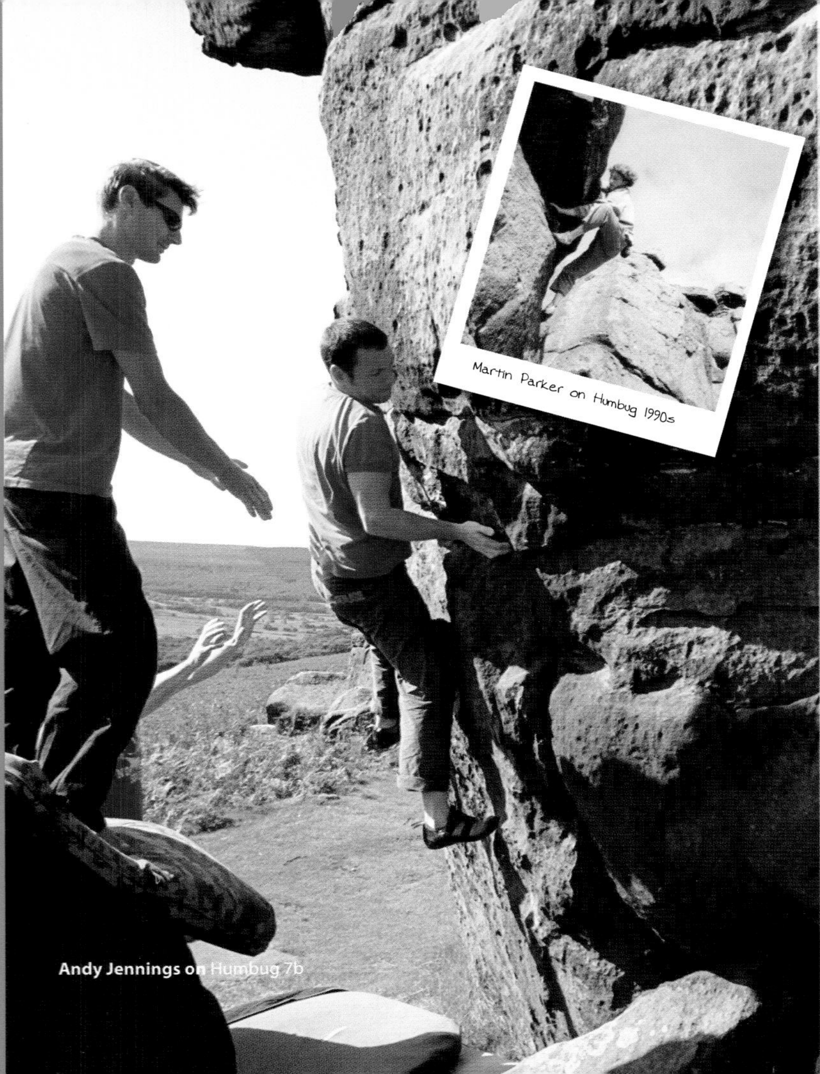

Andy Jennings on Humbug 7b

Drunken Buttress

1. Seamy Side 1 Start up the blunt arête then finish via the left edge of the slab.
2. Bottoms Up 3 Climb the centre of the undercut slab just left of Hangover.
3. Hangover 4 Start at the lowest point of the slab, climb straight over the bulge into a shallow groove and finish up the slab.
4. Tippling Wall 5 The splendid overhanging wall to the right of the slab can be climbed almost anywhere on small holds and deep breaks, though it's easier on the right. Don't sneak left near the top, finish direct.
5. Tippling Arête 5 Climb straight up the leaning edge of the wall to a difficult exit.
6. Humbug 7b (E4 7a) Begin 1m right of the arête, climb the wall following a hairline crack and pockets to a sloping hold to finish over the roof. Maybe the hardest line of the crag.
7. The Shelf 6a (E2 5c) Gain the shelf then pull past a flake onto the slab. Can be sandy in places and for its size requires a cool head.

Pisa Buttress

8. Plumb Line 2 (S) The corner crack between Drunken Buttress and Pisa Buttress, finish up the slab on the right.
9. Pisa Buttress 4+ (VS 5a) Start between Plumb Line and Gravity Wall, ascend the wall on small holds to the break then move right to gain a shelf and finish direct.
10. Gravity Wall 3+ (HS 4b) Start at the blunt toe of the buttress, climb straight to the break then move diagonally left and finish up the top corner.
11. Gravity Wall Direct 4 (HS 4c) A direct start climbing up Pisa Buttress then joining the original route at the top corner.
12. Gravitation 5 (E1 5b) Ascend the narrow wall between Gravity Wall and Galileo's Gully. Start up the left edge of the chimney, climb to the first break then climb straight up to gain the right end of the obvious shelf to a sloping top-out.
13. Galileo's Chimney 2 Climb the outside of the chimney.

Scugdale Buttress

14. Tooth and Nail 3 (MVS 4b) Climb up the wall and move left to finish up the prominent crack.
15. Supine 4+ (VS 5a) Step off the boulder and climb the left side of the right arête on fragile holds.
16. Hybrid 3+ (HS 4b) Start up Scugdale Chimney and traverse round the arête, passing under the overhang of Supine to finish up Tooth and Nail.
17. Scugdale Chimney Eliminate 3+ (VS 4b) Climb up the narrow wall to pass the overhang and finish direct.
18. Scugdale Chimney 1 The chimney.
19. Scugdale Wall MVS 4b Up the wall to finish left, up the chimney.
20. Zeta Wall 4 (VS 4c) Climb up the wall to gain the crack system and once up this finish just right of the chimney.
21. Deviator 6a (HVS 5c) Ascend the shallow groove, then cross the break and follow the faint crack to an awkward finish.
22. Nameless Crack 1+ The crack just right of Deviator.

Low Level Traverse 6c *A traverse from Nameless Crack to Hangover at rarely more than 0.5m above the ground.*

1
2
3
4
Drunken Buttress

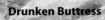

5
6
7
8
9
10
11
12
13
14
15
16
17
18
19
Pisa Buttress

Drunken Buttress

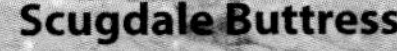
Scugdale Buttress

20
21
22
Scugdale Buttress

Barker's Buttress

1. Cub's Climb 1 The left side of the wall to finish up a shallow corner.
2. Pup's Climb 2 Follow the crack system to finish on pockets.
3. Bonzo 5 Climb up past a break to reach the obvious letterbox hold, once this is gained finish direct.
4. Pet's Corner 3 Climb up the wall and crack just left of the arête.
5. The Arête 4 Directly up the edge.
6. Whippet Wall 4 Straight up the centre of the wall finishing using the crack.
7. Barker's Chimney 1 The corner chimney.
8. Pluto 3 The undercut wall to the right is climbed on its left side.
9. Pluto Variant 6a+ The right side of the wall using small holds to an easy finish.
10. Catwalk 1+ Step off the boulder and traverse along the break to finish up Pluto.
11. Hyena 2 From the top of the boulder climb the steep arête.
12. Cerberus Crack 2 The curving crack just right of Hyena.
13. Peke's Perch 2 The thin crack and small niche right of Cerberus Crack.

Holly Tree Buttress

14. Pingers Left Hand 5 The left side of the wall without using the ledges or left edge.
15. Pingers 5 Climb directly up the centre of the wall past pockets and breaks, brilliant.
16. Pingers Right Hand 5+ The right side of the wall without using anything from Pingers or anything beneath the overlap at the start.

The next two problems are covered by the holly tree which makes them either difficult to get to or painfull to try.

17. Prickly Rib 1+ The wall left of the tree to finish with the rib.
18. Holly Tree Chimney 1 Start right of the holly tree in the corner, climb up and cross the slab beneath the overhang and finish up the hidden chimney.
19. Touch and Go 6c (E2 6b) Start as for the last route but pull over the nose on its left side using small holds and the arête of the nose to a bold finish.
20. Holly Tree Wall 3+ Climb the wall then move into the thin crack just right of the last problem.
21. Holly Tree Hover 4+ Start as for Holly Tree Wall, then pull over the overhang at the left of the crack to a short strenuous finish.
22. Saint's Wall 1+ The wide crack immediately right of Holly Tree Wall.
23. Oak Tree Wall 3 Start in the short awkward corner, then move right using the ledge as little as possible to move up the scoop to a mantelshelf finish.
24. Oak Tree Gully Arête 2 The good arête on the left of the gully.
25. Oak Tree Gully Wall 1 The short wall just to the right.
26. The Mantelshelf 3+ Climb up the polished slab to make a move over the bulge at its left end.
27. Humpty Dumpty 3+ Directly up the right side of the bulge without use of the chimney.

The Razor

1. Left Hand Swing 3+ The left edge of the block. A sidepull is used for the right hand with the left aiming high on the left edge.
2. Central Route 2 Takes the centre of the short wall to a sloping finish.
3. Slashed Wall 1+ The shallow slanting grooves in the right edge of the wall.
4. The Gash 1+ Climb the short chimney.
5. The Gash - Arête Finish 3 Climb The Gash to the ledge, then continue up the blunt arête on the right to finish up the shallow groove.
6. Razor Wall 3+ The centre of the wall keeping away from the flake.
7. Razor Rib 1+ Ascend the wall just left of the arête, to finish up the flake crack. Excellent.
8. Razor Rib Direct 1+ Start as for Razor Rib but don't use the flake, instead climb the left side of the arête to the top.
9. Gillette 4 The right side of the arête using hands on the arête to mantel the shelf. Finish up the rib using pockets.
10. Gillette Variation 6a Follow the wall on small holds, once on the shelf continue straight up without use of the rib or the crack of Suds.
11. The Strop D Gain the shelf from the right side and follow it leftwards to finish round the corner as for Rib Direct.
12. Suds 4+ (HVS 5a) Gain the shelf then climb the hanging finger crack on the left. Bold.
13. Tension 5+ (HVS 5b) Gain the shelf, then climb the wall right of Suds following a hairline crack. Also bold.
14. Tension Right Hand 4+ (VS 5a) Make the first move of the upper part of tension, then step right and climb the edge without using the jammed blocks.

Low Level Traverse 5 *Start at the right side of the shelf beneath Tension, traverse down leftwards onto the wall and on pockets to the arête. Round the arête and across the face to finish up Central Route.*

Beginners Slab

15. Alpha 1+ Start at the left side of the wall and climb direct, to finish up the sloping sandy groove above.
16. Beta 1 Start as the last problem but move right to climb straight up the grooved wall. Pleasant.
17. Gamma 1+ Climb the right edge of the wall and finish up the arête.
18. Gamma Direct 4+ The arête direct.

Curtain Slab

19. Curtain Call 1+ Start 1m right of the crack and climb straight up using flakes.
20. Curtain Crack 1+ Up the crack to finish just right of the bulge.
21. Curtain Corner 1 Ascend the right corner on its left.

Overhanging Block

Barker's Buttress

Barker's Buttress Right

Rowan Buttress

Barker's Crags

Although only a stone's throw away from Scot Crags there is definitely more solitude to be found at Barker's Crags, which possess some popular problems and a fair amount which are much less travelled. The first few buttresses are located just beyond the fence and have some excellent boulder problems with good landings.

Approach: Either cross the fence at the right side of Scot Crags and drop down into the first area or walk down the road from the parking, take the public bridleway opposite Scugdale Hall and continue as it snakes uphill to the gate near Day's End Buttress. ✱ **See page 89**.

OS Map: NZ 520003
Walk: 5 minutes
Faces south

Steven Phelps on Right Wall 5+

The first block you come to is:

Overhanging Block

1. Slab 3+ Up the slab at the left side.
2. Overhang Crack 4 The crack splitting the overhang can prove awkward but good.
3. Flake Route 4 Up the groove at the right side, using the flake.

40m to the right across a small path is the next buttress.

To the left of Barker's Buttress on a large set of blocks are 2 problems. The slab centre passing a break is **3** *and the overhanging arête on the far right from sitting is* **4**.

Barker's Buttress

4. Angel Eyes 3 Follow the blunt arête on the left.
5. Stolen Moment 3 Climb the centre of the slab up a shallow scoop.
6. Roof Route 3 The edge of the main face on sculptured holds.
7. Avalon 5 SS Round the corner is a nice crackline. Make good moves up to an awkward finish, pulling onto the slab. The original from standing is **4+**.
8. Mantra 5 SS Start 4m in front of the last problem, low down in a grassy hole and from a good hold dive up to a sloper just right of a flake, then finish direct. Sandy in places.

8m to the right is:

Rowan Buttress

9. Rowan Tree Wall 2 Climb the blocky wall left of the stump.
10. Rowan Tree Corner 1 The corner just to the right.
11. Left Arête 4+ Climb up the left side of the square-cut arête.
12. Right Wall 5+ The wall right of the arête on small edges to a good hold and an awkward finish.
13. Right Wall Variation 6a Start on the break low down and right, then traverse into and finish up Right Wall.

8m to the right is:

Jackson's Block

14. Left Arête 4 The left arête of the small block.
15. Front Overhang 3+ Straight up over the centre of the front face.

The next similar block is:

Barking Block

16. Barking Mad Fin 5 SS Start at the column beneath the main block to gain and finish up the left arête.
17. Barking Mad 5 Follow good moves up the centre of the overhanging front face.

100m to the right is an excellent little area with some high challenges and several test-pieces.

Amphitheatre Buttress

1. Green Chimney 2 Climb the prominent wide crack up the hill.
2. Hairline 4 Without using the embedded block, climb the hairline crack just to the right of the last problem to the overlap and finish over this.
3. Problem Wall 5+ Climb the centre of the wall on tiny sidepulls.
4. Outer Wall 4 Right of the last problem is a shallow groove in the wall, just left of Pedestal Crack. Move up this then finish up the wall, keeping left of the arête.
5. Pedestal Crack 2 Climb the obvious crack with some nice moves, then finish up the wall above.
6. Walled Out 5 Start just right of the crack and climb the wall by use of small crimps up to the pockets near the top.
7. Walled In 5 Start in the centre of the wall, make difficult moves over the overlap to gain the break, then finish direct.
8. The Nose 1+ Start just right of the nose then move up and left to finish over the nose.
9. Pedestal Chimney 1 The wide crack just to the right.
10. Pedestal Wall 1+ Start up Pedestal Chimney. Gain the small platform, move right onto the face and then finish up the middle of the face.
11. Pedestal Wall Eliminate 5 Straight up the wall past a break and use small holds to finish up Pedestal Wall.
12. Hedgehog Arete 5 The arête to the right.
13. Flake Chimney 1 Climb the wide cleft.
14. Flake Chimney and Wall 1 Start up Flake Chimney then move rightwards near the top, to finish up a crack.
15. Hard Sell 4 Climb the wall to the right of Flake Chimney moving right at the top.
16. Long Chimney 1+ Follow the prominent chimney in the corner.
17. Tall Tales 5+ Immediately right of Long Chimney, cross the undercut to gain a good hold and traverse right for a metre-ish to finish up the short crack.
18. Fairy Tale High 7b A hold has probably gone since the first ascent, so the start is now significantly harder. An easier variation at **6c** starts on the blocks and gains a left-hand crimp.
19. Easter Edge 5+ The bulging arête on small edges to start.

Adrian Mellor on Alan's Wall 5

20. Fairy Tale Low 7a SS Pull over the bulge using two small pockets to start, finish direct.
21. The Nose 5+ The prominent blunt arête just to the right.
22. Snuff 5+ Climb up the narrow sidewall between The Nose and Alcove Cracks. Tricky to work out.
23. Alcove Cracks 2+ Follow the excellent double crack system.
24. Alcove Chimney 3+ The prominent chimney in the corner.
25. Alan's Wall 5 Climb up the thin fragile wall past a deep break, to a high finish.
26. Scoop Wall 6a Start just left of the curving scoop and climb the edge of the wall on small holds, finishing right at the top.
27. Mister Whippy 6a Follow the impressive curving scoop without either arête, finish direct through the roof-crack.
28. Snatch Arête 6a Climb the fine arête forming the right edge of the curving scoop, with difficult moves throughout.
29. Empty Illusions 6a Take the narrow hanging wall round the corner.
30. Pioneer's Chimney 1 The deep chimney.
31. Ancient Pioneer 3+ Climb a blunt flake to finish up a thin crack moving right at the top.
32. Ancient's Ascent 1 Climb the right-hand side of the flake keeping to the left edge.

5m right is a sharp arête.
33. Super Skunk 6b+ SS This arête is climbed using an obvious pocket. The standing start is **6a+**.
34. Natural High 6b+ SS Using the left-hand pocket and a small edge, gain the slanting feature, follow this to finish as for Super Skunk.

Super Skunk Wall

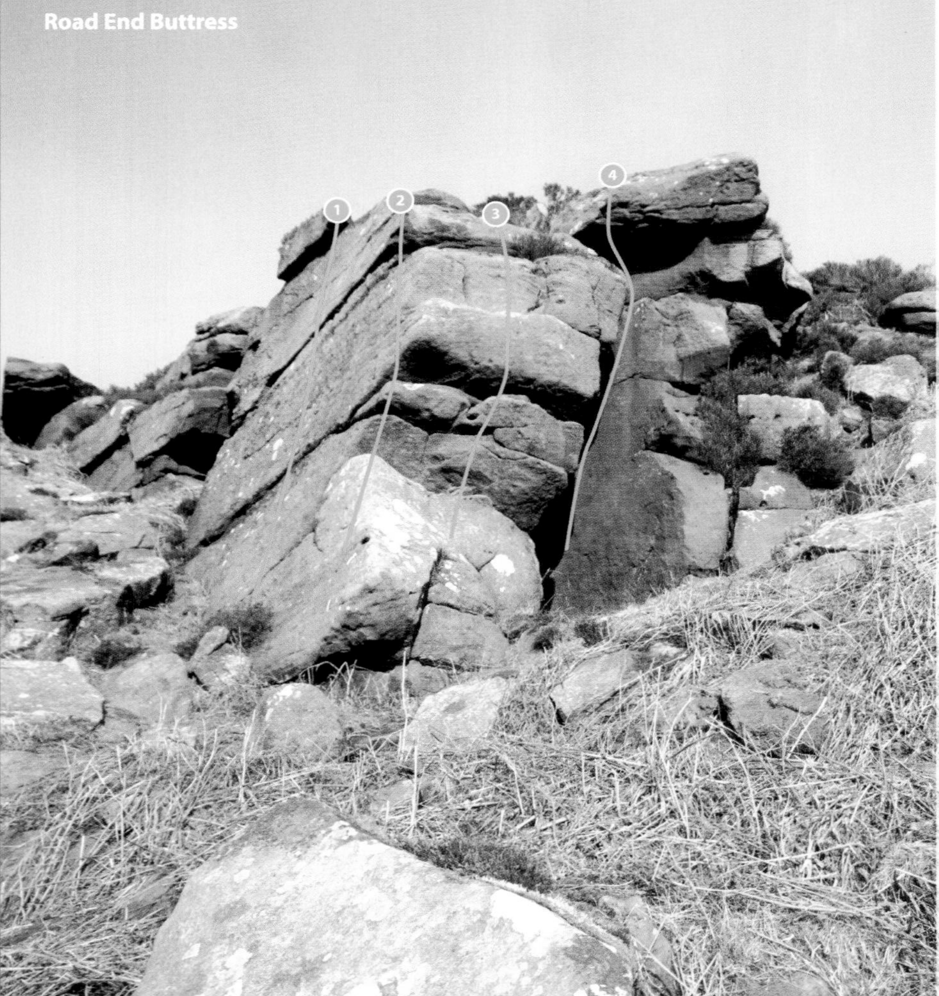

50m to the right is:

Road End Buttress

1. One For The Road 2 Climb the centre of the steep wall.
2. Shandy 1 Climb the nose on its left side.
3. Shandy Variation 3 Start just to the right and climb the wall straight up and over the overhang to the top.
4. Chaser Chimney 2 The chimney in the right-hand corner of the buttress.

10m to the right is:

Last But One Buttress

5. The Frog 5 Start below the overhang, pull onto the slab and escape right.
6. Last But One Buttress 1 Climb the obvious flake-crack over to the right of The Frog.

20m to the right is:

Day's End Buttress

7. Flake Wall 2+ Climb the flakes up the centre of the wall.
8. Joshua's Nose 2 The excellent blunt arête just to the right.
9. Bilberry Cracks 2+ Climb the shallow groove using the cracks.
10. Left Again 5+ Climb the undercut arête without using pockets to the left.
11. Dangerous Game 5 Start on the right side of the right-hand arête, pull up, then round onto the front towards a crack and follow to finish.
12. Safety in Numbers 4 Start round to right of the last problem and climb the wall direct.
13. Breakout 3 Climb up to the diagonal fault, then follow to the top.
14. Belly Chimney 1 Thrutch up the alcove using the cracks.
15. Snippet 5 SS Climb the overhanging arête just to the right of Belly Chimney. From standing is **4+.**
16. Jericho 1 Climb the wall on jugs.
17. Evening Wall 2+ The short wall.

On the large boulder just below:

18. Easy-Going 3 SS The small leaning arête on the block below.
19. Close Encounter 5+ SS Start on the block with one foot on the arête and the other on the ramp, pull onto the wall, then move leftwards along the arête. Use pockets to reach an undercut, then finish using the ramp and the arête.

This block also has a pleasant south facing slab.

Last But One Buttress

Lee Robinson on Snippet 5

This next area is across the bridleway, following the wall just after the gate to the east, for about 100m.

The Eyrie

The Eyrie

1. The Eyrie 5+ A good little problem starting from the pockets at the top of the crack, then gaining the sloping ledge and holds beneath the small roof and moving left to finish.

10m right is:

Bird's Nest Buttress

2. Fragile Wall 4+ The left side of the wall on fragile holds.
3. Smiler 5 SS Climb up the centre of the wall to the good holds of The Bends, then move left on sharp holds to finish.
4. The Bends 6a+ Use the good holds to reach the top. Can be done as a double dyno.
5. Wild 4+ Climb just left of the arête.
6. Flake Arête 5+ SS Climb up using increasingly better holds to a mantelshelf finish. Sharp.
7. Short and Sweet 6a The centre of the front face to the sloping ledge and a difficult finish.
8. Windy 1 Climb left of the chimney.
9. Air Time Traverse 6c+ Traverse the buttress at a high level, then back across at low level.
10. Breeze 3 The face of the boulder on the right of the chimney.

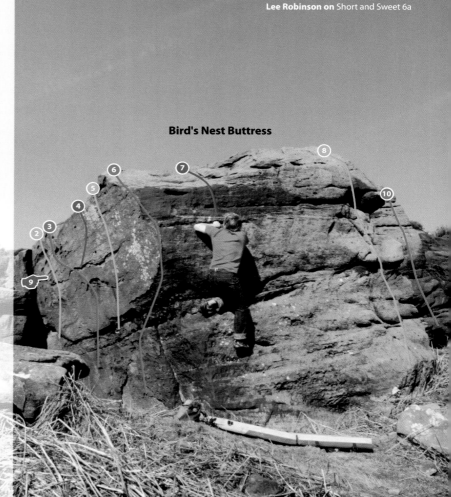

Lee Robinson on Short and Sweet 6a

Bird's Nest Buttress

2 3 4 5 6 7 8 9 10

30m right is:

Arch and Attic

1. Architrave 5+ SS Jam the crack on the overhanging wall, finish direct past the ledge.

2. Arch Rival 6a+ SS Start at the overhanging wall, use the diagonal crack to pull around the bulging wall just left of the gully and then make use of a hidden pocket right of the arête.

3. Arch Gully 1 Scramble up the gully beneath the capstones.

4. Over The Top 4 Climb up and over the capstones to finish on the right.

5. Fallen Arch 5+ Climb up the classic overhanging crack with difficulty.

6. Attic Gully 1 The gully to the right.

7. Atticism 5+ The wall between Attic Gully and the arête. Use a pocket on the arête to help gain a sloping ledge, then finish up a slab.

8. Foot Loose 6a+ Start in the middle of the leaning wall around the corner, pull up and move left to a finger crack to finish.

9. Foot Loose Direct 6a+ Climb straight up to the crack.

10. Attikismos Traverse 6a A low-level traverse starting from Attic Gully, to the right edge and back again.

10m right is:

Hogmanay Buttress

1. Auld Lang Syne 5 Climb the wall left of the wide crack, using a hand jam and pockets.
2. Hogmanay 2+ Gain the ledge by hugging the block, then finish up the cleft.
3. First Footing 1 Start right of the arête and up past two obvious pockets.

Just across the path is an excellent bouldering wall bearing six problems with many different variations and eliminates.

Black Wall

4. Black Corner Left Side 1+ Climb the left arête on jugs.
5. Black Corner Right Side 3 The wall just right of the arête.
6. Black Wall 5+ SS The wall 2m right of the arête on small elusive pockets.
7. Mandela's Day 6a Gain the shallow corner above the overlap using crimps.
8. Timeless Divide 4 Climb the right side, past a good pocket and ledges.
9. Black Wall Traverse 6a+ SS A left to right traverse following the obvious break-system.

Just below is:

Black Wall Boulder

10. Billy No Mates 6a The overhanging arête starting at the flake.
11. Harry Palmer 6a The centre of the boulder using a sidepull. Can be sandy.
12. Big Nose 5+ Make a big jump for the nose and pull over direct.

Black Wall

Mike Adams on Grand Master Flash 7a

The Cleft Buttress

1. Imperial Measurements 2 The crack on the right of the yellow scoop to a good finishing jug.
2. Leaning Wall 5 Climb the wall on a series of diagonal flakes.
3. The Chute 4 Climb a shallow groove to finish at the top of the scoop.
4. Elimination 6c Start left of Finger Jam and climb up a shallow scoop to join Finger Jam at the good hold.
5. Finger Jam 6a The excellent finger crack to move leftwards into The Chute to finish.
6. Finger Jam Direct Finish 6a+ Climb the crack then finish direct over the blunt nose.
7. Monty's Leap 6c The wall between Finger Jam and New Dimensions, then swing across to the jug and finish as for New Dimensions.
8. New Dimensions 6a+ The severely overhanging crackline by use of interesting moves. A Moors classic.

9. Open up and Gurgle 7a+ An eliminate up the wall between New Dimensions and Hangover using an obvious pocket.
10. Hangover 6a The right arête of the wall.

The next two problems are training test-pieces.

***Circuit Training 6a+** Climb New Dimensions to the jug, swing left across to The Chute, then down it and traverse right and low into new dimensions and repeat!*
***Shorter's Circuit 6a+** Start at Elimination and traverse right to the arête with feet above the bottom break. Traverse back left again at the same level to Finger Jam, up Finger Jam to the break then reverse Circuit Training into New Dimensions. Move down to hang off the bottom break, then back up to continue Circuit Training. Enjoy!*

11. Chockstone Chimney 1+ (HD) Up the chimney using the chockstone.
12. Sculptured Wall 4+ (E1 5a) The right wall of the chimney is climbed on small elusive holds.
13. Sculptured Arête 6a (E3 5c) Start as Sculptured Wall but move right onto the arête until 2m below the top, then traverse right around the arête and move up to an awkward finish.
14. Heartbeat 6a (E3 5c) The right side of the arête moving left at the top break, to finish in a shallow groove on the arête.
15 Cannonball Run 6a+ (E3 6a) Climb up Heartbeat until a rising rightwards traverse can be made, then traverse the bulging wall across Grandmaster Flash to a good block ledge.
16. Grandmaster Flash 7a (E6 6b) Take the centre of the impressive concave wall on fragile holds with a high crux.
17. Mother of all Ketchup Bottles 7a (E6 6b) Climb up Grandmaster Flash, but as the angle eases traverse right on pockets to make the most of the bad landing.
18. Night Entry 1+ (VD) Climb up the corner on the right then pull round to finish up the arête of the buttress.
19. Rum Doodle 4+ Layback the corner crack with an awkward finish.
20. Rhum Dubh 6a+ The short wall using a small pocket and a mono. Keep away from footholds out right.

Just down to the right on a large boulder is the next problem.

21. Rum and Raisin 6b SS Start on holds at the top of a small crack and launch for the arête. Follow to finish with feet on the slab.

Lee Robinson on Rum and Raisin 6b

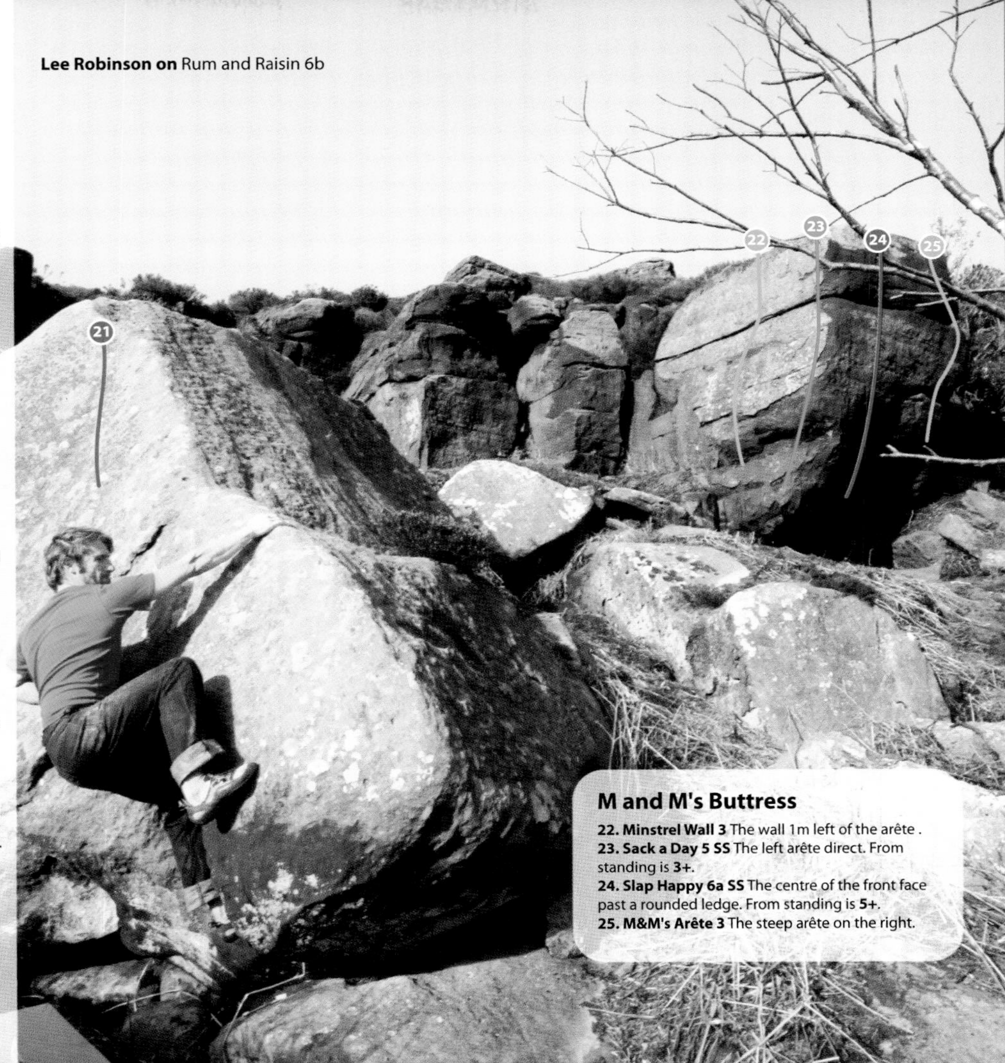

M and M's Buttress

22. Minstrel Wall 3 The wall 1m left of the arête .
23. Sack a Day 5 SS The left arête direct. From standing is **3+**.
24. Slap Happy 6a SS The centre of the front face past a rounded ledge. From standing is **5+**.
25. M&M's Arête 3 The steep arête on the right.

70m right is:

Cinderella and The Ugly Sisters

1. Beware The Thunder 6a (HVS 5c) Climb the wall at the left end of the overhang trending right to finish. Can also be finished up the crack on the left at the same grade.

2. Living in Sin 6a+ (E1 6a) The centre of the wall, making difficult moves passing the undercut.

3. Impressionless Lust 6a+ (E1 6a) Start 1m right of the last problem and make more difficult moves over the overhang, to reach the nose on smooth holds.

4. Cinderella 1+ The centre of the prominent nose starting on the right side and moving left as height is gained.

5. The Slipper 1+ Scramble up the dirty gully and climb up the crack in the wall on the left.

6. Ugly Sister One 3+ Up the arête on its left side.

7. Pantomime 1+ Follow the corner.

8. Ugly Sister Two 2 Climb over the bulges to finish up a slanting fault.

9. Direct Start 2 Up the face to finish as Ugly Sister.

10. Whazzup 5 Climb the undercut arête on its right, without bridging on the boulder.

20m right is:

Virgin Buttress

11. The Virgin 4+ The left wall on flakes.

12. Flaked Out 5 Climb up to a rail, then move up rightwards to a flake above the overhang and near the nose. Finish direct from here.

13. Obsessions of the Mind 6b Start right of the overhanging arête, pull up and swing left to reach better holds around the arête. Finish direct.

14. Hard Play 5+ Start as the last problem, then climb the overhanging wall trending right on fragile edges up to a two finger pocket. From here it's a long reach up and then moves leftwards. This leads to a finish near the nose.

15. Right Wall 2 Use the shallow corner flake to climb the right wall.

16. Hocus Pocus 2+ The blunt arête.

17. Back To Basics 1 Up the wide chimney.

18. Curtain Call 5 The short steep wall passing the left side of the overhang.

19. Final Curtain 1+ The final arête.

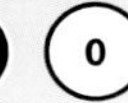

Stoney Wicks is situated a few hundred metres east of Barker's Crag. The rock is hard coarse sandstone and most of the problems are in the lower grades with good grassy landings - a great place to introduce yourself to bouldering. It's a peaceful escape from the the busier parts of Scugdale and has excellent views down the valley.

Approach: As for the right section of Barker's Crag. **See map on page 88**.

OS Map: NZ 527002
Walk: 20 minutes
Faces south

1. Introductory 1 Move up the slab using the arête and finishing left.
2. Layback Slab 2 The steep slab and top block, without use of the rock on either side.

The next three problems have no descriptions, are very close to each other and where possible take independent lines up a number of different cracks.

3. Crackers 1+
4. Loopy 1+
5. Loony 1+
6. Toper's Trouble 1+ The left arête, without use of the boulder.
7. Pick Pocket 2 The slab left of Y-Crack, without straying into the crack.
8. Y-Crack 1+ The excellent crackline.
9. Sober Sides 1+ The right side of the wall.
10. Blue Heather 2 The slab just left of the arête, using the break.
11. Free and Easy 1+ The arête throughout.
12. Nondescript 1+ The slab on the right.
13. Rockfall 2 The wall using the left arête but not the crack.
14. Lambda 1 The crack.
15. Tombstone 1 The tombstone-shaped wall.
16. Sepulchre 1+ The left arête.

Steven Phelps on Waltzing Matilda 1

17. Chagrin Left Hand 6b+ SS The left arête of Sepulchre, as a sit-start with hands on the lowest shelf.
18. Chagrin Right Hand 6b+ SS The right arête, again with hands on the lowest shelf.
19. Hanging Chimney 1+ The wide crack just to the right.
20. Elimino 2 The right arête of Hanging Chimney, without using the side buttresses.
21. Waltzing Matilda 1 Zig-zag up the slabby wall and around the small nose feature.
22. Solitairy 1 The slab on the left side.
23. Solitary 1 Straight up the front face of the small buttress.
24. Corner Climb 2 The overhanging left edge to a mantel.
25. Twisting Crack 1 The twisting crack.
26. Flake Slab 1 The slab to the right of the crack.
27. Pocket Wall 1+ The wall with an obvious pocket on slopey holds.
28. The Wave 1+ Traverse left and up the block from its lowest point, then pull over the centre of the nose.
29. The Wave Machine 1 Start at the lowest point and climb straight up the convex slab.

17 18 19 20 21 22 23 24 25 26 27 28 29

16

3

2

0

0

White Stone Boulders are a concentration of decent-sized blocks in an isolated location at the head of Scugdale. Most problems are low to mid-grade, with some highball challenges on the West Wall and a few shorter harder problems on some of the other boulders. The rock is similar to the rest of Scugdale; but unfortunately it doesn't get the traffic of the northern edges so lichen can be present. Bracken can be a problem in summer.

Approach: From the main parking, walk down the road past Scugdale Hall and go through the gates. About 50m past the woods, take a left onto an old four-wheel drive track. This goes uphill for 10 minutes to where a gate accesses the moor. Follow the track to where another to the right takes you onto a public bridleway. Follow this south and once a bend is reached near the top of the hill, head right so you can drop down just before the boulders. **See map on page 88**.

OS Map: SE 528991
Walk: 25 minutes
Faces west

James Rennardson on The Flutings 6a

White Stone Boulders

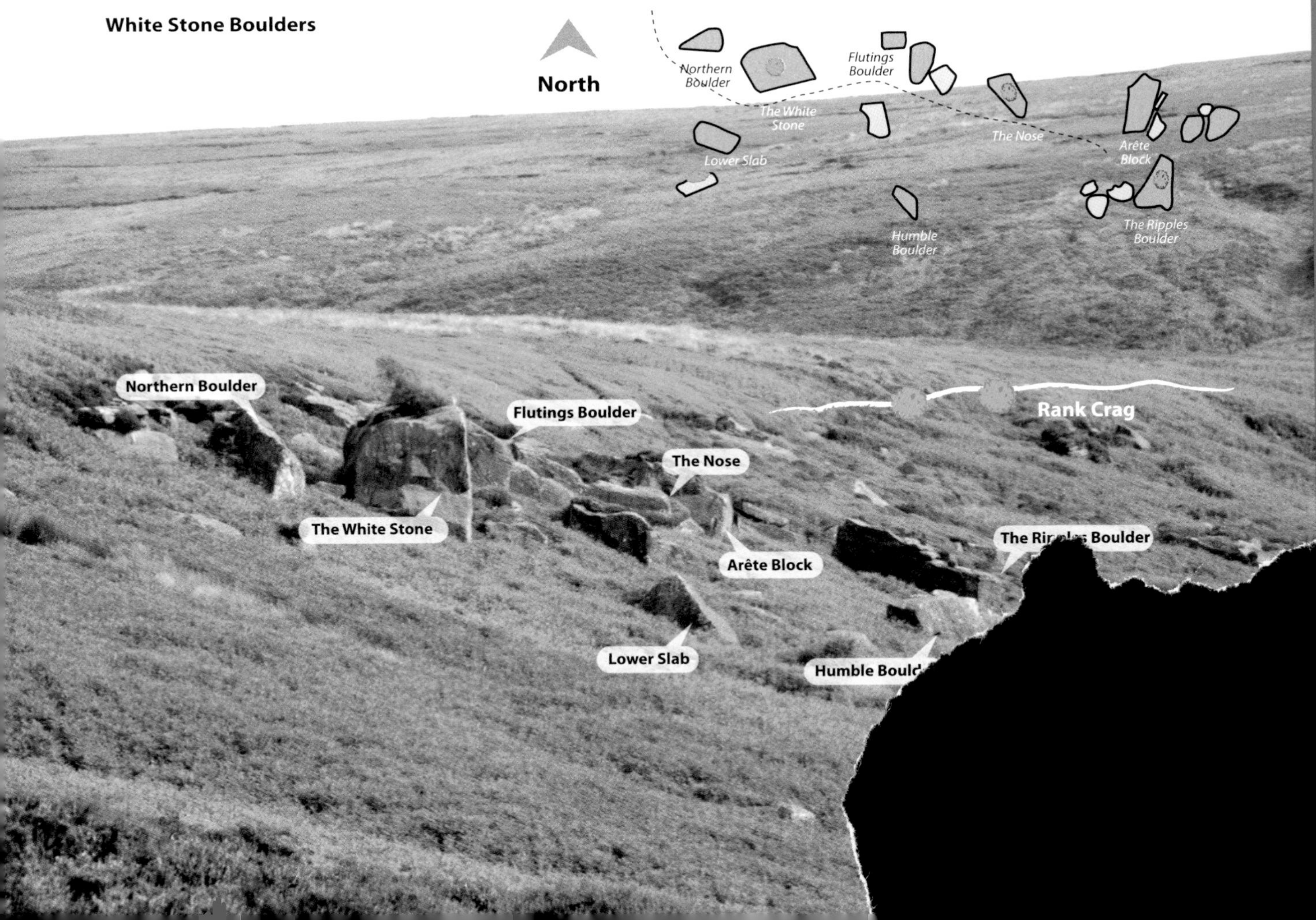

Northern Boulder

1. **Slap 4** Follow the first arête using the sloper out to the right.
2. **Redeemed 6b+ SS** Use a flake on the wall to reach the sloper, then finish slightly left.
3. **Blunt West Arête 6a** Start at a thigh-high incut foothold, move up and then head rightwards to a massive jug to finish.
4. **Arête Direct 4+** The arête to the right.

Lower Slab

5. **Scob 4** Layback the right side of the arête. Can be done from sit at **5+.**
6. **Baby Tic 4+** The centre of the hanging slab.
7. **Ledge 4** The right side of the slab moving leftwards on slopers.

Steven Phelps on Redeemed 6b+

The White Stone (Everest Boulder)

1. Rocking The Show 5+ The right side of the soaring arête.
2. The Buzzard 6b Follow the technical line of holds right of the arête to a heart-stopping finish. No arête at this grade.
3. We Close Our Eyes 6c+ Climb straight up to the sloping shelf on the west face, then mantel and finish direct.
4. The Shelf 6a Follow the line of holds on the left side of the arête to finish as the last problem.
5. South-West Arête 5+ Climb on the right side of the arête without using the crack system on the right.
6. The Slab 5+ Straight up the east face using two shallow horizontal cracks; with no further use of the crack.
7. 6b Use a sidepull and the blunt left edge of the groove to pull onto the slab. Finish with a pop for the top.
8. Short Groove 4 The obvious groove. Harder if done static.
9. South-East Arête 5 SS Up the crimpy arête to gain a shallow pocket, without reaching round to the jug in the groove.
10. East Side 4 SS Start on a low curving flake and climb direct to a large blunt sidepull, keeping out of the dirty groove to the right.
11. North-East Arête 5 Follow the blunt arête rightwards.
12. North-West Arête 5 Climb the arête on its left side to the flake, then up the obvious runnel.

Lee Robinson on We Close Our Eyes 6c+

Flutings Boulder

1. Ironstone 4+ The left side of the short wall on iron nodules.
2. 4 The centre of the short wall.
3. L'arête 4 The right arête of the wall.
4. The Flutings 6a The arête direct to the summit flutings. From standing is **5**.
5. The Nose 4 Over the small bulge direct.
6. Pockets 3 Just left of the arête.
7. Undertone 6b SS Start undercutting the break to another undercut further up on the right. Finish via slopers and the slot-hole.
8. 6a+ Start with a slot for the left hand and a blunt flake for the right. Pull onto the wall and reach for the sloping top. Finish direct onto the slab. Possible sit-start.
9. Nice and Spicy 6a+ SS The wave feature starting on undercuts and making a hard pull to the blunt flake. Move rightwards using the break to finish onto the slab above.

The Nose

10. The Prowler 6a SS The right side of nose without the arête, starting with the break.

Steven Phelps on Problem 8 6a+

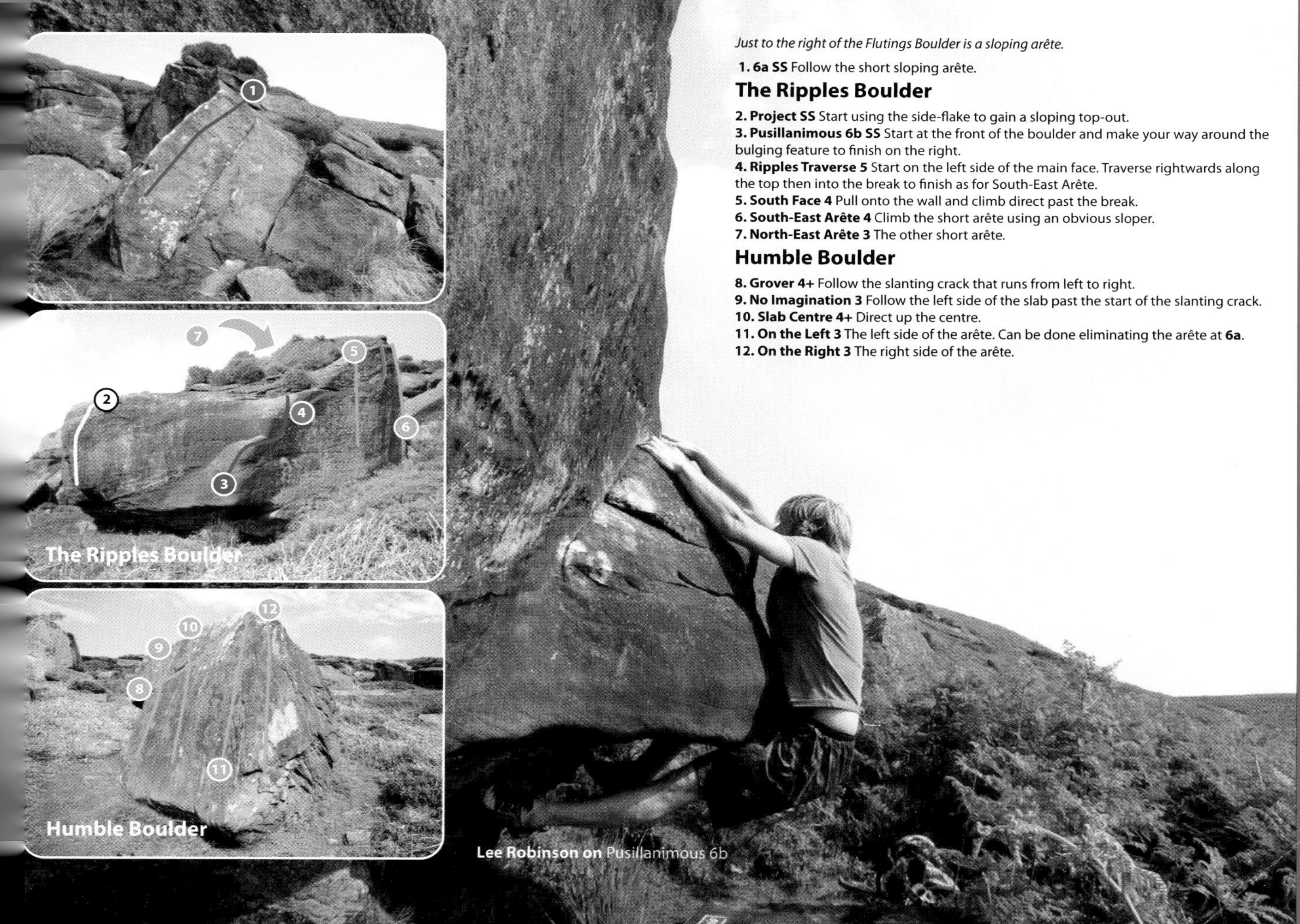

Lee Robinson on Pusillanimous 6b

Just to the right of the Flutings Boulder is a sloping arête.

1. 6a SS Follow the short sloping arête.

The Ripples Boulder

2. Project SS Start using the side-flake to gain a sloping top-out.
3. Pusillanimous 6b SS Start at the front of the boulder and make your way around the bulging feature to finish on the right.
4. Ripples Traverse 5 Start on the left side of the main face. Traverse rightwards along the top then into the break to finish as for South-East Arête.
5. South Face 4 Pull onto the wall and climb direct past the break.
6. South-East Arête 4 Climb the short arête using an obvious sloper.
7. North-East Arête 3 The other short arête.

Humble Boulder

8. Grover 4+ Follow the slanting crack that runs from left to right.
9. No Imagination 3 Follow the left side of the slab past the start of the slanting crack.
10. Slab Centre 4+ Direct up the centre.
11. On the Left 3 The left side of the arête. Can be done eliminating the arête at **6a**.
12. On the Right 3 The right side of the arête.

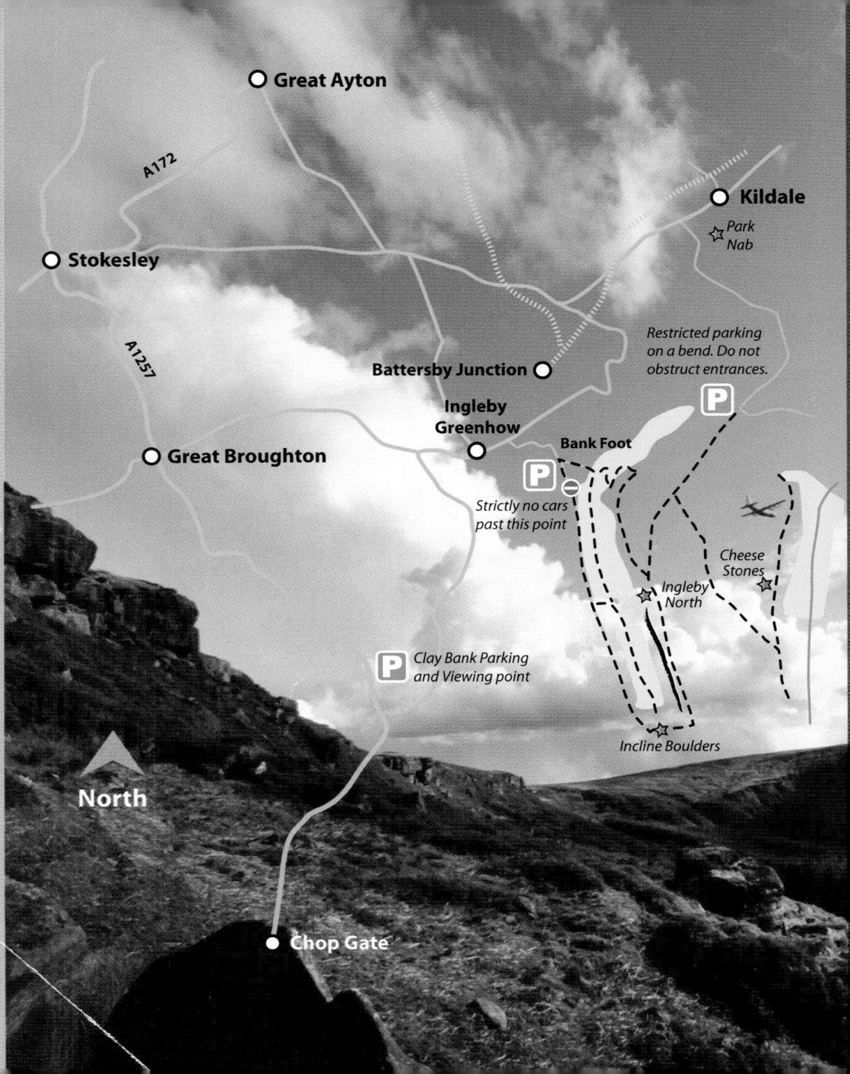

Great Ayton
A172
Kildale
Park Nab
Stokesley
A1257
Restricted parking on a bend. Do not obstruct entrances.
Battersby Junction
Ingleby Greenhow
Bank Foot
Great Broughton
Strictly no cars past this point
Cheese Stones
Ingleby North
Clay Bank Parking and Viewing point
Incline Boulders
North
Chop Gate

Ingleby Incline Boulders are located on an exposed stretch of Greenhow Bank on the eastern side of an isolated valley. The area covers just over a mile of hillside, from The Slug in the north to The Mushroom Boulder just above the incline in the south. Expect to do some walking if you wish to climb the majority of the problems. The boulders are good quality sandstone and stay clean throughout the year, although the few located in the woods may take some days to dry after bad weather. There's a wide variety of problems throughout the grades, ranging from easy-angled slabs and tough sloping arêtes, through to nice cracklines and several worthwhile traverses thrown in for good measure. Details of climbing on the main crag can be found at **www.climbonline.co.uk.**

Approach: Take the road leading east out of Ingleby Greenhow. Approximately 100m after the last house take the right turn which brings you to Bank Foot. At the first house turn right onto an old railway line and park at the left side on the grass. Please do not drive any further as this is a private road. Follow the track for 15 minutes where you will draw alongide a drystone wall in the fields to the right. Take the uphill track to the left where there has been some tree-felling. After about 100m, jump across a small stream onto a faint path on your left which passes a very large oak tree. This will take you up to the main central path and bring you out below The Slug and Waylander Block. If you are wanting to start at the Incline Boulders, continue along the main bottom track past the cottages and half-way up the Incline. This should take about 40 minutes walking from the car.

If you are planning to visit the North Boulders or any of the higher boulders only, an alternative way in is to use the limited parking at Battersby Moor. Take the turn south of Kildale bearing a sign for Baysdale Farm, and also part of the route of the Cleveland Way. This passes Park Nab and goes up Battersby Bank onto the moor. Pass a small cattle grid and then park considerately at the lay-by on a tight corner where the road drops down into Baysdale and the Cleveland Way goes south. Take the Cleveland Way through the gates passing the left turning to the Cheese Stones and after about 20 minutes you'll come to a T-junction. Turn left and follow the path for 5 minutes where blocks are visible to your right, then break off down the hill to reach the North Boulders 100m below the track.

OS Map: Central Woods NZ 598046 - North Boulders NZ 602040 - Carriage Boulder NZ 602041 - Incline Boulders NZ 603031- Cheese Stones NZ 615050
Walk: 25 to 40 minutes
Most of the boulders get lots of sun and are very exposed.
Wooded boulders need a few dry days.

Ingleby Incline was known locally as "Siberia" due to it's exposed position. Workers lived and worked at the Incline throughout the year. The 1891 census records show that two workers, a Joe Featherstone and John Collier lived in houses at Incline top.

Very different to the way it looks today, just a few remains are left of a bygone era.

The Incline was originally constructed as an extension for an industrial narrow-gauge railway in 1858. The line was owned by the Ingleby Mining Company which had started to mine the area for ironstone. Initially the railway extension reached a height of 1,200 feet above sea level and terminated at Ingleby, however in 1861 it was enlarged and extended to the top of the hill and across the moors to serve the much more lucrative but isolated Rosedale Mines. The incline was the scene of many accidents during the lowering of wagons of iron ore down the hillside and sadly several people were killed over the years of operation. The last locomotive was lowered down the Incline on the 8th June 1929, ending the important industrial history of the area. This is a shame as a train ride would speed up the approach to the boulders.

The top of the incline as it is today: Industrial archaeology

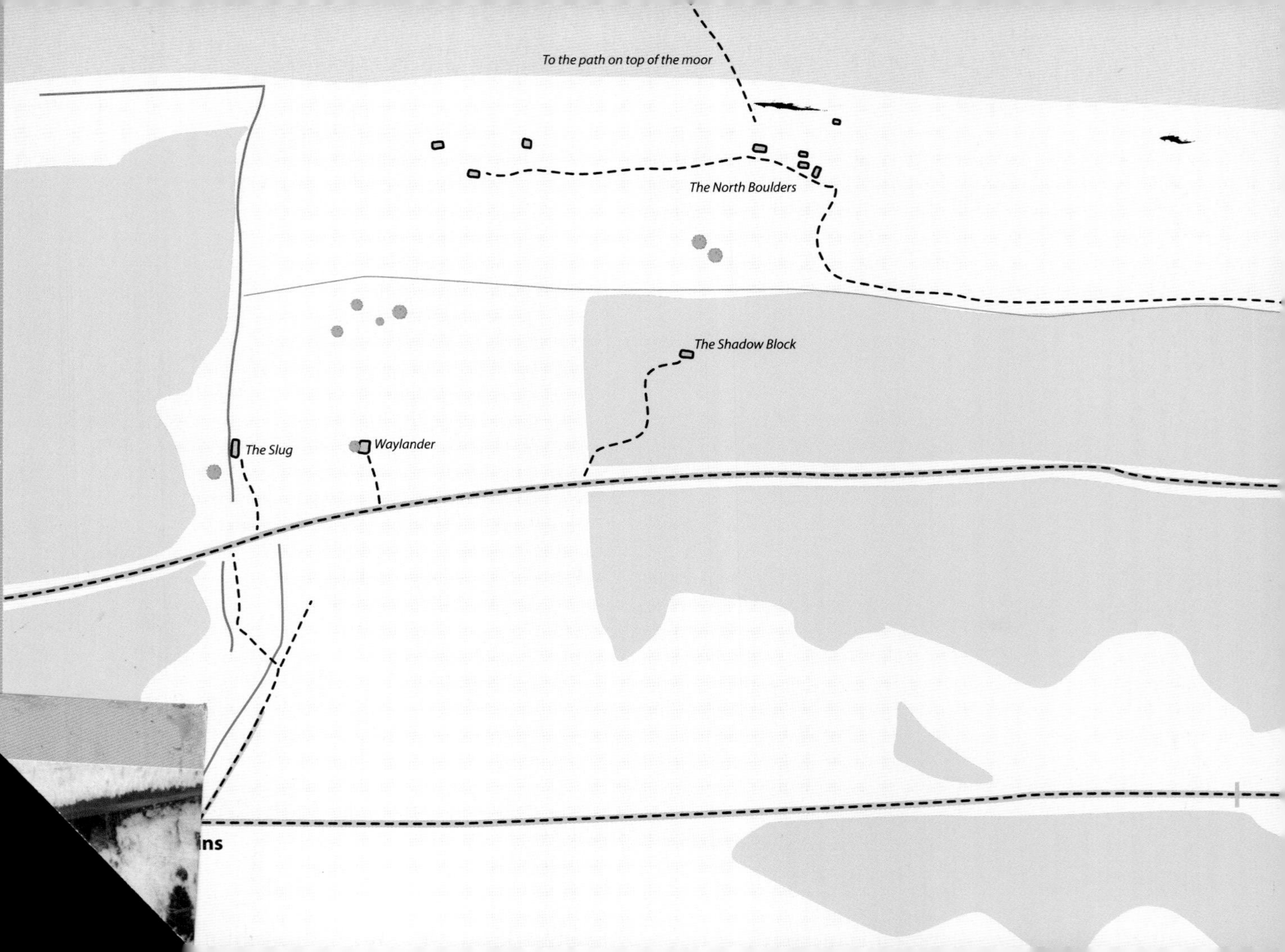

To the path on top of the moor

The North Boulders

The Shadow Block

The Slug

Waylander

ins

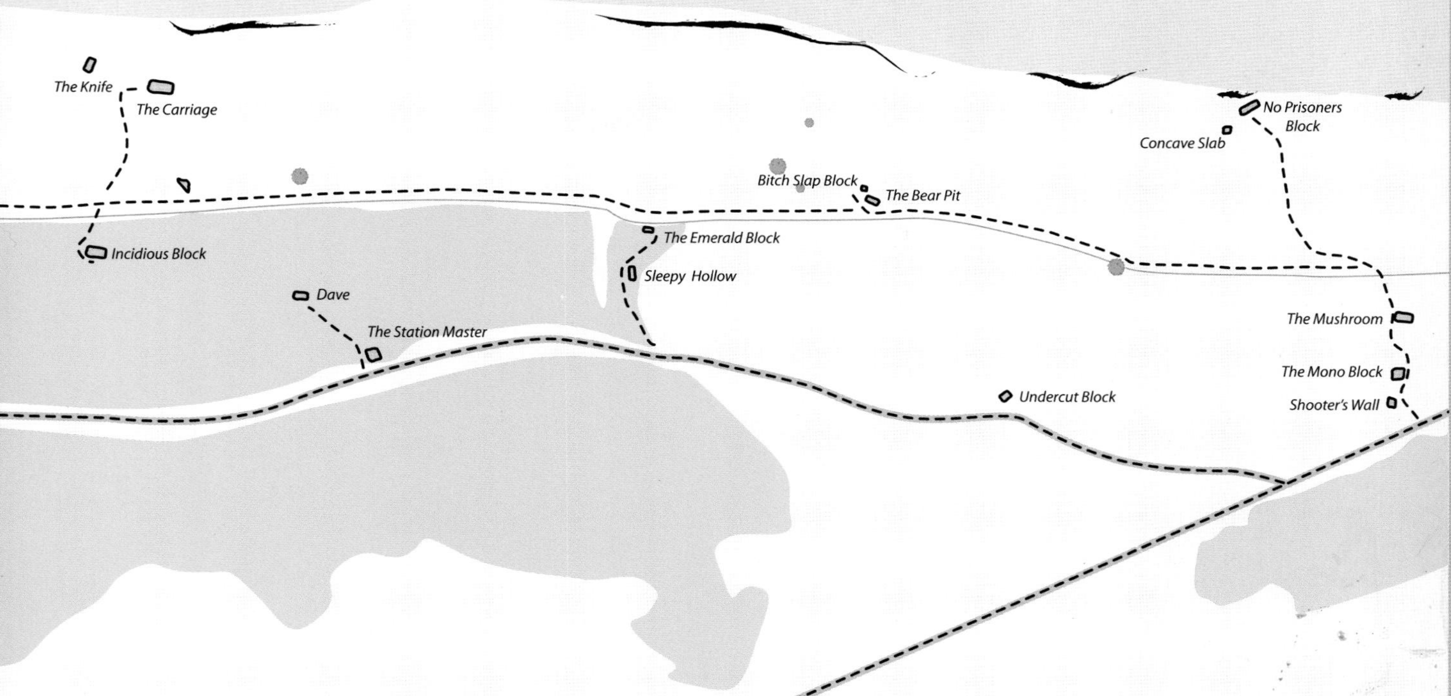
Moorland top track
The Knife
The Carriage
No Prisoners Block
Concave Slab
Bitch Slap Block
The Bear Pit
The Emerald Block
Incidious Block
Sleepy Hollow
Dave
The Station Master
The Mushroom
The Mono Block
Undercut Block
Shooter's Wall
Private houses

Chris Carr on The Lettuce 5+

The Slug

1. Slug Pellet 6b Start 1m right of the wall and gain ledges in the groove, avoiding the wall. Carry on up the slab.

2. Ditch the Car 7b SS Just left of centre of the sloping face. Pull on at the obvious hole and surmount the bulge with difficulty to get established on the slab.

3. The Slug 6c Climb the right side of the bulge using sloping sidepulls. The sit-start is a project.

4. The Right Slug 6c SS Climb the right side of the arête.

5. The Lettuce 5+ The side-wall in front of the tree.

Lee Robinson on The Slug 6c

Waylander

The large block you can see from the road below.

1. Moss Side 5+ The centre of the slab, just right of the tree.
2. Danyal Left Side 6a+ The bulging left side of the arête.
3. Danyal 5+ Follow the arête on its right side. Has a long reach finish.
4. Waylander 6c Climb the centre of the excellent main face by use of a crimp high up.
5. Third Eye 6a Start about 2m right of Waylander at two pockets and climb the wall direct.
6. Five Thieves 6a+ SS With a crimp for the left hand and low pocket for the right, pop for the top. Mantel to finish.
7. Chaos 5+ SS The short overhanging arête on the end of the block.

Steve Ramsden on Waylander 6c

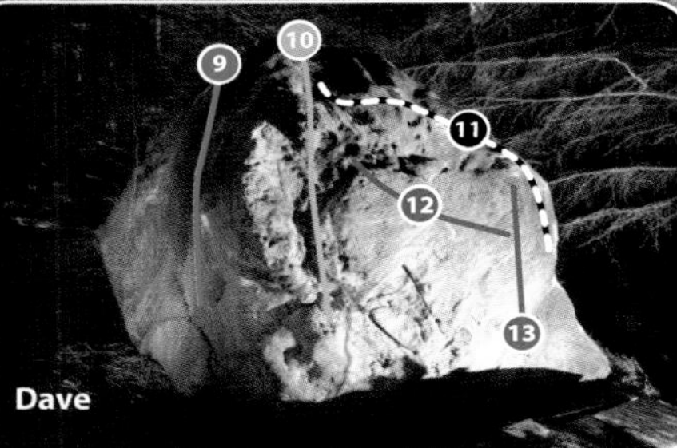

Martin Parker on Jaumermephantang 7b+

The Shadow Block

1. Illusions 5 A direct line straight over the obvious bulge. Often damp.

2. Shadow Caster 5 SS Climb the groove on flakes, starting with pockets. From standing is **4**.

3. Trash Talker 6b+ SS Climb the right arête to gain its sloping top. Move across on slopers to the obvious good flake-hold and finish direct to the highest point. From standing is worthwhile at **6b**.

The Station Master

4. Hannah Ward 5+ Climb the left slab starting at the lowest point.

5. Crack in the Wall 5 Climb the crack using jams or big laybacks. The choice is yours.

6. The Station Master 6b The left arête can be difficult to work out. The timid may jam the crack to finish, which doesn't affect the grade.

7. On Time 6a Gain the slab using the pockets.

8. Subterranea Britannica 6b Use a left sidepull and a right pinch to gain the slopers. Unleash some power and funky footwork to top-out.

Walk uphill and slightly left through the woods for about 60m to the next bloc

Dave

9. Criminal Badger Bonnet 6b+ SS The side-wall left of the arête, starting with obvious pockets.

10. Invisible Light 4+ SS The right side of the arête on bulbous holds.

11. Jaumermephantang 7b+ SS Start using an obvious flake. Follow the lip leftwards on sloping holds to the arête. Finish up this.

12. Teeratuu 6c+ Start at the flake-hold again. This time traverse left using holds on the face to finish up the arête.

13. Dave's Mate 6a SS Using the good flake-hold and undercut, gain the slopers and finish.

Walk uphill for about 10m from Dave. Follow a faint edge of more boulders for about 150m to the next block. It's about 20m from the top of the woods.

Insidious Block

14. Insidious 7b SS Climb the left wall on undercuts and crimps.

15. Big J 6a SS Climb the right wall on crimps.

Lee Robinson on Sleepy Hollow 7c+

The next area of blocks are located at the edge of the forest at its southern end. They look quite green, but clean up quickly.

Sleepy Hollow

1. Headless Horseman 7a Start with the left hand in the crack and right on a small hold out right. Pull onto the wall and finish using slopers either side of the crack.

2. Sleepy Hollow 7c+ SS The excellent sloping arête. Start using holds on the face and finish at the apex. **7b** from standing.

The next block just up the hill and right from Sleepy Hollow.

The Emerald Block

3. Yellow and Blue 5+ SS Gain the faint crack on the rising lip. Rock-up right to the large pocket and finish direct.

4. The Colour of Money 6a+ Climb the slab left of the arête, without use of the right arête. Delicate moves.

5. Envy 6a The sloping right arête has an exciting finish.

The Emerald Block

Incline Boulders

Pete Jackson enjoying the crimps on Aku 6b

Undercut Block

1. **Siberia SS 5** Start at an obvious hold and climb up using old bolt-holes to reach the top, then move right to finish.
2. **Underhand 6b SS** From a low start, aim right to a crimp, gain the undercut, to an easier finish.
3. **The Seat 5 SS** Sit on the block and then climb the flakes.
4. **Boring 6a SS** Better than its name. Climb the right arête on both sides using the bore-hole and some smooth holes to the right.

Shooter's Wall

1. **Beater 2 SS** Climb the left arête.
2. **The Big Flake Out 5 SS** Follow the ramp then finish direct.
3. **Direct Line 5 SS** Straight up.
4. **Hip Flask 6a SS** Start at the ramp and work your way rightwards on the crimps and pockets.
5. **Project SS** A hard start from a right mono!

Shooter's Wall

1. **Cheese Burger 6a SS** Climb the left arête of the slab. **2** From standing.
2. **Gun Dog 2** Climb the slab using the pockets and crack.
3. **Shooter 4** Climb the slab using the pockets.
4. **Boom 4** The right-hand side of the slab, over the bulge.
5. **12 Bore 5** Traverse the slab from right to left below the top.

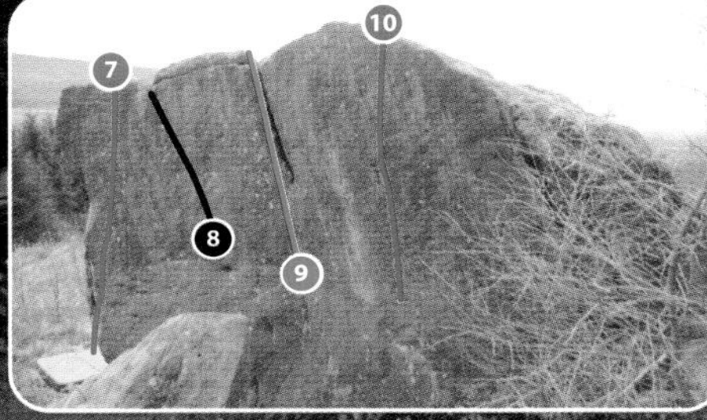

Mono Wall

1. Ronin Arête 6b+ Start at a flake at the extreme left end and work your way rightwards on sloping ledges. **Project from sitting.**
2. Inclination 6c SS Start on the slanting ledge and climb direct via a shallow break and crimps.
3. Samurai Jack 6b Gain the ledge via a side pocket, reach for a crimp and then match another crimp to reach the top (eliminate the crack to the right).
4. Smithy 5 Mantel the ledge then finish up the crack.
5. Aku 6b Start at the right of the ledge and climb the wall using a crimp.
6. Pleasant Arête 5+ SS Climb the right arête with a flake.
7. Avoiding Pleasantries 6c+ SS Start on the left side of the arête then pull round onto its right side to finish.
8. Out of Pocket 7a Starting a the shallow pocket climb via faint holds to the 'V' groove to finish.
9. Hanging Crack 5 The short crack.
10. Mono Wall 6c The concave wall by use of the mono with a long reach finish. Be careful.

James Rennardson on Mono Wall 6c

The Mushroom

1. Love Handles 5 The slab at the extreme left end of the block, without use of either arête.
2. 5+ Right of the crack is a pocket. Use this to climb the slab and join the right arête of the crack near the top.
3. Strict Machine 5+ Excellent moves past the two slits.
4. 6a Start at a sloping ramp and climb the faint crackline moving slightly right.
5. Strict Drill Sergeant 7b SS Climb the arête direct using the arête holds only, then top-out left.
6. Drill Sergeant 7a SS The right side of the arête utilising pockets.
7. Weekend Warrior 7a+ SS Climb the leaning wall on small pockets.
8. Groovy Baby 6a+ SS Climb into groove.
9. The Dish 6b+ SS Start on two obvious holds and reach for the dish, then top-out.
10. Parker's Traverse SS 6b+ Pull up to gain the lip, then head rightwards to a rock-over finish.

Martin Parker on Strict Drill Sergeant 7b

Mike Adams on Circle My Demise 8a

Head uphill from the Mushroom Block to the crag and a bit further north you will find a big leaning block.

No Prisoners Block

1. I Surrender 1 Climb the left side of the arête direct.

2. Circle My Demise 8a Climb the obvious challenge up the right side of the left arête of the face. Finish with a mantel at the top. There is one rule. Stay on the arête and holds just back from it, do not reach back to the very back edge of the block (used on I Surrender). Highball, with committing and difficult moves to finish.

3. Prisoner of War 7c+ The direct version of No Prisoners, using a pocket for the right hand and jumping to the sloping hold as the crack widens.

4. No Prisoners 6c SS The excellent slanting crackline. **6b** from standing

10m northwest below this is:

Concave Slab

5. Smooth Criminal 6b Use two distinct side-crimps and a high left foot to gain the slab and pounce for the left arête. Finish on good holds over the top.

6. Flustered 6a Mount the slab using the sidepull again and make for the right arête. Follow left to finish on the good holds.

Back down the hill, along the fence and to the north are two hidden blocks.

The Bear Pit

7. Big Brown Bear 7c SS The prominent blunt arête, starting in the pit.

8. Big Paw 7a This takes the side wall about 2m to the right using small holds.

Bitch Slap Block

9. Bitch Slap 7a+ SS Start with a hold above the lip and an undercut beneath the roof. Make a stiff pull off the floor and slap for the top to finish.

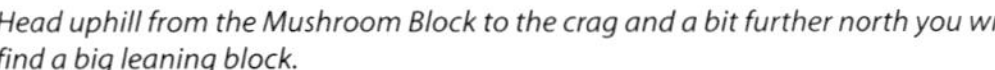

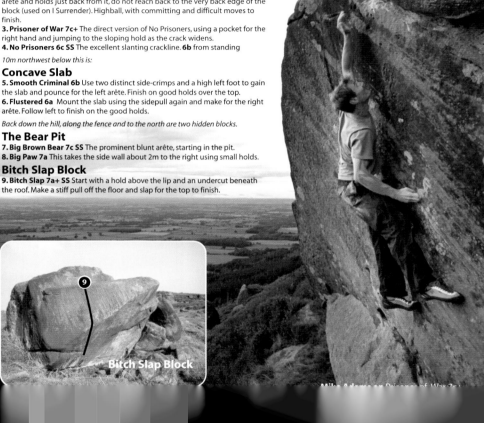

The Carriage

1. Juncture 7b SS Start on the left side of the blunt arête on slopers, then span up to a tiny crimp and finish using more slopers.
2. Expansions 7a Climb up using the crimpy left side of the ledge to gain the sloping right side of the blunt arête.
3. Removables 5+ Layback up the crack, then finish moving left up the slab via a sloping ledge.
4. 3 Start 1m right of the crack and climb up the slab direct aiming for a pocket high up.
5. 2 A direct line up the slab, via the slot.
6. 2 Start where the slab is undercut and take a direct line again.
7. The Signal 4+ Avoid the hole to the right and make precarious moves on small slopers direct to the top.
8. The Passage 3 Climb the arête on its left side.
9. Safe Passage 2 The arête on its right side.
10. Full Steam 5 Up the centre of the wall, without the arêtes.
11. Hard Labour 5 Climb the right side of the wall.
12. Grease Monkey 5 Ascend the groove, tricky.

The Knife

13. Give Blood 7b SS Start on the sloping ledge and pop for the top.
14. The Knife 7a+ SS From the thin crack climb the arête.
15. Like Butter 4+ Climb the layback feature. Can be tricky to figure out.

Steven Phelps on The Signal 4+

The North Boulders
Tank Block

1. Suicide Wasp 7a+ SS Climb the arête, then traverse left along the lip to top-out using a good hold and making best use of foliage!
2. Shorter and Sweeter 6b SS The arête using a pocket and a flake out to the left. Either mantel direct or move right to finish.
3. Western Front 5+ Use a thin undercut flake to pull onto the wall. Pop for the top and mantel.
4. Rhomboid 6a Use a sidepull and an undercut to pull onto the wall. Go for the top and mantel.
5 Boom 6a SS The right side of the wall using crimps.
6. Tank Traverse 5+ Start on the right side and make a traverse left along the lip. Once at the left end, use a pocket to mantel and finish.

Holly Block

7. Holly Arête1 Climb the arête finishing on its right side.
8. Prickly Balls 4 The centre of the slab direct.
9. Holly St 4+** The right side of the block, avoiding the arête.

Undercut Slab

10. Hole In One 4 Climb past the pocket on the slab. Interesting.
11. Bassless 4+ Gain holds in the upper scoop via a hole and finish. A sit-start has also been done using the arête at **6c.**
12. Woofer 1 The slabby right side of the arête.

Spire Block

13. 1 The left side of the slab.
14. Murphy 4+ The right side of the slab, without the right edge.
15. Refresher 3 SS Traverse right across the slab using a seam just below the top. Finish up a groove.
16. It's Just a Ride 6a SS Up the blunt arête past a sloping shelf.
17. Comet Crack 5+ SS The crack finishing as direct as possible.
18. Genesis 4+ SS The right flake-line with a mantel finish.

Martin Whitton on It's Just a Ride 6a

Steven Phelps on Hole in One 4

Edge Slabs

Edge Slabs

Lee Robinson on Pin Ball 6b

Edge Slabs

1. Edge Cracks 2 The cracks at the left side.
2. In Your Tracks 5 Move up to the ledge and climb the bulge above.
3. Allergic Reaction 3 Follow the scoop finishing once the ledge is reached.
4. Conspiracy Theorist 5 Just left of the vague rib using crimps. Heathery top-out.
5. Flake Wall 4+ On the right of the vague rib, past the flakes.

5m to the right is the next slab with just one problem.

6. Route 66 4 Climb the blunt rib in the centre.

Just past the high heather is the next slab.

7. The I.M.F. 4+ Start at a flake and climb the zig-zag feature with a mantel finish.
8. Incredulous 4 The line 1m right of the rib.
9. Route 1 4 The next line starting just left of a crack and passing a break.

The next slab on the main edge is about 5m to the right.

Midnight Slabs

10. Midnight Arête 3 Follow the arête using pockets.
11. The Shelf 5 Using the lowest pocket only, gain the shelf using a faint ramp for feet. Finish direct.
12. Project Straight up the blank slab by way of a small pocket.
13. Midnight Rib 5 Climb the blunt rib using crimps and pockets. Finish using the sloping ramp.
14. Midnight Crack 4 Gain the hanging crack from directly below and follow to the top.
15. Kola Cube 3+ Climb using the flake past the overlap to finish over the top block.
16. Wind Of Change 4 Just to the left of the heathery crack.
17. Way By 3 Start up the heathery crack and finish over the right of the large block.

About 8m to the right are the next set of problems.

Tilted Block

18. Traversity 5 Make a rising traverse leftwards until a runnel. Finish up this or past the large hole.
19. Slab Route 5 Climb to the shelf and finish direct.
20. Pin Ball 6b The right side of the sloping arête. A sit-start would be worth adding.

18
19
20
Tilted Block

150 metres north on the same level is the next area. You'll pass a high ovehanging prow which is unclimbed **(see left)**.

Elements Area

1. The Road to Damascus 5 SS The overhanging right arête on slopers.
2. Incisions 6a+ SS Straight up the overhanging face using a small undercut and a sidepull. Slap for the top and finish direct.

Above this is the another boulder with a thin block perched on top.

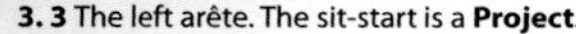

3. 3 The left arête. The sit-start is a **Project**.

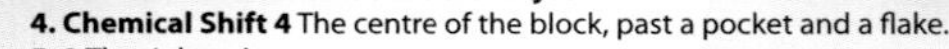

4. Chemical Shift 4 The centre of the block, past a pocket and a flake.
5. 2 The right arête.

Steven Phelps on Incisions 6a

The Cheese Stones

Remote moorland boulders, the best being a large split block with pleasant landings.

Approach: **See Map on page 124** Follow the road south as the Ingleby North directions on the single track road. Park on the corner were the road takes a sharp left turn. Head south-west, then take a left turn up a track that drops into a valley. The rocks become visible on your left.

OS Map: NZ 615050 - Walk: 40 minutes - The boulders get a lot of sun and are very exposed.

1. 2 Mantel the ledge on the left end and finish direct.
2. Pond Wall 4 Mantel the break in the centre of the wall and top-out over the large eroded hole.
3. Trapped in the Eighties 5 Mantel just left of the crack without using it.
4. Big Crack 3 Climb the crack direct.
5. Slippery Nipple 5+ SS Gain the crack and finish direct on a good crimp over the top.
6. The Big Cheese 6b SS Follow the crack leftwards and up on jams.
7. Project SS Starting under the roof, traverse the top lip leftwards to the crack.
8. Blue Cheese 7a SS A frustrating mantel over the centre of the slab, without the use of the right crack. Swearing is allowed.
9. Crackers 2 Climb the crack to gain the slab.
10. The Groove 3 Climb the groove to gain a well-earned jug on the right.
11. The Cheese Factor 5 Climb the bulge direct without the ledge for feet. Has an easier finish to the right in a deep eroded hole full of water, at **4**.

Lee Robinson on The Big Cheese 6b

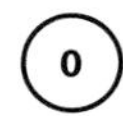

Jason Wood on The Lion King 5+ **Photo Jason Wood Collection**

Park Nab is a small crag just outside the village of Kildale, sitting prominently on the edge of Warren Moor. It is another venue where the line between bouldering and routes is a little blurred. Bold highball problems are the order of the day, mostly with good flat landings; though there are a few bad ones, even with pads. The rock is good solid sandstone, similar in character to that of the Wainstones. Unfortunately some of the crag's best lines were lost in 1995 when heavy rain and storms caused the left side to collapse.

Approach: From the village of Easby to the east of Stokesley and Great Ayton, drive east towards the village of Kildale passing parkland with a metal paling on the left, a National Park sign and two railway bridges: one metal, one stone. After the second bridge as the road goes uphill, Park Nab will be clearly visible up on your right. Take a right on a small road signposted Baysdale Farm (and part of the Cleveland Way) and follow this as it turns a tight corner and passes below the crag. Go over a cattle grid then park on your right at an obvious car park. Cross the stile and follow the path which takes you directly up to the crag.

OS Map: NZ 607086
Walk: 5 minutes
Faces north-west

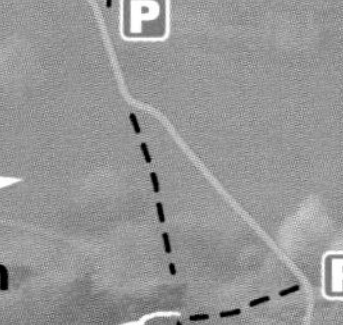

Kildale End

1. Slap Happy 6b The left wall at the far left of the crag, using old peg holes.
2. Weetabix 6a The scoop to the left of Dangle.
3. Dangle 6b The wall and then up the overhang direct. Bold.
4. Martin's Dilemma 6b+ An eliminate up the arête, without using anything on Lion's Jaw.
5. Lion's Jaw 5 Climb the corner then move up the hanging flake.
6. The Lion King 5+ An eliminate up the thin prow, without using anything from the surrounding routes.
7. Zero Route 4+ Make excellent moves up the thin crack and finish direct.
8. Cook's Gully Left Chimney 1 Climb left of the poised boulder.
9. Cook's Gully Table Top 1 The right of the poised boulder.
10. A Step Class 1+ Climb up to and follow the arête.
11. High Stepper 5 The middle of the left wall of the alcove to a good jug and a pocket. From here move up past a break, then finish.
12. Forked Crack 1+ The corner to the crack, after which small edges lead to the top.
13. Achilles' Last Stand 6a (E2 5c) The centre of the wall using pockets, small edges and a cool head. Finish as for Mowgli.
14. Mowgli 6a (E1 5c) From the boulders start up the right arête of Baloo until you can move out and stand in the horizontal crack, where a small edge on the left allows the centre of the wall to be climbed.
15. Baloo 4 The arête all the way.
16. Grumble In The Jungle 1 The forked chimney. Finish on the right-hand fork.
17. Bagheera E1 5c Start in the chimney but climb the wall on the right up to the break, then finish direct.
18. Twister E2 5c The bold arête to the right.

Kildale End

Kildale End

19. Twin Cracks 2 The excellent crack system finishing rightwards or direct to the rocking block. Left crack only **4+**. Right crack **3**. Neither crack **6a**.
20. Dynamo 7a This problem has got somewhat harder over the years due to ground erosion. Climb the wall by use of thin breaks moving left at first then finishing right at a small shelf.

Ladies' Gully

21. Left Gully 1 The gully.
22. Right Crack 2 The crack just to the right.

The Pinnacle

23. Pinnacle Crack Eliminate 4+ The wall between the cracks.
24. Pinnacle Crack Left Hand 1 The curving crack finishing right.
25. Pinnacle Crack Right Hand 1+ Climb up the overhanging crack at the edge of the pinnacle.
26. Pinnacle Face E2 5c The tall front face using the right arête if needed.
27. Chairman's Climb VS 4b Follow the wide crack to the ledge, then follow the leaning wall using a pocket or the arête to the left. The direct avoiding the crack and ledge is **5a**.
28. Chockstone Chimney 1+ Climb up the wide crack that seperates The Pinnacle from Jack's Wall.

Jack's Wall

29. Wall Bar Buttress 2 The excellent steep juggy wall to the right. Using the left crack only is **3**.
Parallel Lines 4 The right crack only.
30. Picture This 4+ The short wall to the right is climbed up to the large ledge then up the arête.
31. Scoop Chimney 1+ Follow the gulley to a choice of two exits, the best being the one to the right.
32. Pessimist E2 5c The excellent blunt arête with a taxing finish. Finishing right of the arête from the thin crack is **5b**.
33. Hara-kiri 4+ Climb the thin crack then follow the break to a point where there are a series of flakes and layaways to exit. The direct start is **5+**.
34. Longbow 4 This excellent feature does not let you down. Follow it to the niche then finish.
35. Bowstring 5+ Follow a thin crack and finish as for Longbow.
36. The Bitter End 5+ Gain the letterbox hold from the right then finish direct.
37. A Harder Start 6a+ A direct to the letterbox.
38. The End 4 The arête on the right.
39. The Very End 1+ The short crack just to the right.

The Traverse 6a+ *Start under the overhang of Slap Happy and traverse low all the way to The Very End.*

The Three Arêtes

40. 4+ The left arête on its right side.
41. 4+ The centre of the slab on good holds.
42. 4+ The right arête on its left.
43. 1+ The left side of the arête on the next block.
44. 2 The right side of the arête.

Steven Phelps on Twin Cracks 2

Martin Parker on Dynamo 1990s

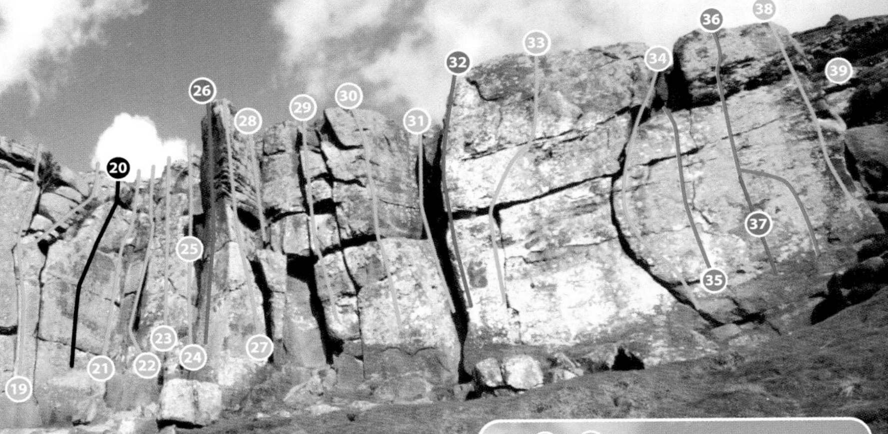

NOS Boulder

Several hundred metres south on the other side of the road from Park Nab is an excellent large boulder with some tesing mid grade problems on solid coarse sandstone. Mainly used for training by locals but any visiting boulderer will not be disappointed and will get a seriously good workout doing the many different eliminates to be found.

OS Map: NZ 609083
Walk: 1 minute
Faces west

The sloping block left of the NOS Boulder

1. Joe Mangel 6a+ Start on the left side at a sidepull. Pull onto the block and across to a pocket, then start moving down and right with feet 'down under', utilising a series of slopers to finish by rocking onto the slab after the good holds. This can be reversed from sitting at **6b+**.

The NOS Boulder

2. Boulevard of Broken Dreams 6b A traverse of the boulder in an anti-clockwise direction starting at a sausage-shaped sloper on the left of the main front face. Follow the ramp to a series of poor horizontal cracks then across to The Prow. Move round this on undercuts to a rest in the crack round the corner and move more easily round to the moor-side and finish where you started.
2a. An alternative diversion to this moves down from the good flake on the ramp to the break and joins back up with the original problem at the arête. This goes at **7a**. This can also be reversed at the same grade.
2b. Project Traverse dropping low, without using the shelf to the big pocket.
3. Westerley 6a Mantel the shelf and finish direct via the break. From sitting is a similar grade.
4. Western Front 6b+ SS Use low undercuts to gain the ramp then finish leftwards. From standing is **6a**.
5. Wild West 6c SS From the same undercuts as the last problem, move right to the waist-height hole, then make a difficult leap to the good flake-hold on the ramp. Finish direct on slopers. From standing is **6a**.
6. Mono 6a+ Climb the groove past the mono to another sloping finish.
7. West Wall 5+ Start at the circular jug and climb the wall right of the faint rib trending right. Can also be done with a dyno from the jug to the top at **6b+**.
8. Zorro 6c Start from the circular jug and traverse left along the low-level break until a dynamic move to gain the flakey ramp which you head down on slopers. Continue back up the ramp to a pumpy top-out finishing up Wild West.
9. The Prow 6b SS The prow topping out left. From standing is **6a**.
10. Rock On 5+ Start 1m right of The Prow and climb the wall using the crack and jug to the left to finish rocking onto a sloper.
11. The Scoop 5 Follow the obvious scoop.
12. The South Face 5 Straight up the high wall.
13. The Final Arête 4 Climb the left side of the arête.

Steve Ramsden on Boulevard of Broken Dreams 6b

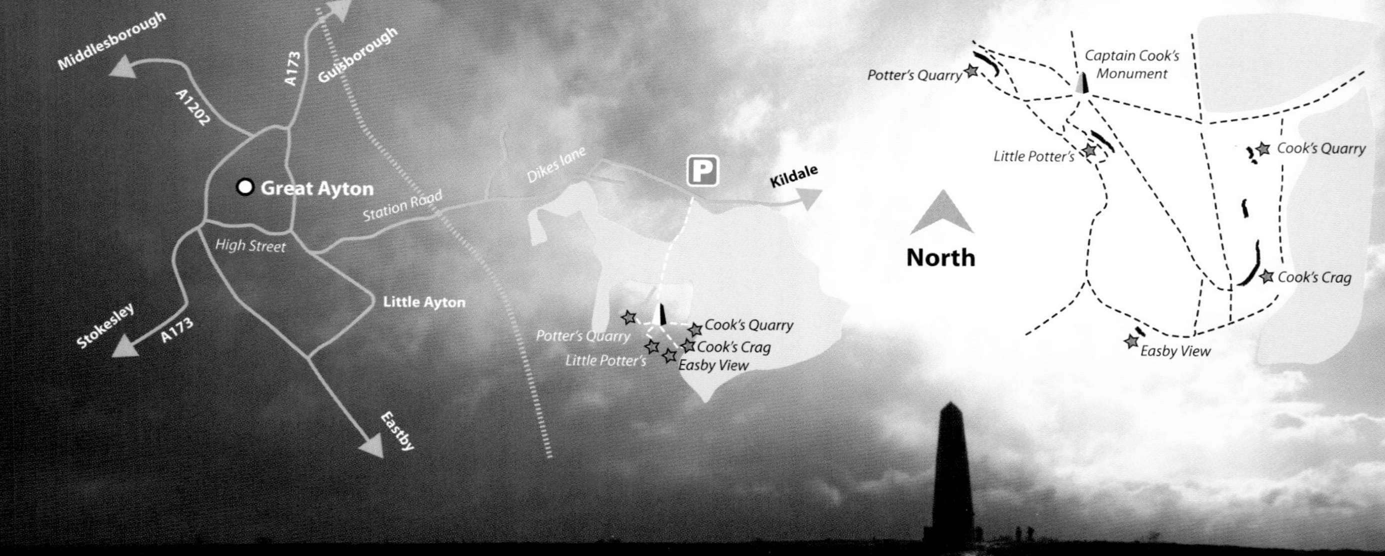

Captain Cook's is a collection of quarries and a crag on the the edges of Easby Moor, which is dominated by the magnificent Captain Cook's Monument, in memory of the great British navigator, explorer and cartographer, Captain James Cook, who spent his youth in Great Ayton. The rock condition varies, but on the whole is good and solid. Potter's Quarry has something for everyone, Little Potter's Quarry to the south-east, posesses a few short powerful problems and Easby View, some several hundred metres downhill, has a small selection of easy problems. The main crag, which is situated above the trees along the south-eastern edge of the moor, holds some excellent problems on fine coarse sandstone.

Approach: Make your way through Great Ayton High Street heading east with the river Leven on your right, pass the locally-famous Suggitt's ice cream shop on the left, after which the road bends leftwards at High Green, with its statue of James Cook as a young man. After High Green turn right into Station Road (you'll see the sign for the station). At the roundabout, take the first left following Station Road which changes its name to Dikes Lane shortly after the station. Continue for two miles uphill on the narrowing lane to Gribdale Gate car park, just after the cattle grid. Go through the gate and walk south on the Cleveland Way, up through Lonsdale Slack Woods. The main track goes directly to the monument. An alternative walk-in can be found by following a public bridleway west after parking just off the road at grid reference NZ 600102

15 6 2 1 0

Potter's Quarry is the first port of call from the main parking. It has fine views across to the Cleveland Hills and the exposed position on the edge of the moor ensures the rock dries quickly. The rock is good throughout and has various different challenges including some good cracks and bold high-ball walls. It's a nice spot to climb and take in the view.

OS Map: NZ 588101
Walk: 15 minutes
Faces south-west

Dave Crofts on First of Many 5

Potter's Quarry

Potter's Quarry

The problems are described right to left, as originally recorded.

1. First arête 2 The short arête.
2. First of Many 5 On the wall at the right side of the quarry. Follow the wall over a bulge on pockets. Excellent.
3. Voyager 4+ Gain the ledge then follow the wall direct past the breaks.
4. Square Corner Crack 1 The obvious corner.
5. Cook's Wall 2 The wall to the left using small holds.
6. Cook's Rib 1 Follow the nice prominent ridge.
7. Endeavour 1+ Climb the wall trending leftwards to a small ledge, then back diagonally right to finish.
8. Resolution Corner 1+ Start as the last problem and gain a wide ledge. Move across left to make an awkward move into a sloping groove and follow to finish.
9. Resolution Direct 2 Climb up into the groove direct.
10. Borboletta 6a The wall 2m right of the corner is excellent - with technical moves.
11. Poison Letter 6a A variation finish to Borboletta finishing on pockets out right.
12. Stretch 5 Follow the excellent crack to an awkward finish.
13. Zig-Zag 4 Start 1m left of the corner and follow the crack in the wall.
14. Potter's Wall 4 Climb the cracks and blocks to finish above the overhang on the left.
15. New World 7a Start in the sandy groove, gain the undercut, work your feet up and reach round the roof to a curved crimp-rail. Match on this to gain the good hold on the right of the arête, then the top, with a mantel finish. Take a couple of pads and a spotter!
16. Jumping Jack Flash 5+ The overhanging groove round the corner is awkward.
17. B.K Wall 5 Start at the initials B.K and climb the wall to finish at the top of Jumping Jack Flash.
18. G.B.G. 4+ Make moves up the wall past G.B.G. and up to the pocket and an excellent finish.
19. Friendly Gully M The obvious gully.
20. Friendly Ridge 2+ The ridge 2m left of the gully.
21. Friendly Wall 3 Follow the wall trending leftwards.
22. Tot 1 The corner on the left.
23. Flanged Wall 1+ Diagonally across the wall to the arête, with a mantel-shelf finish.
24. Flanged Wall Direct 2 Climb direct to the arête.

1
2
5a
3
4
5
6
7
8
9
10

6 3 3 0 0

Little Potter's Quarry is about 150m south-east of Potter's Quarry and although both are similar, the problems here are somewhat shorter. The rock is pretty solid and holds mainly low grade problems with good landings. A good place to spend an hour's bouldering.

OS Map: NZ 590100
Walk: 15 minutes
Faces south

The problems here have been climbed for many years and where possible the descriptions bear the names given by the first ascentionists. Give them a go and enjoy.

1. Don't Talk Coq au Vin 5 A traverse of this buttress using the head-height break. Can be extended to Fixter's Folly at the same grade.
2. I Can Speak English, But I Won't 3 The crack 1m right of the arête.
3. Derrière 5 Use a low undercut to gain the two-finger pocket and mantel to the top.
4. Merd 5+ From an undercut in the first break gain the second break and then mantel.
5. Nonchalant 5 SS Start on two pockets just to the right of Merd, then it's up to the break and mantel the top.
5a. Not So Nonchalant 6a SS Start at the first problem and traverse following the low break to finish up Nonchalant.
6. Claque la Putain 6b SS Start on slopers then move up to a finger pocket and finish.
7. Le Jardinier 6a+ SS Start at the small pinches in the crack and follow to the top. From standing is **2**.
8. A Certain Je Ne Sais Quoi 3 SS The arête from the right side.
9. I Would Speak French, But I Can't 4 Start at a slanting crack and climb straight up the overhanging wall.
10. The Route 3 The boldest line on the quarry, topping out on the upper tier.

There are also some problems on the short wall between problems 9 and 10.

11. Fixter's Folly 4+ The excellent arête at the far right of the quarry.

Tom McClure on The Route 3 Little Potter's Quarry

Lee Robinson on Hawkeye 4

7 3 0 0 0

Easby View is located 200m south-east of Little Potter's Quarry and is identifiable by a small holly tree on the edge of the moor. The rock is fairly sandy compared to the rest of Captain Cook's, worth the walk down as it holds some nice problems with good flat landings.

OS Map: NZ 590098
Faces south

1. Lure 1 Follow the ramp rightwards to the top.
2. Bewit 1 The slabby arête at the left side.
3. Hawkeye 4 The old peg crack is sandy but good.
4. Falco 5+ Climb the wall just right of Hawkeye to a difficult mantel finish.
5. Eyasses 4+The crack on the arête.
6. Jesses 1 The right side of the arête on good rock.
7. Easby Crag 1 To the right of Jesses, following the flakes.

Over to the right are the final problems.

8. Gyr 5 Gain a small shelf then move up the smooth wall.
9. Wild Side 2 The chimney with a large wedged block.
10. Antz 3 Up the wall right of the chimney.

Brandon Copley on Hula Hawke 6b

Cook's Crag is found by following the path south-east from the monument along the edge of the moor and crossing over a stone wall to join a faint path. There are several different buttresses and boulders with some excellent problems on good clean coarse sandstone, although some buttresses can take a few days of good weather to dry out. There's a fine selection of problems throughout the grades, mainly with good flat landings. Some of the larger buttresses are not included in this guide though details can be found at **www.climbonline.co.uk**

OS Map: NZ 592098
Walk: 15 minutes
Faces south-east

Cook's Crag

The first buttress you encounter as you drop off the moor onto the crag.

1. Easby Corner 4+ Up the arête.
2. Arty Farty 5 An eliminate up the wall between Easby Corner and Deviation.
3. Deviation 4 Gain the flake in the groove then step up to move right to a mantelshelf finish.
4. Deviation Direct Finish 5 Gain the two holes in the groove. Climb direct using the flake for the right hand.
5. Hula Hawke 6c A direct route over the nose using the small protrusion.

The wall in the gully.

6. Fibre Optic 5+ Climb to the nose from the slab edge round the corner, then finish up the nose direct.
7. Greasy Wall 2+ The centre of the wall finishing past some good holds.
8. Lambert's Wall 3+ Climb the right side of the wall on pockets.

The wall opposite.

9. Short Wall 1 Follow the diagonal crack on the back wall of the alcove.

The small block below the edge has a short problem.

10. Treasure Chest 6a SS Climb onto the top of the block via a thin seam.

Jason Wood on The Pinnacle Dyno 7a

The Pinnacle

1. The Hard Way 5 Gain the break then use a sloping crimp to finish.
2. The Other Way 4+ Climb direct to the crack and follow this to finish. Or dyno from the break to the very top **7a**
3. No Ledge 5+ SS Avoids a good ledge at mid-height and starts with a left-hand layaway make a balancy move to gain the break. Finish with a tricky mantel. **5** with the ledge.
4. Vague Arête 7a SS Climb the vague arête. Tricky to start. If you're tall and it feels easy, you're starting on the wrong holds.
5. Paul's Party Piece 6a Start at the arête, then traverse along the crimps below the top. Top-out as you reach the main break or carry on round the full block at **6b**.
6. Bag of Bones 6a SS The arête using holds on either side.
7. Seventeen Hands 6c SS The centre of the wall is quite frustrating.
8. Toothpaste Kisses 6a SS From a stretched out start, climb left on crimps to a mantel finish.
9. Trickster 6a A traverse of the block starting and finishing at The Easy Way.
10. The Easy Way 1 Start round the corner and follow the zig-zag crack which is also the descent.
11. The Pinnacle Nose 1 Start at the back of the alcove and climb the arête via the projection.

Christine Close night climbing on The Harp 5

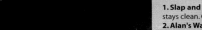

Alan's Wall

1. Slap and Hang It 6a An excellent problem which stays clean. Gain the obvious sloping shelf then finish.
2. Alan's Wall 6a Start at the undercut wall and follow the slanting fault.
3. Pimple Picking 6a+ The knobbly arête across the gully on the right.

Walk round the corner to the next wall.

Pobble Wall

4. Stone Cold 3+ Start from an embedded boulder. Climb the wall direct, finishing up a shallow depression.
5. Pobble Wall 1+ The sculptured wall right of Stone Cold, finishing up a short corner.

Situated below Alan's Wall is:

Harp-Shaped Slab

6. 4 SS From the right end, traverse the wall below the top, and finish up the left arête.
7. Harp Traverse 5 SS Make a stiff pull from the break to the top of the block. Traverse leftwards onto the west wall with hands on the top to finish at the top corner.
8. 5 Climb the bulge on slopers to finish up the slab.
9. The Harp 5 Start up the crack and finish up the slab.

Lee Robinson on Nimrod Variation 6a+

Mark Wilson on Submariner 6a+

The Boulder

Problems start from left to right.

1. The Boulder Ordinary 1+ Start left of the arête and move up past the ledge. Finish using the shallow crack just left of the arête.
2. The Boldest Yet 5+ Start just to the right of the arête and climb the wall.
3. The Boulder Direct 4 Start 1m to the right of the last problem and climb the wall to finish just left of the top block.
4. The Boulder Very Direct 5 Climb direct and finish over the top block.
5. Nimrod 6a Another direct problem. Use two small crimps and pass the deep break up to more small crimps and a high finish.
6. Nimrod Variation 6a+ Start as Nimrod and move right, undercut the break to gain the thin break above. Top-out direct.
7. Baldy 4 Follow the ramp into a scoop, then reach up to some obvious holes to finish.
8. Baldy's Traverse 4 Start at Baldy and traverse left across the break to finish just left of the top block as for The Boulder Direct.
9. Green Slab 3 Start just right of the chimney. Gain the slab and continue up into a shallow scoop to finish.
10. Rampart 1+ Stand on the small boulder to start. Step off into a slanting crack and follow to a small corner, then it's up and onto the slab to finish.
11. Rampant 5+ SS A direct start, finishing up Rampart.
12. The Brown Stuff 6b SS Start just right of the sit-start for Rampart and climb direct to finish using some good holds.
13. The Squeeze 6a SS Start deep between the wall and the boulder and climb up past the sloping break.

Round to the path side of the boulder

14. Low Tide 6c+ SS A low start using the sloping breaks.
15. Bay of Despair 5+ SS Start on a sloping break again. Pull up avoiding the short crack to a hidden pocket in the next break. Finish using the obvious side pocket.
16. Submariner 6a+ SS Start on the lowest break. Move up to the second break and make difficult moves to get to a hole out right to finish direct.

The next problems are in the cleft in the middle of the boulder

17. Project Starting low on the left side of the cleft.
18. Chimney Left Hand Variant 5 Tackle the nose direct from the broad ledge.
19. Chimney Variant 3 Start on the broad ledge again. Move up the shallow scoop to the right of the nose.

The next problems are on the right-hand side of the crag.

Veranda Buttress

Often green but worth it when dry. Give it a clean.

1. Out of Reach 5+ Start under the bulge, climb over this to gain a pocket then finish up the blunt rib.
2. Skulduggery 5 Start at the left end of the wall in front of a tree and climb the sculptured wall on fragile holds to a tough exit.
3. Dirty Tackle 4 From a good starting hold reach for the curving ledge. Step up and finish left up a dirty corner.

Just below is:

The Slab

4. Left Hand 1 An awkward start leads to the top.
5. Centre 1+ Start in a shallow depression. Climb the bulge direct to reach the top.
6. Right Hand 1 Follow the right side to the top.

Back up hill and right is:

Overhanging Buttress

7. Wasps are OK Really 6a Start under the arête and pull up to gain a good hold, then finish direct.
8. Stirrup 5+ Follow the blunt nose on poor holds. Old school tough.
9. Flanker 2+ The hanging scoop just right of the overhang via a ledge.
10 Brittle Band 1+ A traverse starting beneath the overhang, finishing in the gully.
11. Flake Wall 1+ Climb up the wall past a small ramp.
12. Gibber 6a Right of Flake Wall is a curving arête on a boulder. Climb up the left side until it is possible to move round to finish up its right side.

Jason Wood on Stirrup 5+

Cook's Quarry

The small quarry at the right-hand end of the crag contains some good test-pieces.

1. The Watchman 6a SS Quite powerful moves all the way up the arête. **5+** From standing.

2. The Wickerman 5+ SS Start 2m right of 'The Watchman', make a big move right to a ledge, then left to a pinch jug, then use layaways to top-out.

The next block is a slabby prow.

3. Cook's Wall 3 A rising traverse from the left end of the wall.

4. Marr's Attacks 7a An eliminate on the left wall without the ledges for hands and feet. From two small crimps, pop for a pocketed break, some tricky footwork, then pop for the top.

5. Men's Zone 6a Balancy technical moves to gain the arête to the top.

6. Captain Sausage Fingers 6b Straight up the middle of the front face using the sloping rails, starting with feet on the right block. No use of either arête.

7. Forty Years On 5 Climb the slabby block on its right side.

Brandon Copley on Men's Zone 6a

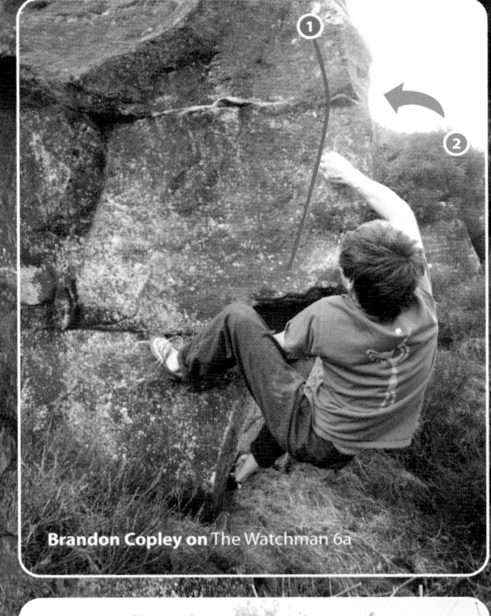

Brandon Copley on The Watchman 6a

28

9

13

9

0

Winter Wonderland Photo Jason Wood

Roseberry Topping is in a spectacular position with commanding views across Teeside, Hambleton and the rest of the Cleveland Hills. It was named after the Norse God Odin as 'Othenesberg' the 'Topping' being added later, and is sometimes referred to as 'The Matterhorn' of Cleveland due to the distinctive shape of the summit. The boulders are all within a small area below the main crag and hold a wide selection of problems from large bold slabs through to short arêtes. There are also smaller west and east-facing edges with some nice easy problems above good flat landings. Some of the rock is solid sandstone, though other parts are extremely friable and the crag above recently had a large collapse in 2010 so care should be taken.

Approach: The main parking for Roseberry Topping is a pay and display car park just to the south of Newton-under-Roseberry, on the A173 between Great Ayton and Guisborough. Follow the public bridleway which goes directly up the hill, through the woods and then out onto the moor. It's rather steep but the quickest way there. The venue can also be reached from the parking for Captain Cook's at Gribdale carpark, from which you head north along The Cleveland Way. A further alternative is Hutton Village on the edge of Guisborough, parking at grid reference NZ 597141 and heading south-west on another public bridleway. Both alternative ways take about 35 minutes.

OS Map: NZ 578125
Walk: 20 minutes
Faces north-west

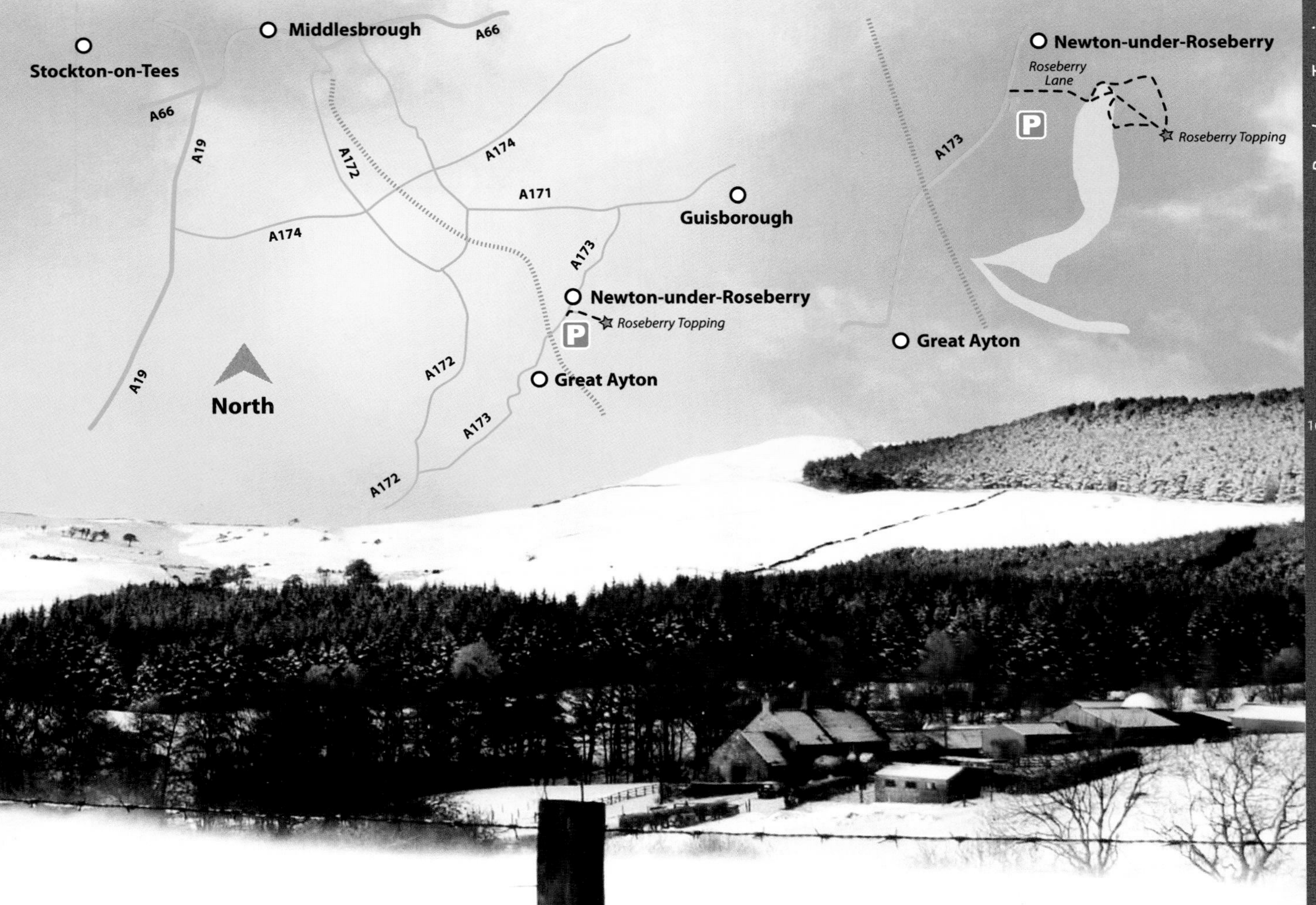
Middlesbrough
Stockton-on-Tees
A66
A66
A19
A172
A174
A171
Guisborough
A174
A173
Newton-under-Roseberry
Roseberry Topping
P
Great Ayton
A19
North
A172
A173
A172
Newton-under-Roseberry
Roseberry Lane
P
Roseberry Topping
A173
Great Ayton

Roseberry resident lizard charging up in the sun

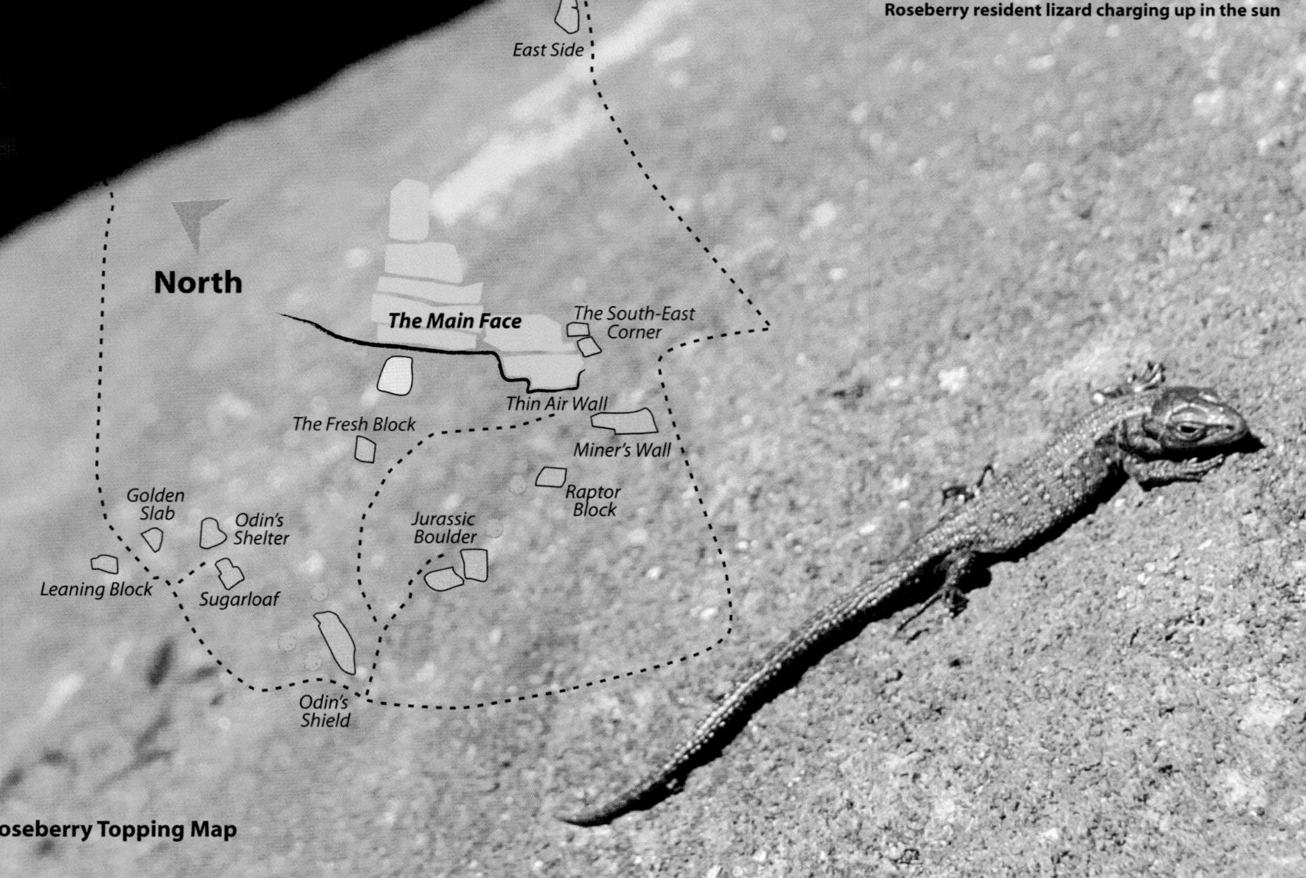

Roseberry Topping Map

Leaning Block

1. 4+ SS The leaning arête.
2. 4+ SS Climb the blunt arête.

Golden slab

3. 4 SS The left arête.
4. 4 The centre of the slab without the arêtes.

The Mighty Roseberry Topping

The Fresh Block

Thin Air Wall

Miner's Wall

Jurassic Boulder

Odin's Shelter

Sugarloaf

Odin's Shield

The Fresh Block

Up the slope below the left-hand side of the crag are some recently fallen blocks. The Fresh Block is uppermost.

The Fresh Block

1. 2 The arête on either side.
2. Organ Wall 5 Climb the centre of the short wall. Use no arêtes.
3. Organ Grinder 6c+ SS The nice arête on its left-hand side.
4. Fresh Meat 7a SS The arête purely on its right-hand side. Use a big pad or two as the landing is not great.

Odin's Shelter

5. 4 The left arête on the leaning block.
6. 4 The centre of the slab, without the arêtes.
7. 4 The right arête.
8. Asgard 7a+ SS Start about 2m inside the cave on holds on the left wall. Traverse out and rock-up left to make a pop for the ledge, then finish. Starting just inside the cave on obvious holds is **6b+**.

Sugarloaf

9. 5+ The short arête. No jumping for the top.
10. 5+ SS The central flake is a delight.
11. 5 The arête climbed on its left.
12. 3 The left arête.
13. 3 The centre of the slab, without the arêtes.
14. 4 The right arête.

Dan Crawford on Asgard 7a+

Odin's Shield

1. Hammer 6a Follow the left side of the block, with a tricky move to get the feet up high.

2. Weather of Weapons 7b SS From undercuts make a long move right to pinch the flake, use this to lock for the left arête and make a tricky move to bring the feet up to an easier finish.

3. Shield Maiden 7a+ Start on the under-cuts just right of the boulder. Pull up to edges, then use these to move leftwards to get established on the shield. Obviously the boulder is eliminated.

4. Odin's Grace 7b+ SS Start just left of the boulder on small crimps, pull up and use a heel-hook and some poor pinches to get the good half-edge. Use this to lock left to the layaway, get the left foot established, then finish precariously up the slab. **7a** from standing.

5. Legend 6a+ SS Start under the nose and finish direct.

6. Crack of Thunder 6a SS Start under the nose, make a strong move then follow the crack rightwards.

Jason Wood on Odin's Grace 7b+ **Photo courtesy of Jason Wood**

Lee Robinson on T-Rex 7a

Just up the hill from Odin's Shield is the:

Jurassic Boulder

1. 3000 BC 6b+ SS Sit on the boulder and climb the short left arête.
2. Shinned 6a+ Using a low sloping ledge with feet under the block, pop-up to the ledges. Rocking over the bulge is trickier than it looks.
3. Rex 6b SS Start on the right side of the arête, pull up to the obvious sloper, then rock around left onto the front face to finish.
4. T-Rex 7a SS The sloping arête on its right-hand side.
5. Stegosaurus 7b SS Climb up the centre of the wall not using either arête. Make a tricky finish using the two small crimps just right of the arête.
6. Newton Groove 4 The right side of the wall using the arête as and when needed.

Just up the hill from the Jurrasic block:

Raptor Block

7. Raptor 7a SS From a low sitting start in the cave, under the left arête, climb up and out using holds in the crackline to the right.

About 30m above the boulders and below the south-east corner is the next area.

Miner's Wall

8. Undercut Arête 6a SS Follow this direct. A standing start gaining the arête from the right side is **4**.
9. Miner's Face 5 Follow crimps up to a curving shelf for the left hand, then more crimps lead to the top.
10. Crack One 3 Follow the high crack without using anything else.
11. Carved Slab 3 The slab between the two cracks.
12. Crack two 3 Follow the short crack, using no other holds.

On the right end of the crag is a large wall with a prominent narrow shelf and attractive arête on the right side. All problems require spotters.

Thin Air Wall

1. The Shelf 6c Climb up on small edges to finish past the shelf.
2. Wings of Insanity 7b+ With the right hand on the small crimp-hold in the crack and the left in a very small pocket, pull up and use small holds to somehow get both hands on the shelf. Finish with the mantel as for The Shelf. Just as intimidating.
3. The Edge of Glory 7c+ SS Ascend the attractive twin arêtes using a tricky set of moves to get the good crimp high up on the right face and then on to a steady finish. An outstanding problem! From standing is **7b+**.

Mike Adams on Edge of Glory 7c+

Dan Crawford on The Model 6c

Next along the edge is:

The South-East Corner

1. Summer House Crack 1+ Start in the corner and climb up a short cleft to finish up an awkward crack.

2. Run From Home 3+ The arête to the right climbed on its left.

3. The Mantelshelf 4+ Round the corner the wall has a curving ledge. Ascend to this and finish direct.

4. The Cleft 3+ Climb up the crack using the narrow grooved wall for help.

5. Airyholme Chimney 1 The obvious wide chimney.

6. Havago 5 The peg-scarred crack without use of the chimney is good.

7. Neb 2+ Layback the flake to gain the ledge then escape up the slab above. Can also be climbed using the nose to the right.

8. The Alcove Left Hand 1+ The left-hand corner of the alcove.

9. The Alcove Right Hand 1+ The crack over to the right.

10. Dangle Direct Start 6a+ SS Straight up to join the finish of Dangle, starting on holds beneath the roof. **4** from standing.

11. Dangle 3+ Start over to the right of the last climb at a horizontal crack and hand-traverse left along the lip until it's possible to gain holds for the top.

12. Dangle Direct Finish 4 A direct finish to Dangle.

13. The Model 6c SS Start low and climb the difficult sidewall on crimps.

The last area is just off the zig-zag path round the back of Roseberry Topping.

East Side

1. Little Gem 1+ Up the centre of the wall using a high foot in a pocket.
2. Cleveland Way 1 The arête and crack right of the last problem.
3. Stook 3 The centre of the wall on good solid sandstone.
4. Eastern Promise 5 The blunt arête direct using anything on or around the line.
5. Pick a Pocket 4+ Start right of a carved cross then climb the steep wall.
6. Stepped Corner 1 Follow steps leading leftwards.

Steven Phelps on Stook 3

Apple Tree Rocks and Tarn Hole are a fine selection of blocks and buttresses spread across the western edge of Bilsdale East Moor, in a peaceful setting. The rock quality is excellent and has some varied features, with problems spread across the grades with harder projects and bold highball solos at Tarn Hole. To top it all the views are some of the best in the Moors. **See map on page 14**.

Approach: Parking can be found at a large lay-by near The Grange on the B1257 between Helmsley and Chop Gate at grid reference SE 573963. Cross the road, walk south and take the farm track to the left. Almost immediately take the left track to High Cowhelm farm until you reach the T-junction. Turn right and pass the farm and also Low Cowhelm Farm. At the next farm (Apple Tree Hurst) a leftwards path by the first barn leads through fields to a gate. Just after the stone wall separating the fields from moorland, take a faint path going left along the top of the fields. After around 10 minutes the first area of Cowhelm View Rocks is up on the right. The rest of the boulders are scattered to the north below Bilsdale East Moor, with the last area lying close to the outcrop of Tarn Hole.

Apple Tree Rocks
OS Map: SE 587967
Walk: 30 minutes
Faces west

Tarn Hole
OS Map: SE 592976
Walk 50 minutes
Faces west

Neil Furniss on Ever Fallen in Love 7b **Tarn Hole**

Todd Intake, Collar Ridge and the Badger Stone

Just north of Kay Nest are a few remote blocks of quality sandstone with a possible circuit for the remote exploring kind. Some cleaning is needed.

Approach: Use the same directions as Kay Nest. **(See map on page 23)** The first blocks at Todd Intake can be seen as you drop over the moor into Kay Nest. Just carry on up the other side of the valley and once at the top of the moor again, head north to reach the blocks. If you carry on east up the valley you will see the Collar Ridge Boulders on the opposite side of the valley. If you continue east on the track from Kay Nest, take the first track north and go straight on at the crossroads, you will get to the Badger Stone.

Todd Intake
OS Map: SE 585994
Walk : 1 Hour 15 minutes
Faces north

Collar Ridge Boulders
OS Map: NZ 587001
Walk : 1 Hour 25 minutes
Faces south

Badger Stone
OS Map: NZ 604004
Walk : Forget it, go on a bike!
Faces south-east

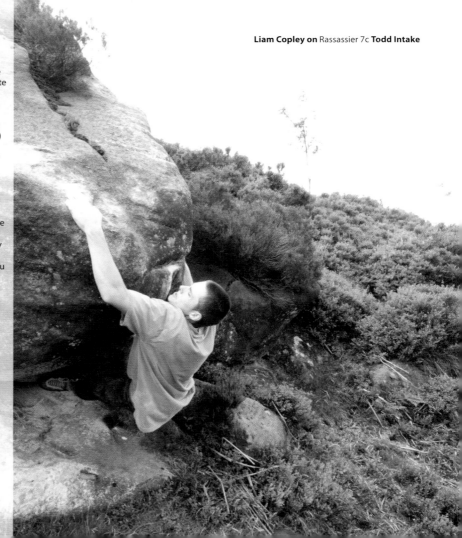

Liam Copley on Rassassier 7c **Todd Intake**

Liam Copley on Badgers 6b **Badger Stone**

Highcliff Nab perches like a castle above the sweeping woodland south of Guisborough. It holds a variety of intricate rock formations with a panoramic view to the north. The bouldering at Highcliff is a physical and technical trip into the history of Moors highball climbing. All the problems are crag-based, with many of these being old traditional routes that are now protectable with pads. Some of the best problems, such as the testpieces of Desperate Den and Moonflower, are climbed up to a logical finish part-way up the crag. With this approach the best moves of these fascinating lines may be enjoyed without the danger once associated with them.

Another nice block with a handful of bold problems in the low to mid grades is The Hanging Stone. OS Map: NZ 591134. A good place to gain your head for heights. The downhill face without either arête is a worthy technical challenge with a bold finish. This goes at **6c**.

OS Map: NZ 610138
Walk: 20 mins
Faces north

Lee Robinson on a Project

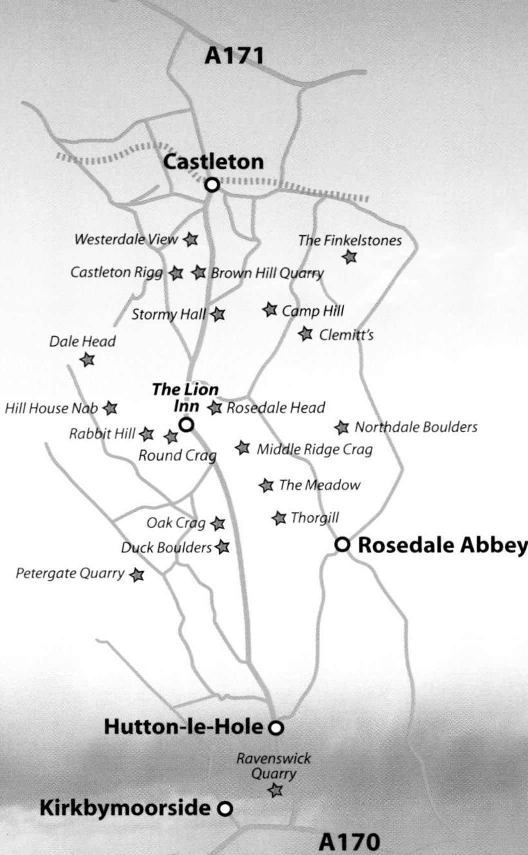

Blakey Ridge

Central Section

The majority of bouldering in this area is on or around the spectacular Blakey Ridge, which is surrounded by the wonderful valleys of Farndale, Fryup Dale, Rosedale, Danby Dale and Westerdale. Most of the venues are located on the edges below the exposed heather moorland and all have a different panoramic aspect of the stunning valleys below. Many of the venues have a short walk-in from the parking, making it possible to enjoy more than one in a day. The area also includes the only limestone bouldering venue on the North York Moors, the hidden quarry of Ravenswick, a good dry bet in wet weather. Beware! It's dark world of painful eliminates that you can easily get obsessed with.

4 6 13 10 1*

Ravenswick Quarry is quite simply a life-saving venue, well maybe not, unless you are obsessed with getting out climbing whatever the weather. The limestone walls are an invaluable training resource and are usually guaranteed to be dry unless there has been some seriously prolonged wet weather. A myriad of holds on a long stretch of slightly overhanging wall are perfect for eliminates and developing stamina. You can easily get obsessed with a hold, move or traverse and the possibilities for harder problems using some quite improbable holds are seemingly endless. The problems have good landings and don't finish too high, as the rock is less stable the higher you climb.

* The eliminate project possibilities are mind-blowing.

Approach: Ravenswick Quarry is situated in Ravenswyke woods on the road between the village of Keldholme on the A170 and Hutton-le-Hole (Gray Lane). About 0.6 miles north of Keldholme there's a small muddy layby on the east side of the road, near the telegraph poles. Park here. The path sloping down to the quarry is on the other side of the road just to the south on the bend, where the telegraph wires cross over the road.

OS Map: SE 711873
Walk: 3 mins
Faces west

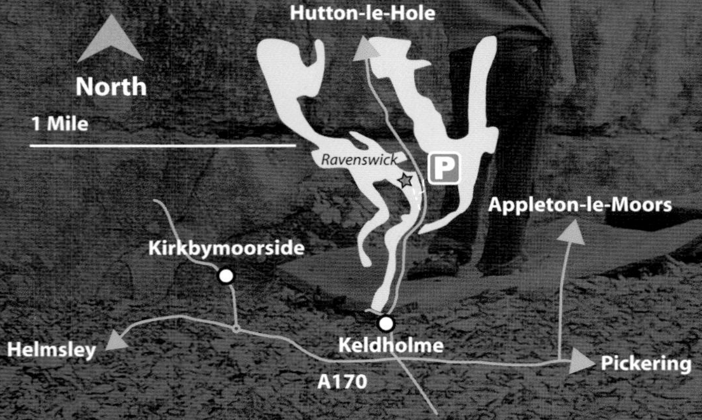

A very social gathering on a wet day

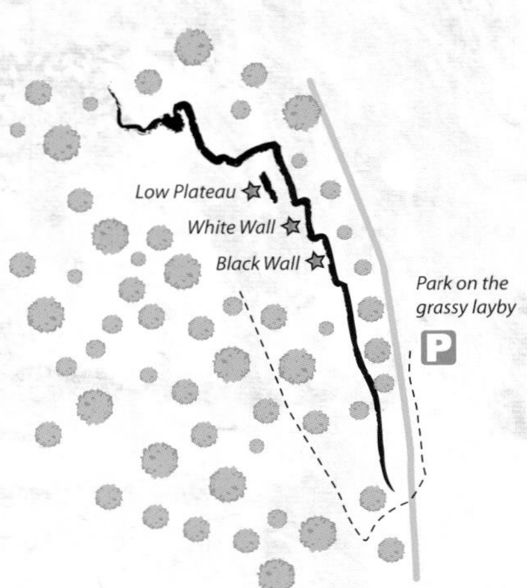

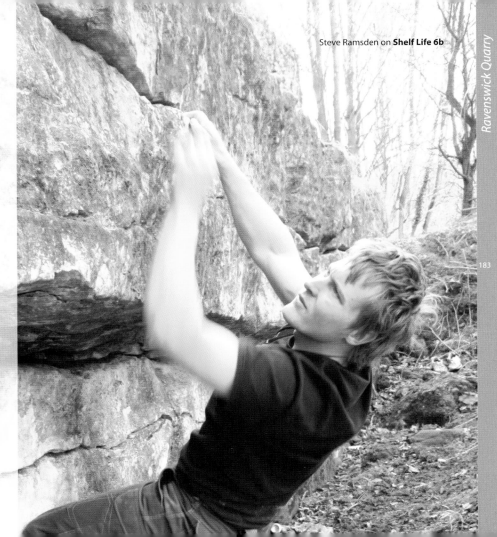

Steve Ramsden on **Shelf Life 6b**

Problems in the quarry start on the Low Plateau . This has an excellent traverse using the mid break of the overhanging shelf.

Low Plateau

Shelf Life 6b SS Traverse the wall from right to left using the thin crack above the roof. Top-out as the roof finishes.

The plateau also has some short 'straight up' problems.

Above this plateau is the White Wall with friendly short route-like problems plus a traverse well worth seeking out.

Beyond this is the Black Wall: the darker side of Ravenswick with its knarly, crimpy, pumpy traverses and frustrating, endless eliminates. Perfect for the obsessive boulderer.

White Wall

1. White Wall Traverse 5+ Start at the crack of the route White Crack (HS) on the left side of the wall and make a rightwards traverse, not going any higher than 3m to finish at the far right arête.

2. 5+ SS The wall 1m right of the crack. Makie a difficult pull off the floor and finish at holds near the crack at 3m high.

3. 4 SS The groove to the right on pockets, finishing at the half-height break, at about 4m.

4. 5 SS The boulder problem start to White Wall (E2 5c) is 2m left of the crack. Finish at the good crimp-hold 3m up.

5. 5 SS Climb the wall 1m to the right of the arête finishing at the half-way break.

6. 4+ SS Ascend the blunt rib just to finishing at the crystallized hold.

7. 4 SS The boulder problem start to Franco's Wall (E1 5b) follows holds around the hairline crack, finishing at a small hold on the crack 3m up.

8. 5 SS Without using the ledge on the right, pull up past an obvious hold to finish at another good hold 3m up.

9. 4+ SS The arête finishing at a small break around 3 metres up.

Lee Robinson on Problem 6 4+

Ravenswick Quarry - White Wall

- 1. **6c** Crack - pocket - cluster - small nobble - pocket - crimps - side crimp/flake - flake jug
- **2. 6b+ SS** Use the break to reach high to the petrified smooth crimp. From this climb direct up any of the crystal clusters.
- **3. 5+ SS** Traverse the low break to the layaway break , finish halfway up.
- **4. The Pigeon 6b SS** Break - pocket - nipple pinch
- **5. Dark Matter 7a SS** Break - side nobble - nipple pinch - side crimp - jug
- **6. Film Noir 7a SS** Break - small left-hand razor crimp - right-hand crimp above pocket - side crimp - jug
- **7. The Condor 7a SS** Break - pocket - poor crimp - jug
- **8. Bio Fuel 6b SS** Break - curved crimp - good hold
- **9. Marooned Eliminate 6c+ SS** Undercut break - crimps - side crimp/flake - flake jug
- **10. Special Brew 7a SS** Undercut break - curved crimp - sloping crimp - hidden jug
- **11. Hidden Treasure 7a SS** Break - curved crimp - twin crimps - sloping crimp - hidden jug
- **12. The Pinch 6c SS** Break - side crimp/flake - faint crystal pinch - top jug
- **13. Sam's Problem 6a SS** As above but using a pocket instead of a pinch: Break - side crimp/flake - left crystal pocket - top jug

Sam Marks eyeing the endless possibilities on The Black Wall

- **14. 6c SS** Crimps - no break - crimps - sloping rail - thin break
- **15. 6a SS** A tricky start - crimps - break - crimps - working up the crack to finish
- **16. Black Magician 7a SS** Side-pull - sloping crimp - left break crimps - break pockets - break
- **17. 6a+** SS Curved crimp - to left crimp pocket - quartz hold past the break
- **18. Destroyer 7a** Traverse the classic horizontal break of Black Wall from right to left, starting from the side-pull of problem **21**. Finish at the flake crack.
- **Project** Start at Problem **1** the **6c** traverse of Black Wall (See page 186), then reverse Destroyer, finishing directly from the sloper on problem **23** to the arête at the end of the wall!

Ravenswick Quarry - Black Wall Eliminates

19. 6a+ SS Sidepull jug - to break
20. Dark Times 6b SS Crimps on break - crimps next break - sidepull - good quartz hold - break
21. 7a SS Break - corner hold - right to a micro crimp - right to side sloper - up left to a quartz crimp - break
22. The Silence 7a Hold the side-sloper and a small crimp cluster - quartz crimp - break
23. 7a+ As problem **21,** but finishing on the arête not the break
There are many more eliminates and traverses not described here, just make them up and enjoy.
P
23
P
23
18
P

Duck Boulders

A collection of boulders about a mile south of Oak Crag, hidden on the slopes of Breckon Bank. There are some large boulders with a wide range of problems all within a 100m stretch of hillside, divided by a stone wall. In addition to bold slabs and highball walls are some excellent sloping traverses on good moorland sandstone. All have reasonable landings although care should be taken when moving around the north side of the wall as there are loose blocks and voids. For such a small venue there's a large amount to do for boulderers of all abilities.

Approach: Parking can be found on the Castleton to Hutton-le-Hole road at grid reference SE 691946.

From the south, leave Hutton-le-Hole in the direction of the Lion Inn and after around 2.5 miles you'll pass the S-bend of 'Stepin Turn'. Just after this park on the wide grassy verge on the left, near the green footpath sign. If you reach the tarmacked lay-by on the right of the road, you've gone too far.

From the north, drive about half a mile past the large tarmacked lay-by on the left and the parking is on your right after the green footpath sign and just before the warning sign for 'Stepin Turn' S-bend.

From the parking, follow the footpath west down the hillside to a wall. Follow the wall to where a small path breaks off to the right opposite a gate. The path goes downhill away from the heather. Take this for a few hundred metres where the top of the boulders will be visible to the north. Don't head there direct, follow the path down the slope and head up to the boulders along the stone wall which divides them.

OS Map: SE 684950
Walk: 10 minutes
Faces west

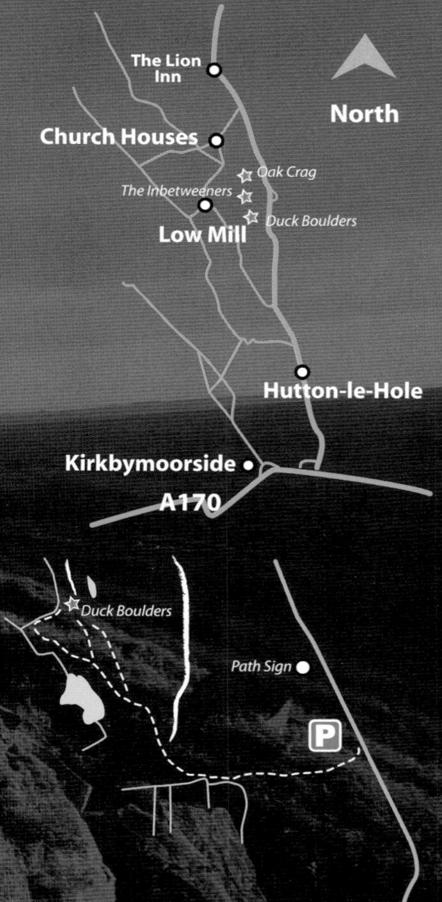

Lee Robinson on Perfect Sunset 6a

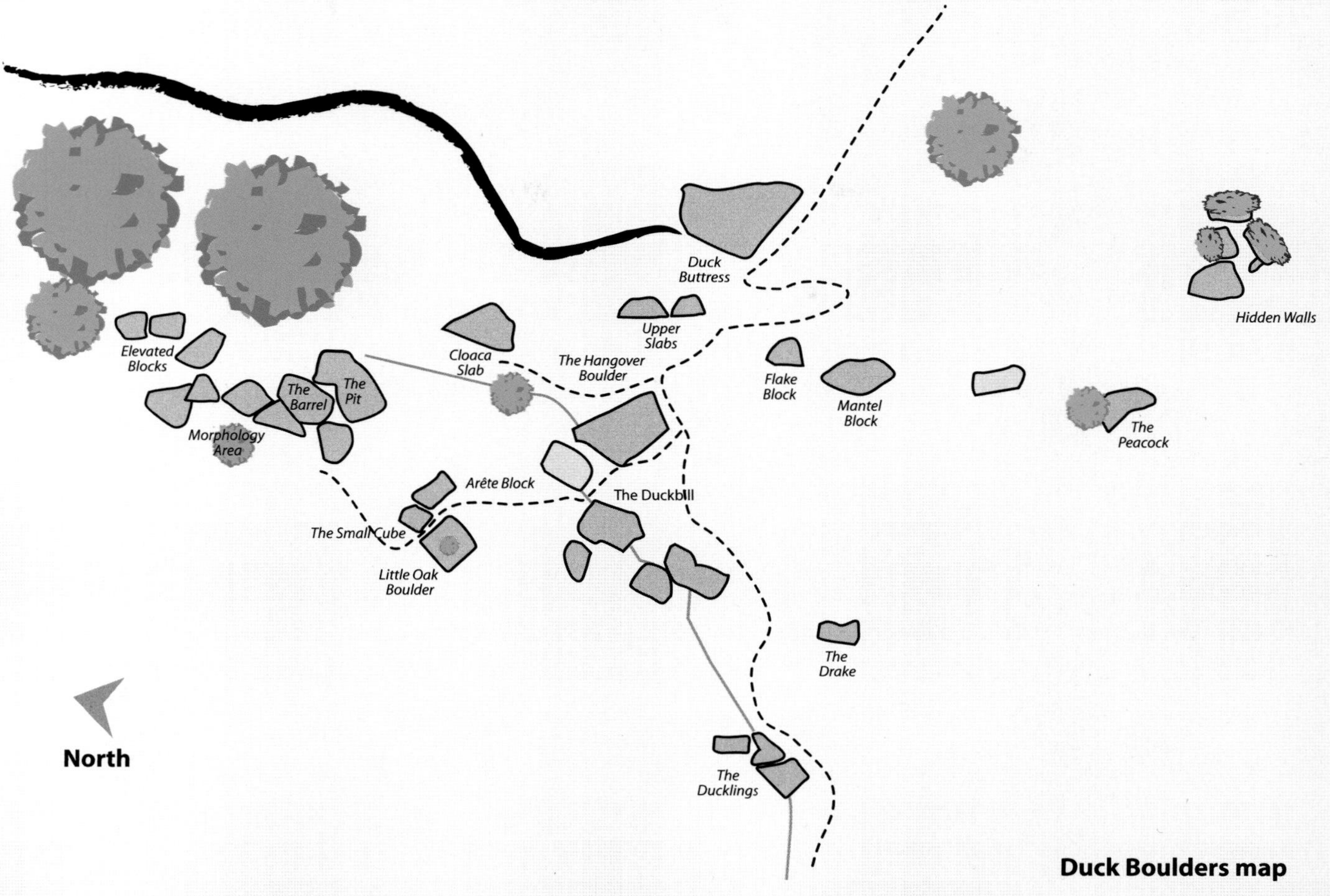
Duck Buttress
Hidden Walls
Upper Slabs
Elevated Blocks
Cloaca Slab
The Hangover Boulder
Flake Block
Mantel Block
The Barrel
The Pit
The Peacock
Morphology Area
Arête Block
The Duckbill
The Small Cube
Little Oak Boulder
The Drake
North
The Ducklings

Duck Boulders map

Mike Adams on True Morphology7c+

Problems are described from the north end of the boulder field. Just set back from the west edge are:

Elevated Blocks

1. Elevated 7b+ SS Start with hands on small holds. Pull onto the face and climb rightwards to the arête to finish.

2. 3 Start using a slanting shelf. Pull onto the wall and climb direct.

The next blocks are on the edge of the cluster.

Morphology Area

3. True Morphology 7c+SS Start on the built-up landing platform in the cave. Make a hard pull-up on small holds to get into a position to slap the good sloper on the lip. Match and make easier moves to finish. A short sharp shock!

The next slabs are to the right.

4. 3 The left arête.

5. 4 Smear up the slab using the left hand layaway and pockets out to the right.

The next block to the right.

6. 4+ SS The blunt arête direct.

7. 1 Direct up the centre of the slab.

8. 2 Climb direct up to the blunt flake, then finish.

Nigel Poustie on Sunbeam Ales 7a+

The Barrel

1. The Barrel 6a SS Using the sidepulls gain the lip and climb the groove to the left.

2. Belly Porker 6c+ SS Starting low in the pit (either standing or sitting on a mat pushed underneath) make powerful moves off undercuts to start and then sidepulls to gain the and climb the 'barrel' of the boulder. Do not use the groove, shelf or arête out left.

3. Sunbeam Ales 7a+ SS As The Barrel, then traverse right along the slopers.

4. Ale Beaming Sunshine 7b SS Reverse the traverse of Sunbeam Ales by starting from sitting at the right arête of the boulder, pulling on and traversing left by staying low at the lip to lock up into the higher slopey holds. Continue along these to finish by rocking around into the corner on the far left-hand side.

Over the top of The Barrel you will find a pit. In here is a long traverse starting as far back into the pit as you can. Will you make it out?

The Pit 7a SS Climb out of the pit starting as far back as possible. There's a tricky mantel finish over the lip.

Another worthwhile roof problem just behind The Barrel near the big oak is:

Fern Bottom 6b SS From a low start climb to the arête. Top-out left or right, the choice is yours.

Nigel Poustie on The Pit 7a

James Kitson on Fern Bottom 6b

Cloaca Slab

The huge slab in the middle of the cluster.

1. Regress 5 SS The left arête up on the blocks. Start at a sloping ledge and climb the arête on its right side.
2. Cloaca 6c SS Start using the lowest slot and the block beneath for feet. Once you've pulled onto the slab, break immediately left via a tough couple of moves on small holds. Teeter up the bulging slab to finish.
3. 6b SS Straight up into the vague scoop. From standing is **6a.**

The next slabs are up the hill below the crag.

Upper Slabs

4. 3 Centre of the slab utilising the small ledge on the left.
5. 5 The right arête starting with a small foothold on the arête. Reach for holds on the left to finish direct.
6. 3 Climb the left arête.

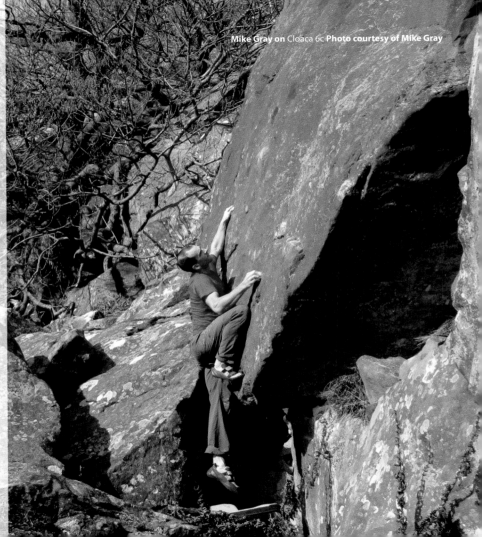

Mike Gray on Cloaca 6c **Photo courtesy of Mike Gray**

Little Oak Boulder

Back down the slope to the edge of the cluster is:

1. Anatidae 3 Climb the centre of the wall on nice flakes.
2. Hook-a-Duck 6c SS Start with the left hand on the arête and right on the bottom of the crack of Crispy Duck. Work your way up the arête. From standing is **4**.
3. Crispy Duck 6a SS Climb the thin crack.
4. Roast Duck 4+ The deep crack.
5. Mallard 5+ Start at crimps on a thin ledge. Climb direct making the best of sidepulls.
6. Drunken Duck 5 Using a thin crack and gaston on the right, pull onto the face and mantel the top.
7. Peking Duck 5 The thin finger crack system with good footholds.
8. Orville the Duck 5+ SS Climb the right arête, mostly on its right side. The blunt flake on the right is **4+** from sitting.
9. I Hate that Duck 5+ Hand traverse the whole boulder using the top of the rock for hands and anything for feet.
10. Duck Soup 6a From sidepulls climb the bulge.
11. Pancake Roll 5+ Over the bulge to the right-hand square pinch.
12. Quackers 4 Start 1m left of the arête trending right on better holds to finish.

The Small Cube

1. The Cube 6b SS Gain the lip and traverse right. Top-out round the corner. Finish up Cubism.
2. Cubism 6a SS The arête on its right.

Arete Block

3 . 2 The left arête.
4 .4+ The arête on its left side.
5. Project SS Very tricky, using small crimps.

The Duckbill

1. I'm So Throwed 6b SS With feet on a small boulder, take a pinch for the right hand and small crimp with the left. Use a heel/toe lock in an attached boulder and a left-foot smear to lunge up to a sloping jug, then progress right along the lip of the small roof on good holds to the arête. Mantel over to finish. **6c** without the block for feet.

2. Brewer's Gold 6b+ SS Start low on the lip working rightwards and top-out on the apex.

3. 6b SS Starting low in the depression using a right pocket and a layaway for the left, make a tricky move to avoid the block to the right, gain the lip and rock onto the slab.

4. 6a+ SS Starting on undercut pockets, gain the lip and rock onto the slab.

5. 6a SS Starting on the good ledge, gain the lip and rock onto the slab.

6. The Duck-billed Platypus 7a+ SS Start with your right foot on the very lowest hold and the left under the roof on a smear, plus your right hand on a large sidepull undercut and left hand on a high crimp on the arête. From here climb the arête direct to the top and finish around the left-hand side, over the top of the dry stone wall.

On the west face of the block is a short roof leading into a groove.

7. 6b SS Make a hard pull to gain the lip, pull onto the slab and climb with care up the groove.

Mike Gray on Problem 7 6b

5

Tony Simpson on The Duck-billed Platypus 7a+

The Ducklings

A

B

2c

3d

Over the Wall

The Drake

The Ducklings

The lowest and first blocks in the cluster.

1. 5+ The arête from standing.
2c. 6c A satisfying eliminate. Use holds A and B, pull on and pop up to hold 2c.
3d. 7a Another eliminate challenge using holds A and B, but then up to hold 3d.
4. Quackers 7b SS The obvious challenge of the centre of the boulder not using any arêtes. Pull on using the undercut edge in the middle of the wall and a small edge just left of the right arête. Dyno to the top and mantel direct to finish.
5. Gone South 6c+ SS The right arête staying on its left side to mantel the lip of the boulder to finish. **6b** from standing.
6. 6b SS The short prow.

Over the wall is:

7. 1 Climb the slab moving leftwards as height is gained.
8. 4 SS Gain the arête and traverse rightwards on the lip to the far end. Finish on some good holds.

The Drake

9. 6b SS From the left side on a sidepull, pop for a good small ledge and mantel this to gain the slab. Can be started on the right at the same grade.
10. The Drake 6c SS Get all your limbs in place then make a hard pull to gain a good hold. Top-out right on the face.

Lee Robinson on Problem 10 6c

The Drake

Mike Gray on The Hangover 6c **Photo courtesy of Mike Gray**

The Hangover Boulder

1.The Hangover 6c SS From the low holds under the arête, climb to the nose and pull onto the slab above.
2. Hanging the Groove 5 SS Start in the V groove, using the left hanging fin and the right edge. Climb out following the crackline.
3. Alka-Seltzer 2 Bridge up the grooved slab via pockets.
4. Hanging Corner 1 The shallow corner to the right, starting at a small ledge.
5. Aspirin 5 SS The left side of the arête. From standing is **3**.
6. Ibuprofen 3+ The right side of the arête past a large flake.
7. Beer Goggles 4+ The left side of the wall keeping left of the thin crack.
8. On the Lash 3+ The right side of the wall using flakes.
9. Grand Slam 4 The right arête on its left side. Classic.
10. Fine Ale 7a+ A hard eliminate on the left side avoiding the arête and the large flake.
11. Hair of the Dog 6b+ SS From undercuts, slap up to the flake and then grab the jug. Heel-rock over and top-out rightwards.
12. Green Gorillas 7a+ SS Without use of the flake, climb the crimpy wall to the right. This has two variations. One starting on a left hold near the flake. The other on a sloper further right. Both similar in difficulty. Harder for the shorter climber.
13. Green Vision 7c SS Start matched on the hold just right of the flake, then traverse right staying low below the good holds until you get your right hand on the good starting edge of Double Vision. Finish up this.
14. Champagne Charlie 6c+ SS Start with your right hand on a long crimp and the left hand on a low crimp, make a stiff pull to gain a layaway. Then fire up to a sideways crimp and pop again to easier juggy holds. Top-out with a smile. You can also do a harder left-hand variation starting with the right hand on the thin crimp, this is **7a**.
15. Double Vision 6b SS Make a long reach from a large crimp to gain the top.
16. Recollection 6c+/7a With the good ledge for feet and the right hand on a thin crimp, make a big move to a thin layaway. Finish up through the bulge utilising a pocket.
17. Crisps 5+ SS Climb the end of the block, bear hugging all the way.

Nigel Poustie on Fine Ale 7a+

Duck Buttress

The main buttress has some dodgy flaky rock on the top but is still worthwhile.

1. Lose the Love Handles 7a SS Climb the prow avoiding the block to your left and without use of the loose jug hold on the prow. Make some stiff pulls to gain a good pocket on the arête, finish leftwards.

2. Eyes Wide Shut 7a Climb the attractive left arête of the buttress, starting initially on the right-hand side. Once you get the good hold switch to the left side to finish using the pockets on the left wall. No feet right of the left edge of the right crack. A sit-start bumps the grade up to **7a+**.

3. Perfect Sunset 6a Climb up via the golden flake and pockets higher up. Top-out right on the ledge. Be careful, the top has some brittle flakes!

4. Beaucoup de Gifles 6c SS Climb the right arête using both sides. Brilliant.

Mike Adams on Eyes Wide Shut 7a

Flake Block

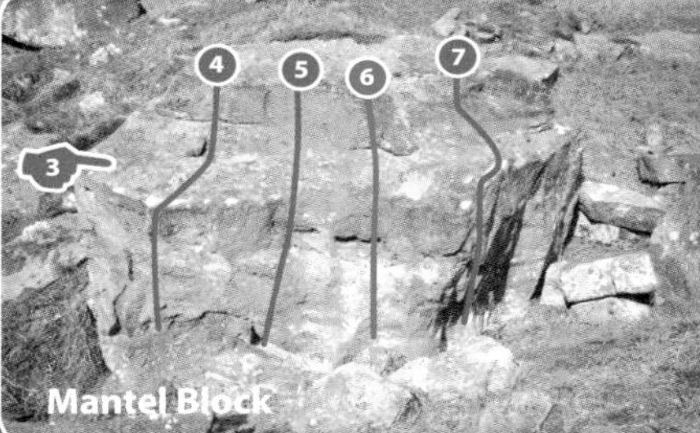

Mantel Block

Hidden Walls

The Peacock

Flake Block

1. 5+ SS Climb the flake feature on the left of the block.
2. 6b SS The right-side flake has a tricky low start.

Mantel Block

3. Leaning Traverse 5+ Start at the pocket at the left side of the block. Make your way along the top to finish as for problem 7.
4. 6a SS Climb up the short layaway feature to a tough exit onto the slab above.
5. 6a SS Start undercutting a large hole. Reach up and right to some small holds and finish direct.
6. 5 SS Climb direct using slopers and some ironstone pockets just left of the blunt arête.
7. 6a SS Climb the right side of the blunt arête using an undercut and an ironstone pocket. Once the top is reached move slightly right to finish.

The Peacock

8. The Peacock 5+ SS Climb the curving arête all the way across.
9. 6c SS The central line on the wall with no use of the arête.
10. 6a SS Make a strong move to gain the slab, then tackle the short roof.

Hidden Walls

11. 6a SS Climb the left side of the wall with a spicy top-out.
12. 6a SS The right side of the wall, just as spicy.
13. 6b+ SS The short technical wall. Don't top-out.

Lee Robinson on The Peacock 5+

Three worthwhile blocks half a mile north of Duck Boulders, just past a small wood. OS Map: SE 683955 **(See map on page 190)**

Best Friend Block

1. Too Close 2+ Climb up the arête trying to avoid the shrubbery.
2. Nothing But Something 7a Starting on the undercut, climb over the bulging arête, finishing up leftwards along the lip. A pumpy **7a+** from sitting.
3. Rogue Trader 6c SS A difficult start with a pinch and an undercut. Make your way up to the shelf using more undercuts, then top-out.
4. Empty Pockets 7a Straight up through the pocket and pointed ledge to the top lip. From this gain a good hold further back on the top. The sitting start adds some nice moves but doesn't change the grade.
5. Bumder 6c SS Start at a layaway and make a difficult move to better holds. From these make an even more difficult move to a sloping top-out.
6. Hand Job 5+ SS Climb the right arête mostly on its right side.

Bus Stop Block

7. The Tramp 5 SS Climb the left wall inside the gully, heading left on good holds.
8. Carli 6b SS From a hard start in the middle of the gully, climb direct to a mantel finish.
9. Tramp's Shoes 7b Start at a rail and climb the prow, with use of the pinch mono. Finish up the slab.
10. Crap Yellow Car 6a Start under the roof, then pull rightwards onto the wall. Finish up the left side of the slab.
11. Sleepy Time 2+ Start just right of the shallow cave, reach for a small sloper then up to a larger one. Finish direct to the highest point.
12. Black Bull 3 Start as the last problem. Reach right to a sidepull then climb up the thin slab, past a break in a shallow to the top.
13. Tara 3 Start as per the last two problems and traverse right keeping feet above the small overlap. Cross to the arête and finish up this.

Just up the hill to the left is:

Hawaii Wall

14. Caravan Club 3 SS Start at the rib where the floor begins to slope upwards. Mantel the shelf and finish direct.
15. Mr Gilbert 3+ SS Start at an obvious sidepull. Climb the shallow scoop via a pocket, then mantel the shelf. Finish direct.
16. 3+ SS Start at a black ledge and use this to climb direct up the slab.
17. 4+ SS Start as the last problem, then move rightwards using undercuts to finish up the crack.

Franco Cookson on Tramp's Shoes 7b

Oak Crag is situated on the edge of Farndale with fantastic views into the valley below. The bouldering described here is mainly centered around North Buttress with a few other boulders scattered below Oak Buttress. There are some good problems to be found on solid sandstone, the highlight of which is the excellent Oak Wall on North Buttress.

Approach: Parking is on the Castleton to Hutton-le-Hole main road on Blakey Ridge. Look for where the grouse butts straddle the road at around grid reference SE 689960. Park on the west side of the road at a small lay-by and follow the grouse butts running down the hill, using a small path to the left hand side. Break off right at the sixth shooting butt to get to North Buttress. **See map on page 190**.

OS Map: SE 684961
Walk: 15 minutes
Faces west

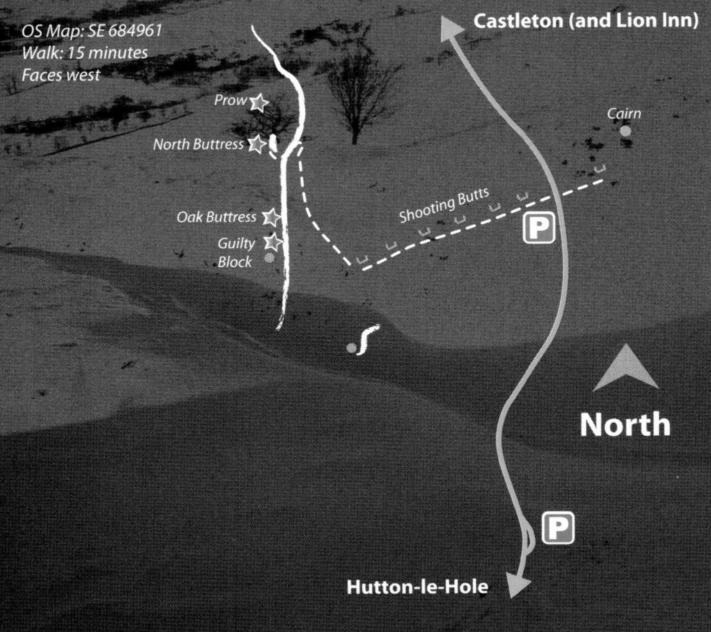

Winter drifts walking into Oak Crag

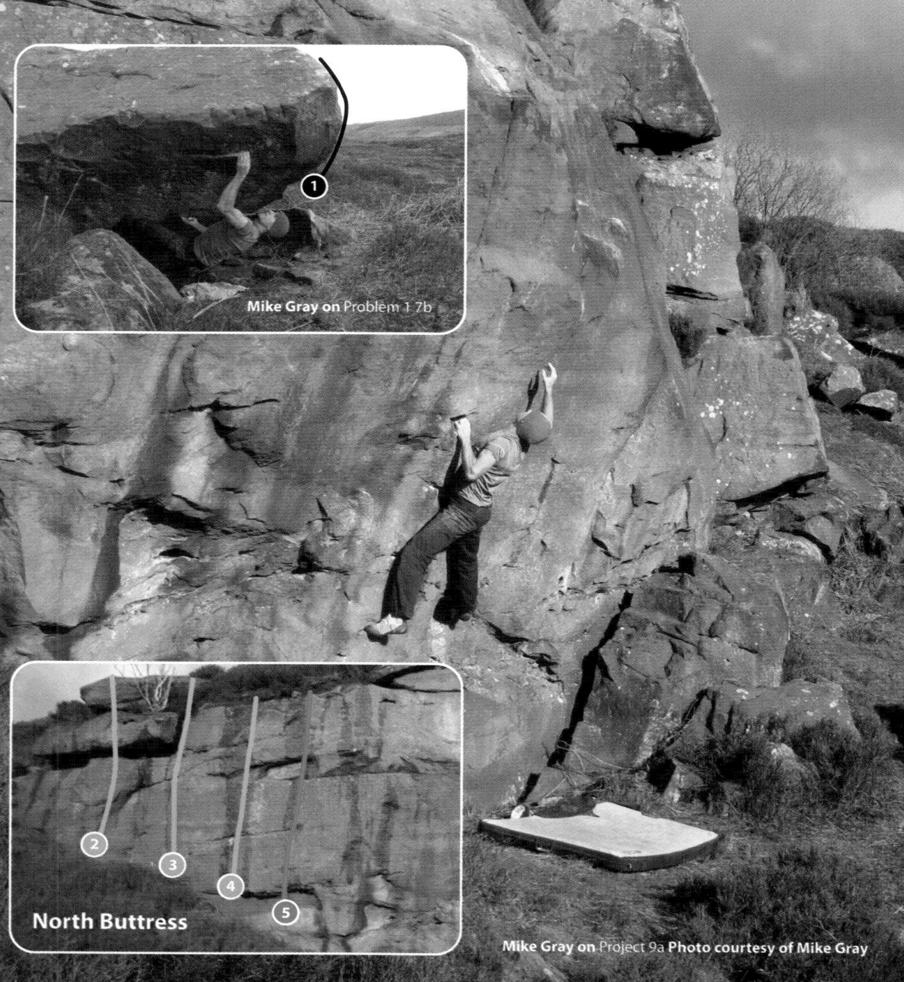

Mike Gray on Problem 1 7b

North Buttress

Mike Gray on Project 9a Photo courtesy of Mike Gray

About 50 metres from the North Buttress lies a block with a small roof.

1. 7b From the undercut climb out of the roof, trending right up the arête. Possible direct mantel finish.

North Buttress

2. Blue Peter 2 Climb the broken wall on the left. Finish over the top block on friable holds.
3. Motley Crew 2 Climb a thin crack just right of the groove and finish up the corner above.
4. Pugwash 4+ Climb the thin crack system in the wall and finish direct.
5. Pokemon 5+ Start at the embedded block, pull over the undercut onto the wall and finish direct.

Oak Wall

An Impressive leaning wall with hard test pieces all the way across. You'll have to make some big reaches from thin holds to gain success on this wall, challenging the limits of any boulderer. The top-outs are spicy so keep your cool and you'll be rewarded with some of the moor's finest.

6. 6c Climb around the arête using the thin crimps to the top.
7. Four Seasons 8a+ The arête on its right via a big left-hand sidepull, avoiding the good holds to the left of the arête.
8. Project Climb up the thin blankness.
9. Mighty Oak 7b Work your way up the wall to a gnarly left pocket and a side-flake crimp. Pop up to the sloper, match and rock-out right. Brilliant!
9a. Project A direct finish to Mighty Oak**,** avoiding the good sloper.
9b. Mighty Oak (LH finish) 7b+ Tougher than the original and feels a bit pokey at the top.
10. One-armed Bandit 7b+ A big move from the crimps to another crimp right of The Mighty Oak.
11. Digimon 6a The excellent finger-crack just to the right of Oak Wall. Avoiding the block beneath is problematic.
12. Captain Birdseye 5 Follow another excellent thin crackline, passing small edges along the way.
13. Popeye 1+ The corner crack to the right.
14. Centre Route 1+ Ascend the centre of the blocks that jut out from the buttress.
15. Get Yer Coat 5 Move up the slab to the left of Coat Crack.
16. The Acorn 6b SS The short arête, using the arête only.
17. Coat Crack 4 From the niche, gain the crack with difficulty then follow to finish.
18. Rigg Slab 1 The easy slab to the right, direct.

*There are several high and low-level traverses on North Buttress not included in this guide. Details of these and more on Oak Crag can be found at **www.climbonline.co.uk.***

Mike Gray on Four Seasons 8a+

North Buttress - Oak Wall

North Buttress

Lee Robinson on Mighty Oak 7b

200m south are:

Slab

1. 2 The right side of the block has a tricky start.
2. 1 Straight up the middle of the slab.
3. 2 A nice sloping arête.

Gollum Block

4. The Pullover 6a SS Start under the nose, rock-up onto the face and finish direct.
5. Gollum 6b Start in the hole with both hands on the block below, then climb out onto the face to finish direct.

Just a bit further south under an old oak tree is:

Guilty Block

6. Twisted Arête 6a SS Climb the arête on its right.
7. Guilty Pleasure 7b+ SS The centre of the boulder making a tricky slap to a hard-to-hold sloper, then gain the top.

Dan Crawford on The Pullover 6a

3 1

Petergate Quarry is a forgotten sandstone quarry on the moorland at the west side of Farndale with some fantastic views over to the east. The quarry reaches to a height of about 6 metres in places, with good solid rock. The problems include thin slabs and overhanging walls from the low to mid grades. The landings are littered with hidden boulders covered with heather, so care should be taken. It's also home to one of the most impressive cairns in the moors.

Approach: Follow the main road north out of Hutton-le-Hole (Blakey Road). After the cattle grid take the next left turn for Gillamoor. After about a mile and another cattle grid, take the right turn after the bridge signposted 'Farndale'. Follow this uphill until the road levels out where there is large car park on your left (OS SE 675927). Take the sandy track winding up the hill, head towards West Harland Farm also signposted 'Low Harland Cottage' Pass the small reservoir and take the track that goes north-west up through a gate. After about 100m turn right onto a public footpath which crosses the main track. Follow this for just over half a mile until the quarry will be visible on your left as the path goes downhill.

OS Map: SE 665944
Walk: 25 minutes
Faces east

Steven Phelps on Red Giant 5

The Lion Inn
Church Houses
Rosedale Abbey
Low Mill
Petergate Quarry
P
Gillamoor
Hutton-le-Hole
Kirkbymoorside
A170

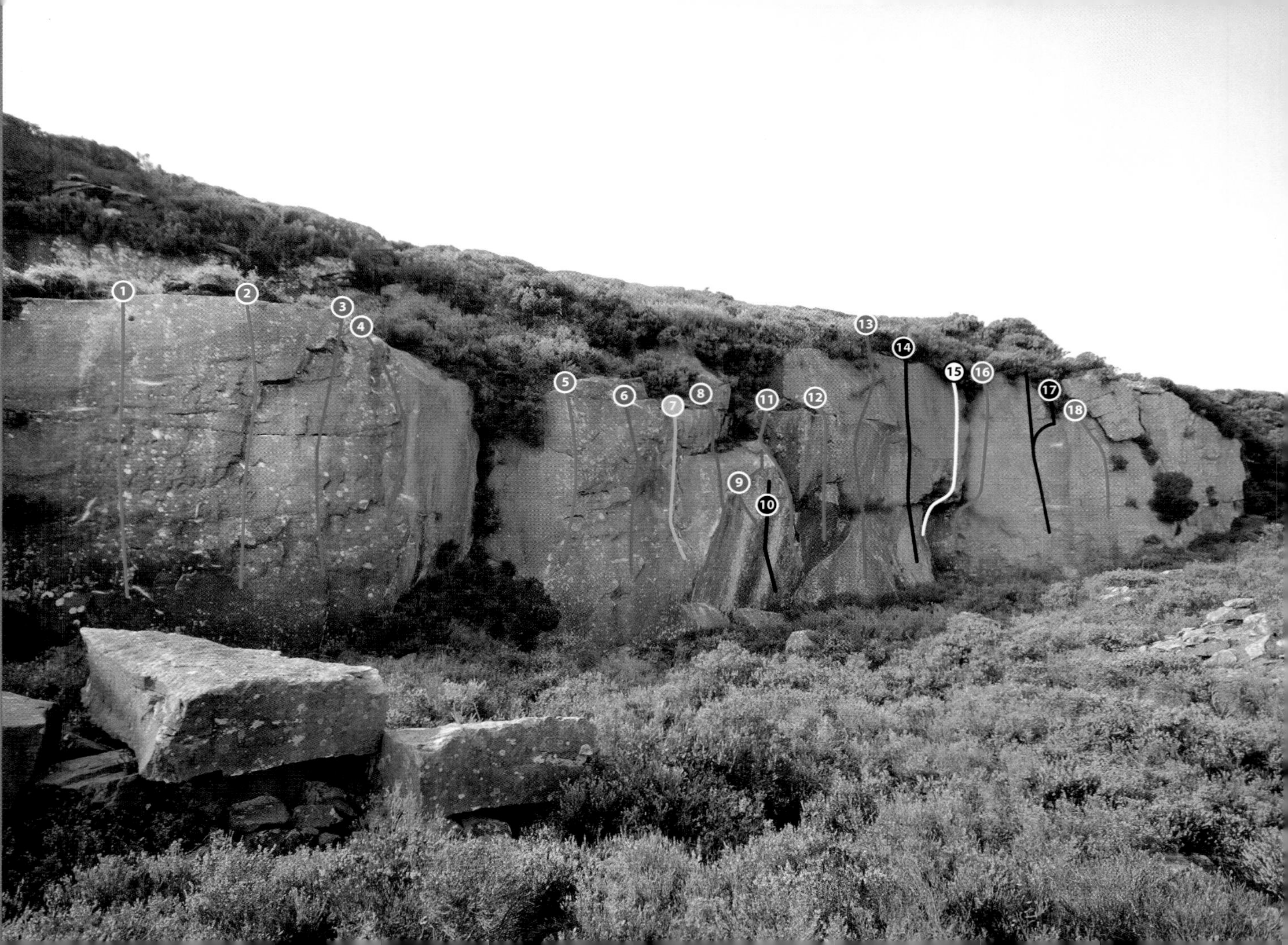
1
2
3
4
5
6
7
8
9
10
11
12
13
14
15
16
17
18

Petergate Quarry

1. Maya 5 The centre of the steep slab without using the ledge on the left. Use the borehole to finish.
2. Eschaton 5+ Climb direct up to the large layaway flake, then make a long reach to the top.
3. Final Fling 6a Up the slab just left of the arête to a good pocket. Finish direct.
4. Pandemic 6b The right arête reaching from crimps up to a good hold on the arête. Finish direct.
5. Red Giant 5 The excellent blunt arête on its right at first, then using holds either side to a bold finish.
6. Silent Spring 6a Up the centre of the wall by the use of small edges, to another bold finish.
7. Cairn Crack 4+ Follow the grooved crackline.
8. Fragile Earth 6b+ SS The overhanging arête with a sit-start on the block. Make an initial hard move to reach a good hold on the face, then finish direct on slopers.
9. Last Flowers 6c Using the obvious pocket, pull up and move out left to use the good face hold. Make difficult moves rightwards up the sloping lip. Finish direct.
10. The Big Dream 7b+ SS Start on holds left of the crack, then climb left to the good pocket, finishing direct.
11. Last Orders 5+ Follow the sloping fault/crack until you can reach up for the high shelf.
12. Saloon Wall 5 Start as for Last Orders. Pull onto the overhanging wall with the flake and finish on the shelf above.
13. Jim Rummy 6a Gain the ledge. From there, climb direct to gain another good ledge and a bold finish.
14. Vanishing Point 7b+ A hard problem right of the mantel ledge. Move up the left side of the bold slab staying right of both ledges.
15. Project Climb the overhang direct. Gain the right edge of the slab to finish, without use of the right sidewall.
16. Crimson Corner 5+ Follow the corner. Climbing eases with height.
17. Black Velvet 7a From a narrow ledge gain thin sidepulls to gain height and stand on the ledge. Finish rightwards on a good ledge (beware of the dislodged block to the right). Very perplexing if you cannot reach the next ledge when standing on the narrow ledge. Can also be finished direct.
18. The Last Word 5+ Climb up to the dislodged block. Layaway leftwards to finish as for Black Velvet.

More problems exist to the right but have not been included as they stay dirty due to run-off from the moor above.

Steven Phelps on Eschaton 5+

Thorgill is located on the southern west side of Rosedale and consists of a number of large boulders below a crag containing some excellent problems. The boulders are clustered just below the main crag and the lower boulders are a short walk down the hill. Most of the problems are in the mid to high grades and the rock is in the main good and solid with a few lesser quality sandy problems on some of the lower boulders. The area suffers from bracken in the summer months; but paths are usually worn enough to get around without a problem.

Approach: **(See Map on page 181) From the south**, take the turn off Hutton-le-Hole high street signposted Lastingham and with a sign for the coach and car park (which has loos!). After the cattle grid, take the left at the fingerpost and large blue sign for Rosedale Chimney Bank. After 3 miles across the moor there's a car park on the left just before and another just after the blue dangerous hill sign for Chimney Bank (the steepest public road in Britain!). Either car park will do, though the lower one is closer and will take you via the old Rosedale West Kilns, a popular local tourist spot and important site for industrial archaeology. The kilns were used for roasting iron ore prior to smelting in blast furnaces and there was once a large chimney to the rear, a dominant local landmark until demolition in 1972.

From the north, follow Castleton High Street south 4 miles along Castleton Rigg towards Hutton-le-Hole until a left turn for Rosedale Abbey, just after the stone cross. Pass the church and village green and take the right turn signposted 'Hutton-le-Hole via Chimney Bank' and with a blue Chimney Bank sign. Drive up Chimney Bank (1 in 3, do not attempt in winter) to the two car parks near the top on your right and park. **From the Parking**, Head north and you will pass above or below the kilns and follow the disused railway north as it curves round the valley. About 150m after passing a large wooden bench, take a right onto a diagonal path which goes down the hill. Follow this until the path becomes sunken. A series of faint moor tracks break off left where large oak trees mark the location of the crag. Take one of the paths that crosses beneath the crag to reach the boulders.

OS Map: SE 712959
Walk 20 minutes
Faces east

The Rosedale Chimney demolished in 1972

The old kilns on the way to Thorgill

Steve Ramsden shaking out on Bermuda 7a

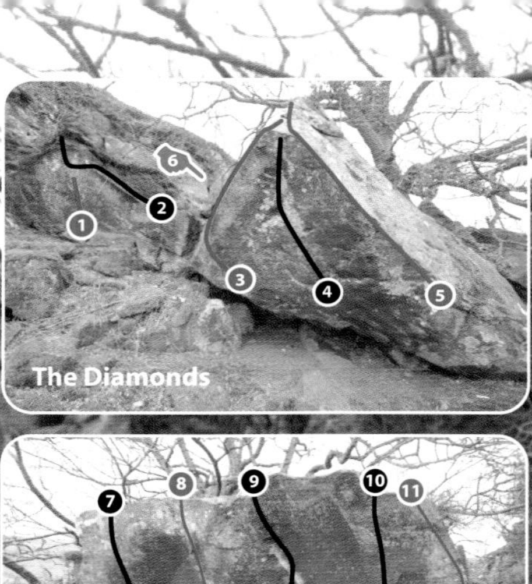

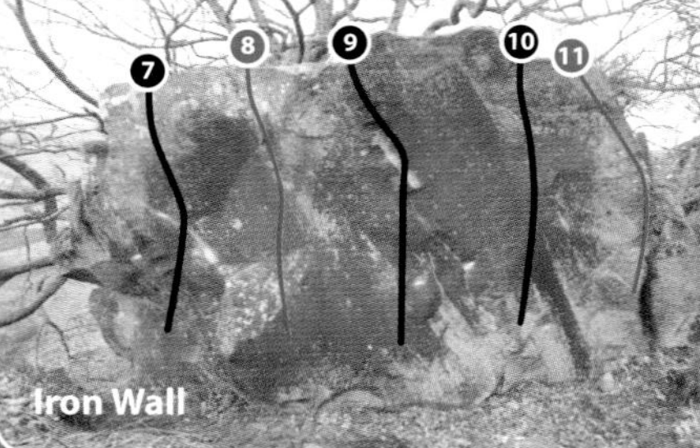

Steven Phelps on Torsång 6c

The Thorgill Diamonds

The first block just to the left of the large leaning triangular block under the tree.

1. 6b SS Climb the short arête from a tricky start.
2. Brilliant Cut 7a SS Starting low, climb the lip on sharp crimps, finishing on the left side of the arête.

The large pyramid block under the oak.

3. Thorsminde 6c+ SS Start under the left side of the block, climb the arête to the apex and top-out right of the apex. Hands on the arête only at this grade!
4. Bermuda 7a SS The central line to the apex, topping out right of the apex.
5.Torsång 6c SS The right arête, top-out right of the apex. Hands on the arête only at this grade.

Behind these two blocks you will find:

6. Secret Service 5+ SS Follow the overhanging arête leftwards using holds on the lip only. An awkward finish awaits.

Behind this is the:

Iron Wall

7. Stalingrad 7a SS The left side of the wall using a flat left hand hold and an obvious sidepull to start. Once off the floor make a dynamic move for the top and rockover. Only one rule, don't use the small ledge at any point.
8. Iron Curtain 6c SS This time use the small ledge and a small hold out right to rock-over for a long reachy finish.
9. Cold War 7c SS A direct line up the centre of the wall starting on crimps and using the excellent layaway feature.
10. K.G.B 7b SS Climb just just to the left of the arête without using it.
11. Red October 6a SS The obvious overhanging arête.

Below and to the left of Iron Wall is an overhanging arête.

12. Facet 5 From a good ledge mount the arête and gain the top. The sitting start will be hard.

The Ore Boulders

Lee Robinson on Roasted Ore 6a+

30m down the hill is a large block with some spicy high problems.

The Ore Boulders

1. Narrow Gauge 5 SS Make your way up the smaller block, mostly by use of the right arête.

2. Magnetite 6c+ SS The overhanging left arête using holds on either side.

3. Roasted Ore 6a+ A tricky start then up the scoop to gain the jugs on the groove at the top.

4. Project Start under the arched overlap. Move over this and take a direct line onto the slab.

5. 6a Start left of the crack. Make a difficult initial move into the flake system, then transfer onto the slab aiming for the pocket. Finish using the runnel and avoid the shelf.

6. Guts For Garters 6b SS The crack on the right with a difficult start. Finish via the shelf.

Down the hill and left from The Ore Boulders are:

The Calcine Boulders

1. Crossing the Rails 5 Start at the left side and traverse rightwards across the wall to finish before the arête.

2. Direct Rails 4+ Gain the pocket on the wall and move right to finish as for the last problem.

3. Derailed 7a+ SS Start with your left hand on the lip and right hand on a crimp under the lip and climb the arête direct.

4. Gully Arête 5 Follow the right arête using the slab features for feet, then make a high rockover exit above a bad landing.

5. 4 SS Climb the arête on its left.

6. Project Gain the shelf. Top-out via the flake on the top.

7. Stoke the Fire 6b The overhanging right arête utilising a pocket round the corner and near the top.

The final block is south just above a stone wall.

Work Break Boulder

8. A Chisel, a Pick and a Walking Stick 6b+ SS
Start low down in the diagonal break. Climb direct using the layaway.

9. 6a SS Start just to the right of problem 8 and make a stiff pull onto the arête. Follow left to finish as for the last problem.

Jake Hampshire on Crossing the Rails 5

Sam Marks on **A Chisel, a Pick and a Walking Stick 6b+**

3 5 7 1 6

The Meadow is a luscious grassy circuit unlike anywhere else in the moors, holding mostly mid grade problems including some nice traverses on excellent boulders. It's also bracken-free in the summer and a good place to have a peaceful and chilled out day's climbing.

Approach: Park as for Oak Crag **(see page 203)** but cross the road and head north-east on the footpath lined by grouse butts. As it goes downhill you'll walk past the remains of an old miner's house and a fenced-off mine shaft known as Sheriff's Pit. Cross the dismantled railway and continue on the footpath as it goes north-east. Eventually you'll drop down to a small quarried area. Turn left and walk along a small plateau then over a wire fence to drop into the boulders. Please be discreet and keep to the rocks below the edge.

OS Map: SE 698966
Walk: 20 minutes
Faces north-east

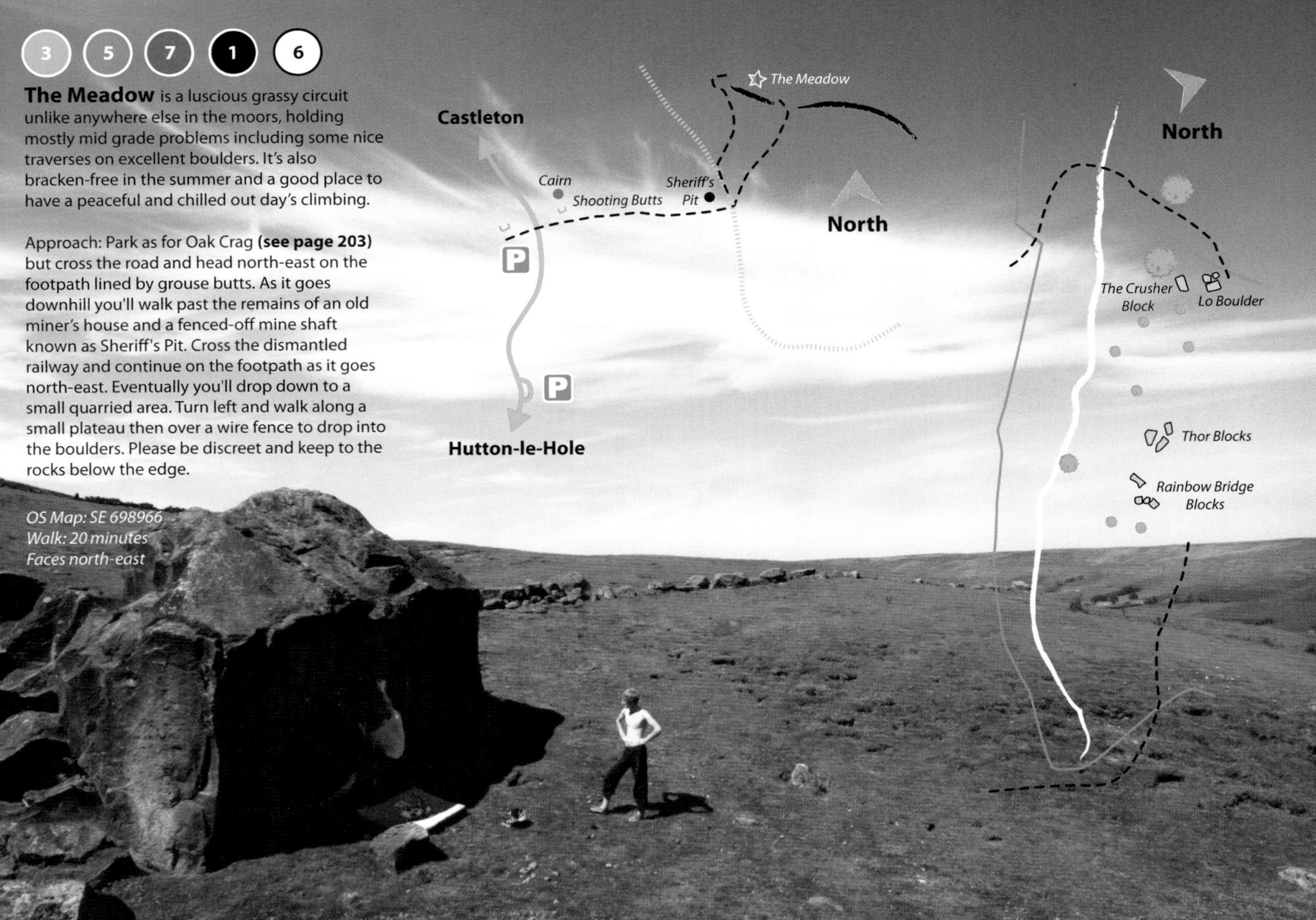

The first cluster at the south end of the meadow.

Rainbow Bridge Blocks

1. Loki Arête 4 SS The left arête.
2. Loki 6a SS Dyno to the top from the good ledge.
3. Bilskirnir 6b SS From the good ledge traverse right topping out on the incut ledge.
4. Ridill 6b SS Climb the arête on its left on thin crimps.
5. Regin 4 The right side of the arête.
6. Volsunga Saga 3 Climb the right side of the slab
7. Nordic Arête 5+ SS Start at a small shelf and a pinch. Move up rightwards to a break, then climb the right side of the high arête.
8. Rainbow Bridge 6b+ From the undercut ledge gain the small pocket and bring your feet up to gain the next sharp pocket, then it's up to the break and the top.
9. Project Good holds on the left upper wall. Just needs a little clean.
10. Project SS After a cramped start, this could be a good little problem.

Billy Lawrence on Bilskirnir 6b

Rainbow Bridge Blocks

Steve Ramsden on Thor 7a

Thor Blocks

A fine collection of problems in the middle of the cluster.

11. Storm Sword 5+ The rising left to right arête is an excellent challenge. Top-out at the right.
12. The Sword 4 SS Climb the arête and mantel.
13. Project SS The short arête.
14. Thor 7a SS A low start trending left, popping up to a sloping hold and avoiding the arête.
15. Thor's Arête 6b SS The arête direct.
16. Project SS A hard pull to a sloping top-out.
17. The Hammer 6b+ SS A stiff pull leads to the lip and a rockover.
18. Marvel Traverse 5+ A right to left traverse of the block. Start at the right arête with a heel-hook and follow the lip to finish at the arête variation of Thor.

Lee Robinson on Thunder 6a+

Lo Boulder

Lo means meadow in Old Norse. The block is very photogenic, but is quite dirty and snappy in places. It just needs some TLC.

1**9. Lo 5** A standing start in the middle of the block. The sit start will be a lot harder.

A few more problems on this block need a clean. There is also a short slabby block behind it.

The Crusher Block

(Mjölnir - Thor's Hammer) The largest leaning block in the meadow holds a few projects.

20. Project A bold lip-traverse up the arête. Looks steady but needs a little brush.

21. Thunder 6a+ Trickier than it looks. Using a right layaway and a left crimp, gain a two-finger crimp with the left hand to gain the top mantel. The sit-start will be worth adding.

22. Project The right end of the block may hold a good line.

The Crusher Block

Lo Boulder

Middle Ridge Crag is situated in a pleasant moorland setting in the valley of Rosedale and is one of the smaller venues in the area. Most of the problems are on a small edge of compact solid sandstone above good flat landings and are at the lower end of the grade range. It's fairly sheltered and gets any sun going from about midday onwards. Some of the finishes involve negotiating heather.

Approach: Park at Blakey Junction, where there are two car parks with tourist information boards, about half a mile south of the Lion Inn on the main Hutton-le-Hole to Castleton road along Blakey Ridge. Follow the public footpath east from the smaller car park over the the dismantled railway until it meets a large track at the bottom. Turn right onto this and come off at a corner onto sheep tracks heading south. The crag's position is marked by a tree and is about 5 minutes across the moor, passing a large boulder and the highball wall of Kettle Howe on the way.

OS Map: SE 689983
Walk: 15 minutes
Faces west

Middle Ridge Crag

1. Goaf Arête 6b+ Layback up the arête. Make a delicate move to finish.
2. Curlew 5+ Start at the small ramp in the centre of the wall. Move right at first, then left with a long reach to gain the top. Fingery.
3. Groove Crack 3 Layback the crack system using the groove for the feet.
4. Project SS The slanting arête may need a dynamic solution.
5. Bilberry Chimney 2 Head up the chimney moving left to a heather finish.
6. Kiln Tower 2+ Straight up the mini tower by use of small ledges. Followed by a mantelshelf top-out.
7. Ironstone Flake 2+ Starting at the slab, reach round onto the flake, then make your way up to cross over left and finish as for the last problem.
8. Ironstone Arête 3 Start with both hands on the sloping flake. Reach right to continue to the top for another heather finish.
9. Sheriff's Drift 3+ Right of the trees is a slab which is climbed using a series of small steps. Heather top-out.
10. Sheriff's Groove 3 An eliminate climbing the groove feature on crimps. Finish slightly leftwards.
11. Sheriff's Pit 3 Climb the cracks, then traverse rightwards along a break to finish using a sloping ledge and a flake crack.
12. Sheriff's Pit Eliminate 6b SS Climb into the last problem, without the crack to the left.

The Shield

13. Left Arête 5 Start at the left side of the front face of the shield. Move leftwards onto the arête and climb direct. Possible sit-start.
14. Perseverance 6b Using a small ledge for the feet and some nice holds, climb directly into the faint ramp-line above and follow this rightwards to finish.
15. Project SS Just right of the last problem on thin holds avoiding the ramp-line.
16. Shield Route 1+ Starting at the small slab, take a direct line to finish up the brown lichenous slab above.
17. Brown Arête1 Start as for the last route. Once positioned on top of the small slab, reach right onto the arête and finish up this.
18. Brown Arête Direct 3 Tackle the arête direct. Good moves.
19. Boot Route 1 The easy-angled slab at the right side of the crag.

Matthew Ferrier on Perseverance 6b

5 1 10 3 1

Rosedale Head boulders are in an attractive setting below the dismantled railway at the north end of Rosedale and are part of a small boulder-field. Although not huge in quantity, the boulders make up for this in quality, bearing some good crimp problems in the mid to high grade range on clean solid rock.

Approach: Parking can be found at the famous 16th century Lion Inn on the main Hutton-le-Hole to Castleton road along Blakey Ridge. Cross the road and walk leftwards along the stone wall of the house. At the corner where the wall ends is a small path signposted Rosedale Railway North. Follow this down to the dismantled railway, which takes you north and contours round the head of the the valley to the opposite side. Just before a boggy section is reached on the opposite side and as you are in line with the top of some trees, turn right on a faint path which takes you down a gully to the boulders.

OS Map: NZ 684007
Walk: 25 minutes
Faces west

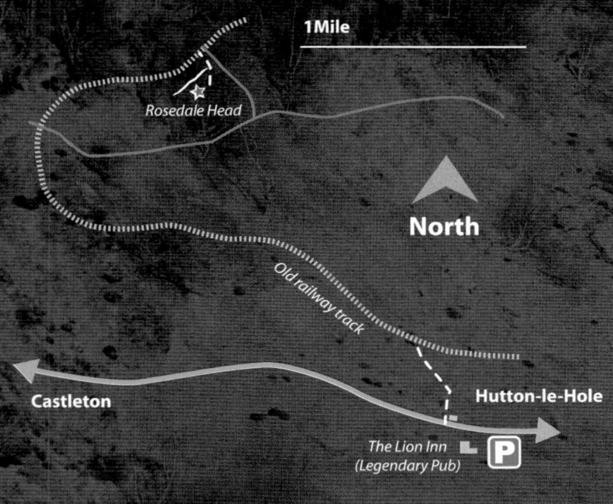

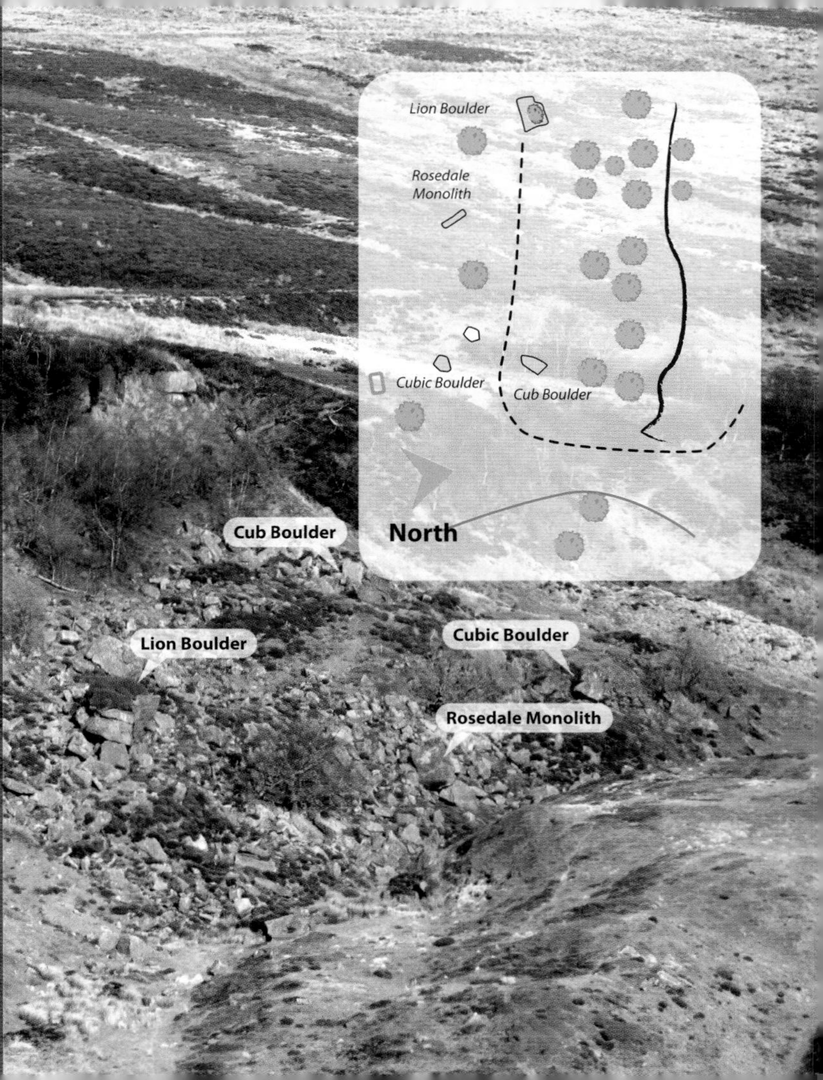

Lion Boulder
Rosedale Monolith
Cubic Boulder
Cub Boulder
North

Cub Boulder
Lion Boulder
Cubic Boulder
Rosedale Monolith

Lion Boulder

The largest block in the cluster is a little gem.

1. Badge 6b+ SS From a good hold on the lip and the block beneath for feet, climb the wall via a large layaway and small ledges. Can also be started lower without the block and using holds on the lip at **7b.**

2. Lioness 6a Start just left of a block and make a long reach using the horizontal cracks. Bold.

3. Project SS Start at the arête, traverse left to the crack and finish as the last problem.

4. Lion Arête 6c+ SS Start low using the arête and the sidepull out right. From standing using the ledge on the main face is **6a+**.

5. The White Room 7a Climb the wall right of the arête via thin crimps.

5a. The Dark Room 7b SS The sit-start for the last problem starting near the arête with small edges. Move up to the ironstone break to finish via the crimp.

6. Whiter Than White 7b+ SS Make the first few moves of the last problem, but this time traverse the face of the boulder taking the line of least resistance.

7. Bitter 6c SS Using the curved rail, climb the wall leftwards past a shelf to finish.

8. Beer 6b SS Using the curved rail, fight and mantel to gain the small hold out right that leads to success.

Lee Robinson on Lion Arête 6c+

Lee Robinson on Rosedale Monologue 6b+

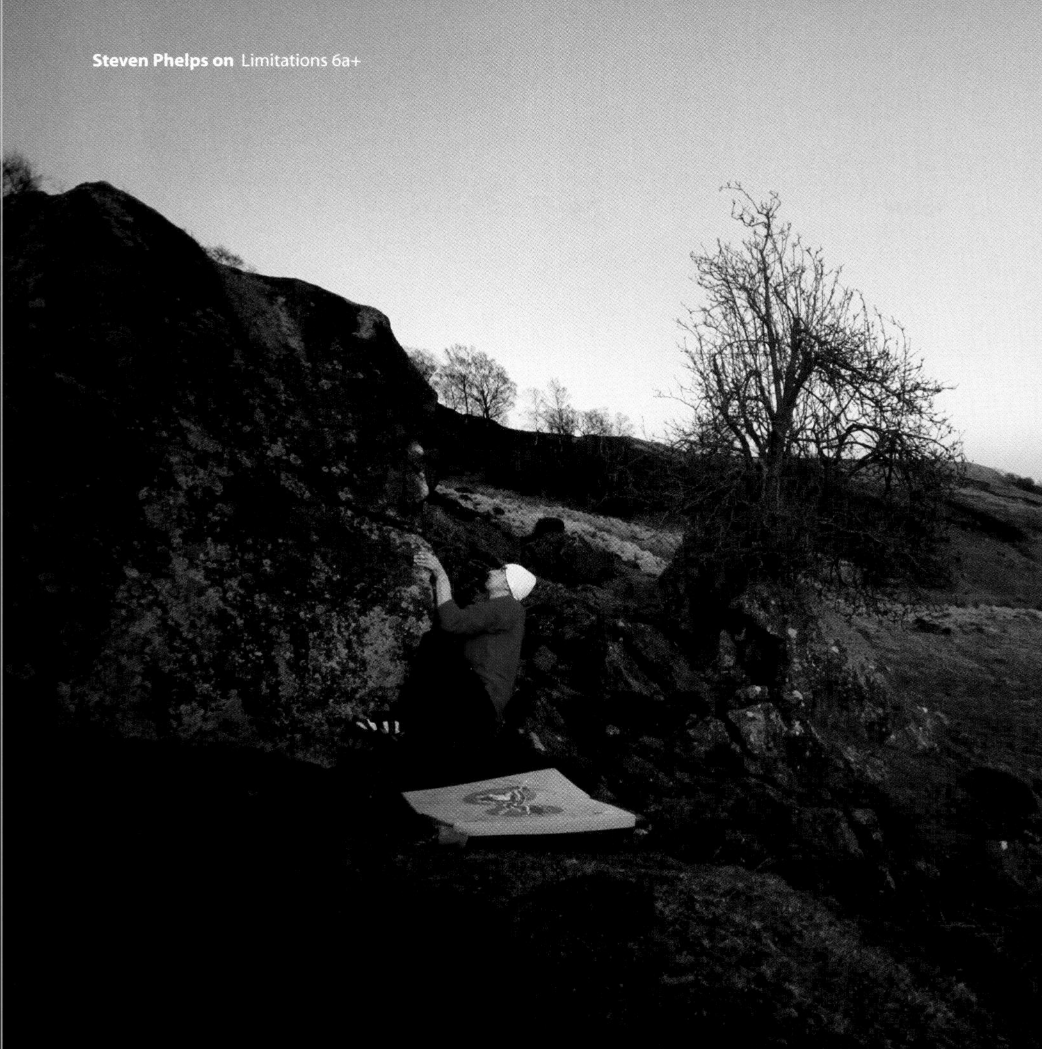

Steven Phelps on Limitations 6a+

Rosedale Monolith

A proud upstanding block with some good test-pieces.

1 Chinese Whispers 6a SS The left arête starting with right hand on a sidepull and left on the arête. Make a tricky pull up to get the easy-angled part of the arête and finish on the right side of the arête to the top.

2. Straight Talking 7a+ SS On low edges climb up using the curved sloping rails, then head towards the left arête. Finish more easily to the highest point of the block. **6c** from standing, by hanging an edge just above head-height.

3. Outcry 7c SS Climb up the centre of the block using curved sloping rails, then it's a big dyno for the top edge. Strictly no arêtes allowed.

4. Rosedale Monologue 6b+ The right arête. Start direct from the lowest point, then climb the left side to the top. Slightly easier using holds on the face.

5. Dialogue 3 The narrow sidewall using both arêtes.

About 20m up and right are more problems on a tilted boulder with the initials I.G. carved into the front face.

Cubic Boulder

6. Sprag 6a SS Start left of the carving with a good left hand hold and right hand on the arête. Using edges under the small roof for feet, follow the left side of the arête to a better hold and finish.

7. Wedge 3 The short slab via the break.

8. Limitations SS 6a+ The overhanging arête on its right side is harder than it looks.

About 30m up and left of these is the next boulder. There are several easier eliminates with only the obvious lines described here.

Cub Boulder

9. 2 The left side of the slab without the arête.

10. 3 The centre of the slab.

11. 3 The right side of the slab without the arête.

12. 5+ SS Move up the sidewall via slanting shelves.

13. 4+ SS Start with hands on a sloping ledge, traverse up leftwards then around the corner using the heather-filled break to the other end.

Round Crag Pinnacle, one for the highball junkies

Round Crag situated on the flank of Blakey Ridge and extending for over 800 metres has excellent views into Farndale. Whilst not originally known for its bouldering, recent developments have led to an excellent collection of problems throughout the grades on quality sandstone. Only the small edges and boulders are described here.
There are also several good highball problems on the pinnacle and in the surrounding area, details of which can be found at:
www.climbonline.co.uk.

Approach: Parking can be found at The Lion Inn on the Castleton to Hutton-le-Hole road. Walk north along the wooden fence in front of the pub, then follow the outer wall and path westwards down the hill. This takes you down to the dismantled railway, where the crag is directly below. Alternatively park at Blakey Junction and follow the dismantled railway north.

* There are further project possiblities on the crag and blocks below which are not listed in this guide.

OS Map: SE 674995
Walk: 10 minutes
Faces west

Micro Quarry
Bear Wall
Hidden Walls
Chocolate Box Blocks
Rainbow Wall
Pannierman's Block
The End Blocks
North

Mark Wilson on Bear Breaker 5+

The first small quarry at the far north hold some short but challenging problems.

Micro Quarry

1. 5+ Hand traverse the lower of the two breaks from left to right, finishing around the corner just before the holly bush.
2. You Are Here 5 SS Climb the arête with a mantel top-out. Start by using flakes on the left side. From standing is **4**.
3. Second Nature 4 SS Ascend the cracked arête to a mantel top-out.
4. Variety Crack 4 SS The crack to a mantel top-out. Variations using just the left or the right side of the crack have been sent. Using the left side only is **6a** and is the hardest and most satisfying variation. The right side goes at **5**
5. 4 SS The small crack to the right with a heather top-out.

Just a bit futher along the edge is:

Bear Wall

6. Bear Breaker 5+ Traverse the wall rightwards to finish up Bear Edge.
7. Gamekeeper 5 SS Start using the obvious layaway at the left side of the wall to reach better holds. Finish past two holes and a ledge.
8. Hound 4+ SS Start about 1m to the right at a small flat left hand-hold and any of the rounded flake holds for the right. Move up the wall direct.
9. Bear Edge 4 SS Start at the rounded flake in the small corner and climb up the wall using the right edge when needed. Finish leftwards.

Lee Robinson on Sleeper 6b+

Steve Ramsden on Orgasmatron 7a

Hidden Walls

These problems are just below the micro quarry.

1. Sidekick 7a SS Start at the back of the roof with right hand on a good undercut and left on a low pinch edge. Without using the back wall for feet, climb directly out to finish up the nose. Do not use the right edge.

2. Orgasmatron 7a SS Start on the good undercut, without using the back wall for feet. Climb the right edge of the roof by use of a small cracked pocket. Finish straight over the nose.

3. Rift 6a SS Start at an obvious rounded sidepull and small footholds. Move up the wall passing sidepulls and a deep break to finish over the capping stone.

4. Sleeper 6b+ SS Starting on the low break and use sidepulls to gain the top. Finish using the capping stone.

5. The Event 6a SS Hand traverse the block leftwards to finish over the capping stone.

Just round to the right are:

6. Chuck Rock 6b+ SS From the low break down in the hole, span out to slopers and move right. Chuck for the top.

7. Spaghettification 5+ SS Climb the arête on its left.

The Chocolate Box Area

The leaning spike block has a great little problem.

1. Busting Some Moves 5 SS Start using good holds to work your way leftwards and reach the spike at the top of the boulder.

The block behind may hold problems. As yet none have been recorded.

Little Slab

2. 2 The left side of the slab on good holds.
3. 3 The centre of the slab using the weakness.
4. 4+ The right side of the slab using the right edge.

Baby Arête Block

5. 3 The centre of the small slab utilising an iron pocket.
6. 4+ SS Climb the small arête on either the left or right side (both the same grade).

Just up the hill is the next problem.

7. 4+ Climb the centre of the slab on good holds. Finish rocking out rightwards once the top is reached. A pleasant problem.

The Chocolate Box

The tilted block, short but entertaining.

8. Pure Madness 6b SS From an awkward start with feet in a hole, pull up using side-slopers to the ledge. Follow this to finish.
9. Coffee Cream 5+ Climb the arête on its left-hand side.
10. The Candy Man Can 6b SS Climb the centre of the block using a pocket for the right hand, to an interesting mantel top-out.
11. Can You Do The Can Can 6a SS Climb the right-hand arête on its left side.

The slab on the right-hand side of the block can be climbed in several places.

James Rennardson on Fight or Flight 6b+

Smooth Wall

1. Smooth Talker 5+ Mount the spike, then move leftwards on the slab to finish.

2. Mr Smooth 5+ Mount the spike and climb the slab to a break, from which a big span gains the top.

Undercut Wall

3. Flight of the Concords 6a SS Make difficult moves up the wall using the arête and sidepulls. Escape leftwards.

4. Flight Path 6b+ SS Starting at a layaway, make difficult moves up the flake system. Escape leftwards. From standing is **5+.**

5. Flight Facilities 6a+ SS Make a powerful move from positive holds to mount the overhang. Continue up to finish and escape leftwards.

6. Fight or Flight 6b+ The groove in the hanging wall direct. Undercut to a sloping ledge, then rock rightwards to another hold. Escape leftwards.

7. Spitfire 5+ Climb the crack and groove past the high hold used on the last problem. Escape rightwards.

On the small slab about 20m to the right is:

8. 5 Follow a thin flake and small holds in the centre to a heather finish.

About 15m below below at a the bottom of the slope is a small arête.

9. 5 SS From a low start traverse the lip topping out at the apex.

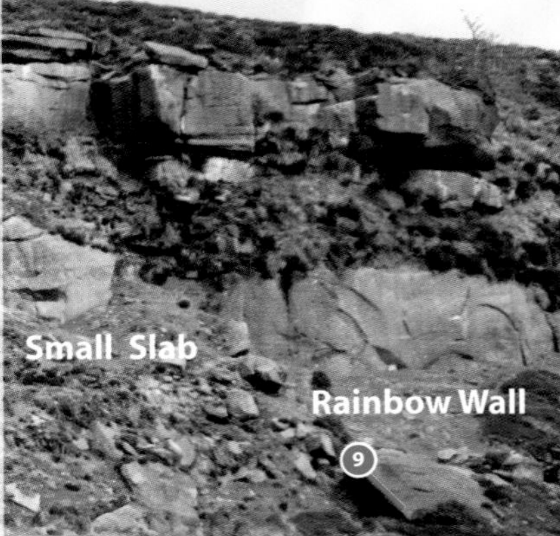

Rainbow Wall

1. Prism Crack 5 Climb the crackline, to the heather. Drop off.
2. The Colour Wheel 5+ Up the shot holes to the heather top. Drop off.
3. Colours of the Mind 8a Make some stretched-out moves to gain a sidepull pocket with the right hand, place the right foot on the sloping sidepull and the left on a choice of poor smears and make a hard dyno pop to the top. Morphologically hard but brilliant.
4. Chasing Rainbows 7c Start on the slopey sidepull in the middle of the wall. Pull up to gain small edges, place the heel on the sidepull and finger-mantel to gain the top lip. An outstanding problem!
5. Ultraviolet 6b+ Mantel the shelf to gain a left-hand curved crimp. Top-out left.
6. Shadow Illusion 6a Nice moves gain the layaway and the top. Drop off.
7. Liquid Refraction 7b On the right side of the wall make tricky moves to climb up just left of the right edge of the crack. Use the hold just in from the crack. Do use the crack at all. Top-out.
8. 1 The pleasent crack/arête.

Just below the pinnacle is:

Pannierman's Block

1. Slabbierman's Arête Font 5+ The arête on its left-hand side.

2. Pannierman's Arête 6b+ SS The arête on its right is a classic of the crag. **6b** from standing.

3. Fat Cactus 6a SS A tricky start just around the right arête.

4. The Rig 7b+ From a hanging start, climb the pillar on its east face using hugging techniques. No use of any other blocks at this grade.

The Rig is on a pillar at the north end of Round Crag Pinnacle

Steve Ramsden on Pannierman's Arête 6b+

At the far south end of the crag are a few boulders with good problems.

The End Blocks

1. The Brave 6a SS The left side of the overhanging wall. A hard start gains the big ledge, followed by bold moves to mount the ledge and top.
2. Falling Arête 6b The arête mainly on its right, with a long reachy finish.
3. 3 Climb the arête to the right.
4. Project SS Follow the lip of the block leftwards.
5. Mystic Marsh 6a Climb the widening slab using both arêtes, without use of the adjacent blocks.
6. Zig-Zag 4 Start from the slanting ledge. Move right to the arête and finish using it.
7. Hard Labour 6a Pop from the central flake to the lip. Mantel with the help of a sidepull.
8. 1 Just right of centre of the easy-angled slab. Very interesting without hands.

Lee Robinson on Falling Arête 6b

My favourite lonely moorland tree, en route to Northdale

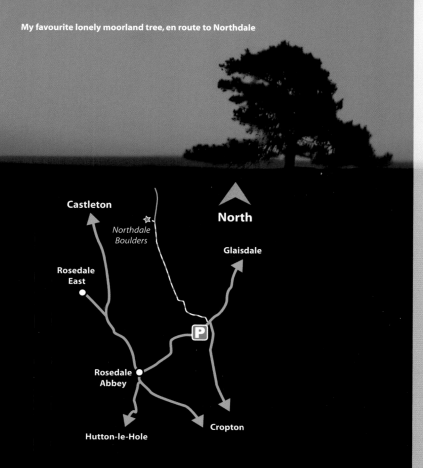

Castleton
North
Northdale Boulders
Glaisdale
Rosedale East
P
Rosedale Abbey
Hutton-le-Hole
Cropton

Northdale is a secluded valley that runs north from the eastern side of Rosedale. The boulders are near the head of the valley in the midst of a blanket of bilberries after, a fairly long but flat walk that starts just outside Rosedale (a small village where refreshments can be found). There are many boulders on the hillside, with the documented blocks interspersed with much smaller ones. Good problems are on offer and although some do require a brush, the rock is generally clean and solid sandstone. It can be rather exposed on the moor top but on a calm summer's day there's nowhere better to pass a few hours. Most grades are low to mid, though a few harder projects remain.

Approach: **From the south,** turn off Hutton-le-Hole High street signposted 'Lastingham'. After the car park (and loos) and over a cattle grid, take the left turn onto a lonely moor road which eventually drops down Rosedale Chimney Bank (an infamously steep 1 in 3, so not for winter driving). Pass the popular White Horse Inn and once at the bottom take the second left signposted 'Castleton'. Very soon after and still in the centre of the Rosedale Abbey take the right turn just before the Milburn Arms Hotel, which goes up Heygate Bank to 'Egton'. Pass the cattle grid and stone cross and park at a small grassy lay-by on the right, opposite the track with green metal gate to the boulders and just before the junction.

From the north, take the main Castleton to Hutton-le-Hole moor road along Castleton Rigg until a left turn signposted 'Rosedale Abbey', about 4 miles south of Castleton. Follow this for about 5 miles into the village and take a left turn up Heygate Bank signposted for Egton. Follow to the green metal gate and grassy lay-by mentioned above.

From the parking, take the track north through the green gate. Keep on this, ignoring the first two tracks going right but taking the third after about 10 minutes walk from the car. Follow this track for another 10 minutes and take the right fork. After another 10 minutes look out for two large rocks, one either side of the track. Both are feeding points for grouse. Go left down the hill between these to the boulders.

OS Map: SE 726988
Walk: 30 minutes
Faces west

North
Bilberry Crag
Satsuma Slab
Iron Prow
Satsuma Area
Sunset Slab
The Banana
Carambola Block
Kiwano Wall
The Lip
Cherry Slab
Papaya Block
The Orange
Kiwano Area
The Pear
The Lime
Mulberry
Mulberry Area

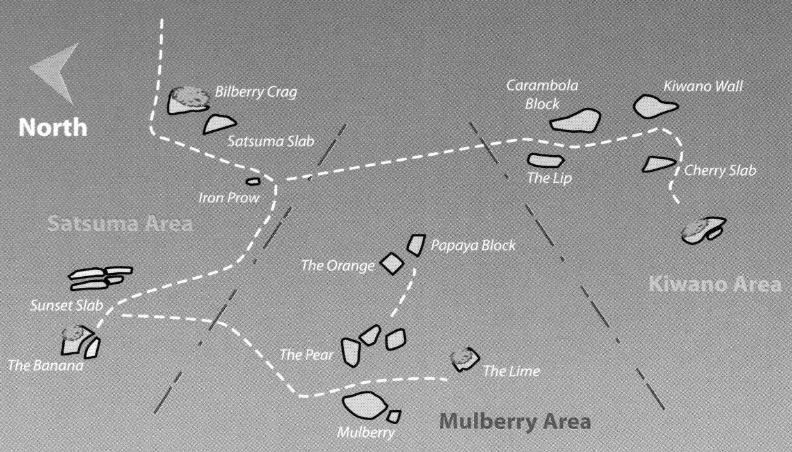

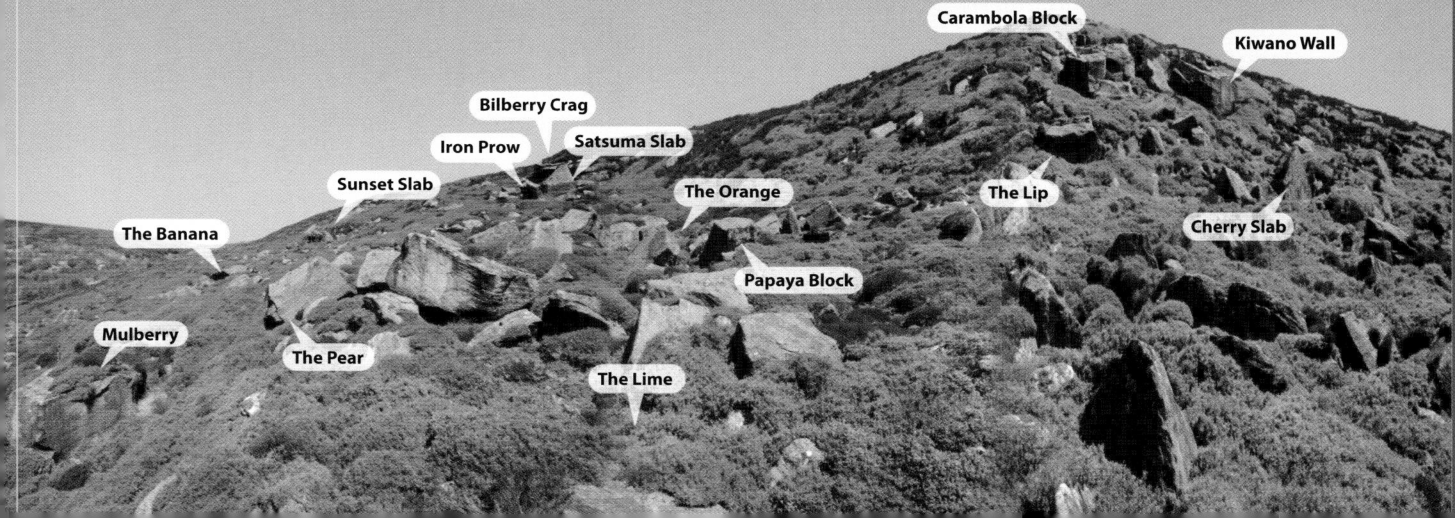

Carambola Block
Kiwano Wall
Bilberry Crag
Iron Prow
Satsuma Slab
Sunset Slab
The Orange
The Lip
The Banana
Cherry Slab
Papaya Block
Mulberry
The Pear
The Lime

Satsuma Area

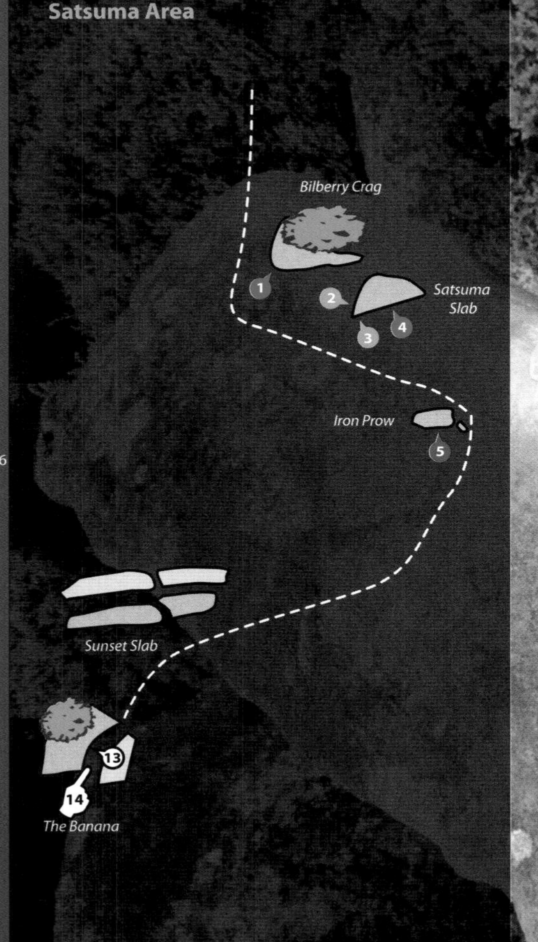

Lee Robinson on The Iron Prow 6c+

Bilberry Crag

The little buttress as you drop into the blocks.

1. Carbon Bathtub 5+ The centre of the overhanging wall, past the breaks to a high crux finish on slopers.

Satsuma Slab

2. Crushed Mango 4+ Up the arête above the cave. Once at the good hold pull round to finish.

3. Orange Arête 4+ Start at the left side and follow the arête all the way.

4. Satsuma 5 Climb up to a curving rail and mantel. Then it's a long reach for the top.

10m below the slab is a leaning block.

Iron Prow

5. Iron Prow 6c+ SS Climb the prow finishing leftwards, using the block below for the feet. Eliminating the block will add a couple of grades.

Sunset Slab

A tall west facing block down the hill.

6. Slice 'n' Dice 3+ Start at a small ledge. Undercut all the way leftwards to a jug, then finish.

7. 4 Start with hands on the good slot and climb direct.

8. 4 Start 1m right of the last problem. Finish direct.

9. Sour Arête 4+ The arête has good climbing on the left.

10. Bitter 5+ Climb the arête from its right until you are forced out on the front face.

11. Sunset Arête 5 The left arête of the smaller slab.

12. Sunset Slab 5+ Straight up the slab past an obvious hold, then over the bulge.

The Banana

A short, steep, curving wall.

13. Traverse Project Traverse the lip of the block, footless some of the way.

14. Short Dyno project Starting on a crimp rail.

Steven Phelps on Nice Pear 6b

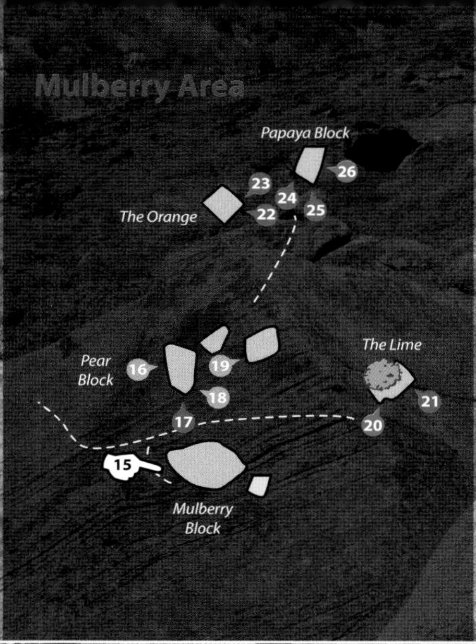

Mulberry Area

Lee Robinson on Sweet Orange 6b

Mulberry Block

15. Operation Mullberry Project Traverse The block from left to right. Start moving across the first side on sharp crimps to a rest at the first rib. From here cross to the lower shelf, then move round and up to the lip of the final wall to mantel at the far right end. Very boggy on the first section.

The Pear

16. The Pear Bureau 2 The centre of the slab - pure friction.
17. Nice Pear 6b SS Gain the right arête from good holds. Top-out and tip-toe across the top of the block to finish. Classic.
18. The Wonder of Pears 3 Climb from the left end traversing across rightwards to top-out at the right end.
19. 2 Climb the slab opposite.

The Lime

20. Fruit of the Loom 5 SS Start at the jug at the left end. Climb up and move right to the arête, then finish.
21. Dragon Fruit 6a SS From good holds with feet under the roof, pull your torso over the slab. Harder than it looks.

The Orange

22. Chinese Apple SS 6b+ From the same start as Sweet Orange, head left and climb the left arête. Sloping blissful climbing.
23. Sweet Orange 6b SS From good crimp rails, head rightwards on the sloping arête. Top-out at the apex.

Papaya Block

24. The Finer Things in Life 6a The arête utilising good footwork.
25. Forbidden Fruit 6a+ The right arête is gained by a wild move, then it's a slap for the top.
26. Kiwi 5 SS Up the wall using fragile flakes.

Kiwano Area

The Lip

1. Project Start by hanging the left side and make your way right to a mantel finish at the right end.

Carambola Block

2. Pear Halves and Soul 6a SS Start with feet on a small ledge and climb up using the large flake on the wall.

3. Compot Shot 5 SS The blunt arête just to the right. Don't stray onto the sloping ledge.

Uphill and right of this is:

Kiwano Wall

4. 4+ SS Start at the left side on crimps and climb direct to jam the large slot. Mantel to finish.

5. The Date 6c Undercut the low slot and climb the blunt rib feature using crimps and a sloper out left.

6. 4 Undercut the large slot and finish direct.

7. Carboniferous 5+ Start to the right of the larger slot and climb the layaway/flake feature.

8. The Slot 6b One of the highlights of the venue. Climb direct from the slot.

Cherry Slab

9. Broken Berry 5+ SS Start at the left side and make a fierce pull up to the good jug, then finish up the arête.

10. Purple slab 5 The centre of the slab using crimps and a pinch for the right hand.

11. Um Bongo 1 The right arête on its left side.

About ten metres down and right is a small overhanging block.

12. Proven Prow 5 SS Start at the left side and traverse round the prow to finish on the right side.

There are further blocks below here that could have potential, if given a clean.

Sam Marks on The Slot 6b

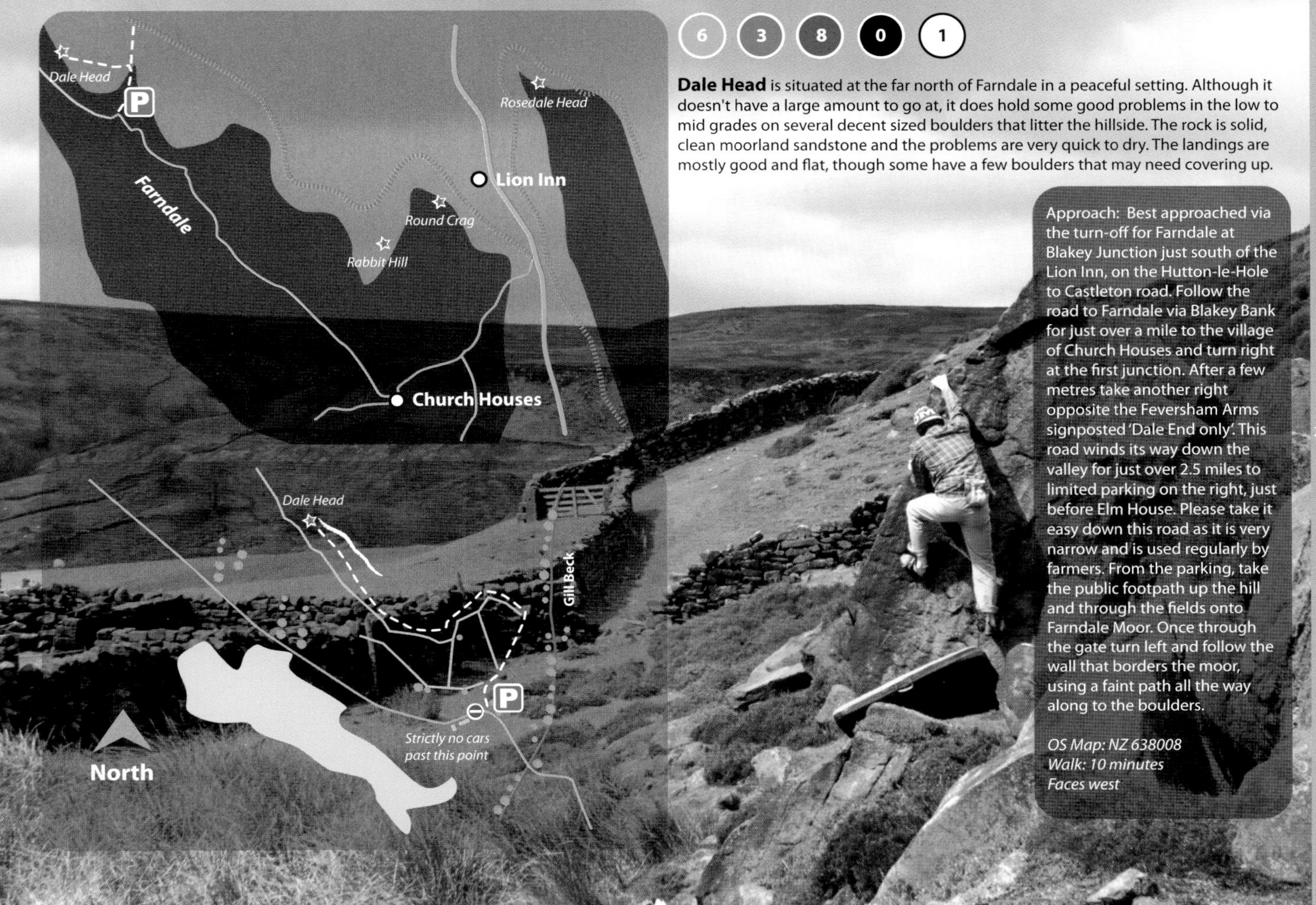

Dale Head is situated at the far north of Farndale in a peaceful setting. Although it doesn't have a large amount to go at, it does hold some good problems in the low to mid grades on several decent sized boulders that litter the hillside. The rock is solid, clean moorland sandstone and the problems are very quick to dry. The landings are mostly good and flat, though some have a few boulders that may need covering up.

Approach: Best approached via the turn-off for Farndale at Blakey Junction just south of the Lion Inn, on the Hutton-le-Hole to Castleton road. Follow the road to Farndale via Blakey Bank for just over a mile to the village of Church Houses and turn right at the first junction. After a few metres take another right opposite the Feversham Arms signposted 'Dale End only'. This road winds its way down the valley for just over 2.5 miles to limited parking on the right, just before Elm House. Please take it easy down this road as it is very narrow and is used regularly by farmers. From the parking, take the public footpath up the hill and through the fields onto Farndale Moor. Once through the gate turn left and follow the wall that borders the moor, using a faint path all the way along to the boulders.

OS Map: NZ 638008
Walk: 10 minutes
Faces west

Lee Robinson on Venom 6c

The Wedge

1. Wedge Edge 4+ Follow the left edge/arête of the block.
2. Wedge Face 5+ Climb up the front of the block, without either arête.
3. Arête Left 6a+ SS The left side of the arête, hugging to start! From standing is **5**.
4. Arête Right 2 The right side of the arête.
5. 4 The narrow slab without use of the arête.

Traverse Boulder

6. Do androids dream? 6a SS Start at the lower corner and follow the lip as it rises leftwards. Possible hard extention starting at problem 7.
7. Electric Sheep 6a SS Start at the lower corner and follow the lip as it rises rightwards.

Small Roof

8. The Clamp 6c SS Climb the hanging prow with difficulty.
9. Venom 6c SS Start with a good hold for the left hand underneath the roof and another good hold on the nose for the right. For feet use a detached flake for left and wedge for your right. Make a stiff pull for the crimp on the face and follow the square-cut arête to finish. **6c+** if you start with both hands on the flake under the roof.
10. 4 The short side-wall on crimps, avoiding the block on the left.

Streamside Boulder

11. The Adjustment Bureau 6b+ Traverse the lip of the block from right to left.
12. 3 Mantel, then tip-toe up the slab above.

About 20m up the hill are more problems starting with a highball buttress on the left.

Hopeful Buttress

13. Painter 3 The side-wall direct, just left of the bulge.
14. Project Climb the centre of the wall.
15. Topless Robot 5 Climb the right arête to sneak off up the right side.

A bit below this and to the right is another problem on a low block .

16. Sorrow 5+ SS Keeping feet on the wall or on the lip, traverse leftwards finishing up the left edge using a useful pocket.

About 10m to the right are the next problems.

Dream Boulder

17. Thought Control 6a+ SS Climb the short arête making a long move to a sloper above the lip. Short but satisfying.
18. Dream Stalker 6b SS Follow the excellent sloping arête leftwards to finish as the last problem.

Hopeful Buttress
Dream Boulder
The Wedge
Traverse Block
Streamside Block
Small Roof
12
11
Streamside Block
13
14
15
Hopeful Buttress
17
18
Dream Boulder

Located above peaceful fields on the western edge of the beautiful and secluded Fryup Dale are the exceptional **Clemitt's Boulders**. These hold some classic boulder problems on good, clean, coarse sandstone, divided into three very different areas.

The first area documented here is **Clemitt's Out**. This area is on the far left of the hillside, with the blocks at the base under a small craggy edge. Unlike the other two areas there are some lower grade problems, therefore it's both an excellent spot for beginners and a good place to warm up before entering the woods. There's a lot of variety, from small steep overhangs to easy-angled slabs and the rock is usually dry and stays clean throughout the year.

The next venue is the jewel that is **Clemitt's in the Woods**. Once you enter through the gate you're confronted by several large boulders, giving you a sign of things to come. All are in a magical woodland setting with each offering something different, including features which are rare for the moors. The woods offer few problems in the low grades; though mid to high grade problems abound, including local classics not to be ignored. There are steep slabs, tough arêtes, overhanging walls and testing traverses throughout this excellent circuit, making it one of the bouldering highlights of the moors.

The third area is **Clemitt's North**. Here some of the climbs blur the boundary between highball bouldering and routes. Despite the committing nature of some of these problems, many of the lines are of impeccable quality. It's one for the explorers out there.

Although Clemitt's is fairly popular it can still feel isolated and you'll often have the place to yourself. Through the summer months bracken can be a problem and after wet weather the areas in the woodland can take a few days to dry out. All areas are sheltered from westerly winds.

Andrea Lalley Treasure on Stairway to Heaven

Castleton
Clemitt's North Parking
Camp Hill
Stormy Hall
Clemitt's
North
Rosedale Head
Lion Inn
Round Crag
Hutton-le-Hole
Rosedale Abbey

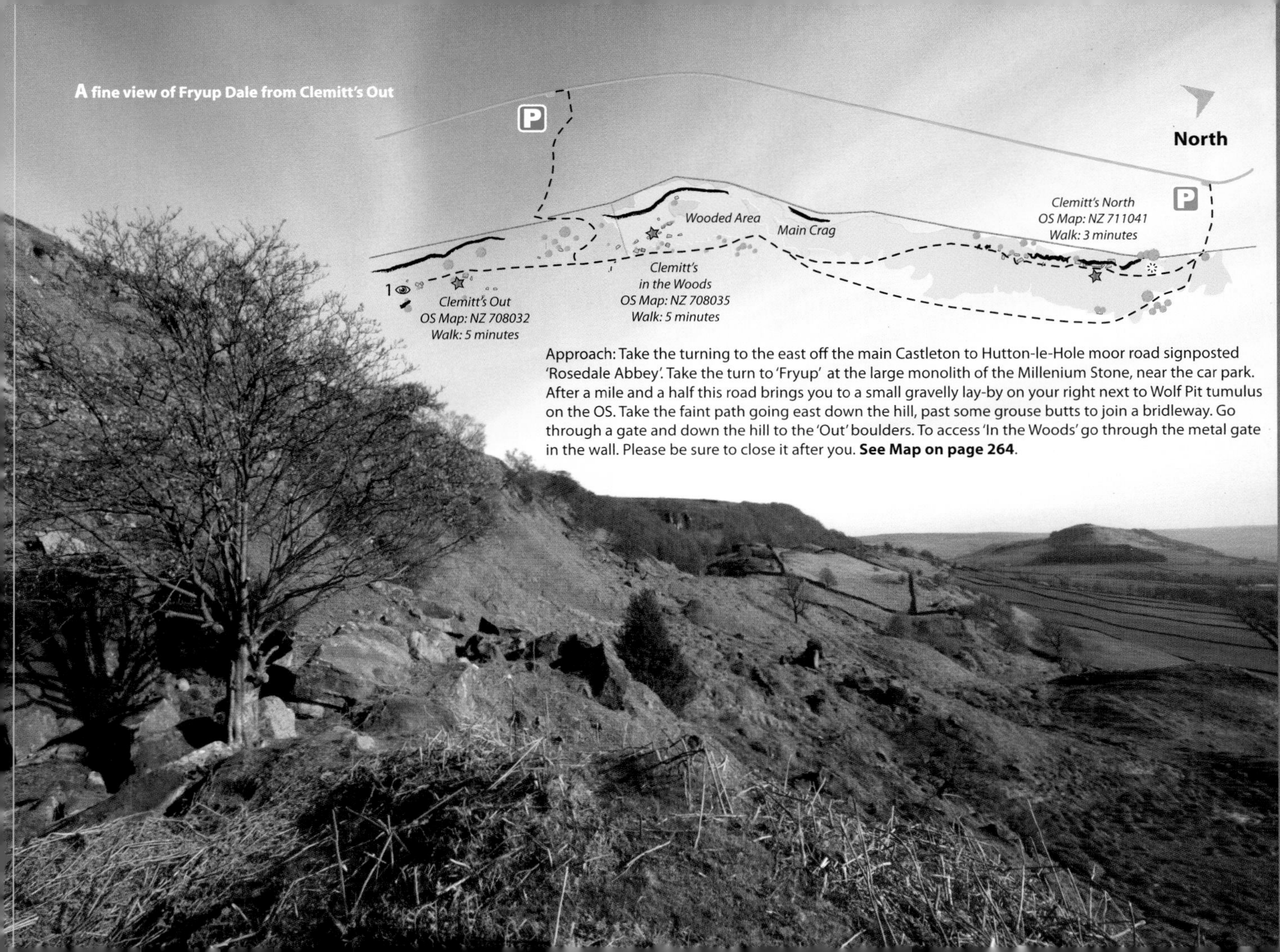

A fine view of Fryup Dale from Clemitt's Out

North

Wooded Area

Main Crag

Clemitt's North
OS Map: NZ 711041
Walk: 3 minutes

Clemitt's
in the Woods
OS Map: NZ 708035
Walk: 5 minutes

1

Clemitt's Out
OS Map: NZ 708032
Walk: 5 minutes

Approach: Take the turning to the east off the main Castleton to Hutton-le-Hole moor road signposted 'Rosedale Abbey'. Take the turn to 'Fryup' at the large monolith of the Millenium Stone, near the car park. After a mile and a half this road brings you to a small gravelly lay-by on your right next to Wolf Pit tumulus on the OS. Take the faint path going east down the hill, past some grouse butts to join a bridleway. Go through a gate and down the hill to the 'Out' boulders. To access 'In the Woods' go through the metal gate in the wall. Please be sure to close it after you. **See Map on page 264**.

The first blocks described are at the far south end, outside the woods.

The Mobile Phone

1. 4 The front face using a blunt flake.
2. 3 The arête mainly on its right side.
3. 5+ SS The wall to the right, on crimps and ledges.

5m to the north are more problems.

The Lump

4. Lump Arête 6b SS The sloping arête on its left side. **5** from standing.
5. 5+ Gain the slab without using the arête, then move rightwards using the sloping shelf to finish direct.

Directly behind this is:

Paparazzi Block

6. Paparazzi 7a SS Climb the overhanging left arête.

Dave Warburton on Paparazzi 7a

Franco Cookson on a crimpy project

Hidden Wall

About 30m north and a bit down the hill is a long wall.

Hidden Wall

1. 5+ SS Move rightwards up the sloping ledges.
2. Project SS Direct up the wall on crimps.
3. Happiness 6a+ SS Start on an obvious sloping edge and climb the blunt flake.
4. 6c SS The right arête is harder than it looks.

Just to the right is another boulder, above very boggy ground.

5. 6a SS The short left arête round onto the lip.
6. 5 SS Follow the lip leftwards.

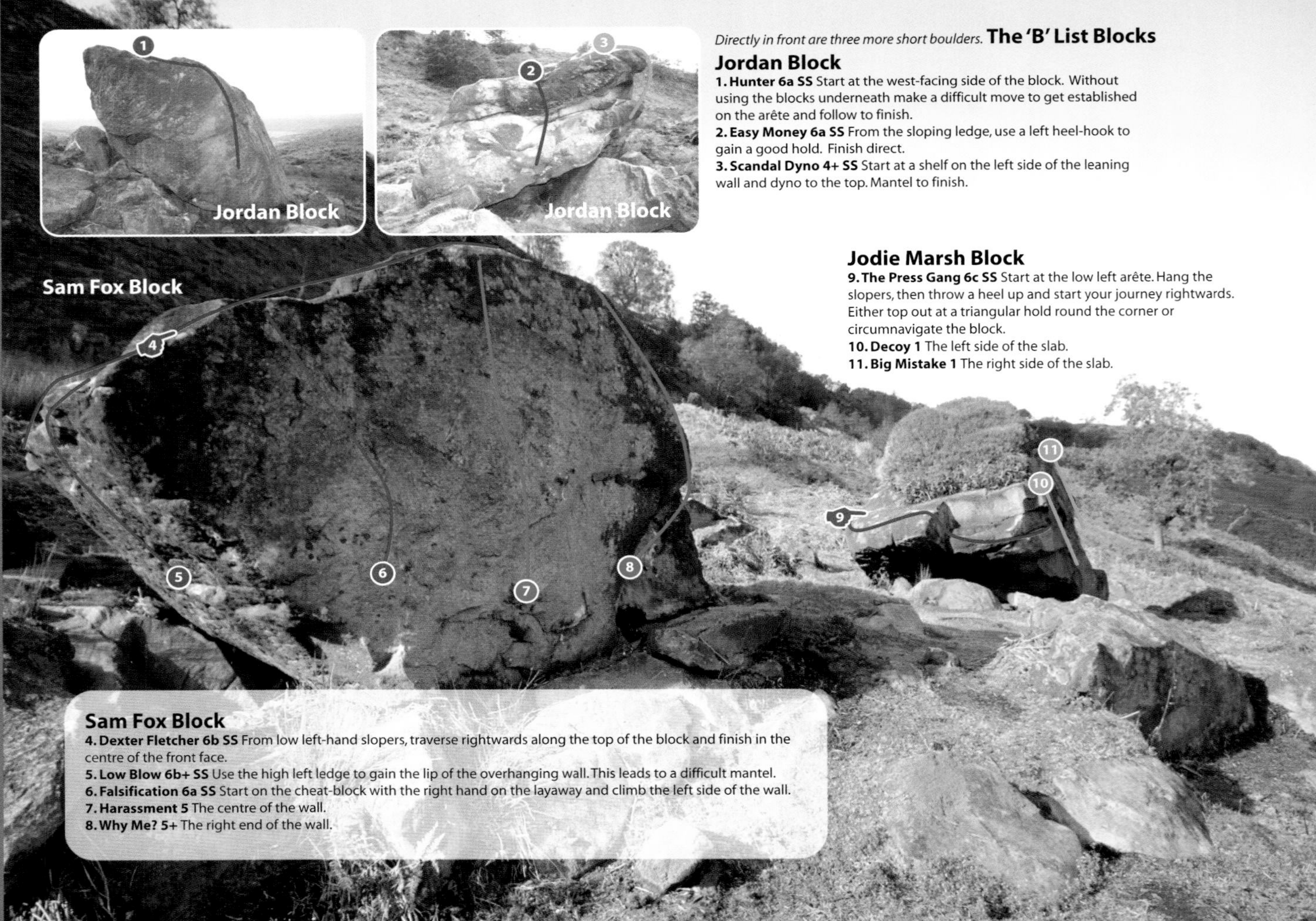

Directly in front are three more short boulders. **The 'B' List Blocks**

Jordan Block

1. Hunter 6a SS Start at the west-facing side of the block. Without using the blocks underneath make a difficult move to get established on the arête and follow to finish.

2. Easy Money 6a SS From the sloping ledge, use a left heel-hook to gain a good hold. Finish direct.

3. Scandal Dyno 4+ SS Start at a shelf on the left side of the leaning wall and dyno to the top. Mantel to finish.

Jodie Marsh Block

9. The Press Gang 6c SS Start at the low left arête. Hang the slopers, then throw a heel up and start your journey rightwards. Either top out at a triangular hold round the corner or circumnavigate the block.

10. Decoy 1 The left side of the slab.

11. Big Mistake 1 The right side of the slab.

Sam Fox Block

4. Dexter Fletcher 6b SS From low left-hand slopers, traverse rightwards along the top of the block and finish in the centre of the front face.

5. Low Blow 6b+ SS Use the high left ledge to gain the lip of the overhanging wall. This leads to a difficult mantel.

6. Falsification 6a SS Start on the cheat-block with the right hand on the layaway and climb the left side of the wall.

7. Harassment 5 The centre of the wall.

8. Why Me? 5+ The right end of the wall.

The next block is about 40m uphill on the path.

The Camera Block

1. Space Invasion 7a SS A cramped start from a side-crimp flake. Pull hard and pop for the top. Finish left.

2. The Chase 5 Start round the corner, right of a block and traverse the lip rightwards.

3. Shutter Speed 6c From a small undercut, get established, then pull for the top.

4. Dirty Prince Harry 6b From the big ledge and left incut, climb direct to join the top arête.

5. Vegas Pool Party 6a Start as the last problem, then climb rightwards to the arête and finish up this.

6. Kate's Knockers 5+ SS From the low, sloping ledge head left to finish on the end face.

7. Have I Got News For You 5 SS Start as the last problem, but climb direct.

8. Papped 2 Feels bold up the front face.

9. Punched In The Face 6a Mantel over the lip to the right. A good tip is to watch someone else do it first!

10. Dirty Tricks 6b SS Climb the arête starting with a high right heel.

Lee Robinson on Space Invasion 7a

James Rennardson on Flash 4

The Slab

A further 20m along is a prominent slab.

1. Stalker 6b SS A tricky low start gains the bulge to easier climbing up the slab.
2. La Dolce Vita 5 SS Traverse the block from left to right finishing up the arête.
3. Flash 4 Mantel a sloping ledge and finish up the slab.
4. Click Click 6a SS Use an undercut, a green flat edge and a good toe-hold to reach up to a good slanting hold. Finish direct.
5. Headline 5+ SS Climb the arête on its left side.

Just uphill outside the entrance to the woods is a low block with some short wrestles.

The Outcast

1. **Transfusion 4+** Start on the obvious flake and trend right to an easy top-out.
2. **Direct Transfusion 5** Start as Transfusion and climb direct to a mantel finish.
3. **Give Blood 5 SS** Start on a low pocket, then climb to finish using a boomerang-shaped sloper.
4. **Black Pudding 5+ SS** Climb straight through the vague scoop without using any hold outside the scoop.
5. **True Blood Traverse 4+** Without using the top block, traverse right to left to finish up Transfusion.
6. **Nose Bleed 4** Mantel over the hanging nose.
7. **Don't Push Me 6a SS** Start at the right end of the hanging lip. Traverse leftwards to top-out around the uphill face.
8. **First Blood 6b SS** Move up the east facing wall on crimps to escape over the left arête.

Mark Wilson on Direct Transfusion 5

The Sentinel

Just downhill from the Outcast block is a climb that is a right of passage at Clemitt's. If you can climb and stand upright on the top, you are worthy to go into the woods and face the mighty circuit within - if not, you are banished to the boulders outside the wood (only joking, the woods have something for everyone).

1. The Sentinel 6a SS Climb the downhill-facing side of the pinnacle.

Lee Robinson on The Sentinel 6a

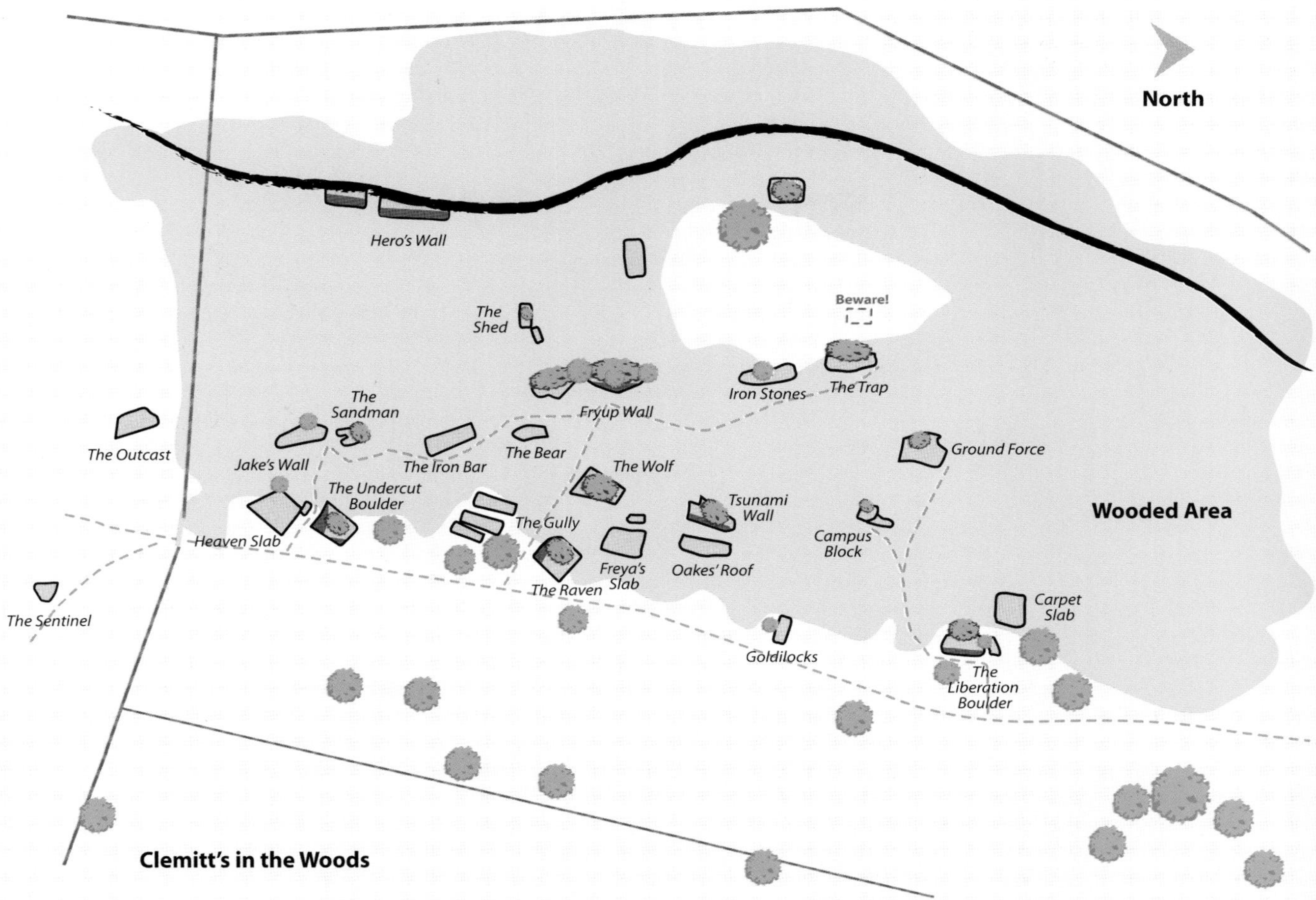

North

Hero's Wall

The Shed

Beware!

Iron Stones

The Trap

Fryup Wall

The Sandman

The Outcast

Jake's Wall

The Iron Bar

The Bear

Ground Force

The Wolf

The Undercut Boulder

Tsunami Wall

Wooded Area

The Gully

Campus Block

Heaven Slab

Freya's Slab

Oakes' Roof

The Raven

The Sentinel

Carpet Slab

Goldilocks

The Liberation Boulder

Clemitt's in the Woods

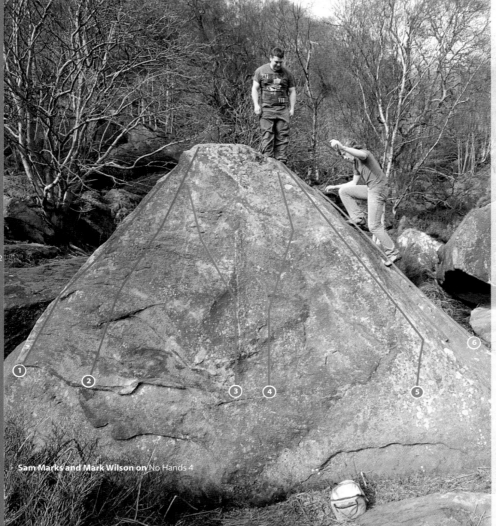

Sam Marks and Mark Wilson on No Hands 4

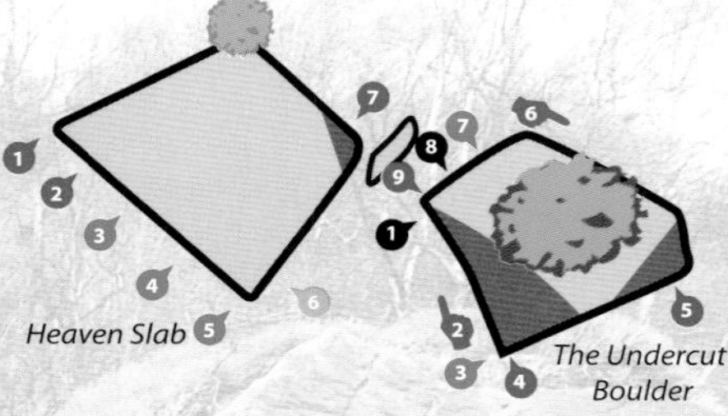

The first blocks you come across when you enter the woods.

Heaven Slab

1. Cloud Nine 6a Starting with a high foot and the undercut, climb the arête on its right.
2. Princess Leia 6c Delicate slab climbing just to the right of the arête, without using it!
3. The Finger Print Preservation Society 5+ Start in the middle of the block and top-out just to the left or on the very top, if you dare!
4. Halo 5+ Start in the middle and top-out just to the right.
5. Stairway to Heaven 5+ The arête on its left-hand side.
6. No Hands 4 Walk up the tricky slope.
7. Palm Tree 6c SS Pop up to the edge of the slab then mantel onto it.

The Undercut Boulder

1. In The Bag 7b SS Start on the block and with good heels work around the left of the arête to finish up the left side. An alternate finish up the right side has also been done at **7a+** using holds out right.
2. Underworld 6a Cross the face using the undercut rail.
3. Overlord 5 Straight up the nice ribs.
4. Arrogance of Youth 6c SS The arête on its right-hand side. Do not escape left of the sloping shelf, finish up the arête.
5. Off the Rails 6b+ SS Rail to rail.
6. Free as an Elk 6b Traverse from right to left on the rails. Also you could try reversing it, **Elk as a Free.**
7. Cop-out 5+ From the left sidepull '7' and the crimp '7' pop for the top. **See photo on page 253.**
8. Imperial Biker Scout 7b Using both the '8' holds, sort the foot out and hit the top. **See photo on page 253.**
9. Seal of Approval 6c The arête on its left side.

James Rennardson on Imperial Biker Scout 7b

Jake's Wall

This rising wedge has some tasty lines. The block is so-called as it was believed to have been first climbed by Jake Hampshire. In fact this is a myth, as Jake endeavoured, tried and cleaned the line but sadly failed. Unlucky Jake.

1. Beautiful Mind 7b+ SS The full lip traverse from the left to the very right. It has a tricky central section which is harder than it looks.
2. Wookiee 6a+ SS Straight up the groove.
3. Jake's Wall 5+ SS Start with feet on a flake protruding from the ground and hands on the ledge. Reach into the diagonal crack of the rising traverse. Finish straight up the flakes. Also can be done finishing up problem 5. **7a** if climbed static.
4. T Rex 6b+ Dyno from the break to the sloper and top-out.
5. Dyno Saw 6b+ Dyno from the spike to a blind hold.
6. Dilemma 6b SS Start at from the sidepull, make a big reach to the spike and finish up Jake's Wall or Dyno Saw.

The Sandman

A short but worthy prow.

1. Mandy Dingle 6a SS Start at the back of the overhang, climb direct to the lip and traverse right to top-out, or mantel the nose.
2. Tuskan Raider 6b+ SS Start on the left arête. Follow the low holds to the right-hand arête and mantel.
3. Project SS The mantel direct .

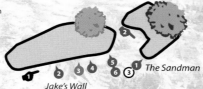

The Iron Bar

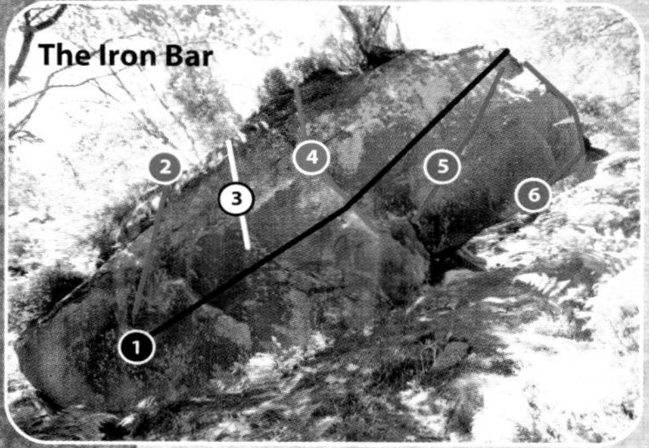

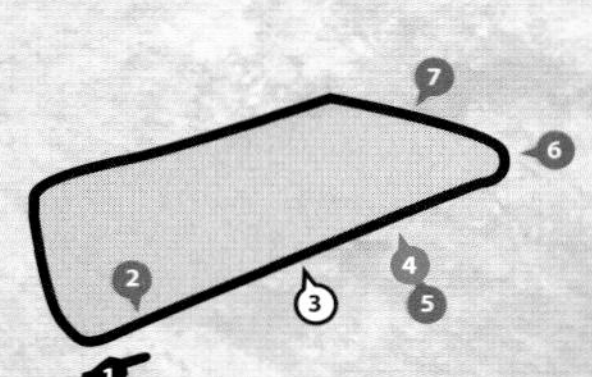

The Iron Bar

A big rectangular block partially raised out of the ground.

1. The Iron Bar 7b SS Work your way across the block using the rails, pockets and crimps and not using the top of the block. Very tricky. Finish on the arête. **7a+** from a couching start on a higher rail.

2. Iron Bru 6b+ SS Tackles the start to The Iron Bar then finishes direct.

3. Project A direct line without the ledges.

4. Greedo 5+ SS Follow the left-hand ramp.

5. Admiral Ackbar 6a SS Make a long move for the pocket.

6. Underbelly 6b SS From under the prow pop over and finish up the left side of the arête.

7. New Life 6a SS Starting low and on holds above the lip, traverse leftwards around to the arête finishing as Underbelly.

Franco Cookson on The Iron Bar 7b

The Raven

The largest boulder at Clemitt's, with quality rock holding some spicy problems.

1. AT AT Walker 6b SS With your hand at the bottom of the left-hanging crack and your other hand on the arête, climb to a hard mantel (without using the holds round the right arête). **1a. The Force 7b SS** The obvious lower start to AT AT Walker. Start right at the back of the roof matched on the good jug and climb out to join and finish as for AT AT Walker. Use the right arête but not the good holds around to the right of the arête and do not use the big shelf for the feet.
2. In the Dark SS 6b Starting low on the block in the bivi cave, gain the arête then make a long reach to a good flake-hold. From this reach the ledge.
3. The Wave 5 Climb the flakes via the weakest line.
4. The Wave Direct 6a SS As the Wave but finish direct via crimps.
5. A Black Heart 6b Climb to the right of the flakes, without using the flakes or the ledge.
6. Forgotten 5+ SS Use the right side to gain the ledge, mantel it with help from the curving weakness then mantel again to finish.
7. Star Arête 6b SS Climb the corner direct without the ledge.
8. The Groove 5+ Mount the slab and climb the groove.
9. Sam's Slab 5+ Straight up the middle of the slab.
10. The Raven 6a+ The right-hand end of the slab, climbing in from the right then direct up the right-hand end using the thin crimps and sidepulls.

The Gully

Just south and into the woods behind the Raven.
1. Wedge Antilles 6c+ SS on the marginal holds, then climb to the slanting flake and upwards.
2. Wicket Arête 5 SS Climb the arête.
3. Project Traverse The block either way.
4. Goodbye Cruel World 6a SS Climb the short arête.

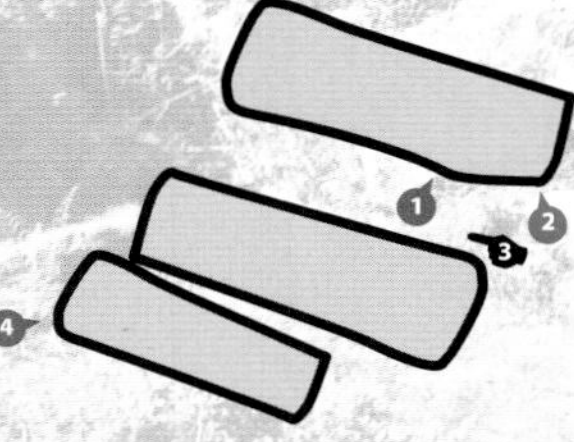

Sam Marks on Sam's Slab 5+

James Oakes on Oakes' Roof 7a

Freya's Slab

Delightful friction and not too steep.

1. Princess Leia's Golden Bikini 4+ the arête on its left side.
2. Jawa 4+ The groove.
3. Free as a Bird 6b Using the blunt rib for hands only.
4. Crossroads 5 Start at the far right of the slab, then climb diagonally left to the highest point. Loads of variations can be done on this block. Mix it up a bit.
5. Jabba's Butt Plug 7b SS Start with the left hand on the obvious good slopey edge and right thumb in the pocket. Pull up and grind out a mantel to get both feet on the slab and gain the much easier finish.
6. Project A short roof block behind Freya's slab.

Oakes' Roof

1. Oakes' Roof 7a From the undercut flake and feet on the block, climb out the roof to a mantel finish.
2. Project There may be a hard project on micro-holds to the right.

Tsunami Wall

1. Wave Dodging 6a On the left end of the block, from the undercut make moves left to rails on the side of the block.
2. Tsunami Arête 7c+/8a Start from standing (no blocks) and use only the small holds to climb up the arête to gain a slopey finish. Eliminate the the jug rails for both hands and feet on the left side wall.

3. In the Barrel of the Wave 6b+ SS Start on the large brittle flake. Get high feet and gain the small undercut above. Reach the sloping lip and then a good hold before a the scary top-out.

Freya's Slab

Tsunami Wall

Franco Cookson on
In the Barrel of the Wave 6b+

Goldilocks

The small boulder on the way to The Liberation Block.

1. Goldilocks 5+ SS Ascend the short block using hugging tactics! (best climbed when it's not too hot and not too cold!)

The Wolf

A large wedge with more lines to be uncovered.

1. Little Red Riding Hood 6b+ SS From the rail use heels to work rightwards, finishing on the highest point of the block.

2. Iron Double 7c SS On small pockets make a stiff pull-up to get the small undercut pinch. Sort out the feet, then double dyno the good left arête of the block.

3. Iron Heart 7c+ SS From the same start pull up and gain the pinch, but this time traverse right following the vague iron streak and make some very tricky moves on small holds to gain the right arête of the boulder. Eliminates the left arête that the last problem jumps to.

4. Coconut Mono 6b SS Start directly below the obvious mono and climb straight up to the top ledge, then the left arête to the top

5. R2D2 and CP3O 6a+ SS The arête from a low sit on the right just on the corner. Make a hard start to mount the arête, then onto the flat ledge (R2D2). Carry on up the arête to bag CP3O. The good hold on the top is a bit further back.

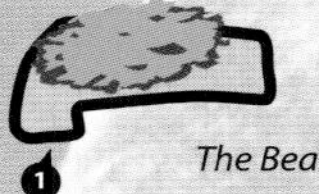

The Bear

Just south and up from The Wolf.

1. The Bear 7a SS Perfect fridge-hugging.

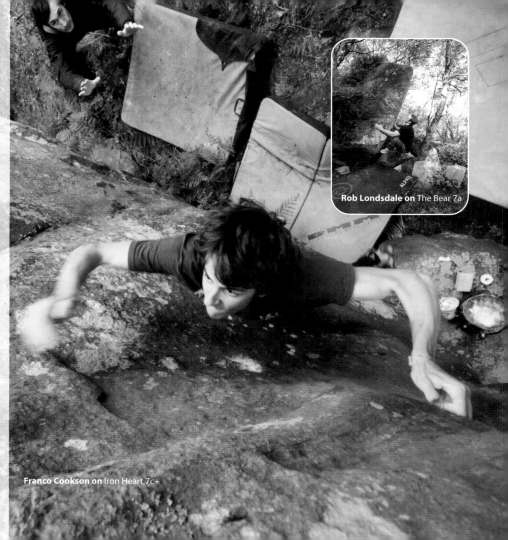

Rob Londsdale on The Bear 7a

Franco Cookson on Iron Heart 7c+

Sam Dewhurst on Plum Tomato 7b

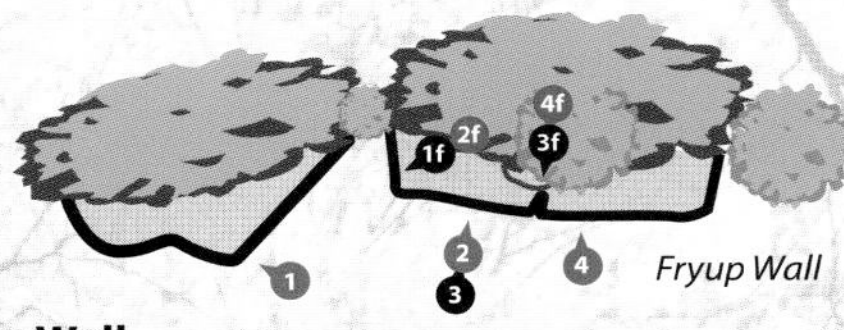

Fryup Wall

Four great lines at a nice angle, sometimes wet.

1. Fried Bread 6c+ SS From the left block, traverse the block rightwards with hands on the lip only. Swinging onto the main wall, climb the arête then use the high jug to finish up Full Breakfast.

2. Full Breakfast 6c SS From the lowest curved rail crimps, move up to the ramp then a jug out left to a sidepull and up to sloping jugs. Top-out leftwards, via a faint runnel on the ramp.

3. Plum Tomato 7b SS Head rightwards from the start of Full Breakfast, then straight up topping out left at the tree root.

4. Veggie Sausage 6b+ SS The obvious crack, topping out left at the tree root.

The Shed

The Shed

1

Try some other lines up this lonely block.

1. The Shed 6a SS Start inbetween both blocks to gain The Shed. Short but sweet.

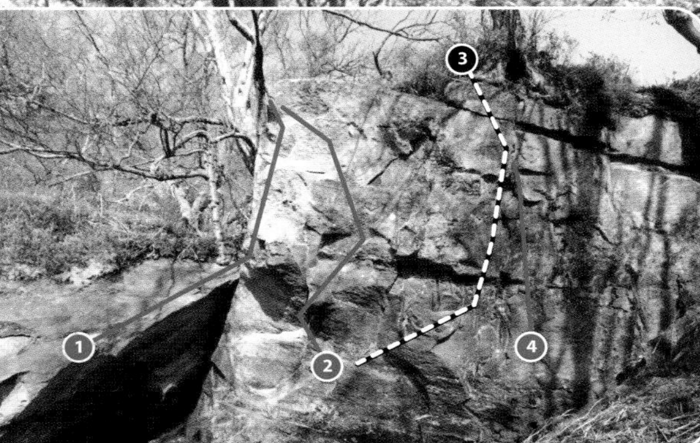

Mick Radford on Mick's Extention

Iron Stones

1. Project Traverse the lip from the left, topping out at the right end. Some of the stones are solid, honest!

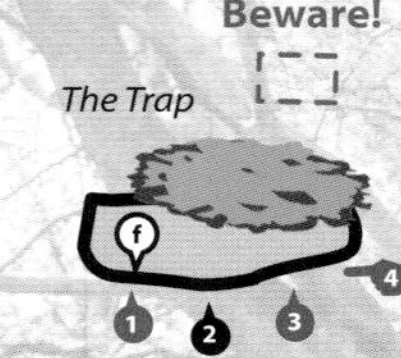

The Trap

1. The Trap Left-hand 6c SS
Reach the arête from the undercuts and faint footholds, then finish up the arête, **6a** from standing.

2. The Trap Right-hand 7a SS
A very tricky start gains a good pocket then finishes up the arête. **6a+** from standing.

3. Mick's Shortcut 6a+ SS
From the curved scoops pull onto the slab and finish up the arête.

4. Mick's Extension 6a+
Traverse into the arête from the far right-hand end.

Martin Parker on The Trap Left-hand 6c

Lee Robinson on Liberate 6c

Liberation Boulder

1. The Lip 7b SS Traverse the lip from the far left and finish up Liberate. Classic.
2. Lip Sink 6a SS From the large pocket climb over the lip direct, via the thin rib.
3. Liberate 6c SS From the large pocket head right until you can pop up to a right-hand crimp over the blunt arête.

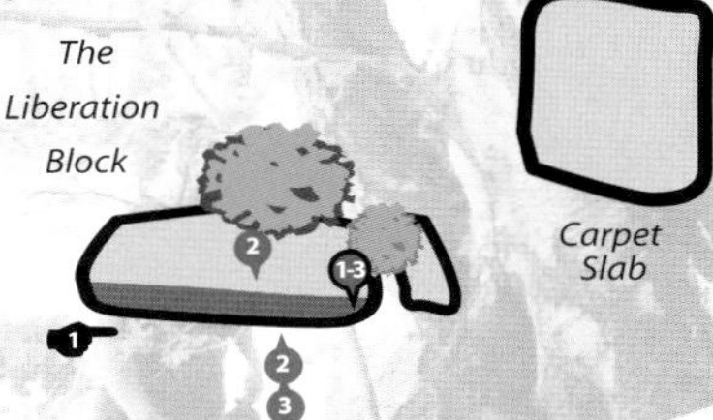

Carpet Slab *A few problems have been done on this block.*

Martin Parker on The Lip 7b

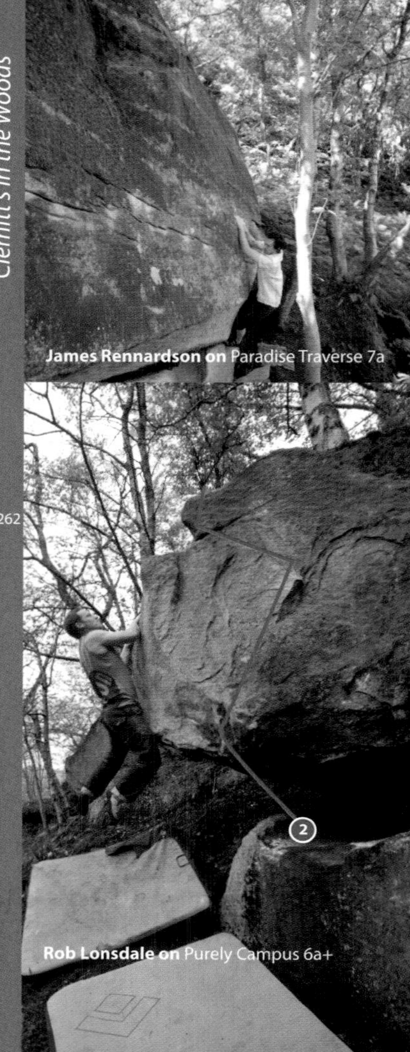

James Rennardson on Paradise Traverse 7a

Rob Lonsdale on Purely Campus 6a+

Campus Block

Perched nicely on another block.

1. Purely Campus 6a+ From a kneeling start campus the rising lip from left to right. Finish with both hands on the highest point.

2. The Friendly Fat Robin 6b SS From the block gain the undercut and follow with a tricky foot swap to reach up the face.

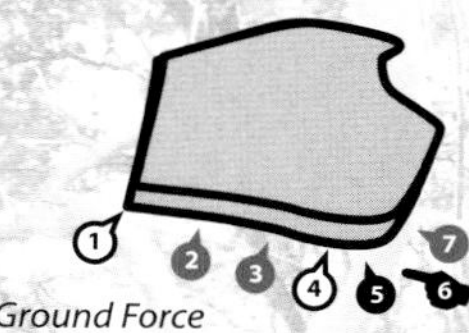

Ground Force

Needs a bit more of a clean.

1. Project The arête from sitting.

2. Little Ewoks 6a SS Climb the groove using super slick footwork.

3. Big Red Riding Hood 6c SS Start behind a tree and move up to good crimpy rails. Get a high right foot and rock upwards to the large shelf. Difficult for the short.

4. Project SS Climb the arête on its left! The tree is slightly in the way but it may be possible.

5. Spotless 7a SS Under the left of the arête gain the ledge, swing right to a good hold, then use the rib on the arête and higher rib gaston to gain the further ledge.

6. Paradise Traverse 7a SS From the right end, traverse with feet under the block then gain the arête from low down and follow to finish.

7. Cleaner 6b+ SS Start right of Spotless, pull up to the undercut and the use the layaway for the left hand to gain the ledge.

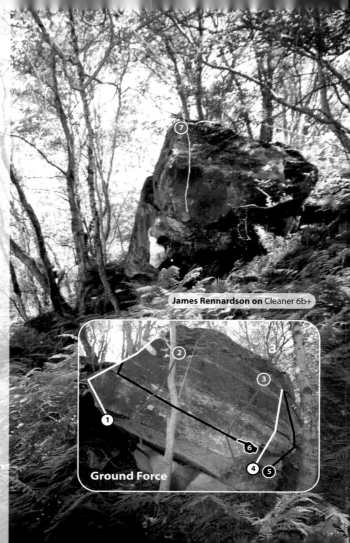

James Rennardson on Cleaner 6b+

Ground Force

Clemitt's North is situated on a high plateau at the far north end of Clemitt's Woods. You will find a good handful of problems on little buttresses bearing quality sandstone. It's best from late autumn until early spring. There are also uncompleted projects here, on a hard iron-rich wall, with a boggy landing.
A connoisseur venue for the lovers of deep, dark places. Take a brush-stick and enjoy.

Approach: Park half a mile further north than the main Clemitt's parking at the side of the road. A track leads east down to a gate. Once you have passed this, head south into the woods. The craggy edges will soon appear on your right.

See map on page 243

OS: NZ 711041
Walk: 5 minutes
Faces east

James Kitson on Smiling Arête 7a

5

Camp Hill is situated above the village of Botton on the flanks of Danby Dale. There are several areas featuring a combination of boulders and edges with some excellent problems within a 600 metre stretch of moor. The Main Crag area has most of the large boulders scattered below and further north are other boulders and small edges. The rock is simply some of the best around with only a few sandy boulders. There is something for everyone here with a fair proportion of problems in the lower grades and a good handful of harder problems.

Approach: Take the turning off the main Hutton-le-Hole to Castleton road signposted 'Rosedale Abbey' and follow it for a mile and a half until a tight left turn can be made onto a small single-track road to 'Fryup' (just before the car park for the Millenium Stone). Follow this for nearly two miles and use the same parking as Clemitt's at the Wolf Pit tumulus layby. Cross the road and follow the marked bridleway that heads north-west for about five minutes, then take the faint path along the top of the edge, which should bring you out above the crag.

OS Map: NZ 701043
Walk 10 minutes
Faces west

Centuries of Graffiti on the Strict Boulder

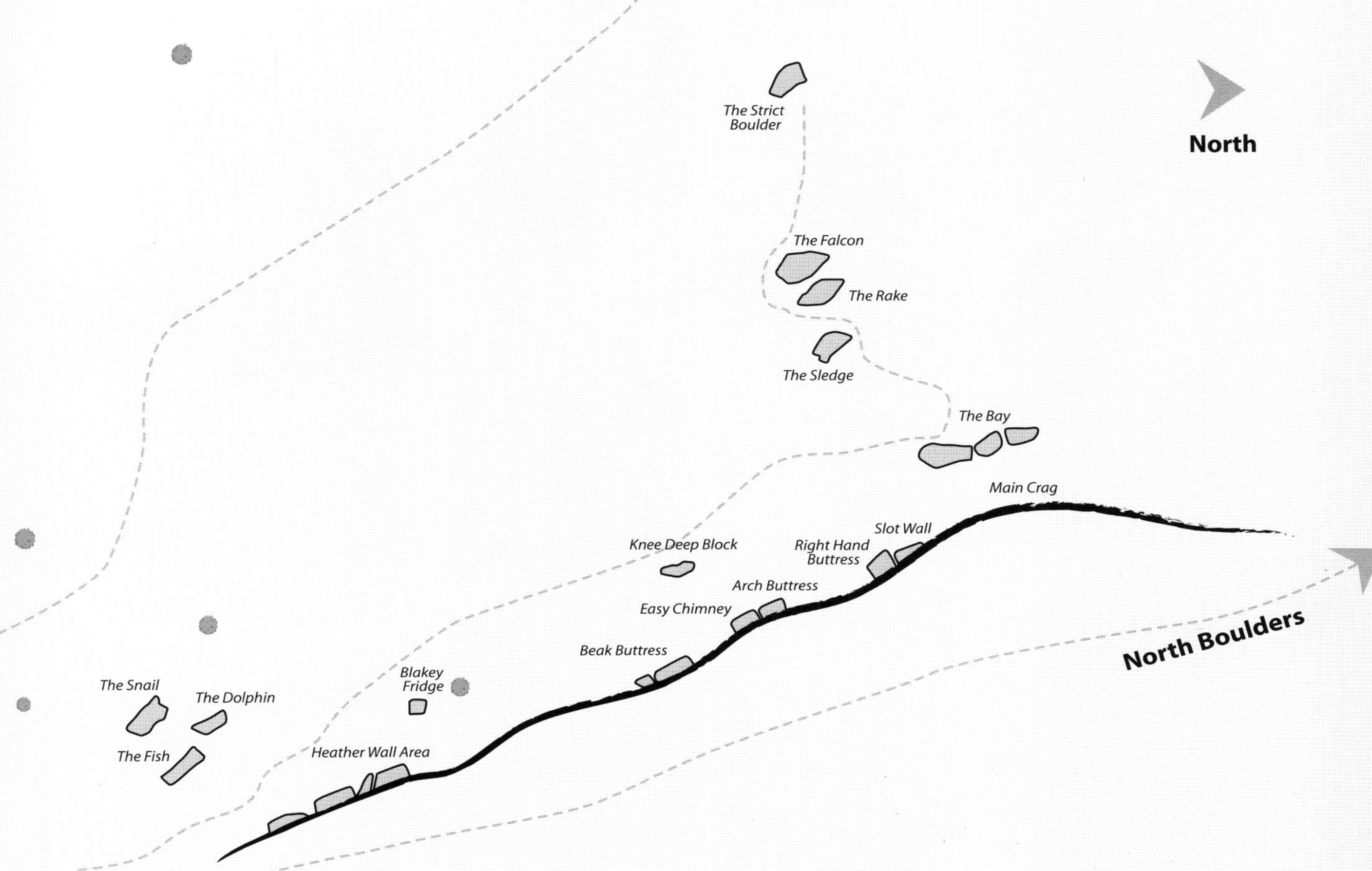
The Strict Boulder
North
The Falcon
The Rake
The Sledge
The Bay
Main Crag
Slot Wall
Right Hand Buttress
Knee Deep Block
Arch Buttress
Easy Chimney
North Boulders
Beak Buttress
Blakey Fridge
The Snail
The Dolphin
The Fish
Heather Wall Area

The Strict Boulder

The lowest block at the bottom of the hill, with a flat top.

1. 4 SS Start using the large flake-hold and move up direct.

2. 6a SS Layback the short crack with a long reach to finish.

3. 4 SS Follow the slanting flake-crack then finish left of the groove.

4. The Arête 6b+ SS Follow the arête using crimps or anything else on either side. The stand is **6a.**

4a. Strict Arête 7a SS Use the arête only for hands, starting on the left side. The standing start with the pinch is **6b+.**

5. On Edge 6a SS Gain the break using the thin crack and dyno or reach up static.

6. Captain Slapstick 5+ SS Follow the sloping rail then rock-out rightwards. Finish as On Edge at **6a+.**

Lee Robinson on Strict Arête 7a

Lower Boulders

Just up the hill from The Strict Boulder are further low problems with good landings.

The Falcon

1. Project Traverse SS Start at the very left side of the boulder and traverse rightwards along the lip.
2. The Falcon 6a+ SS Start below the cracks, gain the lip, then top-out about a metre to the right.
3. 5+ SS Climb the excellent thin crack.

Just behind The Falcon and next to the path is a short worthwhile problem.

The Rake

4. Red Arête 6a SS Climb the arête using anything else along the way.

The Sledge

5. Minimalist 5 SS Climb the short flake-crack to finish on good holds.
6. Fortune 6b From a crouch, stuff your fingers underneath the bulge and use the flared crack to finish direct.
7. Black Mirror 6a+ SS Start using the break and slot to latch the top and then finish.
8. Cold Morning 5 SS Start sitting on a boulder and use the break and small pocket to go for the top.
9. Sledge 4 SS The undercut arête starting from the low break.
10. Despise 6a SS Start with feet below the roof and hands in some shallow pockets. Gain the left arête and use to finish.

Steve Phelps on Black Mirror 6a+

9
10

Just below the main crag in a sheltered bay are some hard little test-pieces.

The Bay

1. **Left Arête 5** Climb the arête using pebble footholds to start.
2. **Centre Wall 5+** A tricky start leads to a mantel finish.
3. **Baby Arête 6c+ SS** The small arête on thin holds.
4. **Bay Arête 7a SS** A Camp Hill test-piece.
5. **Bay Wall 7a SS** Start as Bay Arête but stretch across to the centre of the break and finish direct.
6. **Arête 6c+** Climb the slanting arête to the break, then finish direct.

There are a few more isolated problems behind The Bay.

Across to the right of the crag is:

Slot Wall

Difficult to get a mat on the ledge. It's safer without it as it slides off. Be careful!

1. **Left Slot 5+** From the good slot reach for the top, then finish direct.
2. **Slot and Pocket 6a+**. A tricky problem and fairly bold. Top-out left or right, not direct.

Right Hand Buttress

3. **Flakey Wall 5** Climb left side of the buttress using flakes.
4. **Pickpocket 6a** The centre of the wall on pockets up to larger holds.
5. **Allain's Arête 5** The arête to the right is pleasant.

Steven Phelps on Pickpocket 6a

Pete Jackson on Knee Deep 6a+

Knee Deep Block

1. Knee Deep 6a+ SS Start low on pockets, gain the blunt arête, then follow this right to the top.

Arch Buttress

2. Lost Cause 2 Start on a boulder and follow a flake in the groove.
3. Lost Crack 4+ The thin crack on the left side of the front face.
4. Lost Wall 5+ The centre of the wall passing breaks.
5. Lost Groove 1+ The shallow groove left of the chimney.

Traverse 6b *Traverse the buttress in either direction using the slopey rail, going no higher than 2m.*

Easy Chimney

6. Hookey 4+ The right wall of the chimney via a break and a pocket.
7. The Good 'Un 4+ The wall just left of the arch via a single pocket.
8. The Arch 4+ Climb the centre of the wall through the arch.
9. Silly Arête 3+ Up the short arête.

Beak Buttress

10. Who Cares 3 The wall at the left side of the ledge.
11. The Mantel 6b SS Directly mantel the ledge without sneaking off right, which reduces the grade significantly.
12. Eliminate Wall 6a The wall to the right.
13. Blunt Arête SS 6b+ The undercut arête starting with the arête and a good left-hand crimp. Harder or not depending on which block you start with for your feet. The standing start is **6a**.
14. Who Nose 3+ Layback up the arête.

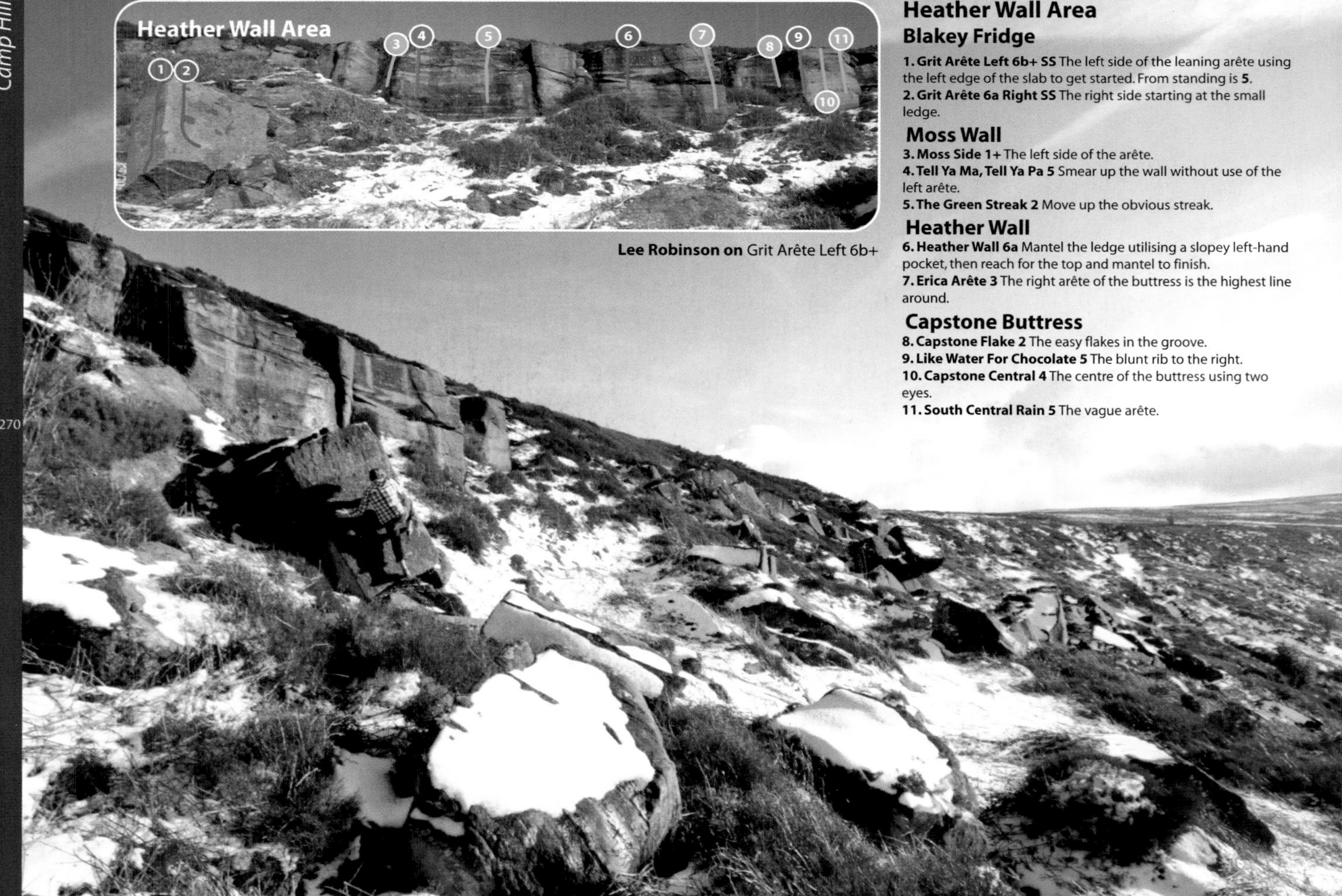

Lee Robinson on Grit Arête Left 6b+

Heather Wall Area

Blakey Fridge

1. Grit Arête Left 6b+ SS The left side of the leaning arête using the left edge of the slab to get started. From standing is **5**.

2. Grit Arête 6a Right SS The right side starting at the small ledge.

Moss Wall

3. Moss Side 1+ The left side of the arête.

4. Tell Ya Ma, Tell Ya Pa 5 Smear up the wall without use of the left arête.

5. The Green Streak 2 Move up the obvious streak.

Heather Wall

6. Heather Wall 6a Mantel the ledge utilising a slopey left-hand pocket, then reach for the top and mantel to finish.

7. Erica Arête 3 The right arête of the buttress is the highest line around.

Capstone Buttress

8. Capstone Flake 2 The easy flakes in the groove.

9. Like Water For Chocolate 5 The blunt rib to the right.

10. Capstone Central 4 The centre of the buttress using two eyes.

11. South Central Rain 5 The vague arête.

The Southern Blocks

Three boulders at the far south of the crag hold some good short problems.

The Fish Boulder

1. Fish Head 6c Climb a small slab, jam a foot in and reach onto the lip. Cut loose and make a difficult mantel to finish.

1a. 6a Start with hands below the top and climb the hanging arête.

*The slab to the right can be climbed from standing at **6a** - by stepping off the block and starting below the top.*

The Dolphin

2. 3+ Follow the short flake on the left side.

3. The Dolphin 6a+ The centre line using the sharp hold also used on the next problem.

4. 5 Use the sharp hold for the left hand to gain better holds near the top, then finish.

The Snail

5. 6a SS Start underneath the low roof, then mantel.

6. 6b Use a sharp hold for a difficult pop for the top.

7. 6a SS Start at the low break and traverse leftwards until you are below a crimp edge on the small slab with a slopey finish.

8. 6a SS Start as the last problem. Move left then up the layaway feature using anything else along the way to another slopey top-out. Just using the layaway is **6b**.

9. 6b SS Move up the wall by use of friable protrusions to yet another slopey finish.

10. 6a SS Make a long reach across to the right to finish.

Steven Phelps on Problem 8 6a

Steve Ramsden on Phileas Fogg

North Boulders

5 minutes further north are some good problems, worth the walk.

Overhanging Buttress

1. Flat Cap SS 6b Start on the ledge and climb through the roof to make a long reach from the pocket or arête to finish.

2. Athletes Don't Eat Yorkshire Puddings 6b+ Layback up the vague arête right of the scoop.

3. The Grand North Face 4 Climb on ledges to a crack and finish.

Phileas Fogg Wall

4. Away From The Smog 7a+ SS The left arête starting at the big hole.

5. Jules Verne 7b+ SS Undercut the large hole and slot, then make a long reach to a thin crimp out left. A flat hold from the next problem is used for the right foot.

6. Phileas Fogg 7a SS Start at pockets and take the excellent direct line up the wall via sidepulls, flat holds and a break. **6c** from standing.

7. Passepartout 5+ The arête using pockets to a slopey finish. Old-school grade.

8. South Face 5 Up the wall on pockets to a thin crack.

9. Right Arête 3 Tackle the right arête.

10. On the Ledge 6b SS Start on the ledge and climb the groove, without feet on the ledge.

11. Fix 5 Starting from crouch undercutting the arête, gain the lip then top-out left of the nose.
12. Project SS Start low and climb over the bulge.
13. 5+ SS Using a good slot and a block for feet, gain a higher slot then the top.
14. Project SS Using a 'bird's foot' feature and the blunt arête.
15. Project SS Mantel onto the slab.
16. Project Hang the slot and sloping undercut under the lip, gain the lip and finish up the arête.
17. 5+ Up the right side of the slab, with no hands.
18. 5 SS The right arête.
19. 4 SS Climb just right of the arête without using it.
20. 4 The left arête.
21. 5 Reach or jump for the break then finish via a flake.
22. Reform Club 6c SS Start at a large sidepull and move leftwards across the wall to some thin holds. From here pop for an edge then finish direct.
23. Perform Club 6a SS Start as the last problem, but reach out to the right arête. Finish direct.

Dave Warburton on **Fix 5**

The Finkelstones are a collection of small edges and boulders on the wooded eastern edge of a plateau in the secluded valley of Fryup Dale. Although not plentiful there are some worthwhile problems on good solid sandstone, mostly in the mid grades. Due to tree cover and bracken growth the venue is probably best avoided during summer; however it's a great venue to visit from autumn through to the spring.

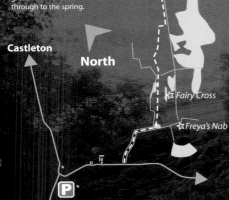

Approach: Use the same directions as Clemitt's North **(See page 242).** From there, drive north for about half a mile to a flat grassy parking spot just before a T-junction, where the road heads off Danby Rigg into Little Fryup Dale. **From the parking**, walk east down the road to Fryup. 200m after Stonebeck Gate Farm, take the public bridleway (a green lane) through the gate on the left. This leads to the next gate and then take the turn to the right to yet another gate . The path then goes through a few copses and through another gate onto the moor. Follow the path north-east across the field and after about 5 minutes take a right on a faint path going through the heather to reach a wall. Follow the wall north to where it bends round rightwards to a gap, where part has collapsed. About half way down into the next field go through another gap in the wall. Walk diagonally down between the location of an old gate in the wall and into the trees on a well-defined path going downhill. After 100m break off left to the boulders. Do not approach from below as the land is private.

OS Map: NZ 732061
Walk: 30 minutes
Faces south-east

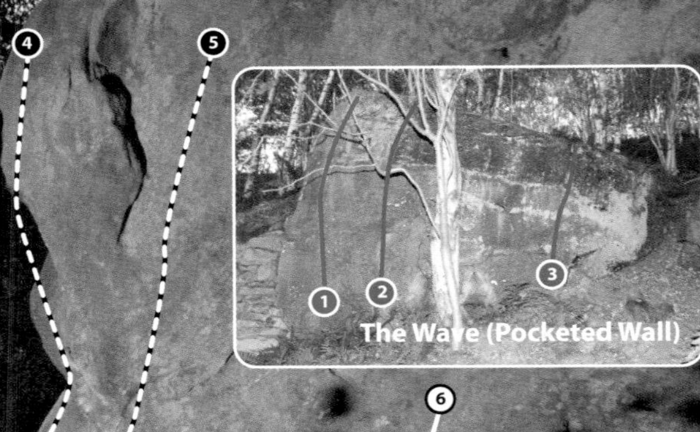

Lee Robinson on Aurora's Encore 7b+

Zillertal Block

The first little buttress you come across is:

The Wave (Pocketed Wall)

1. Stone Wall 5+ SS Start on the left side of the wall and climb direct using the layaway/arête feature.

2. Where The Wild Things Are 6a+ SS Start at a flake and move up the slab using pockets.

3. Wizards of the Night 6a SS Start in the centre of the wall, to the right of the tree. Move up on pockets rightwards to a difficult sloping finish. A variation with the same start, but moving leftwards on pockets to another difficult finish is **7a.**

Just 10m down the hill.

Zillertal Block

4. Labyrinth 7a+ SS Start by jamming the crack beneath the roof with the right hand and left hand on the sloping arête. Make difficult moves up the arête using anything else along the way. From standing is **6a**.

5. Aurora's Encore 7b+ SS Start by jamming the crack beneath the roof with both hands. Climb out onto the face without the arête, using a variety of different techniques including crimping, long reaches and thuggery.

6. Project SS Under the block but climb rightwards on the crimps avoiding the good holds on the previous problems.

The next set of rocks are just to the left of the stone wall, some 50m further than the hole in the wall.

The Warren

7. Thumper 6b+ SS Start on the left side at sidepulls. Make your way up past the shelves and across to the arête, up which the problem finishes.

8. Bambino 7a SS Start with a thumb mono and sidepull and climb direct using branches to finish.

9. Bambi Crack 5+ SS Jam the crack.

10. Project SS Use the undercut then climb the arête on small crimps, avoiding the crack.

11. 4 The left side of the next wall using the tree to finish.

12. 3 The right side of the wall moving left to finish at the tree again.

Back through the wall and down the hill is:

Porthole Wall

13. Port Arête 5 SS Follow the short but satisfying arête.

14. Port of Call 6c SS Make a difficult starting move to the hole. Finish direct without the arête.

Below this is a long low block with a hard project - a left to right traverse avoiding holds on the top lip, topping out at the right end.

About 20m downhill is another boulder.

Deer Wall

15. 5+ SS Start at the left side of the wall and climb direct. Finish rightwards up the slab.

16. Chain Gang 6a+ SS Same start as the last problem, but make a rising left to right traverse of the wall.

17. 6a SS Climb the centre of the wall to the traverse ledges. Finish as the traverse.

About 100m south, just above a shooting hut is another series of problems including an unclimbed highball prow and some smaller problems. If you follow the woods south-west on the same level for about 10 minutes until you reach a clearing there's a large slab just above the fields (grid reference NZ 726054). This is Finkel Slab and it holds some good lower grade problems on clean sandstone, in a nice setting.

Matthew Ferrier on Bambino 7a

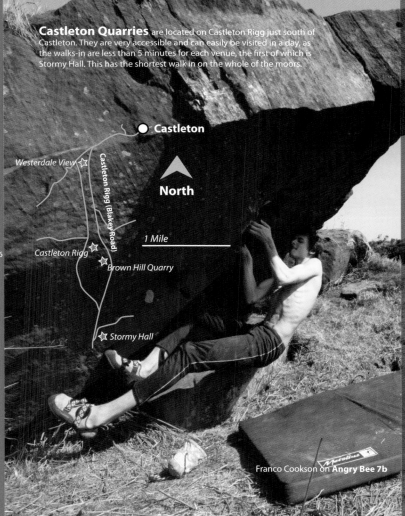

Castleton Quarries are located on Castleton Rigg just south of Castleton. They are very accessible and can easily be visited in a day, as the walks-in are less than 5 minutes for each venue, the first of which is Stormy Hall. This has the shortest walk in on the whole of the moors.

Castleton
North
Westerdale View
Castleton Rigg (Blakey Road)
1 Mile
Castleton Rigg
Brown Hill Quarry
Stormy Hall

Franco Cookson on **Angry Bee 7b**

Stormy Hall is well worth a visit if passing, that's not just because the walk in is minimal. The blocks may not be tall, but they hold a few brilliant test-pieces.

OS Map: NZ 683040
Walk: 30 seconds
Faces east

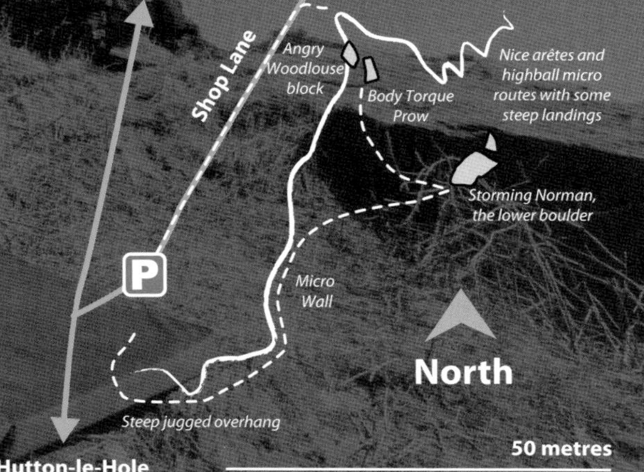

Body Torque Prow

1. Body Torque 7a+ SS The prow is tackled via a large undercut hold, crimps around the arête and a poor left-hand fingerlock. Powerful.

2. Angry Bee 7b SS From the undercut without use of the arête.

3. Small Torque 5+ SS Mount the block direct. A lower start has been done using an obvious undercut under the roof at **7a+.**

4. Endless Torque 6a SS Start at Small Torque, traverse left and top-out round the corner.

Angry Woodlouse Block

5. I Hate Vertebrates 5 SS Use the big pocket to gain the top.

6. Angry Woodlouse 6c SS Using a slanting jug and a crimp, rock across to the sidepull and pop for the top.

7. Arête 3 SS Spicy top-out.

The next two problems lie on the short wall to the right.

8. 4+ SS Climb the wall, initially using pockets, then up the vague arête.

9. 4 SS Start on the small shelf and climb direct.

Steve Ramsden on **Body Torque 7a+**

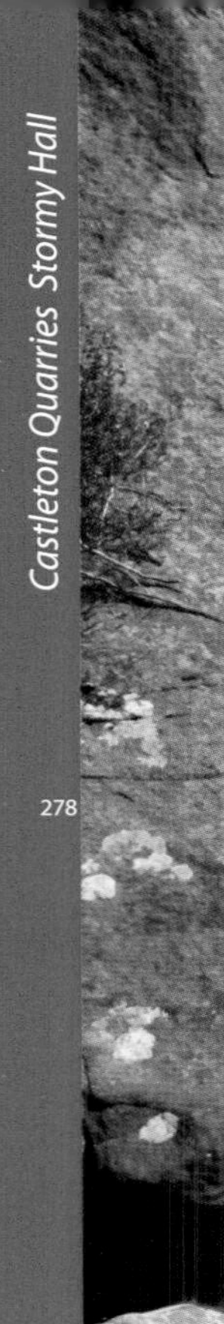

Storming Norman Boulder

At the bottom of the hill is:

1. Dooge 5+ SS Pop and rock left to the big slot on the right edge.

2. Dawes Couldn't Do It 6a+ A palming rock-over onto the slab.

3. Goes With Toes 6a+ SS The right of the scoop at the bottom. Move leftwards on the sloping arête to find the mono for success.

4. Storming Norman 6b SS Start left of the heather, traverse leftwards on slopers on the lip at first, then use better holds further back and rock-over to top-out on the good scoop. Can be extended to finish up the left of the scoop.

5. Direct Storm 6c SS Start with both hands on an undercut at the back of the roof. Move direct to a sharp hold, then the lip and finish as Storming Norman.

6. Left in Storm 7a SS Start at the same undercut at the back of the roof, but this time move left on small pockets to the lip. Finish left of the scoop.

Franco Cookson on Goes With Toes 6a+

Lee Robinson on Problem 6

Micro Wall Area

1. 6b Traverse from the crack on the right to the left arête using holds around the sloping lip.
2. Sidepull Slab 5+ SS The slab using a right-hand crimp and left-hand edge. Finish direct.
3. Jagged Arête 4 SS The sharp arête. Escape direct.
4. Micro Slab 5+ SS Start on the small shelf and lunge for the thin edge on the slab. Use the crack to finish.
5. Triple Cracks 5 SS Starting on a another small shelf, make your way up the obvious cracks at the right end of the buttress. Mantel to finish.

Prow

6. 4+ SS Start at the left side on the ledge and climb up to finish at the left side of the overhang.
7. 5 SS Start at the same ledge, but this time climb the wall underneath the roof rightwards to scale the roof direct.
8. 3 SS Start the same again but instead of scaling the roof move right to finish up the right side.
9. 6b SS A hard start to gain the good edge, finish more easily up the shallow scoop.

Brown Hill Quarry is a small east-facing quarry of smooth clean sandstone in a nice moorland setting. It includes several highball boulder problems of grade of 5 and above, the best of which are on the main central wall. It's a good place to climb on a hot sunny day, as it tends to be in the shade.

Approach: The parking is a little over half a mile north of Stormy Hall and just over a mile south of Castleton on the main Castleton to Hutton-le-Hole moor road. Park at a large lay-by and viewpoint over looking Danby Dale. The top of the quarry can be seen on the opposite side of the road up the hill. Walk up either side of a spring to reach it. **See map on page 276**.

OS Map: NZ 685054
Walk: 1 minute
Faces east

Lee Robinson on Forgotten Angel 6b+

Brown Hill

1. 5 Start just to the right of a heather-filled corner. Climb up the slab to some good holds, gain the top then pull over direct using a useful edge for the left hand.

2. 5 Climb the small wall using the arête to start. Once at the halfway ledge move up the chimney on the left to finish.

3. Forgotten Angel 6b+ The overhang direct, gaining a small slot and a tiny left crimp. Dare you pop for the top?

4. 5 The groove to the right starts using a curving corner crack and finishes using heather-pulling techniques.

5. Main Wall Traverse 6b Start to the right of a thin crack at a good hold. Traverse low and rightwards on nice crimps and layaways to finish with both hands on the square-cut layaway of Brown Hill Wall. Can be reversed at roughly the same grade.

6. Central Wall 5+ Start at the good hold right of the thin crack. Climb rightwards up the wall to the jug at two-thirds height. Either finish here or continue up and right across to the capping stones.

7. Sam's Wall 6a Start at the head-height sidepull and use this to gain the centre of the wall up to the two-thirds jug. Again finish here or continue to the top.

8. Brown Hill Wall 6a Start at an obvious square-cut layaway at the right side. Move up to a loose looking hold at some heather and climb direct to a break, then finish by moving right to the capping stones.

9. Brown Hill Wall Direct 6a Start as the last problem up to the loose looking hold, but this time break off slightly right to a sloping rail and finish direct to the capping stones (without using the right edge).

To the right is a corner crack, but due to its loose finish it's not really worth it.

10. 5 Climb into a groove and trend leftwards to a point where you can pull round onto the slab at some good holds. Finish direct.

11. 5 SS Start the undercut slab using the arête and small holds out to the right. Finish direct, with a heather top-out.

16 3 2 0 0

Castleton Rigg is a small quarry on the eponymous ridge, north of Blakey Ridge. It holds some nice, easier grade, highball boulder problems mainly with good flat landings. The rock is good and solid, though there is the occasional suspect flake.

Approach: Situated just over a mile south from the village of Castleton, on the Rigg. You can park either beneath the quarry on the small road near Hollins Farm and walk uphill or on the main Castleton to Hutton-le-Hole road (Blakey Road), after which you follow faint tracks across the moor. **See map on page 276**.

OS Map: NZ 681057
Walk: 2 minutes
Faces west

Far Right Buttress

Just south of the main quarry are some harder challenges on a sound buttress.

Problems are described from right to left, as originally recorded.

1. Route One 1+ Climb the arête at the right end.
2. The Face 6a Start where the overlap meets the ground and climb straight up past a shallow slot.
3. Two-Faced 6+ Start on a small ledge and use crimps to get high enough for a left-hand sidepull, to get established halfway. Next aim for a pocket, then continue up (keeping inbetween the green streaks).
4. 3+ Start where a diagonal crack meets the floor and climb up, bearing slightly right of the upper crack.

Steven Phelps on The Face 6a

Castleton Rigg Main

The sheltered north end of the quarry has the most climbs.

1. North Wall 3 Follow the crack in the wall, rightwards.
2. Face Route 4+ Climb the face to the left of the large hole, without use of the crack on the left.
3. Hole in the Wall 3+ Reach the hole, then ascend directly between the two flake cracks.
4. Groovy 3+ Start in the sentry box and climb out leftwards into the flake crack above.
5. Sentry Box Crack 4 Climb out of the right side of the sentry box and follow the thin crack above.
6. The Arête 3 The arête on its left side. Can be made more difficult using the arête for hands only.
7. The Overlap 2 The slab just to the right of The Arête, surmounting an overlap.
8. Short Slab 2 Climb the right side of the slab,1.5m right of the last problem.
9. The Narrow Slab 4 Up the centre of the triangular slab, 1.5m right of the last problem.
10. Yellow Streak 4 The yellow-streaked slab, crossing leftwards onto a hanging slab which is climbed on its left side using the edge. Fairly bold.
11. Eraser 4 On the taller part of the buttress is a series of flaky holds. Climb these without deviation.
12. The Crack 2 Follow the crack from the lowest point of the buttress.
13. Green Streak 5 Climb up to the ledge then ascend direct to a long reach for a hold at the top of the streak. Finish as The Crack.
14. The Slab Variation 5 A direct variation of the next problem up small but positive edges.
15. The Slab 4 Start as the last problem and follow a series of holds rightwards to a point where you can move up leftwards.

10m to the right is a lone slab.

16. Red Slab Arête 4 Climb the arête using thin smears for the feet.

5m right of this is:

17. Scrambled Egg 5 Climb the arête without stepping out right.

10m to the right are several low grade scrambles.

Lee Robinson on The Arête 3

Castleton Rigg Main Quarry

Right End

Westerdale View is a small venue with fantastic views over to Westerdale and is worth a visit, being only a short walk from the parking. There are a few good problems on coarse quarried sandstone, with a high iron content. The amount of climbing is limited, so it's best combined with the other venues on Castleton Rigg.

Approach: Park at a series of lay-bys just after a grass field on the east side of the main Castleton to Hutton-le-Hole road (Blakey Road) and about 200m after the cattle grid, as you leave Castleton. Cross the road and keep well left of the fenced off area to follow a series of faint paths over the crest of the hill, which will take you to the quarry. **See map on page 276**.

OS Map: NZ 680072
Walk: 1 minute
Faces west

1
2
3
4

1. Lokal Yokel 7a+ SS The first hard looking section of the main wall, up a blunt nose. Start from undercuts. The standing start is **6b.**
2. Jack and the Beanstalk 7a The diagonal crack from standing, although you might do better looking for sidepulls on either side rather than using the crack itself. The sit-start is a project.
3. The Craic 5+ SS Start using undercuts and cross rightwards up into the crack to finish up the loose groove. The standing start is **5**
4. Something Special 6b+ SS The right-most line of the quarry. Start at a vertical crimp, then gain the down-pointing flake by several methods and top-out using crimps. The standing start is **6a+**

Steven Phelps on Something Special 6b+

Rabbit Hill is a small collection of blocks and edges on the hillside opposite Round Crag. It is so-called because the hills leading round into Farndale have thousands of rabbit holes. Obvious really!

Approach: Use the same approach as Round Crag. Follow the old railway line north initially, then trend back to the south, following the moor top down to the blocks. More problems can be found along the west-facing edges of Farndale.

OS Map: SE 670989
Walk: 35 Minutes
Faces south-east

Brandon Copley on Depravation 7a

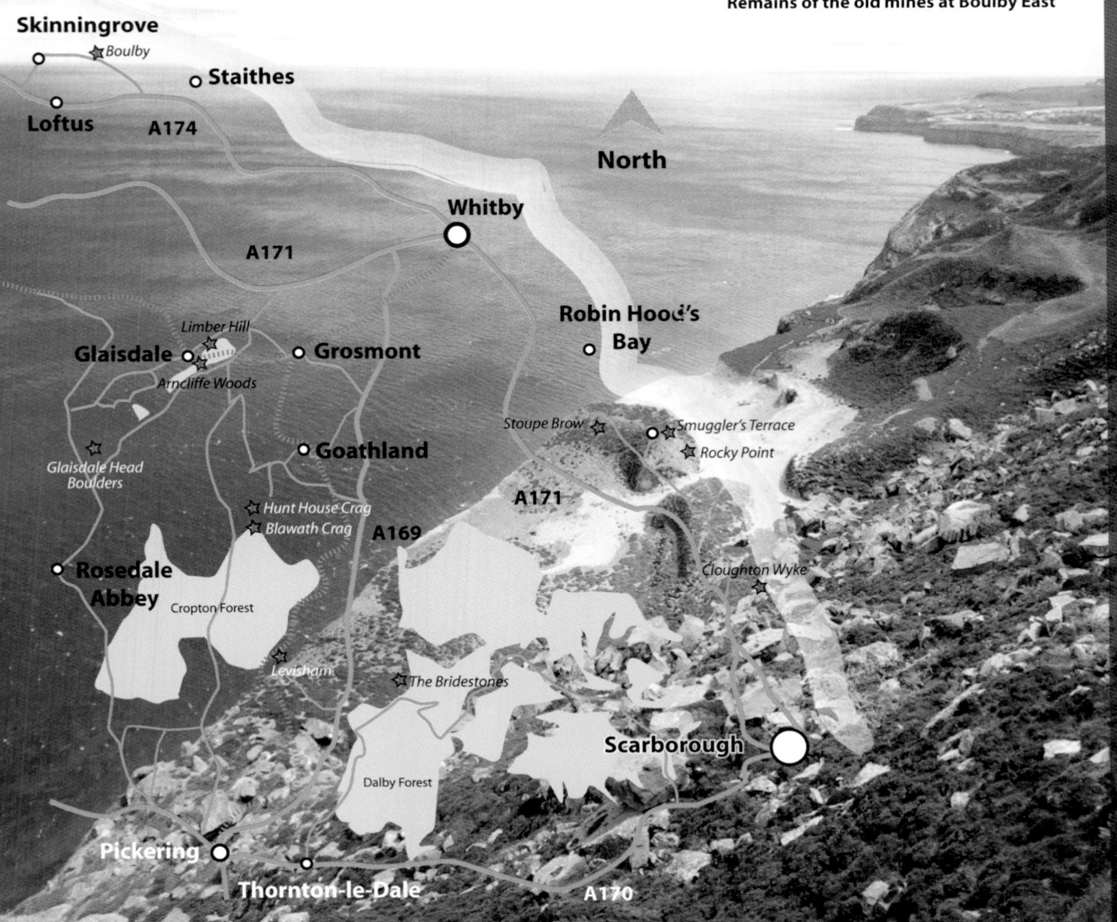

Remains of the old mines at Boulby East

Eastern and Coastal Area

Although there's not a huge amount of bouldering on this eastern side of the moors there's a good and diverse variety of venues. This ranges from the magical Arncliffe Woods in the Esk Valley to the obscure pinnacles of The Bridestones just outside Dalby Forest and all the way over to the coastal bouldering of Smuggler's Terrace high above the North Sea. Most of the venues have only recently been discovered and many are not well known as a result, but a visit in good bouldering conditions or a nice sunny day can rival a trip to more popular areas further west. This area is also home to the largest boulders on the moors, which are 'The Two Sisters' of Stoupe Brow, one of which goes by the name of 'Barry'.

The Bridestones are situated high above the valley of Staindale, in a beautiful setting on the boundaries of Dalby Forest and are divided into two areas. The Low Bridestones have five pinnacles and two small buttresses possessing problems mostly in the low grades. One of the rock formations here is the famous and photogenic Pepperpot, on which some of the best of the problems are found. The High Bridestones have two pinnacles and four large buttresses holding most of the higher-graded problems and also some excellent traverses around the mid grades. Most of the pinnacles have similar styles of climbing, with short sharp problems and awkward rounded top-outs. The majority of the buttresses are somewhat higher, bearing hard moves up to high roofs. The rock can be sandy and some buttresses may suffer from seepage, which can take a few days of good weather to dry out. Holds do occasionally break here as a result. Bouldering is permitted but traditional climbing with ropes of any kind is not. The Bridestones are managed by the National Trust and are very popular with walkers and day-trippers, so don't expect to have them to yourself.

Approach: **From the north,** follow the A169 out of Sleights, up Blue Bank and over the moors eventually passing RAF Fylingdales. The next landmark is the spectacular Hole of Horcum. About 3.5 miles after the large car park above this, turn left immediately after the Fox and Rabbit pub. After 2 miles take the left turn at the brown Dalby Forest sign.
From the south, either take the A169 (Whitby Road) out of Pickering for 4 miles to turn right at the Fox and Rabbit pub or follow the A170 into Thornton-le-Dale and follow signs for Dalby Forest going north. There's unfortunately a £7.00 toll road from the start of the forest drive, but it does pay for the forest's upkeep including the mountain bike trails. From here drive for 4.5 miles through Low Dalby village and past the visitor centre to the car parks. Park just before the reservoir in Staindale at grid reference SE 877904.
From the parking, follow a footpath to the second gate, which goes north into the forest. Continue and take either the path that goes uphill steeply or the other path left taking you gradually uphill. Both take the same time and bring you out at the First Pinnacle. The first gate, to the left takes you up Dovedale to the High Bridestones, though this takes longer and is steep; but is recommended for a nice walk out. **See map on page 290.**
Alternative ways in are by driving to the outskirts of the forest using David Lane just off the A169 or by parking at the Hole of Horcum car park and taking the public bridleway (Old Wilf's Way) to the east. Both take about 30 minutes.

OS Map: SE 874910
Walk: 10 minutes
Open aspect

* *There are more variations and problems here, some of which may have been done, though not recorded.*

Eighties Pete taking a rest on The Pepper Pot - Photo Jason Wood

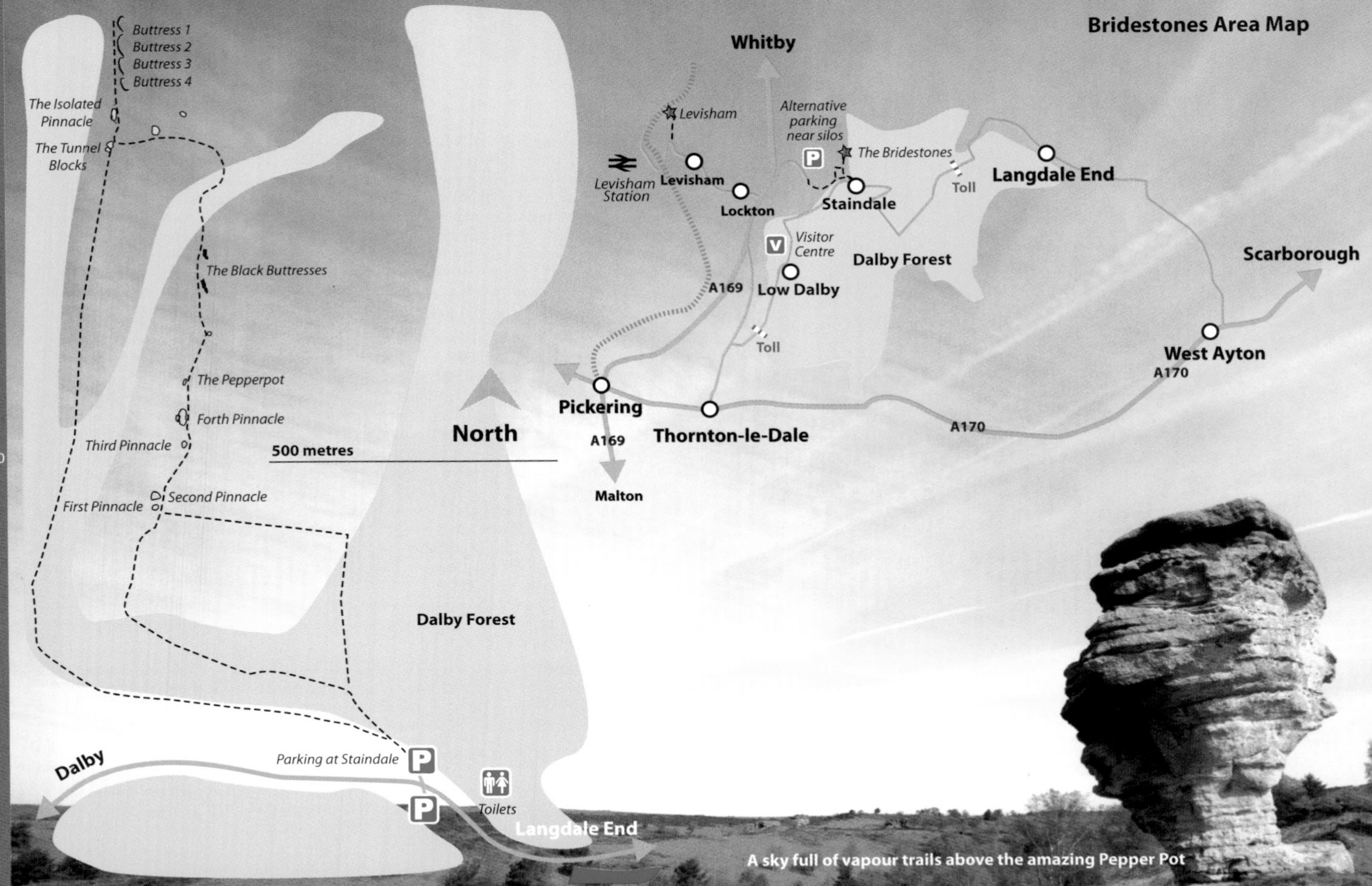

Bridestones Area Map
Whitby
Levisham
Alternative parking near silos
The Bridestones
Levisham Station
Levisham
Lockton
Staindale
Toll
Langdale End
Visitor Centre
Dalby Forest
A169
Low Dalby
Scarborough
Toll
West Ayton
A170
Pickering
Thornton-le-Dale
A170
A169
Malton
North
500 metres
Buttress 1
Buttress 2
Buttress 3
Buttress 4
The Isolated Pinnacle
The Tunnel Blocks
The Black Buttresses
The Pepperpot
Forth Pinnacle
Third Pinnacle
Second Pinnacle
First Pinnacle
Dalby Forest
Parking at Staindale
Dalby
Toilets
Langdale End

A sky full of vapour trails above the amazing Pepper Pot

First Pinnacle

1. Cave Route 5 From a low start in the cave, climb straight up or slightly to the right, which is a tad easier.
2. Descent 2 Use the holes but anything goes.
3. Big Round Jugs 3+ Start at the arête then move left on pockets.
4. Passion Play 3 The crack just to the right.
5. The Small Overhang 5+ The overhang, right of the crack.
6. Accidents Will Happen 5 The overhang in the centre.
7. Guano Wall 5 Start at the pocket, then move up on prominent flakes.
8. Side Pockets 5 Up pockets awkwardly, using sidepulls about 1m to the right.
9. Monkey Business 6a A direct line up the smoothest part of the wall using crimps and slopers.
10. Don't Grab the Bracken 5+ The steeper bulge finishing right.
11. What No Bracken? 5+ The bulge 1m to the right.
12. Pockets With Holes 5+ Use the pockets to gain the top. Tricky!
13. Unlucky For Some 5 1m to the right of the last problem.

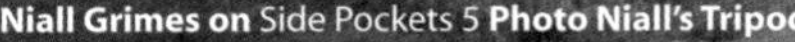
Niall Grimes on Side Pockets 5 **Photo Niall's Tripod**

Second Pinnacle

A good block with some bolder problems.

1. 5 The crack and roof.
2. 5 Climb the roof past two holds.
3. 5 The roof on two holds again.
4. 4+ Use the rib just before the scoop/cave, then hand jam.
5. 5 The scoop/cave to finish right.
6. Nosey 6a Climb the nose on its right side.
7. The Puzzle 6a Gain sidepulls for a lunge. Brilliant.
8. The Crack 5 Climb it!
9. 5+ Just left of the crack.
10. 4+ The steep wall.

Third Pinnacle

A good handful of problems. The traverse is very pumpy and a must if passing.

1. **North Face 3+** Large layaways on the north face lead to an awkward exit.
2. **Great Western 3+** The wall finishing left of the capping roof.
3. **West Way 3** The centre of the west face trending right to exit.

3a. **West Way Direct 5+** As above but finish via a mantel over the capping roof.

4. **Dinner Plate 5** Climb over the capping roof direct.
5. **South Face 3** Prow adjacent to the path.
6. **West World 4** Traverse the boulder but keep off the large ledge on the path side.

Lisa Robinson on West World 4

Tom Metcalfe on Horcum Traverse 5+

Fourth Pinnacle

1. 3 3m left of the chimney using a flake to a mantel finish.
2. 3 The arête to the right.
3. Horcum Traverse 5+ A traverse from 2 to 10, not going above 1m with feet until crossing the chimney crack, where height is gained to use undercuts and small pockets.
4. 4 The scoop moving right to exit.
5. 3+ Shallow roof to ledge.
6. Fast and Sloping Wins The Race 5+ SS Climb the overhang bulge at the corner on the left-hand chimney wall.
7. Chimney 2 The wide chimney crack.
8. Roof Route B 3+ Roof via an undercut.
9. Roof Route A 3+ The triangular roof via a hole.
10 Small Crack 2 The short crack, stepping left to finish.

The Pepperpot

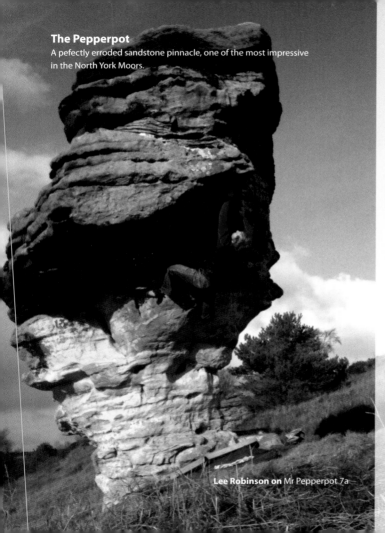

A pefectly erroded sandstone pinnacle, one of the most impressive in the North York Moors.

Lee Robinson on Mr Pepperpot 7a

The Pepperpot

1. Mrs Pepperpot 7a Climb the roof then traverse the lip rightwards. Finish up Mr Pepperpot.

2. Mr Pepperpot 7a SS Tackle the steepest part direct. Find the hidden hold!

3. Professor Pepperpot 6c SS Start as Mr Pepperpot going right along the break, up to a good hold. Reach high left to a small hold and top-out direct. Commiting and difficult to reverse.

4. Central Goove 6a Nice climbing. Watch out for bird droppings!

5. Chilli Pepper 5 Climb just to the left of the overhanging flake.

6. Master Pepperpot 6b The overhang via a pocket.

7. Peter Piper Picked a Peck of Pickled Pepper 5+ The left side of the block on the path side, moving right at the top

8. The Descent 5 Satistfiying, acending and descending.

9. Pot Belly 6a A Steep line on good flakes.

Juicy bilberries on the Initial Buttress

*Walk past another pinnacle to **The Black Buttresses.***

Initial Buttress

1. 6b A right to left traverse from the pinch.

2. 6a SS Start at the hole, then straight up the weakness.

3. 5+ SS Low start on pockets then straight up.

4. 6b SS Start in the cave, not using the jug or thread.

Just a bit further along the path is the:

Final Buttress

1. 4 SS Start at the lowest point of the buttress. Climb the bulge to gain a hollow break, then moving right jam 'the eyes' and mantel to finish.

2. Final Traverse 5 A right to left traverse of the buttress.

You have to descend across the valley and walk back up via steps to get to the next blocks. The first problems are in a small cave facing the path, the others are round the back. All of these problems are on weaker rock, so care should be taken.

The Cave Block

1. The Cave 5+ SS Start at the hole at the back left of the cave. Use slopey holds and make your way out into the centre of the roof on good holds. Finish direct, straight over the front edge.
1a. Left Finish 5 Same start as the last problem, but use the left wall of the cave. Top-out on the left.
2. The Hobbit 6a Starts at the back right-hand side of the cave with both hands in a break and feet in two obvious large holes. Climb straight out using heel-hooks and good holds, then make a strenuous move up and over the front of the cave. **2a. The Bad Hobbit 6a** Same start as The Hobbit but move right and top-out right.

Round to the left of the cave is a wall with two problems.

3. Nettle Wall 5 SS The centre of the wall starting on slopers.
4. Sandy Prow 5 SS Climb the prow at the left end.

The next block has a tunnel right through it with a classic roof problem, though it's rarely dry!

The Tunnel Block

5. The Tunnel 6b+ SS Start on the left side of the entrance, then work your way through the tunnel, for 7.5 metres of enjoyable roof-climbing.

Steven Phelps on Sandy Prow 5

The Isolated Pinnacle

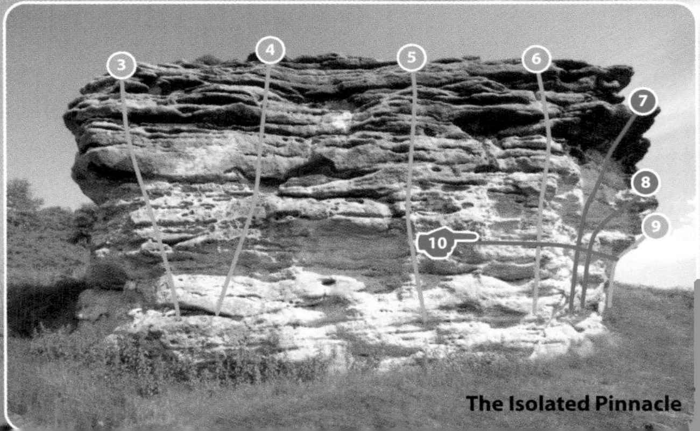

The Isolated Pinnacle

Rob Lonsdale on *Big Dog's Cock*

A very large block with some highball problems.

The Isolated Pinnacle

Problems left to right.

1. Wrong Time of the Month 4 The overhanging north wall on the left side.
2. Vin Rouge 4 The overhanging north wall on the right side.
3. Honeycomb 3 Start on a small ledge, then climb the right side of the arête trending left.
4. Scoop Wall 3+ Start on the small ledge again, then climb the scoop on the west face.
5. Red Flash 3+ 3m to the right of the last problem, up the left side of the bulge, on pockets.
6. Strawberry Fields 4 Start 2m to the right of the last problem. Ascend the right side of the next bulge on good holds.
7. Big Dog's Cock 5+ About 2m right of the last problem, climb into a scoop then over the roof.
8. Scarlet Pimpernel 5+ From the scoop of Big Dog's Cock, climb out right to the arête.
9. Red Light 4 Climb the arête starting on the right.
10. Little Red Robin 5 A left to right traverse. Start at Red Flash and finish at Red Light.
11. Southside 3 SS The right-most wall climbing past a large thread-type hold for both hands.

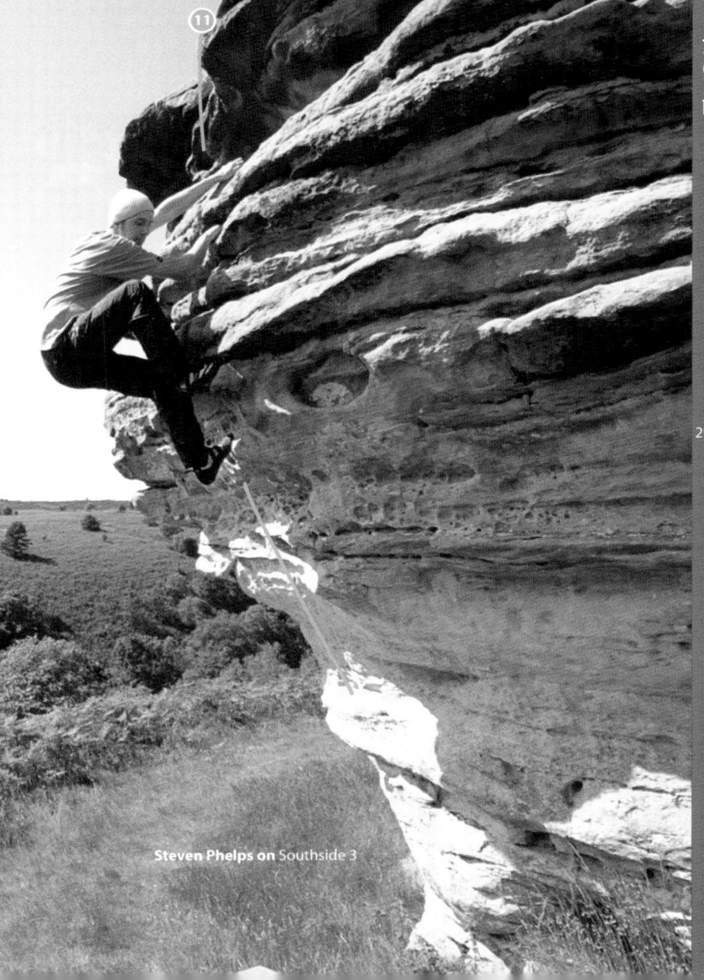

Steven Phelps on Southside 3

Buttress Four

Buttress Four

Problems left to right

1. Just For The Record 4 The arête at the far left end.

2. It's Just a Passing Phase 5 The steep wall, right of the arête. Crimps lead to a sandy layaway and direct finish.

3. Ain't No Lullaby 5 Climb the wall to a small triangular roof, then finish direct.

4. Where It All Began 5 Take a direct line up past an obvious undercut.

5. Wind Up 5 Just to the right is a shallow cave. Start at the left side of this using a big flat hold, then move up past an undercut to a prominent slot. Finish direct.

6. Gordini 5 Start at the right side of the shallow cave and climb direct.

7. Oh Carol 5 The wall at the right end of the buttress using sandy layaways, then over the roof.

8. Party Animal 5 Climb up and over the roof direct, utilising a dinner plate jug below the top.

9. Misplaced Childhood 3 Climb the short wall direct to the sapling.

10. Girdle Traverse 7a Start at the right end of the buttress then move into the corner of Oh Carol. A hard sequence of moves leads left around the bulge to gain sloping holds. Heel-hooks on broken rock enable a reach to undercuts to be made, then drop down to a big flat hold and a frantic rest. From here a rising traverse left is made using painful hand swaps on small edges. Lunge up and left to a good sidepull and continue more easily to the arête.

Lisa Robinson on Oh Carol 5

Buttress Three

1. Changes 4 The bubbly wall left of the crack.
2. Squeeze and Squirm 3 The wide crack separating the walls.
3. Juggler 4+ The wall in between a crack and the recess.
4. Audi Quattro 5 Start 2m right of the wide crack, climb the centre of the recess and the roof above.
5. Turbo Charged 5+ 5m right of the wide crack. From the back of the shallow cave climb the wall up to an undercut, then over the roof.
6. Theft 5 Climb up into a shallow recess, then exit right around the overhang.
7. Larceny 5 A direct start to Theft.
8. Standard Traverse 6b+ Start at the right end of the buttress at the initials J.O. Climb easily left to a good flat hold then use hard moves to an obvious knob or 'tennis ball' feature and on to another flat hold. Continue up following 'dinner plates' into a recess, round a bulge into Squeeze and Squirm and up to a break until a drop down below the final bulge to finish.
8a. Low-level Traverse 7a+ Start as Standard Traverse until the obvious knob or 'tennis ball' feature, drop down to a three-finger flake, then use technical and powerful moves through the recess and up to join Standard Traverse as Audi Quattro is reached (near the centre of the recess).
9. For Someone Very Special 2 The obvious leftwards-rising traverse.

Griff's Variations *A number of harder problems are based around the 'tennis ball' feature.*

Buttress Three

Buttress Two

Buttress Two

1. Northern Frights 5 The bulge to a rounded finish.
2. Super Low Traverse 4+ A left to right traverse, low in places.
3. Aurora 3+ Pull on good pockets on the bulge to the left of Northern Lights.
4. Northern Lights 4+ Rounded flakes lead through the bulge.
5. Borealis 4+ Start at the yellow sandy patch 3m to the left of the boulder in the ground. Climb direct from here.
6. Higgs Boson 5+ Takes the bulging wall 2m left of the boulder in the ground.
7. Winter Wonderland 5 Climb the wall directly in front of the small boulder at its base.
8. Toll Road 6a Start 3m to the right of the small boulder. From a good hold reach slopers, then up to the obvious break. Continue up juggy pockets to the hole near the lip, then move right to a sapling.
9. Nürburgring 7a SS Start 1.5m right of the last problem. From a right-hand flake go to crimps and a right mono, left to good holds, then slopers at the break following with the right-hand sloping undercut. Next it's a big reach left to a good large crimp (control the swing) and finish direct at the sapling.
10. Lucky Man 5+ Climb up to undercut the roof, then continue to fragile flutings.
11. Tainted Love 5 Climb directly up to a hanging flake.
12. Sambo Pati 4+ Climb up the bubbly weakness.
13. Griff's Traverse 6a A good right to left traverse.
14. Walk a Thin Line 4 The right-hand bubbly weakness up the slope.

Buttress One

The northern-most buttress

1. The New Number One 3+ The short wall on the north face, up the steep bulges.
2. Hoedown 3+ The short wall at the left side of the front face, using the good holds on the steep bulges.
3. Bat Out of Hell 5 Climb the bulge to the right of Hoedown.
4. Dingly Dell 5 Start as the last problem and trend right to just left of the central roof. Slightly easier than Bat Out of Hell.
5. Going For The One 5+ Bold climbing up fragile holds in the centre of the wall to finish over the roof.
6. Right Side of The Law 5 The wall and smaller roof.
7. Going Up North 5 A pumpy right to left traverse finishing up Hoedown.
8. Bird Shit Groove 3 The prominent groove at the right side.

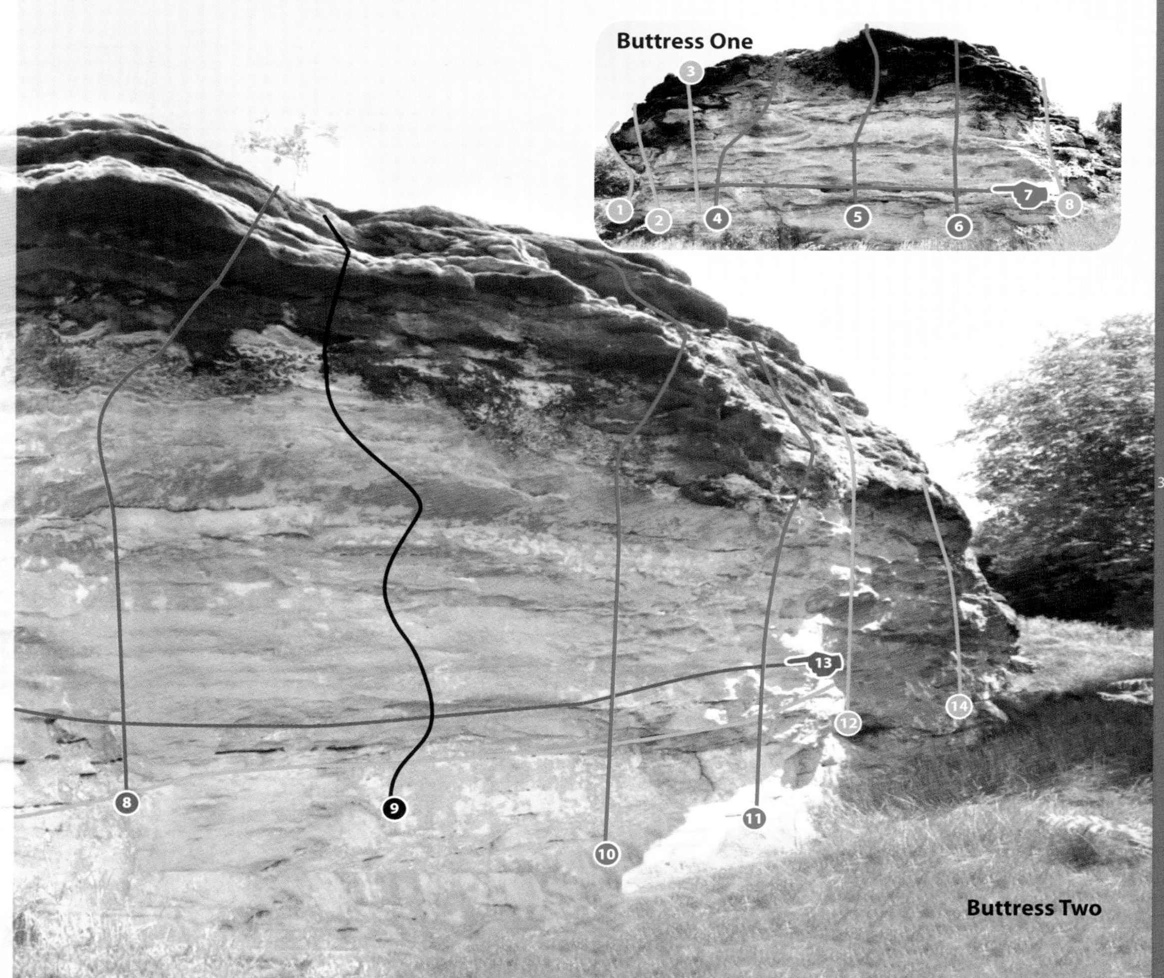

A perfect place to picnic at the tower ruins

Levisham

North of Levisham village via a flat walk-in are two little blocks. It's also a good place to have a picnic and watch the steam trains go by.

Approach: Park on the grassy car park with tourist information sign at the sharp bend on the road between Levisham village and the railway station. Follow the path north until the remains of Skelton Tower are on your left. The blocks are below the tower on the north-facing edge. **See page 290 for the map.**

OS Map: SE 821928
Walk: 15 minutes
Faces north

The North York Moors Railway

Lee Robinson on Powered by Steam 6b

The first block is about 100m east away from the tower.

1. Jolly Roger 5+ SS Start in the large pocket and climb over the roof to gain the top.
2. Exit Left 6a SS Start on the good holds beneath the roof and move leftwards up the crimpy wall to a mantel finish.
3. Powered By Steam SS 6b Start on those good holds again, but this time climb the blunt rib direct on more crimps located to either side.
4. In Case of Emergency 6a The slab on yet more crimps. Possible hard sit-start.

The next block is about 30m east, away from the tower and just down from the edge.

5. The Scoop 6a SS Start at the centre of the wall, climb direct then left to a good pocket on the top, then move round the left side to top-out.
6. Project SS Direct problem through the centre of the downhill face. Top-out on the blank slab!
7. Le Visham Station 6c SS From the left arête, traverse low across the face, then finish around the right arête.

Other problems/traverses have been done on this block. The full traverse is still a project.

Hunt House Crag is a hidden gem just outside the north end of Cropton Forest. It's a little oasis of bouldering in an area posessing few edges. At first glance the rock appears friable, but don't let that put you off, as on the whole the area is worthwhile and not as it first seems. Wander into the woods and you'll find **Blawath Crag**. This has a large block with a 5 metre horizontal roof, a very rare occurrence for the Moors. The venue gets the evening sun but suffers from high bracken during the summer months.

Approach: Head to the village of Goathland on the A169 north of Pickering. Goathland was used as the village of 'Aidensfield' in the popular TV show Heartbeat. **If you enter the village from the south**, take the left at the mini-roundabout for Egton Bridge and the Roman Road (worth seeing) and follow this to the next left for Hunt House. This eventually leads down to parking at a small lay-by near a junction with a tourist information board. **From the north**, follow the A169 out of Sleights, up Blue Bank and onto the moor. Take the second right turn signposted 'Goathland'. Continue on this road through the village and at the mini-roundabout by the church take the right for Egton Bridge and the Roman Road. Follow as above to the parking. **From the parking**, walk south down the road past Hunt House hamlet to join a track passing some more houses. After 150m or so a footpath breaks off to the south and as you reach a rocky hillside follow it slightly rightwards down the valley. The rocks are easily seen on the hillside before the forest.

OS Map: SE 811978
Walk: 15 minutes
Faces west, south and north

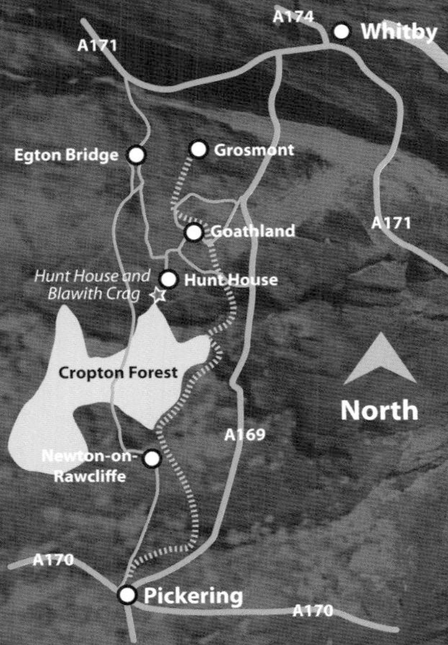

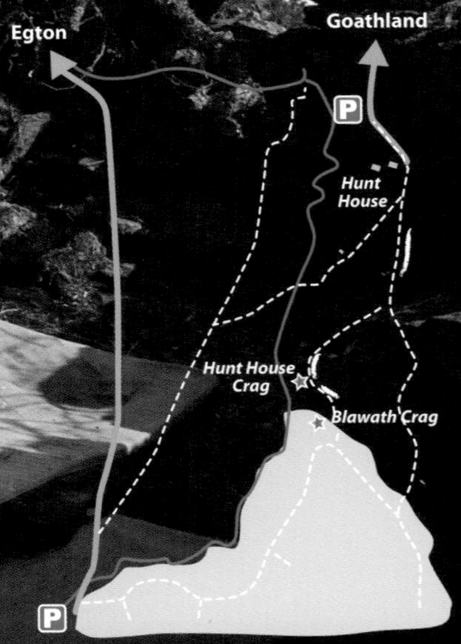

The Shooting Butt

The first small buttress is multi-purpose - a shooting butt, a bivi and now some bouldering.

1. **The Butt Hole 5+ SS** Start as far back as you can in the bivi hole on a ledge to your left. Climb out of the hole and finish up the groove. Jug-pulling bliss.
2. **Keep Flake 3+ SS** Climb up the groove on good holds.
3. **Project** Eliminate on pockets.
4. **Deer Stalker 6a SS** A low start and a strong pull lead to easier moves to the top.
5. **Bang Goes a Halfpenny 5+ SS** A strong start, then onto to some nice steady moves to the top.
6. **Diversion 2** Start on the ledge and climb direct to pull over the top block.
7. **Three Black-faced Sheep 6a+ SS** Use the far right pocket for your right hand, lock-off and gain the ledge. Can be done on the holds further left, though the grade gets lower the further left you go.
8. **Project** Traverse from Three Black-faced Sheep and finish up The Poacher.
9. **The Poacher 6c SS** Start on a low ledge and climb up the bulge on the crimps to the ledge. Keeping your cool when gaining the shelf is tricky.

The Huntsman Block

A stand alone boulder, that looks surprisingly out of place. Just down from the main edges.

1. The Huntsman 7a SS Gain the crack-flake and head right without using the top of the block. Work your way round the next groove to gain a rising crack. Top-out as this ends.
1a. The Hunted 7a+ SS A harder start to the Huntsman.
1b. Project Traverse the full block!
2. The Hunt 4+ The shortest problem on the block.
3. Hounds of Love 6b+ SS Climb direct finishing up the groove.
4. Gun Dog 5+ SS Start under the groove, then top-out on the left.
5. Beaters 5+ SS As above, then finish up the groove
6. Down Comes Half-a-Crown 6a SS As Gun Dog, then traverse right topping out on The Pheasant Plucker.
7. The Pheasant Plucker 4 SS A long reach gains the top.

Lee Robinson on The Huntsman 7a

Mark Wilson on Splat 5+

Hunt House Crag

The south facing edges have a handful of problems. Check the top-outs first. A spotter is essential.

1. 5 SS Climb up and over the roof, finishing left of the block at the top.
2. 5 The side wall, finishing between the top blocks.
3. 1 Climb the arête on its left side.
4. Splat 5+ Tackle the slab to gain the block that looks like it may topple off at the finishing mantel.

The next broken edge:

5. 5 SS Starting on the right side, climb round to the left finishing up the arête.
6. 6a SS The arête on its right side.
7. 6b SS A tricky dyno with a spicy landing.

Blawath Roof

Hidden in the woods is a large roof at the east end of Blawith Crag

1. Honey Jugs 5 SS Climb up to a large flake, then traverse leftwards finishing up a crack.
2. 5+ SS A lower variation climbing under the large flake.
3. Project Tackles the steep roof on large flakes, finishing up a groove in the centre of the roof.
4. Project Start on a large flake and make hard moves leftwards to finish up the arête. Could also be finished up the next problem, avoiding the arête (also a project).
5. 6b Using crimps, climb the centre of the sidewall without use of the arête.

Glaisdale Head

Looking out over the western end of Glaisdale are several boulders which were previously hidden in woodland. They hold a good circuit of problems in the low to mid grades on excellent fine-grained sandstone and include some pleasant slabs and satisfying short arêtes. The boulders are best visited on a sunny evening. The landings are fine on the whole, although some tree stumps have been left over from felling so care should be taken.

Approach: **From the south**, approach from Rosedale Abbey. Take the turning off Hutton-le-Hole High Street for Rosedale Abbey. After the village car park and cattle grid, turn left onto the lonely moor road which eventually drops down Chimney Bank. Once at the bottom take the second left onto the main road signposted 'Castleton'. Follow this to the centre of the village and take the next right turn just before the Milburn Arms Hotel which goes up Heygate Bank signposted 'Egton'. Follow this up onto the moor for about 3 miles crossing a small bridge to a left turn. After roughly half a mile down this road, park at the small gravelly lay-by on the right on a long bend.

From the north, take the turn for Danby on the A171 Guisborough to Whitby road. Follow down into the village and turn just after The Duke of Wellington pub onto Briar Hill, signposted 'Lealholm'. This goes past the Moors National Park Centre and under a rail bridge. Just short of 2 miles later turn off to the right for 'Fryup'. At the T-junction turn left for Lealholm and Glaisdale and follow this for just shy of a mile passing two farms to a crossroads just after a cattle grid. Take a right at the crossroads and continue for just over 4 miles to a small gravelly lay-by on your left on a long bend.

From the parking, follow a faint track through the dense heather in a north-easterly direction keeping right of a line of stone waymarkers. The boulders are just below a small group of spruce trees.

Also see the map at the front of the guide.

OS map: NZ 743015
Walk: 10 minutes
Faces north

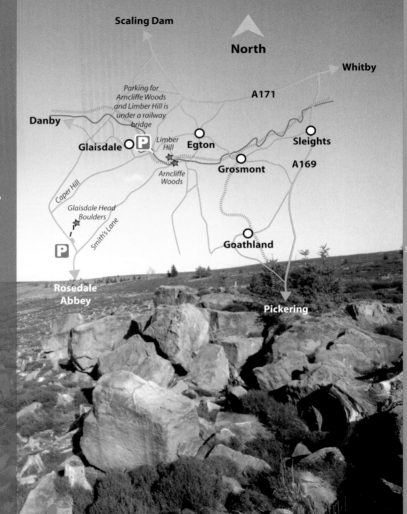

Scaling Dam
North
Whitby
A171
Parking for Arncliffe Woods and Limber Hill is under a railway bridge
Danby
Glaisdale
P
Limber Hill
Egton
Sleights
Arncliffe Woods
Grosmont
A169
Caper Hill
Glaisdale Head Boulders
Smith's Lane
P
Goathland
Rosedale Abbey
Pickering

The Witches Area

Mostly consists of blocks forming a micro crag. Some landings have tree stumps or blocks so a spotter is needed.

1. Tumulus 5 Start 1m left of the right arête and gain the slab using pockets, then follow the arête to the top.
2. Oor Seth 5 The left side of the wall using the arête for the start.
3. Caper 5 The right side of the wall using the arête.
4. Swang 3 A one move wonder up the lone slab.
5. Basskin 5 Nice moves up the left arête.
6. Trial by Ordeal 6b Gain the flake, then dyno up to a sloper and top-out (strictly no arête).
7. Maleficium 6b+ The right arête with the large stump beneath needs some careful composure to gain the top sloping pocket. Be careful, it's not over when you get it!

Witches Slab

8. Witchcraft 6a Avoiding the hole at the bottom climb the left arête. A dyno to the top aiming for an obvious hold is more fun than doing it static.
9. The Witch 6c+ Up the centre of the slab without the arêtes. Use the small crimp and right-hand sidepull, gain the finger crack choosing your footholds carefully and finish directly up the crack. Classic.
10. Project The Ramp, then up the arête on its left side. Dodgy landing!
11. The Ramp 4+ Pull up onto the extreme left edge of the short slab and head straight up.
12. Spells 4+ Gain the right edge of the ramp, then move directly up using an incut shelf for your right hand.

The undercut block might hold another short hard problem.

13. Moon Craters 6b SS Climb the strange looking moon-like prow on the iron features. Take care, it can be snappy.

Further right along the micro crag:

14. Tranquility Slab 4+ Start in front of the stump and gain the slab, smear rightwards to the arête and follow to the top.
15. Lunar Arête 5 The blunt arête without use of the block beneath.

Below The Witches Area are a short block and large slab.

Glaisdale Slab

16. Cunning Folk 6a SS Start just right of the tree stump, gain the arête and climb carefully.
17. Saunter 4 Follow the obvious weakness at the left end.
18. Glazed 5 Follow the faint crack 1m to the right of the last problem, spring for the jug then the top.
19. Pyroclastic 6a Use flakes and a sloper to gain the shelf close to the right side of the slab. Finish direct.

Supernatural Block

20. Supernatural 6b+ SS On the ledge, heel-hook up to the centre of the block. Mantel this out direct. **6a** from standing
21. Low Arête 4+ SS Start at the hollow and make your way up the arête to finish with the curious dish feature on top.
22. Low Crack 4+ SS Hang the low crack then crimp and finish.

Mark Wilson on Witchcraft 6a

Steven Phelps on Orr Seth 5

'The Witch' 6c+
Carved into this slab are a 'W' and a devil or witch-like figure, or is it a dragons head? Beware! Only the black of heart will succeed.

Mountain Ash Blocks
The Three Witches

23. White Witch 2 The right arête.
24. Dark Witch 3 The centre of the short slab.
25. Witch Way Down 1 The left side of the slab.
26. Project A low start traversing right and up over the leaning slab.

Mountain Ash Block

27. The Axe 6c SS The arête next to the stump climbs on its right via a long reach, then a nice mantel. The standing start is **6a**.
28. Black Ash 4 Choose your feet carefully to gain the top.
29. Black Crack 5 SS Make a hard move off the floor, then follow the blunt rib rightwards.
30. Mountain Arête 2 Perfect arête climbing.
31. Ash Slab 2 Fine slab climbing.
32. Ash Arête 5 SS Climb the arête on its left side.
33. Calcification 6a+ SS Tackle the crack, then gain the undercut to reach the top.
34. Cut Loose 4+ Start with the left arête and a crimp, pull onto the slab then cut loose for the arête. Follow this to the top. Sharp!
35. Learning to Lean 5 The very pleasant left arête.

The East-facing Slab

36. Glaisdale Traverse 6a+ SS A rising right to left traverse of the whole block.

Lee Robinson on The Axe 6c

Mountain Ash Blocks
36
34
32
31
33
36
35

Mountain Ash Blocks
29
30
28
31
23
24
25
27
26
32
33
34
35
36

9 11 11 5 4

Arncliffe Woods is situated in a secluded valley high above the river Esk and just outside the picturesque village of Glaisdale. Some of the boulders are glacial in origin and are scattered either side of the Esk Valley Long Distance Walk as it winds its way through the trees on an ancient pack horse path. The rock is excellent fine-grained sandstone which holds some brilliant problems throughout the grades including good crimpy walls and excellent arêtes. It's a good winter venue after the trees have lost their leaves and the rising sun reaches the rock from the east. A dry spell is required to get a good circuit whatever the season.

OS Map: NZ 789048   Walk: 10 minutes   Faces north

Approach: **(See map on page 313)**

From the south, best approached from Rosedale Abbey. From the A170 take a turn north to the village of Wrelton and continue through the village on Main Street following the sign for 'Cropton, Harcroft and Rosedale'. Once out of the village the road becomes Cropton Lane. Continue on this road all the way to Rosedale, where you turn right onto Heygate Bank, signposted 'Egton'. Follow this road across the Moor and after the small stone bridge take the left turn for 'Glaisdale'. After this take the next right turn down Caper Hill, passing a '25%' hill warning sign. This road takes you down into Glaisdale to a left turning at the next junction to continue down the valley. After about 2.5 miles take a right at the village green onto High Street/Carr Lane, the main Glaisdale Village road. After a gap where the houses are sparse, you'll pass 'Arncliffe Terrace' stone cottages on the right and the Arncliffe Arms pub. Just after the train station, go under the rail bridge where the parking is on your right by the River Esk. Alternatively you can approach from the A169 following signs for Grosmont and Egton.

From the north, follow the A171 Guisborough to Whitby road east and about 4 miles after the large car park at the eastern end of Scaling Dam take the right turn for Egton and Grosmont, on the left-hand bend in the road. After 200m on this road, take a right at the crossroads for Egton Banks and follow this for 2 miles. Once into the wooded valley turn right at the next junction at the give-way sign and follow the road over the River Esk to the parking under the rail bridge.

From the parking, go under the rail bridge and across a foot bridge to join the picturesque Esk Valley Walk footpath as it heads south following the river. After a few minutes the path breaks off uphill and not long after that you'll pass the Wishing Stone, a bench and the first rocks of Sleeping Buttress will be on your right. The boulders can also be approached from the limited parking at the delves further south.

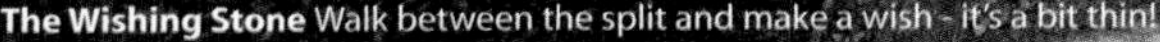

The Wishing Stone Walk between the split and make a wish - it's a bit thin!

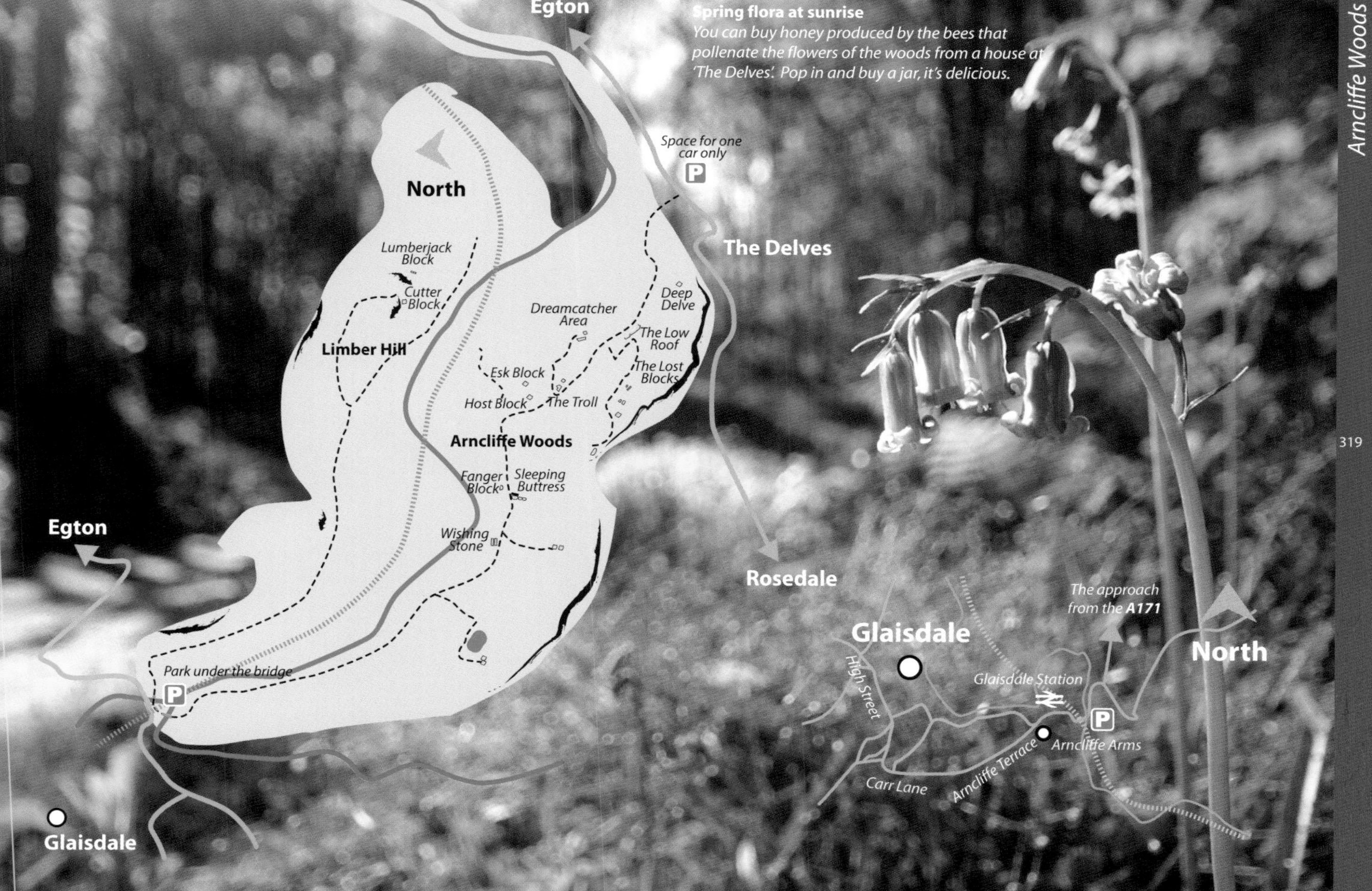

Spring flora at sunrise
You can buy honey produced by the bees that pollenate the flowers of the woods from a house at 'The Delves'. Pop in and buy a jar, it's delicious.

Topping out on Jaw Dropper 6b+

Sleeping Buttress

The first cracked buttress on the right, viewed from the path.

1. First Contact 5 SS The groove using crimpy ledges, mantel top-out.
2. Underverse 6a+ From the break without the right arête. Make use of the undercut to gain the top. Mantel finish.
3. Reckoner 5+ Climb the arête on its left, using an undercut and shuffling carefully left to top-out.
4. The Wrong Turn 6a Climb the arête on its right. Mantel top-out on the right side.
5. Wild Flowers 5+ The central line on the cracked block, with exciting moves to finish. Keep your cool.
6.Sleeping Giant 4+ Climb up the steep wall to finish up the groove.
7. Jaw Dropper 6b+ SS The left side of the upper block from a low start. Gain good holds over the bulge, from here the fun begins.
8. Ground Beetle 6a SS Move up the short wall past small edges.
9. Lucky 6a SS Gain the top without using the good sidepull around the arête and mantel to finish.
10. 5 Sulk SS As 'Lucky' but using the good sidepull around the arête. Mantel to finish.
11. The Fear 6c SS The right arête is short and quite exciting.

Fanger Block

Just past the Sleeping Buttress, on the other side of the path.

1. Suki 5 SS Start on the jug beneath the roof. Climb direct passing a rail on the lip.
2. Stackhouse 5 SS Climb the arête from a low start.
3. Fang Banger 5+ SS Traverse the block to top-out at Suki.
4. Fang Wall 3+ SS Move up the side-wall.

Fanger Block

Steven Phelps on Wild Flowers 5+

The first dry visit to the woods Fallen Angel 5+

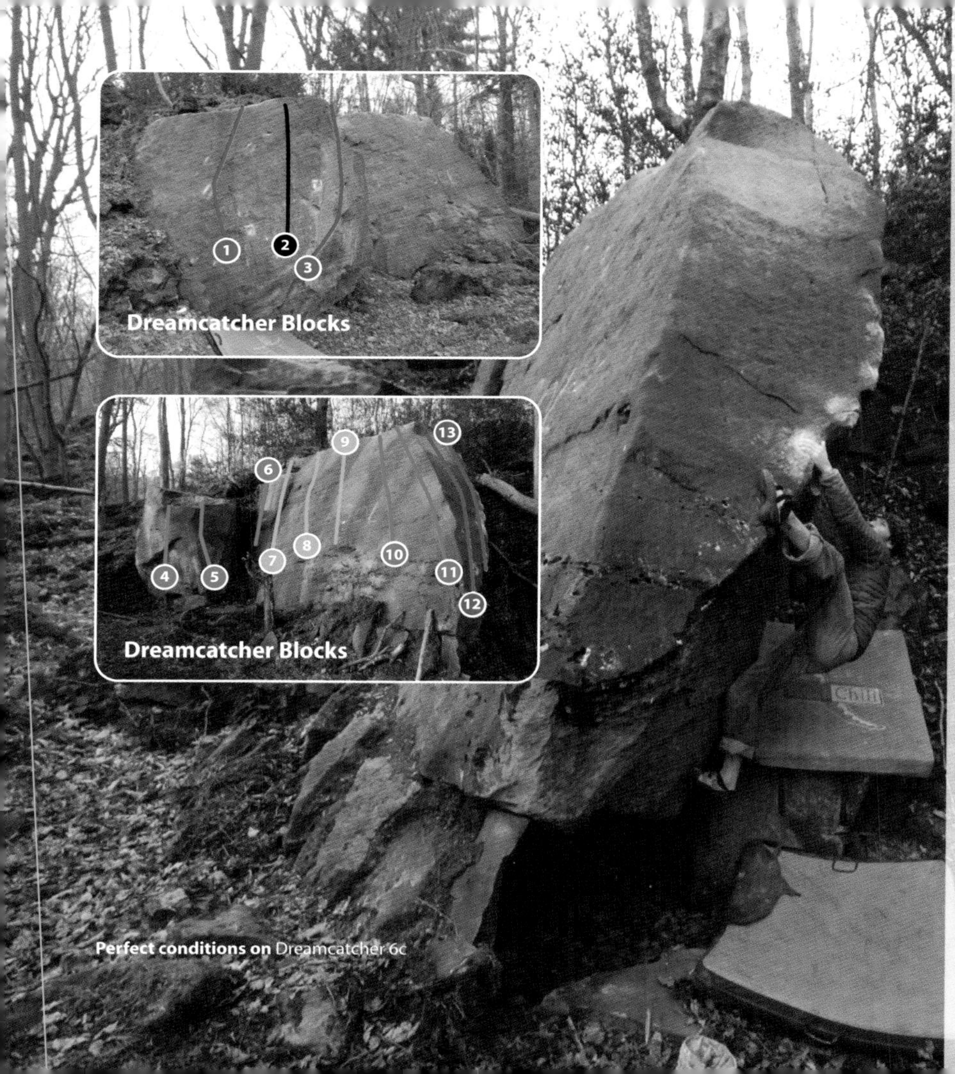

Dreamcatcher Blocks

Dreamcatcher Blocks

Perfect conditions on Dreamcatcher 6c

The next area is about 50m up the path on your left.

The Host Block

1. Demografique 5+ SS Start using two small holds and gain the left arête/rib to an easy finish.

2. The Host 4+ Start using two small sloping holes and climb direct up the arête/rib.

3. The Hostess 4+ Start as The Host, then make for the right arête to finish.

Esk Block

1. Eskimi 7b SS The centre of the thin slab, with extremely sharp holds. Standing start is **4.**

2. Eskovia 5 SS The arête is good although it's over too quick.

The Troll

1. Fallen Angel 5+ SS Start in the corner and make difficult moves to gain the lip. Move right to gain the arête around the corner and follow to finish. Almost perfect.

2. Troll Hunter 5+ SS Start at the embedded boulder. Make moves leftwards to finish up the arête.

3. Blood Sucker 5 SS Start at the embedded boulder again and climb the centre of the wall on pockets.

Dreamcatcher Blocks

The smaller block.

1. Hunting Bears 6b The left wall without the arête.

2. Simon's Alphabetical Beard 7a The arête on its left from standing. The sit-start is **7a+.**

3. The Bony King of Nowhere 6b SS The right side of the arête using the pockets on the wall.

4. Legion 5 Undercut the curving overlap to reach the ledge. Finish direct.

5. There There 5 SS Start at the good ledge and climb the corner.

The large slab and arête block.

6. Angel Dust 5+ Climb the slab left of the groove using a small crimp for both hands. Finish via ironstone pockets.

7. We are Watching You 1 Climb the groove.

8. Rainchime 2 Climb one metre to the right of the groove.

9. Street Spirit 2 Start at the remains of a wall and climb the slab finishing past a small shelf.

10. My Iron Lung 5 Climb just left of the arête avoiding using it.

11. No Surprizes 5 The left side of the arête has a nice finish.

12. Trickster 6a SS From the powerful start on the right of the arête, strictly using the block only, gain the face then tip-toe up the centre of the twin arêtes.

13. Dreamcatcher 6c Start from standing without using the block to your right, then climb the hanging arête until better holds on the right help you top out. Can also be done from sitting and climbing with the hands on the arête only at **7a**. Brilliant.

The Lost Blocks

Mike Adams on Sleepwalking 7b+

The Lost Blocks

(11) (12) (13) (14)

(15) (16) (17)

Lee Robinson on Hellraiser 6c+

The Lost Blocks

The next section is up the valley side above a clearing in the trees and just off the main path. To the left you will see 'Low Roof'. Only one problem has been recorded on this.

1. Through the Heart 5+ SS Start left of a good ledge, work your way right, then climb up the right arête. Mantel to finish.

The next blocks are up the hill and to the right.

2. Sleepwalking 7b+ SS Climb the centre of the block to gain the mono and top. The arête and the left block are out of bounds. **6b** from standing.
3. Go to Sleep 6a SS Start with the right hand on the arête and the left undercutting the block, then gain the arête using holds on the front face and follow to the top. A harder purer variation can be done using only the arête for hands **Deep Sleep 7a SS.** Awkward but satisfying. **5+** from standing

The slab behind.

4. The Sky is Falling 6b SS Start on the iron pocket and use the crimps to gain the top avoiding the good flake holds to the left.
5. The Hole 5 Using only the hole for hands gain the top (just hope nothing is living in there!).
6. Scatterbrain 5 SS Climb the arête on its left.

Keep going uphill and right.

7. Project SS The left arête.
8. As Dead as Leaves 5+ SS Gain the right arête using the pockets on the front face and top-out on the apex.
9. Squelch Arête 4 SS Follow the arête to the top and a rockover finish.
10. Project SS A low lip traverse.

Further uphill and right is an large block with a low roof.

11. The Slab 2 From standing. Needs doing from a sit-start.
12. Hellraiser 6c+ SS Starting on the good ledge, traverse right to gain and follow the arête to the top. **6a** from a standing start holding the arête and the left-hand sidepull-crimp
13. Hellbound 8a SS A hard link from the back of the roof. **See photo on page 326.**
14. Butterball 7c SS Starting under the roof climb out onto the slab above.
15. Nails 6a Start just under the roof, climb out and finish up the arête.
16. Uncovered 5 Up the slab between the arête and the groove, using good edges.
17. Branch Out 4+ Move up the groove left of the tree.

The last block is best accessed further down the path past a broken crag. It can be seen up the hill just before the path turns left.

Delve Deep Block

1. Evade Arête 5 SS The sloping left arête laybacking the right side, with feet on the slab.
2. What's That Noise 6b The right side of the prominent right arête.

Mike Adams on Hellbound 8a

Limber Hill is an obscure venue high above the River Esk on the opposite side of the valley to Arncliffe Woods. There's a broken edge with several boulders beneath. Although some problems have been done along the edge, it lacks the quality of the boulders so the problems are not included here. The rock is excellent solid sandstone bearing occasional strange features. Some lines may need a pre-ascent brush due to fallen pine needles from the surrounding trees. Being a small venue with limited climbing it is probably best combined with a visit to another venue in the vicinity.

Approach: Use the same approach and parking as Arncliffe Woods **(see maps on pages 313 and 319)**. Cross the 'Beggar's Bridge' to the other side of the river. Once into the woods make a right turn and follow the track south-east. After several hundred metres the path goes uphill and past an old quarry on the left. Ignore the first left turn at the top of the hill and continue downhill until a left turn can be made onto another track which runs uphill. After 200 metres take a very faint path that runs off to the right into the woods, which will bring you out just above the edge. The Cutter Block is about 50m below, with the Lumberjack Block round to the east.

OS Map: NZ 792050
Walk: 20 minutes
Faces south

POST CARD

Beggar's Bridge has a fine tale to impart of love conquering social difference. Folklore tells of Tom Ferris, a poor man, son of a sheep farmer, who hoped to wed the daughter of a wealthy local landowner, the fair Agnes Richardson. To win her hand, Tom managed to persuade her father to permit the wedding if he became wealthy man. Around this time, Tom received his orders to join the English fleet, serving during the Spanish Armada with Sir Francis Drake. Tom went to inform Agnes of this, but could not get across the river because it was in flood. So, he unfortunately departed without even a farewell kiss and sailed from Whitby with a heavy heart. Tom luckily returned from his adventures a wealthy man, wed his true love and set about building the bridge so that no other lovers would ever be torn apart by a swollen river, or so the tale goes.

Heading to Limber Hill over Beggar's Bridge

There are more blocks and problems in these woods than are shown here. Since the problems below were initially climbed it has become apparent that they are on private land. The descriptions here are therefore shown as a historical record of what was climbed at the time and do not indicate any current right to climb at this venue.

The Cutter Block

1. Colony Disturber 6a SS Starting with a mono for the left hand and the curving feature for the right, gain the rails on the wall above and use these to reach the sloping top-out.

2. The Arc 6c SS Starting on monos gain the curved feature, follow this rightwards and finish at the highest point.

3. Project The left side of the arête may fall to a dynamic approach.

4. The Cutter 6c Climb just to the right of the arête, making a big move to a small crimp. Top-out left or right.

5. Desert Rose 5 The centre of the wall passing slanting breaks. Finish using crimps.

6. The Bears are Coming 4+ Climb up to the slanting break, traverse rightwards to the blunt arête and continue to the top.

7. Space in the Woods 4 Climb the wall to finish up the blunt arête.

The Lumberjack Block

8. Lumberjack 7a SS Start at the right side of the block under a quarried arch. Make a stiff pull-up to slap the top of the block and traverse the arch feature keeping feet underneath until you can top-out near the centre of the block.

James Rennardson on The Cutter 6c

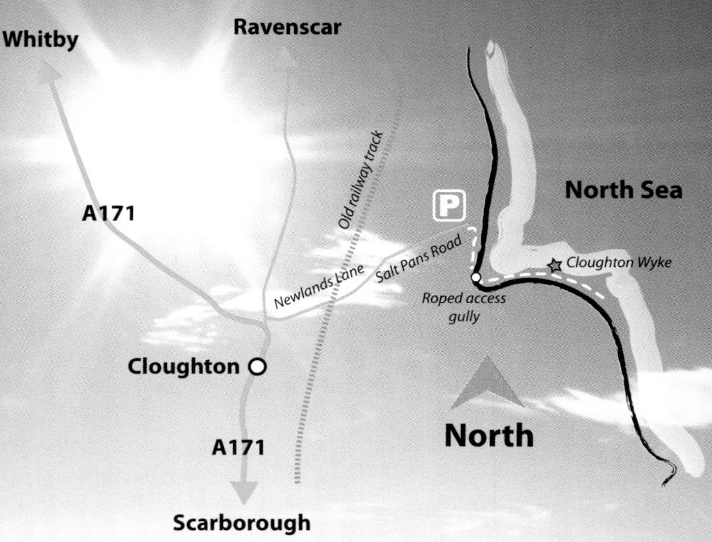

Cloughton Wyke holds coastal bouldering on fine-grained sandstone, in an old smuggler's cove. The area also has a history of industrial usage, as blocks that fell from the cliff were removed for building material. The blocks are only marginally in the tidal zone, so some stay dry when the sea has been calm. The sun creeps over the cliff in the afternoon and dries everything up quickly making the rock look golden red in summer. It's perfect warm weather bouldering, especially at low tide (take your swimwear).

Approach: The village of Cloughton is on the A171 between Scarborough and Whitby.

From the south, drive through the village until the main road bends very sharply round to the left, where you take a right turn, then another immediate right turn onto Newlands Lane which becomes Salt Pans Road, with parking where the road ends at the clifftop.

From the north, take the left turn after the stone village sign for 'Cloughton' onto Newlands Road. Immediately after take another right onto Newlands Lane/Salt Pans Road and park at the end, as above.

From the parking, take the path round the field to join the Cleveland Way as it heads south. After a few hundred metres the path drops down between some trees. As you emerge from these a faint path breaks off left down the steep hillside to a series of rope drops. Once at the bottom follow the shoreline to reach the boulders clearly seen below the cliff.

OS Map: TA 021949
Walk : 10 minutes
Faces north and east.
At its best after dry spells and easterly winds.

* Cloughton still has scope for unclimbed lines, particularly in summer at low tide as the lower plateaus are exposed and have chance to dry.

Warning - The cliffs are a mix of sandstone and mud, which suffers from rockfall and landslip. Some holds are also brittle. Climb with extreme caution.

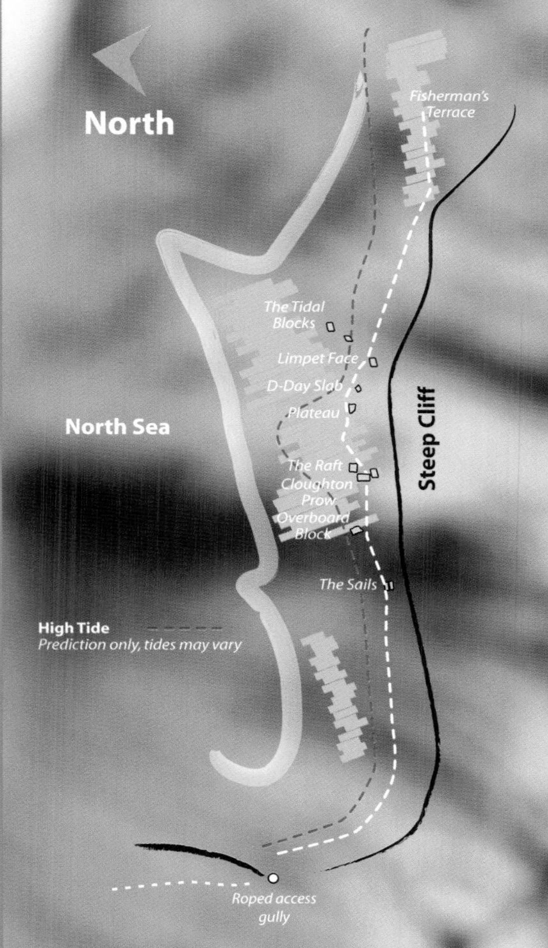

Hardy lichen on The Raft

Mike Adams on Before the Rain 8b

The Sails

The terrifying looking slab!

1. Wayfarer 7b+ SS Climb the tricky back arête without using the left arête.

2. Sheet to the Wind 6c+ SS The front arête on its right side. Do not use the right arête.

3. Main Sail 7a+ The slabby front face just to the right of centre. Quite highball, with a less than ideal landing.

Overboard Block

The block just past The Sails.

4. Brandy Smuggler 6b+ Traverse the block rightwards using holds under the top. Finish up the right side of the seaward face.

This block also has a right to left traverse on the shore face at about ***5+****.*

Cloughton Prow

Sometimes blocks fall the right way.

5. Black Lake 6b+ SS Traverse the lip leftwards, finishing up the arête.

6. Black Spot 6a SS (crouch for the short) The short right wall starting in the crackline.

7. Left at Shore 6b SS The right wall from a low start, without the right arête.

8. Before the Rain 8b Start from standing next to the boulder on the right, with the left hand on a low edge sidepull and the right on the apex of the arêtes. Pull on and make some very trick slaps following the arête to an easier top-out. Brilliant climbing. It is possible for the tall to start from reaching up to the base of the rock slab at **7b+.**

The Sails

Overboard Block

Cloughton Prow West Side

The Raft

Just opposite the prow is a large block with shot-holes all the way round it, not too high but holding some tricky little problems.

1. A Hole Lot of Rum 6b SS From the good ledge gain the top. Which hole to use? The choice is yours.
2. The Funk 6b Start at the arête, traverse rightwards without use of the top and exit up the ramp.
3. Spin the Yarn 6a SS Climb the ramp.
4. Old Gregg 6b SS Start on the low ledge, reach high and left to the sharp hold, climb to the nose and top-out direct.
5. Black Lake 5+ SS Climb the wall using the shot-holes.
6. Baileys 5+ SS Start as Black Lake and traverse the block to the right arête.
7. The Landing Party 4+ Also the descent.
8. An Unjust Trick 6a SS Just left of the arête, a tricky start eases up once you have stood upright.
9. Mangina 6b SS Make a stiff pull and climb the wall using the shot-holes.
10. Cut-throat Prow 6b SS Climb the short menacing prow.

The traverse of the whole block has yet to be done.

James Rennardson on Old Gregg 6b

Lee Robinson on Cut-throat Prow 6b

Past 'The Raft' is a small block on the edge of an undercut sea-washed plateau. This also can be climbed in dry spells at low tide.

Plateau Block

1. 200 Casks of Brandy 4 SS Gain the shelf and mantel up and over the block.

Just past this is:

D-Day Slab

2. Downfall 5+ SS The overhanging left arête on its left side. Finishing left.

3. Omaha 4 SS Climb the left side of the slab to its highest point.

4. Gold 3+ SS The right side of the slab without the arête.

5. Sword 3 SS The right arête.

The next blocks can be found further east before the cliffs turn south.

Limpet Block

6. Gregg's Place 6a SS The larger arête on its right-hand side.

7. Motherlicker 6a SS Start with both hands on the right edge of the corner. Go directly up, staying right of and eliminating the arête.

8. Mini Groove 4 Start on the crimp in the middle of the wall, trending right up the vague groove.

9. Smaller Sister 6c SS At the base of the short arête make an awkward pull-on and pop up. Trickier than it looks.

10. Catch the Day 7c SS Snatch up small crimps, then throw for the lip and rock-over to finish.

11. Bear Claw 7c+ SS Climb the right arête of the overhanging face via a hard pull and slap to a bad hold. Awkward.

The Tidal Blocks

12. Comet Crack 7b SS Climb the hanging crack via some tough moves. A great problem. Possibly a harder project just to the left.

13. 6c+ SS With left hand on the layaway and right on a crimp, pull on and slap the lip. The arête to the left will give a hard project.

14. Rise of the Idiot 6b+ SS Climb the lip leftwards on the Jurassic seabed features.

15. Let Your Hair Grow Short 6b SS Hang the lip with feet under the roof, choose wisely to gain the best holds and gain the slab above.

16. 7 Bottles 6a + SS Just to the right is another slab mantel, thankfully it's a bit easier than the last problem.

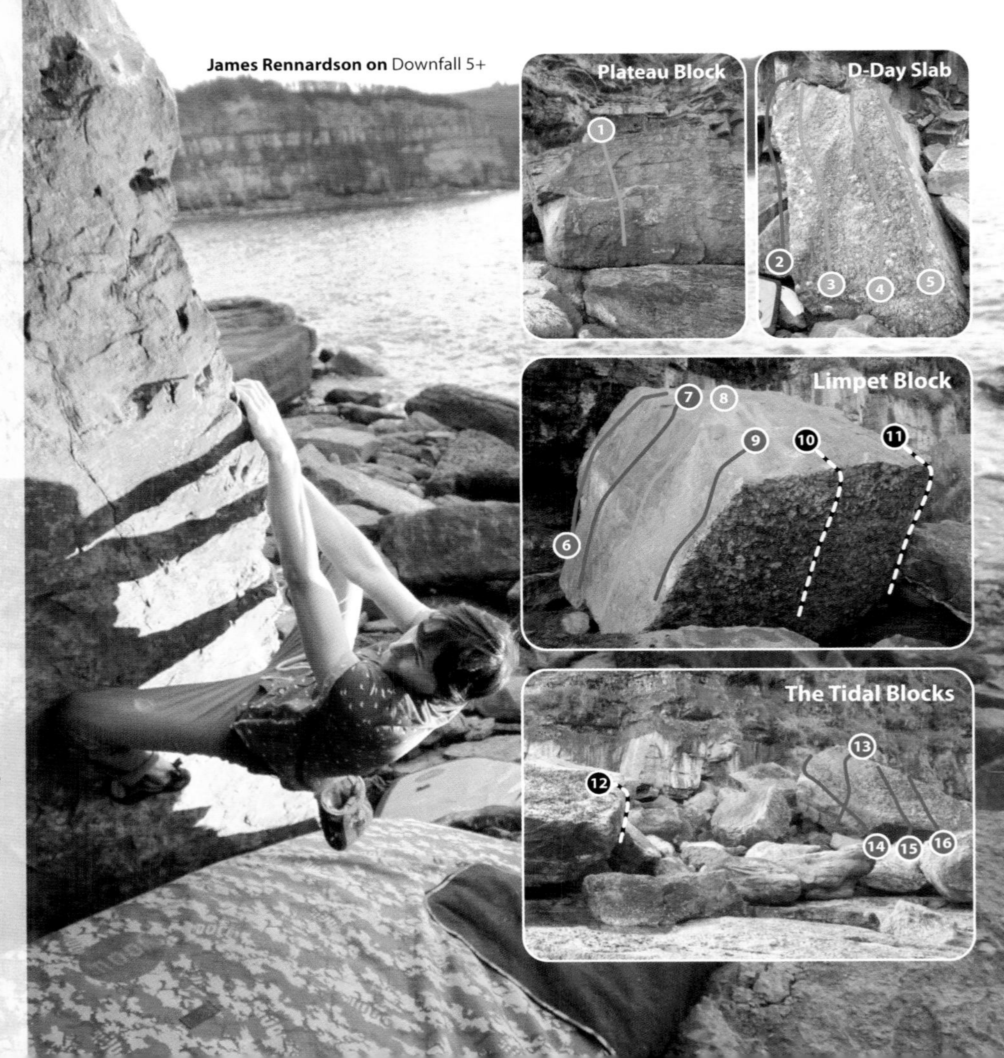

James Rennardson on Downfall 5+

Fisherman's Terrace

Fisherman's Terrace

Just around the corner is a terrace. This has various blocks and slabs, some of which are in the tidal zone. Catch it on a low tide in summer with easterly winds and you are onto a winner. Below are a few of the good problems from this terrace. These are easily found without a topo.

1. Finka 7c SS Climb the little and attractive overhanging fin. Use only the fin feature for hands and feet.

2. Cracker 7a SS The crack to the left of Finka. Climb left out of the cave following the crack feature to a worrying finish.

3. Fuzzy Tingle Time 6c SS Starting on the far left, traverse the prow to the arête, then top-out up the arête.

James Rennardson on Fuzzy Tingle Time 6c

Mike Adams on Finka 7c

North

Old railway line

Rocky Point

Plateau

Beast Cliff

Plateau

Rope Drops

Ironstone Pavement

Old Train Station

Rope Drops

Smuggler's Terrace

Ravenscar

Raven Hall

The Rope Drop at Smuggler's Terrace

3 9 13 5 3

Located in a commanding position high above the North Sea is **Smuggler's Terrace**, where several large boulders are situated on a plateau below a large crag. There's also a micro-edge hidden in the trees. The terrace holds a wide variety of problems, with few in the low grades. The rock is excellent solid sandstone and includes some great arêtes and short difficult walls. The venue is best avoided during the summer months as bracken makes navigating the boulders very difficult, though it's a perfect winter venue as it doesn't seem to take long to dry.

Approach: Parking for Smuggler's Terrace is at the village of Ravenscar, on the coast and off the A171 between Whitby and Scarborough. Take a turn to the east off the A171 signposted for the villages of 'Staintondale' and 'Ravenscar'. This is just near the Falcon Inn if you are coming from the north and around three miles after Cloughton if coming from the south on the A171. Follow signs for Ravenscar. When you reach the village drive down the main street and past the Raven Hall Hotel. Continue until the road ends at a grassed square. Turn left onto a gravel track and park on the right. From the parking, follow the fence-line on a faint path to the Cleveland Way. From here there is a faint path going into the woods bearing slightly left and over some tree stumps. This then turns right to reach the descent ropes. There are two large ropes separated by a shale bank. Once near the bottom of the last rope a faint path breaks off north and drops down into the woods. The micro edge is on the left almost immediately. To reach the boulders outside the woods, carry on north.

OS Map: NZ 985015
Walk: 5-10 minutes
Faces east
Gets the sun early morning. Suffers from high bracken in the summer

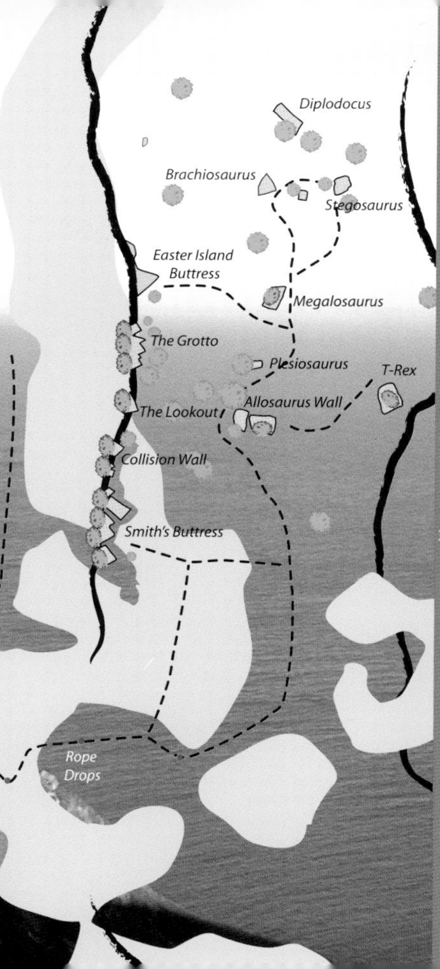

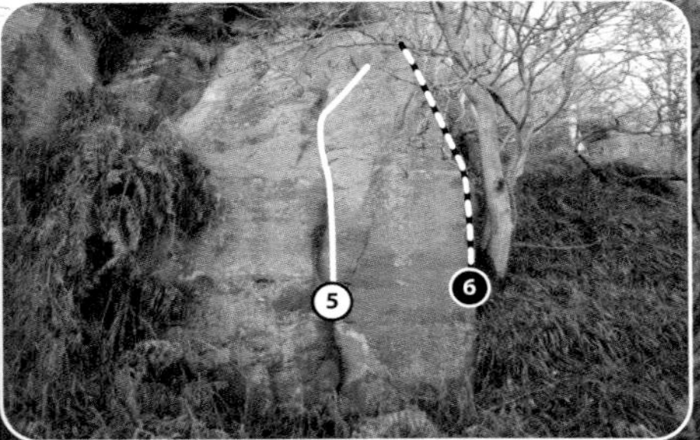

Smith's Buttress

The first hidden wall you come across around the boulders.

1. Machette 5 SS Climb the arête to the pocket.
2. Gondwanaland 5 SS Climb the left arête from an obvious finishing jug on the arête. Continue up Pangaea for the full work-out **6c** tick.
3. Pangaea 6c The highball central line on the face. Treat holds with caution! After topping out descend to the right and beware of the steep slope and loose rock!
4. Anterior Portion 6c The slanting arête on its right-hand side.

Further along the edge is:

Collision Wall

5. Project
6. Africa Collides 7b Climb the arête from a standing start.
The wall right of the arête is:
7. Strata Smith 5+ Climb the side-wall from the bigger central hold and a standing start. Lower starts increase the grade.

James Rennardson on Africa Collides 7b

The next buttresses along are.

The Lookout

1. Tertiary Tension 5+ SS Start just left of the tree at a good hold and follow the striking crackline on the sidewall to its end. Then traverse right at the top to finish.
2. Fossil Hammer 5+ SS Climb the the arête using both sides.
3. Ammonite 6a Make long moves between small edges on the left side of the slab.
4. The Roar 6b+ Similar long moves between small edges on the right side of the slab.

The Grotto

5. Wolffish 5 Climb the groove and finish at the hanging crack.
6. The Lookout 6b From crimps gain a left hand-hold in the crack, then finish up the arête to the second break.

Steven Phelps on Ammonite 6a

Allosaurus Wall

The first hidden wall you come across around the boulders.

1. Clever Girls 6b+ From the jug traverse the wall and exit at the second rail.
2. Devil's Toenail 4+ Traverse the top of the boulder from left to right.
3. Feathered Friends 5 Climb the wall direct using an undercut and small edge.
4. Biotic Crisis 6c+ SS Pull on to the undercut on the wall and follow the sloping layaway past the ledge to finish without use of the right edge.
5. Chaos Theory 6c SS The wide crack on its left side.
6. Toarcian Turnover 6c SS Climb the narrow leaning block direct using a number of different techniques.

Plesiosaurus

The short pointed block. All climbs finish via a cool mantel on the apex.

1. Monkey Puzzle 6a SS The left arête. **6a+** From a laydown start on the lower rail. **5+** from standing
2. Supratemporal 6b SS Tackle the sloping lip leftwards.

Steven Phelps on Biotic Crisis 6c+

Lee Robinson on Amber 6b+

Megalosaurus

The monster of all blocks on the plateau.

1. Sands of time 3 The pocketed slab left of the arête, passing the slanting feature.
2. Beachcoma 6a SS The left of the arête initially starting on holds on both sides. Pockets on the slab are out of bounds. **5** from standing.
3. Amber 6b+ SS The arête on its right side. **5** from standing start.
4. DNA 5+ Directly up, then over the hanging block via a thin slot.
5. Extinct 5+ Start at the bottom of the slope, climb up to the slanting seam and a good hold, then aim for a double mono finish using crimps out to the right. Don't blow the top!
6. Whitby Jet 4+ Climb the groove to the large pocket and top-out.
7. Belemnite 6a Standing start at the direct line, using holds out to the left.
8. Belemnite Dreams 6b+ The direct line up the slab from a standing start and using no side holds. Also possible from sit.
9. Anticline 6b Stiff pulls rightwards along the rail and then small holds to the top-out.

James Rennardson on a T-Rex project

T-Rex

Hidden on the plateau edge looking out to sea.

1. Pale Rider 7c SS From a low layaway crimp and small crimp just above, pull on and make a very difficult slap to get more crimps below the overhang. Trend left to a sidepull then lock to the lip and mantel. A fall from the mantel could be quite serious, so take care!

2. Project SS The rampline rightwards.

Brachiosaurus

A pointed roof block holds this hard test-piece.

3. Mad Dog 7c SS Climb from under the roof on undercuts and slap out with difficulty to the twin lips of the roof, then finish up the arête above.

Stegosaurus

The inverted stepped block on the cliff. Be careful some blocks are loose.

4. Coprolite 6a+ SS A tricky start up the centre of the block.

Three other problems have been done on this block though we have not included them, due to the loose nature of the rock.

Diplodocus

Futher north is a long arête block with a project roof at the base.

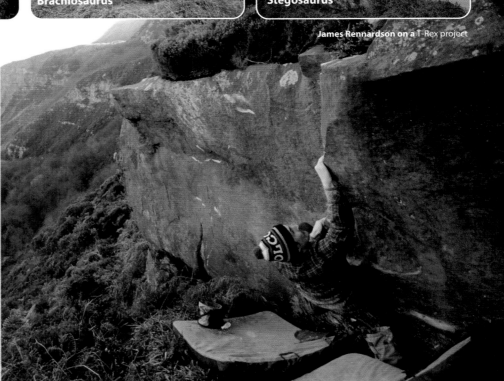

Easter Island Buttress

On the main crag is a a stunning arête, with other possibilites needing some cleaning and top-outs sorting.

1. Life is Life SS 7b Climb the attractive arête à cheval finishing at the break.
2. Leaning Block Project Looks possible?

Smuggler's Resident Robin "Got any food"

The most difficult venue to access in this guide is **Rocky Point**. The blocks are located on the clear blue coastline below Beast Cliff, one mile south of Ravenscar. Care must be taken if you decide to access this area as the blocks have all fallen from a constantly eroding cliff. You will also have to clamber over blocks to get to the main bouldering area. Avoid in winter and when seas are ough as the rocks can be slippery. Try a trip in summer to escape from the midges and experience the spectacular sunrises, if you decide to bivi. It's also a great place to go fishing, so take some Peeler Crab bait. Beware of the tides and please check the tide times beforehand. The problems here have not been published in the guide due to the difficulties of access and potentially dangerous location. Climb at your own risk.

Approach: Use the same parking at Ravenscar as that for Smuggler's Terrace **(see page 336)**. From the parking follow the Cleveland Way south. After a ight-angled turn around the corner of a field boundary there is a faint footpath eading down Common Cliff. You'll be able to see the old coastguard lookout hut and remains of the RAF Radar Station built in 1941, in the next field.
You'll eventually reach several rope drops for the final steep part. Once at the bottom of these, head south along the shoreline for about 30 minutes to the boulders. Beware in summer, as bracken can get beyond head height most of the way down and it's obviously very steep when you're on your way home.

Alternative Approach: An alternative though longer southern approach without he rope drops is via the Hayburn Wyke Inn. From the A171 at the village of Cloughton turn north at the sharp bend with traffic islands onto 'Newlands Road'. Follow this road north for around 1.4 miles to the turn off for 'The Hayburn Wyke'. Use the parking at the Hayburn Wyke Inn, also an excellent place for a bite o eat and a pint of Black Sheep.

From the parking, follow a small track going just left of the way you came in, on a public bridleway. Cross the field to enter the woods and follow the path going traight down to the bottom. This brings you out on the rocky shoreline of Hayburn Wyke, which is followed north for about an hour and a half to the boulders. Take care whilst navigating the approach and on the boulders themselves.

OS Map: NZ 998004
Walk: 50 minutes from Ravenscar – 1.5 to 2 Hours from Hayburn Wyke
Faces east

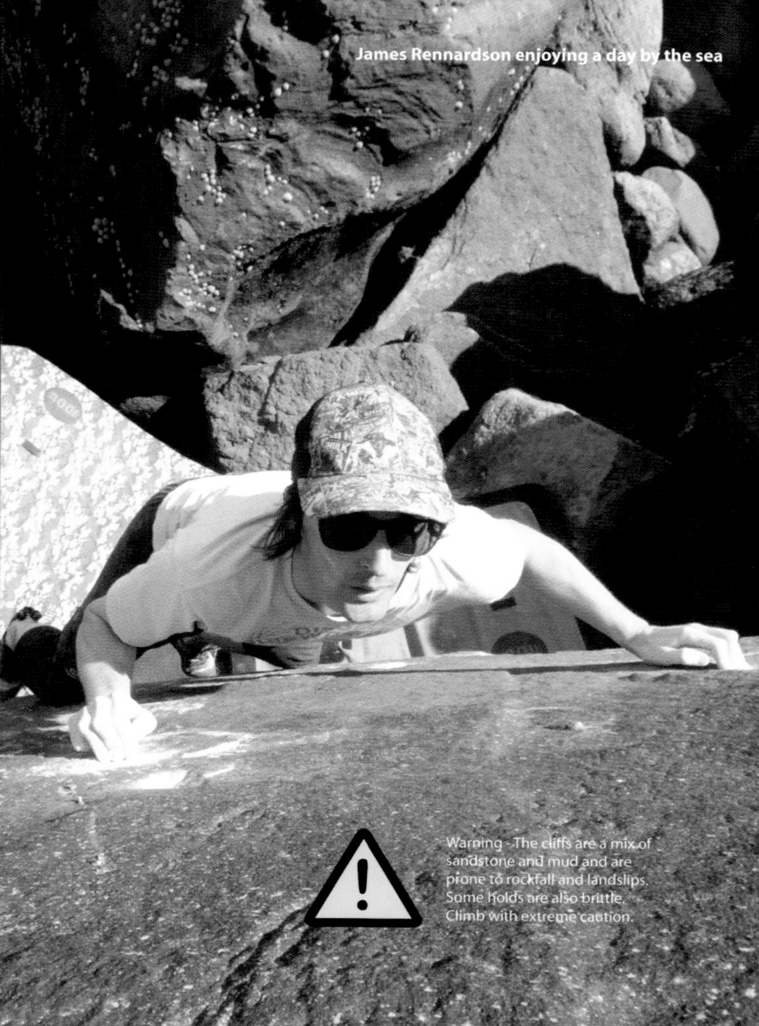

James Rennardson enjoying a day by the sea

Warning - The cliffs are a mix of sandstone and mud and are prone to rockfall and landslips. Some holds are also brittle. Climb with extreme caution.

Stoupe Brow is a delightful north-facing quarry high above the North Sea with excellent views over to Robin Hood's Bay: Home to the impressive and enigmatic 'Two Sisters' boulders along with a few other smaller blocks. The problems are mostly in the mid to high grades, with a few hard projects still left to do. There's a variety of features on very different boulders with slopers, crimps, pockets and thin cracklines above excellent flat grassy landings and the north facing aspect gives grip even in high summer.

Approach: Stoupe Brow Quarry is between the villages of Ravenscar and Robin Hood's Bay, off the A171 between Whitby and Scarborough. Take the turn east off the A171 signposted 'Staintondale' and 'Ravenscar' and follow the signs for Ravenscar. After the old windmill take the left turn on the sharp bend in the road at the Smuggler's Rock Bed and Breakfast, heading towards the radio mast and follow this all the way down for about a mile and a half to the parking, which is just before where the road forks.

Grid Ref: NZ 958023
Walk: 3 Minutes
Faces north

Little Sister Block

A nice block with many hard problems, as well as some highballs.

1. Panda Pops 6a+ SS From a layback to two small crimps, then pop for the top.
2. ASBO Pops 6c Standing start, from a left-hand undercut and right-hand sloper, then pop for the angled side-rail. Rock over and top out leftwards over the arête.
2a. ASBO Pops can be continued up the arête at **6c+**.
3. Nigel's Special Pop 7b Start just right of ASBO Pops, climb up and left of the crack without using any holds right of the crack, then go for the top.
4. Piton Crack 6c Follow the crack to a bold top-out.
5. Fox 6b+ Follow the crack along to a right-hand sloper above the crack. Reach up to another right-hand sloper and top-out around the arête.
6. Untitled 6a SS Climb over the overhang, then straight up via pockets to the obvious jug. Top-out if you're feeling bold.

The north face has a hanging roof.

7. Project SS Links the finish to Keyhole Surgery.
8. Scarface 6a SS Take the thin fingercrack, rising rightwards.
9. Keyhole Surgery 7a+ From a standing start take a direct line over the overhang via a small two-finger pocket. Desperate! A true test-piece.
10. Project Variation finish up the arête.

Rob Lonsdale on ASBO Pops 6c

Little Sister Block

Lisa Robinson on Scarface 6a

Barry the Boulder

The largest and most imposing block in the quarry.

1. Desperate Dan 7a SS From a pocket and angled right-hand sloper, pull hard to slopers and then rightwards to a crimp. Rock-over left to a crimp sidepull to finish on the sloping rail. Can also be started under the roof on a flake at **7a+**, or topped out boldly on good crimps.

2. Requiem for a Dream 8a SS Start at the base, climb the overhanging prow arête on crimps and a mono, staying just above the lip. A North York Moors classic!

3. Blue Eyes and Exit Wounds 8b SS The steep right arête starting from the obvious flake. Compression climbing is followed by a hard move to gain the better but slopey ledges on the arête leading to an airy top-out.

4. Project Stack your pads and attempt some front-face madness.

5. Barry 6a From the corner head up left to the undercut, then rightwards to the jug. Drop off here or carry on to tick the route **Barry E4 6a.**

6. Dark Angel SS 7c+ Start with your left hand on the large layaway and right on a very poor undercut. If you manage to pull off the floor, slap to the jug on the shelf and move left to get into the perfect ramp-line and finish up this. A great hard classic. Climbing just the ramp from a standing start is about **7b+**, but is easier the higher up the ramp you start.

7. Precision 7b From a reachy start with left hand on the flake, pull on with difficulty, slap to the lip and then mantel.

8. Cool 6b+ Using the juggy flake gain the rising lip, then climb leftwards. Rock up and over as you reach the first corner.

Daniel Turner on Blue Eyes and Exit Wounds 8b **Photo Rob Lonsdale**

Jordan Buys on Requiem for a Dream 8a **Photo Mike Hutton**

Limpet Block *This has a sloping arête and can be seen uphill from The Little Sister.*

1. Delusional Reality 7a SS Start with the left hand on the lip and right on the undercut, make a stiff pull to the thin right crimp then gain a good hold. From this traverse around the right of the block on slopers to a good sidepull, finishing up the blunt arête. **1a. Project** A lower start will add a couple of grades.

Cheese Block *The pockmarked block uphill and looking down on Barry.*

2. Cheese Wagstaff 6a+ SS The line of crimps and pockets starting from the dip, about a metre from the left arête.
3. Mini Cheddar 5 SS Sraight up the block where the top edge dips. Top-out over the dip.
4. Hard Cheese 7a SS Start at the left-hand end of the block. Head upwards and rightwards via any of the myriad of small pockets, avoiding use of the top of the block. Drop down to finish around the right-hand arête. A sustained challenge with bewildering choice of tiny holds. Harder than it looks.

99 Block *(A bit flaky) The block with visible flakes below the main face. Caution, very brittle.*

5. Two Scoops 6b SS take the short arête on the left-hand side. Rock onto the face to finish.
6. Death Star 6c Start with the left hand in the painful two-finger pocket - where you place your right hand is up to you. Somehow gain the bigger pocket, then make a bid for the top. Try to avoid the hollow flakes.

Smuggler's Block *Over to the right are two obvious lip traverses.*

7. Smuggled In 6a SS The overhanging left arête using the lip and ridges. Finish up the second ridge, left of the groove.
8. Bread and Butter 5+ SS Follow the lip of the easy-angled right arête to finish using good holds and a sloping ledge for feet.

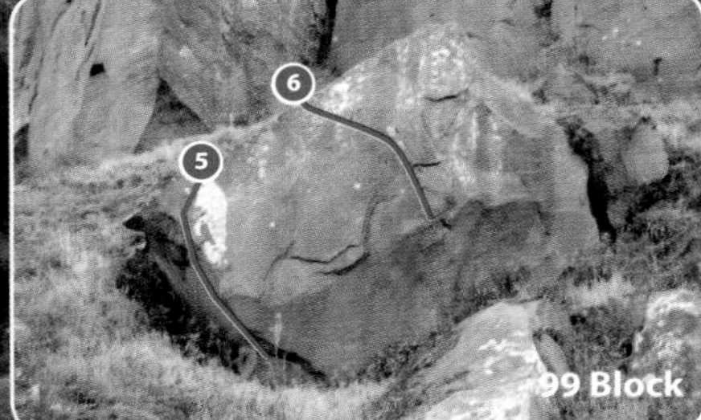

Tom Crane on Cheese Wagstaff 6a+

Boulby is the most northern venue in this guide. Located between the small town of Loftus and village of Staithes in East Cleveland, it stretches for nearly two miles along a coastal plateau which was once part of a large alum quarry and is split into three different areas, Eastern, Galleon and Western. A lot of rock has come away from the soft and unstable cliffs above, which continue to drop large boulders onto the quarries below. Some problems have even suffered as a consequence of this. Most of the boulders documented here are fairly solid sandstone, although softer in nature compared to the other venues further south. There are some surprisingly good problems in each area, including some real test-pieces and character-building exercises above rocky landings. Care should be taken when making your way around, as there are small voids and hollows hidden in the undergrowth throughout the quarried area.

OS Map: Eastern area NZ 750197, Galleon area NZ 739200, Western area NZ 737199
Walk: 10 to 15 minutes
Faces north
Dries very quickly

Warning - The cliffs are a mix of sandstone and mud, which suffers from rockfall and landslip. Some holds are also brittle. Climb with extreme caution.

* *More problems have been done and a few projects are left to do at Boulby. Only the most accessible blocks have been recorded in this guide.*

Approach: The bouldering at Boulby lies between the town of Loftus and fishing village of Staithes, just off the A174 coastal road from Whitby.

From Staithes, after passing through the village on the A174 you'll see Cleveland Potash Works up ahead on the left, after which take the second right turn to 'Boulby'. Parking is at four different locations depending on which area you wish to climb **(see map on opposite page)**. For the Eastern blocks, the first parking location is very close to the turn off on the A174 after Staithes. Please park very considerately at all these locations, especially where the parking is close to houses and mainly for residents. All of the parking spots are at the locations of the public footpaths north which meet the Cleveland Way path and give access to the bouldering areas.

From Loftus, turn left after the clock tower on Loftus High Street onto the narrow North Road and take the next right onto Cleveland Street, becoming Micklow Lane on leaving the town. Take a right at the T-junction. The first parking area you will come across is the limited parking on the left side of the road, just before the green public footpath fingerpost and is useful for Western and Galleon Blocks. **See map on opposite page** for other parking. Please park with care, particularly when parking is close to houses and mainly for residents' use.

Boulby Area Map

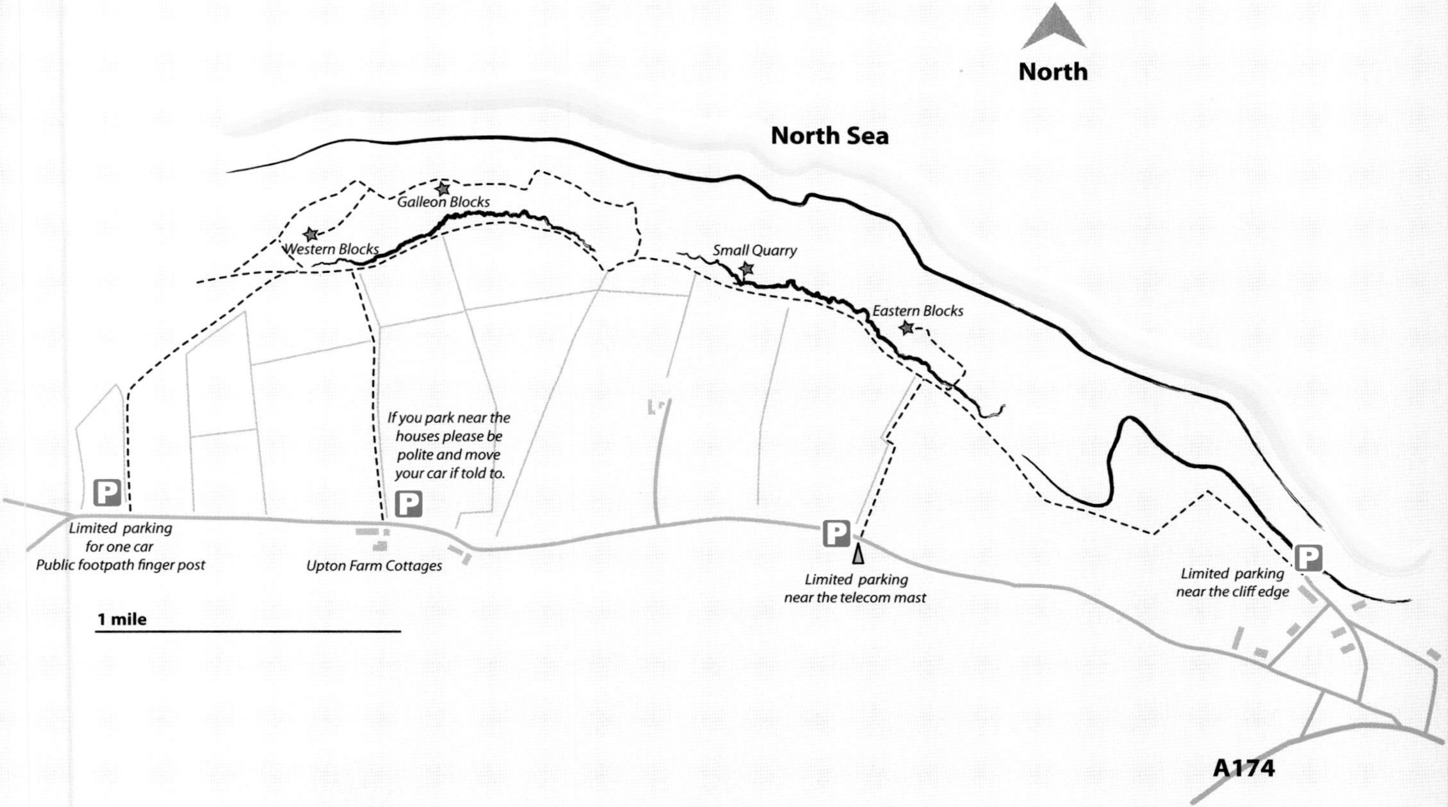

North
North Sea
Galleon Blocks
Western Blocks
Small Quarry
Eastern Blocks
If you park near the houses please be polite and move your car if told to.
Limited parking for one car
Public footpath finger post
Upton Farm Cottages
Limited parking near the telecom mast
Limited parking near the cliff edge
1 mile
A174

Boulby Western Area

St. Elmo's Slab

1. St. Elmo's Slab 5 The left side of the slab using small holds.
2. Sea Sick Steve 3+ The centre of the slab using the curved feature.
3. Bounty 6a Smear up the excellent right edge of the slab using the arête.

About 30m west is the next block.

4. The Puzzle 6a+ SS Move up the short left arête on its right side.

30m up the hill is:

Hangman's Block

5. The Hangman 6a Start by hanging the end of the block, rock onto the side-face and traverse right along the arête to the end of the block.

Steven Phelps on Bounty 6a

The Roof

1. 4 SS Follow the lip of the roof from left to right.
2. Pocket Watch 6a SS Over the sandy roof on large pockets.

Just to the left of these problems is another block with an east-facing slab.

The Slab Block

3. 3+ Follow the left arête on its right side.
4. 4 Straight up the centre of the slab finishing as the last problem.
5. 4+ Start on holds on the ledge. Follow the ledge rightwards until an exit above a bad landing is required.

About 6m up from this block are the next problems.

Mantel Area

6. 4 SS Climb the arête trending right.
7. 6a Mantel the lip direct.
8. Shell Shock 6b SS Start at the left side at a shelf. Traverse rightwards using the top/lip of the block across to a difficult mantel at a natural finishing point, using a blunt spike.
9. Mantel 6b+ Hang the low small edge. Make a stiff pull to a crimp on the blunt arête and pop for the flat ledge. Mantel this to finish. Can be done using the block beneath for feet at **6a+**.
10. 5+ Make a hanging start to gain the large shelf using holds on the right arête.

Lee Robinson on Pocket Watch 6a

Green Fin Block

Steven Phelps on Yellow Polka 5+

About 20m across the hillside from the last area is a cubic block with a prominent arête.

The Cube

1. 5 Gain the left side of the arête and make a long reach left to holds on the face. Finish direct.
2. Genetic Stress 6c Climb the overhanging right side of the arête.

About 30m below this is a large undercut block. Start at the side facing uphill.

Green Fin Block

1. 6a SS Move up the arête and groove to a difficult exit.
2. Itsy Bitsy 1 The easy groove just to the right of the arête.
3. Teenie Weenie 5 SS Start with hands on the small ledge and feet under the small roof. Mount the slab and finish direct.
4. Yellow Polka 5+ SS Using a crimp for the left hand and pinching the lip with the right, make difficult moves to get established on the slab. Finish direct.
5. Dot Bikini SS 6a Make a difficult pull up the right edge/arête then follow left to finish.
6. 5 The slab on the right via the central shelf. Avoid the left arête and finish to the right of the apex.
7. Avocado 5 The blunt arête to the right.
8. 5+ Up the undercut slab to a mantel finish.
9. 5+ SS Start below the finish of the last problem and follow the green lip all the way to the top.

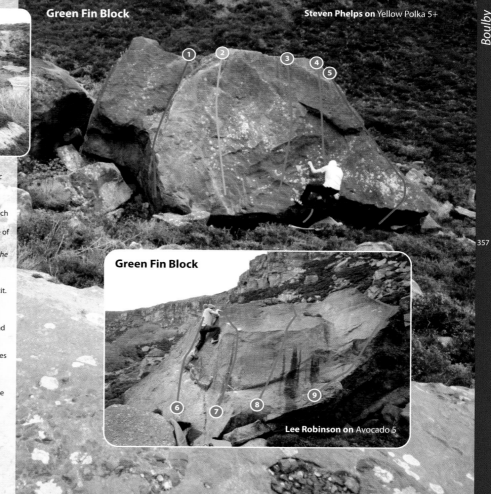

Green Fin Block

Lee Robinson on Avocado 5

Further East

The next section of problems in this guide are four minutes walk west along the lower path, at the Galleon Area. This contains the most accessible bouldering at Boulby.

Those of an adventurous and exploratory nature will not fail to notice the blocks inbetween. These hold varied climbing on rock of mixed quality. So if you're still hungry for more have a look, but be careful of holes under the heather and brittle holds.

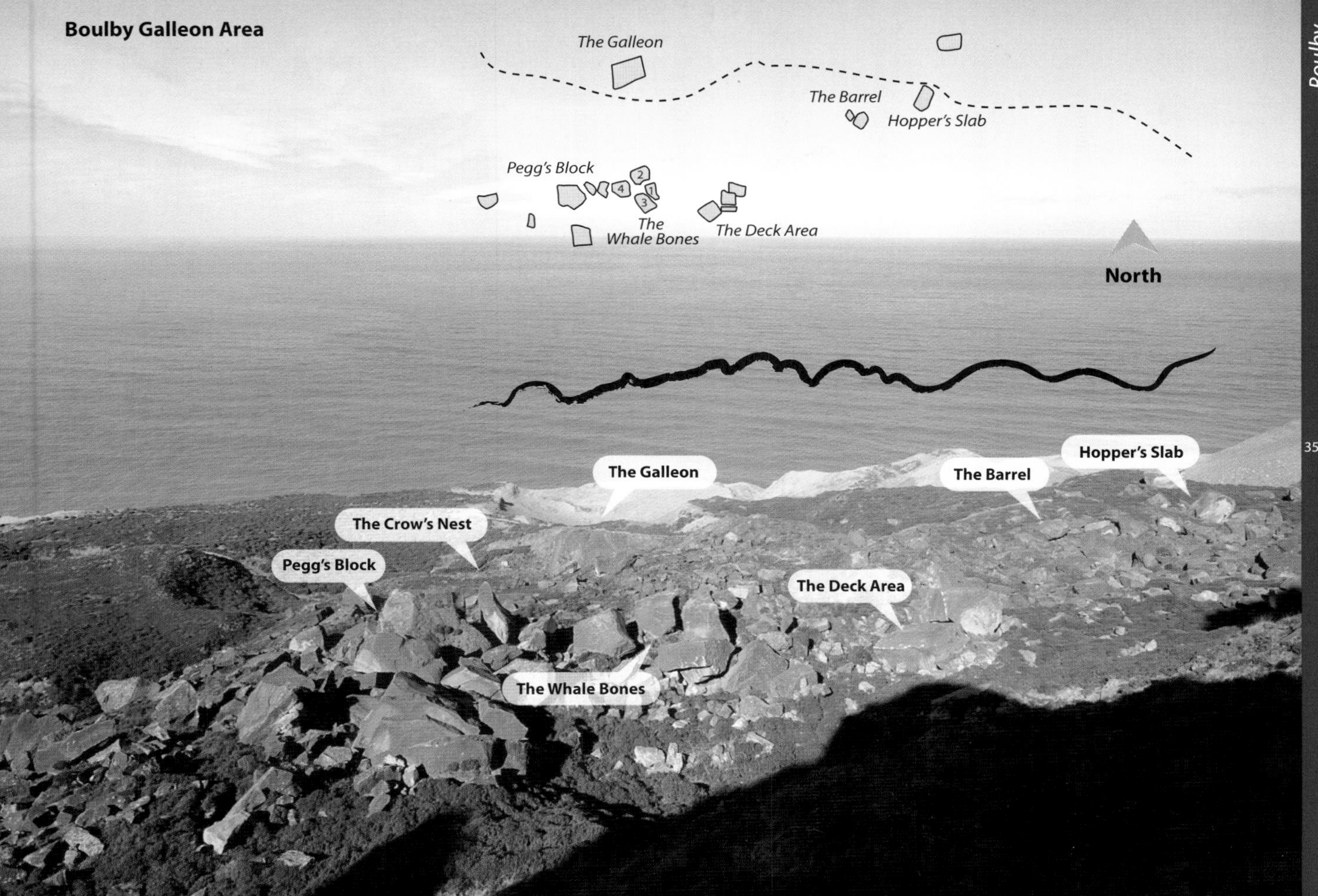
Boulby Galleon Area
The Galleon
The Barrel
Hopper's Slab
Pegg's Block
2
4
1
3
The Whale Bones
The Deck Area
North
The Galleon
The Barrel
Hopper's Slab
The Crow's Nest
Pegg's Block
The Deck Area
The Whale Bones

Hopper's Slab

Hopper's Slab

1. 3 The left side of the slab without the arête.
2. Cupid 6a Thin holds gain the top.
3. 4 Climb the right arête on its left side.

The Barrel

4. Rocket Rainbow 7c SS Starting on a low undercut under the block, climb onto the arête avoiding the shelf to the left. Top-out to the right. This can be done using the left shelf topping out left at **7b+**.
5. 6a Double Barrel SS Starting on the right-hand block, cross onto the left block and keep heading left onto the good diagonal shelf. Gain the top arête and top-out on its left side.

Mike Adams on Rocket Rainbow 7c

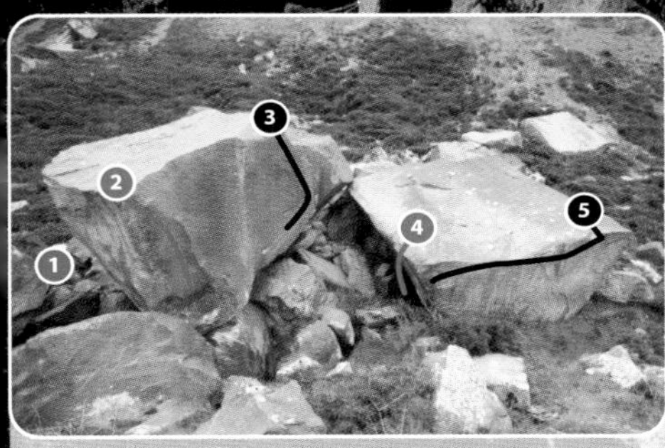

The Deck Area

Just left is a low mantel block.

1. 6a SS Starting on lower crimps, gain the lip and mantel.

The next block with an obvious arête.

2. 6c Climb the awkward left arête.
3. Masquerade 7c+ SS Boldly tackle the right arête, using pure faith and friction.
4. 6b SS Starting low on the left of the arête, gain the lip and finish direct.

The large flat block.

5. Gulliver's Travels SS 7a Traverse the lip of the block from the large sharp crimps and finish at the right arête with an energy-sapping mantel.

Owen McShane working the extention of Gulliver's Travels

The Whale Bones

Short but sweet problems on great little blocks.

1. 4 The left arête. **5+** from sitting.
2. Blow Hole SS 6a Starting under the incut using the rail crimp, climb direct to gain the top.
3. 4 SS The arête on its left. **3** from standing without the arête. **4** from sitting on the right side.
4. 4 SS The right arête on its left side.
5. 5+ Start below the top, get established and gain the top.
6. Wood 6b+SS The arête on its left side. Tricky. **6a SS** on its right side.
7. Pygmy 6a SS Climb the arête from the slot-pocket on the right. A crouch start for the shorter climber.
8. Whale Oil, Beef, Hooked 6c Start on the crimp with feet on the good ledge, gain the arête, then the top.
9 Stig of the Dump 7a+ SS Start low and climb the right side of the arête.
10. Captain Ahab 3 The centre of the slab.
11. Goblin 7a SS Climb the green sloping arête. Excellent.

Owen McShane on Stig of the Dump 7a+

Pegg's Block and The Crow's Nest

The sea-facing side of the blocks.

1. The Crow 6c Climb the flaked front-face, finishing with a bold rockover left.
2. Take Your Brain Out 6c Climb the flaky face and arête all the way. Bold.
3. Hook 5+ Highball arête, hugging from a low start.
4. Fly by the Seat of My Pants 7c+ SS Tackle the arête to gain the lip, traverse right and top-out just before the right end of the block.

The cliff-facing side of the blocks.

5. Loser 4 Climb the left arête.
6. Losing My Edge 6a The centre of the thin slab.
7. Disco Infiltrator 6a+ SS using the crack and sloper.

The west-facing side of the roof has a large slabby face.

8. Pegg's 5+ Gain the shelf then finish direct.
9. Pegg's Arête 4 Climb the right arête.

There are many other problems are in this area. We have just documented a selection to see how the venue develops as it gets more traffic. Take care, climb precisely and be safe.

Mike Adams on Take Your Brain Out 6c

The Galleon

A qualilty coastal beauty with plenty of problems.

1. The Magpie 6b SS Tackle the left arête on its right side, then mantel the right side to finish.
2. Haul Away 7c SS A hard start avoiding the arête on undercuts and small crimps.
3. Blown Away 7a+ The centre of the wall on small holds.
4. After the Storm 7c SS Climb the left arête using holds on the right face, then top-out on the right face.
5. Gazing Out of the Shop Window 6c SS From a good sidepull gain a big undercut, place the fingers in the crimpy slot then gain the juggy rail, and continue to the the top. Drop off here if you want, topping out direct will be tricky.

The next part of the steep wall looks snappy, though it's not as bad as it looks and it may hold a hard project.

After this the rock improves and holds some fine coastal climbing.

6. New Horizon 7c+ SS A stunning arête with a hard start and a bold finish. Rock onto the right face when you reach the top. **7b** From standing
7 Permanent Colour 6a The left of the slab without using any of the good features to the right.
8. 4 Up the features left of the arête.
9. 2 The descent.
10. Kippers 5 Climb just left of the groove.
11. Jet 5+ Up the groove and the ripples above.
12. Ambergris 4 To the right of the groove, finishing at the top of the snaking feature. Good fun without hands at **6a+.**
13. Alum 4 The slab just left of the arête.

Mike Adams on New Horizon 7c+

Steven Phelps on Jet 5+

Boulby Eastern Area

The Cutlass
The Pirate Ship
Dolly 1
Dolly 2
Dolly 3

Arête Blocks

1 2 3 4 5

Seaward Slab Area

6 7 8 9 10 11 12 13 14

Arête Blocks

1. Project Arête and undercut dyno.
2. Arête Left 2 The left side of the arête.
3. Arête Right 5 Climb the arête on its right side.
4. Slab and Pocket 5+ Move round rightwards with the shallow pocket onto the slab. Finish direct past a sloping ledge.
5. 4 SS Climb the short sandy overhang using pockets.
6. 6a SS Starting at the right side of the block traverse left on the lip and top-out round the corner.

Seaward Slab Area

7. 2 The left edge of the slab on good holds.
8. 4+ Start just to the right at a small ledge. Move up to a small crimp and then a good hold out to the right. Finish direct.
9. 4 The right arête, finishing right of the top block.
10. 6c From a hanging start, campus to the lip and mantel the top.
11. 5 SS Climb over the hanging nose. Trickier than it looks.
12. 7c SS The awkward bulge over the lip and up the arête.
13. Split Arête 7a SS Climb the arête on its right. **6c** from standing.
14. 5 The arête on its left side.

There are more problems up the hill, but these blocks are quite brittle.

Lee Robinson on Split Arête 7a

The Pirate Ship

1. 3 The centre of the south-facing wall using the large slanting feature, without the small ledge on the right.
2. 6a SS Climb the overhanging feature direct on sharp pockets.
3. Half-mast 6b+ SS Start on two distinct crimps. From here, pull over the awkward bulge via a tenuous rockover and slap for the top. Avoid the crack to the right.
4. 4 SS Start at the arête and follow to the the top of the block, finishing at the right end.
5. 3+ Using obvious holds, climb the short wall.
6. 3+ The shallow scoop to the right.
7. 3 Pull onto the wall and climb the right edge.
8. 5 SS The short overhanging arête.
9. 5 SS Start on the block and move up the overhanging wall via ledges.
10. 2 SS The right edge of the wall.

The block uphill and to the left of The Pirate Ship:

11. 6a SS Climb the left arête.
12. 2 The left slab.
13. 3 The right slab utilising the arêtes.

Scott Wood on Half-mast 6b+

James Rennardson on Pieces of Eight 6c+

The prominent and tentatively-balanced leaning block up the hill holds some excellent problems.

The Cutlass

1. Sun Rusher 7c SS Start on low crimps and make a dynamic bid for the lip. If you are successful mantel the lip direct.
2. Pieces of Eight 6c+ SS Just to the left of the arête, without using it. **6b+** if you use any holds around the right of the arête.
3. Cutlass 6a SS Climb the arête on its right side.
4. Don't Look Down 6a The right arête is not for the faint-hearted.

Mike Adams on Sun Rusher 7c

Down the slope are many other varied blocks, most holding a problem or two. If you are thirsty for more, have a wander.

The Dolly Mixtures

1. 6a SS Start on the lowest jug-ledge. Work up onto the left arête, then gain the top.
2. 5+ SS The centre of the face.
3. 5 SS Climb the right arête on its left side.

Both of the next blocks face east.

4. 6b Start low in a hole and climb the arête on its right, avoiding the other block.
5. 6a From a hanging start on crimps, up the centre avoiding other blocks.

Dolly 1

Dolly 2

Dolly 3

Lee Robinson on Problem 1 6a

Scan here for more information
Red Goat Climbing Wall
6 Redeness Street
York
YO31 7UU
Tel: 01904 731548
Email: info@redgoatclimbing.co.uk
Website: www.redgoatclimbing.co.uk
Goat
RED GOAT
York Climbing Wall
We have 6,000sq feet of indoor bouldering with a competition wall, large roof, overhangs and prows to keep the most aggressive of climbers happy, combined with a slab and vertical climbing for some technical wizardry. Why not try our circuit board, for those of you who never stop thinking about routes.
The icing on the cake is our coffee shop, where you will be greeted with a smile and the smell of the finest fresh ground coffee in York, so they say....
Red Goat offers climbing courses for all abilities to polish up or learn how to climb. We also offer kids clubs, discount nights, lunchtime happy hour climbing and much more.

Rock Antics
Middlesbrough Wall
Only 2 minutes from the A66
Less than 30 minutes away from the North York Moors
200+ problems, font style circuits
Grade range: Font 3 to Font 8
Top rope area with 13 lines
Separate kids area
Cafe
Free parking
Scan for info
Unit K
Warelands Way
Longlands Road
Middlesbrough
TS4 2JY
01642 232236
www.rockantics.co.uk

A selection of choice problems to seek out

Oranges

Cook's Rib 1 Potters Quarry (Captain Cook's)
Frank's Slab 1 Cold Moor
Y-Crack 1+ Stoney Wicks (Scugdale)
Zoot Route 1+ Scot Crags (Scugdale)
Wall Bar Buttress 2 Park Nab
Brown Arête Direct 2+ Middle Ridge Crag
Alcove Cracks 2+ Barker's Crag (Scugdale)
Sleepy Time 2+ The Inbetweeners
The Route 3 Little Potter's Quarry (Captain Cook's)
Passion Play 3 The Bridestones
Beak Ridge 3 Cold Moor
Stook 3 Roseberry Topping
Erica Arête 3 Camp Hill
Pet's Corner 3 Scot Crags (Scugdale)
Three Tier Climb 3 Cold Moor
The Bulkhead 3+ Scot Crags (Scugdale)
Ibuprofen 3+ Duck Boulders
Grand Slam 4 Duck Boulders
Strawberry Fields 4 The Bridestones
Sleeping Giant 4 Arncliffe Woods
Long Bow 4 Park Nab
Deviation 4 Cook's Crag (Captain Cook's)
Classic Rock 4 Cold Moor
Capstone Central 4 Camp Hill
Saunter 4 Glaisdale Head
Hawkeye 4 Easby View
G.B.G. 4+ Potter's Quarry (Captain Cook's)
The Signal 4+ Ingleby Incline
Pingers 4+ Scot Crags (Scugdale)

Tom Crane on Grand Slam 4 **Duck Boulders**

Karin Magog on Passepartout 5+ **Camp Hill** Photo Steve Crowe

Blues

The Crack 5 Wainstones
Tippling Wall 5 Scot Crags (Scugdale)
The Prow 5 Scot Crags (Scugdale)
Basskin 5 Glaisdale Head
Red Giant 5 Petergate Quarry
Fallen Arch 5 Barker's Crag (Scugdale)
First of Many 5 Potter's Quarry (Captain Cook's)
The South Face 5 NOS Boulder
Sunset Arête 5 Northdale Boulders
Desert Rose 5 Limber Hill
Tank Traverse 5+ Ingleby Incline
Jake's Wall 5+ Clemitt's in the Woods
Stone Wall 5+ The Finkelstones
The Craic 5+ Westerdale View Quarry
Nordic Arête 5+ The Meadow
Troll Hunter 5+ Arncliffe Woods
The Finger Print Preservation Society 5+ Clemitt's in the Woods
Strict Machine 5+ Ingleby Incline
Garfoid 5+ Garfit Quarry
Jet 5+ Boulby
Stairway to Heaven 5+ Clemitt's in the Woods
Pleasant Arête 5+ Ingleby Incline
Sam's Slab 5+ Clemitt's in the Woods
Reckoner 5+ Arncliffe Woods
Pickpocket 5+ Camp Hill
Eschaton 5+ Petergate Quarry
No Limits 5+ Cold Moor
Curlew 5+ Middle Ridge
Big Dog's Cock 5+ The Bridestones
Passepartout 5+ Camp Hill
The Arch 5+ Earthworks Rocks

Alan Taylor on New Dimensions 1977
Long before bouldering mats!

Steven Phelps on New Dimensions 6a+ Scugdale

Reds

Stewker 6a Scot Crags (Scugdale)
Men's Zone 6a Cook's Crag (Captain Cook's)
The Face 6a Castleton Rigg
Cloud Nine 6a Clemitt's in the Woods
Witchcraft 6a Glaisdale Head Boulders
The Flutings 6a White Stone Boulders (Scugdale)
Silent Spring 6a Petergate Quarry
Red and White 6a+ Earthworks Rocks
White Star Line 6a+ Thimbleby Crag
New Dimensions 6a+ Barker's Crag (Scugdale)
Roasted Ore 6a+ Thorgill
Pythagorianism 6a+ Tranmire Rocks
Submariner 6a+ Cook's Crag (Captain Cook's)
Cold Sweat 6a+ Cold Moor
Pebble Climb 6b Wainstones
Rosedale Monologue 6b Rosedale Head
The Bony King of Nowhere 6b Arncliffe Woods
A Black Heart 6b Clemitt's in the Woods
Perseverance 6b Middle Ridge Crag
The Slot 6b Northdale Boulders
Dark Times 6b Ravenswick Quarry
Falling Arête 6b Round Crag
Super Skunk 6b+ Barker's Crag (Scugdale)
Trash Talker 6b+ Ingleby Incline
Pannierman's Arête 6b+ Round Crag
Arrogance of Youth 6c Clemitt's in the Woods
Beaucoup de Gifles 6c Duck Boulders
Seal of Approval 6c Clemitt's in the Woods
Dreamcatcher 6c Arncliffe Woods
Waylander 6c Ingleby Incline
Torsang 6c Thorgill
Elephantitus 6c High Crag
Garfit of Passion 6c Garfit Quarry
Inclination 6c Ingleby Incline
Mono Wall 6c Ingleby Incline
ASBO Pops 6c Stoupe Brow
Lion Arête 6c+ Rosedale Head
Biotic Crisis 6c+ Smuggler's Terrace
The Witch 6c+ Glaisdale Head
We Close our Eyes 6c+ White Stone Boulders (Scugdale)

Blacks

Goblin 7a Boulby
Simon's Alphabetical Beard 7a Arncliffe Woods
Expansions 7a Ingleby Incline
Nothing But Something 7a The Inbetweeners
The White Room 7a Rosedale Head
Thor 7a The Meadow
Stalingrad 7a Thorgill
The Prow 7a Wainstones
New World 7a Potter's Quarry (Captain Cook's)
Corpus Hypercubus 7a Low Water Stones
Nürburgring 7a The Bridestones
Phileas Fogg 7a Camp Hill
Paparazzi 7a Clemitt's Out
Black Velvet 7a Petergate Quarry
Grandmaster Flash 7a Barker's Crag (Scugdale)
Blue Cheese 7a Ingleby Incline (Cheese Stones)
Stig of the Dump 7a+ Boulby
42 7a+ Tranmire Rocks
Psycho Syndicate 7a+ Wainstones
The Duck-billed Platypus 7a+ Duck Boulders
In The Bag 7b Clemitt's in the Woods
The Iron Bar 7b Clemitt's in the Woods
Ever Fallen in Love 7b Tarn Hole
Mighty Oak 7b Oak Crag
Africa Collides 7b Smuggler's Terrace
The Thief of Always 7b+ High Crag
Aurora's Encore 7b+ The Finkelstones
Chasing Rainbows 7c Round Crag
Cruel Intentions 7c Wainstones
Rassassier 7c Todd Intake
Sun Rusher 7c Boulby
Edge of Glory 7c+ Roseberry Topping
Sleepy Hollow 7c+ Ingleby Incline
Oblivion 7c+ Cold Moor
New Horizon 7c+ Boulby
Colours of the Mind 8a Round Crag
Hellbound 8a Arncliffe Woods
Requiem for a Dream 8a Stoupe Brow
Circle My Demise 8a Ingleby Incline
The Cannon 8a+ Kay Nest
Four Seasons 8a+ Oak Crag
Blue Eyes and Exit Wounds 8b Stoupe Brow
Before the Rain 8b Cloughton Wyke
Mixed Emotions 8b+ Kay Nest

Lee Robinson on New World 7a **Potter's Quarry**